THE ORIGINS OF PHILOSOPHY

THE ORIGINS
OF PHILOSOPHY

Its Rise in Myth and the Pre-Socratics

A COLLECTION OF EARLY WRITINGS
SELECTED, EDITED, AND WITH EXPLANATORY ESSAYS

Drew A. Hyland

CAPRICORN BOOKS
G. P. PUTNAM'S SONS, *New York*

Acknowledgments:

Sandars, N. K., tr.: *The Epic of Gilgamesh*; copyright © N. K. Sandars, 1960, 1964. Reprinted by permission of Penguin Books Ltd.

Lattimore, Richmond: *Hesiod*; University of Michigan Press, 1959. Reprinted by permission.

Lee, H. D. P.: *Zeno of Elea*; Cambridge University Press, 1936. Reprinted by permission.

Freeman, Kathleen: *Ancilla to the Pre-Socratic Philosophers*; Harvard University Press, 1948. Reprinted by permission of Harvard University Press and Basil Blackwell Publisher.

Wheelwright, Philip, ed.: *The Pre-Socratics*; copyright © 1966 by the Odyssey Press, Inc. Reprinted by permission of the present publisher, The Bobbs-Merrill Company, Inc.

Hicks, R. D., tr.: Diogenes Laertius, *Lives of Eminent Philosophers*; Vols. I and II. Reprinted by permission of Harvard University Press and the Loeb Classical Library.

Putnam SBN: 399–10922–6
Capricorn SBN: 399–50290–4
Library of Congress Catalog Card Number: 72-86465

PRINTED IN THE UNITED STATES OF AMERICA

This is a book about the manifold meaning of origins.
For this reason I wish to dedicate it to:

> *My parents—Catherine and Arthur Hyland*
> *My teacher—Stanley Rosen*
> *My wife—Anne*
> *My sons—Christopher and Craig*

Preface

THE title of this book is intended as a concise statement of its general theme. I wish to raise the question of the origins of this remarkable and even strange human possibility known since the time of the ancient Greeks as philosophy, and to reflect on what those origins might be. This might at first glance seem a sufficiently easy question to pursue, even if the actual answer should turn out to be more complex or difficult. One might reasonably suppose, for example, that to ask after the origins of philosophy is to ask *who the first philosopher was*, or alternatively, to ask what came *before* philosophy which gave birth to, was the cause of, philosophy. But as I hope to show in the Introduction, the very question of the origins of philosophy is, if anything, more problematic than any answer. This book, then, is as much an effort to be reflective about what it means to ask after the origins of philosophy as it is an effort to defend some specific answer. To do so, I have chosen to reflect specifically on that group of ancient philosophers whose dates range from around 600 B.C. to around 450 B.C. known as Pre-Socratic philosophers, ostensibly because they conducted their investigations prior to the great philosopher, Socrates. I choose them in part because they are generally considered to *be* the origins of philosophy, that is, those thinkers who *originated* philosophy, and who were also *original* philosophers. But I do so also because I find visible in them, sometimes implicitly, sometimes explicitly, reflections on the very questions which concern me in this book: What does the question of the origins of philosophy really ask? Are the origins of philosophy historical? Are the origins themselves philosophic, or are they somehow prephilosophic—say, mythical—and if so, what is the relation between the prephilosophic origins of philosophy and philosophy itself? And if the origins of philosophy are historical in this or a similar way, how can we

7

understand the plausible belief that each man must *originate* philosophy within himself? How, if this were so, could any philosopher after the first be an *original* philosopher? Let me reiterate that my intention is more to reflect *about* these questions than to offer definitive answers. I am far from sure that I or anyone has any such answers. To take what is perhaps the most obvious example, my discussion of the relation between the so-called mythic origins of philosophy and philosophy itself is intended not so much to give my answer to the relation but to show that the question itself is immensely complex, since it assumes that one's conception of what myth is and what philosophy is is already carefully formulated. In the spirit of the Platonic dialogues, then—one of which, the *Charmides*, concludes this volume—and also in the spirit of certain contemporary philosophers such as Martin Heidegger, I will be satisfied if in the course of this book I and the reader become clearer on what the fundamental questions are.

There are an increasing number of books available in English on Pre-Socratic philosophy. The present work originates in a desire to present an alternative to what I consider a fundamental uniformity in the present literature, notwithstanding the many significant differences among them in other ways. This uniformity might be expressed as the decision that the fundamental concern or even duty of the thinker on the Pre-Socratics is to say with as much historical accuracy as possible what these early philosophers meant in their cryptic and for the most part fragmentary writings. Precisely because of the fragmentary character of the Pre-Socratic literature, the challenge of historical accuracy is an immense one, and much of the finest and most controversial scholarship on Pre-Socratic philosophy has involved the effort, often admittedly speculative, to determine with some accuracy what these historical figures really meant. As will be evident from my interpretations, this is not my main concern. The fundamental intention of my interpretations will be to reflect on the *philosophical* rather than historical significance of the Pre-Socratic philosophers, to reflect, that is, about what is philosophically interesting and true about their thought regardless of whether I can "prove" that what I find of interest is actually what those historical figures intended. I happen to believe for the most part that my interpretations do penetrate to their real intentions, but my arguments for this historical accuracy are not part of this book. The great danger of the "historical" approach, especially when it is coupled as it nearly always is with the extrinsic thesis of progress in philosophy, is that it often underestimates the insight and sophistication of these thinkers because such and such a thinker "could not" have had such a thought so early in history. This concern too often results in an interpretation of the Pre-Socratic philosophers as primitive thinkers. The corresponding danger of my orientation is that, by studying these thinkers in the light of the subsequent history of philosophy, I may attribute to them more than they historically *could* have meant. I readily acknowledge this danger and argue that even if from time to time it were shown to be true of my interpretations, it would not necessarily be destructive of my intentions. What will be destructive is if what I say is philosophically uninteresting. To the extent that I am successful, I would hope that one consequence of this book might be to engender a dialogue about how best to think about Pre-Socratic philosophy.

I wish to acknowledge a special debt of thanks to my friend and colleague at Trinity College, Howard DeLong, who has consented to bring his immense logical abilities to bear in an interpretation of Zeno for the present work.

Because much of our information about the Pre-Socratic philosophers comes from other classical writers, many of the selections presenting the views of a particular thinker contain not only the extant fragments of his own works but also a report, or "testimony," by someone else. These are usually referred to as Testimonia. In some cases, as will be seen, we do not have any original material, but only Testimonia about the thinker in question.

The following translations are used: *The Epic of Gilgamesh*, translated by N. K. Sandars (Penguin Books, 1960). The translation from Homer's *Odyssey* is that of Alexander Pope, *The Odyssey of Homer* (1851). The selections from Hesiod are from the translation of Richmond Lattimore, *Hesiod* (University of Michigan Press, 1959). The translations of Diogenes Laertius are from his *Lives of Eminent Philosophers*, translated by R. D. Hicks, two volumes, The Loeb Classical Library. All translations from Plato's dialogues are those of Benjamin Jowett, *The Dialogues of Plato* (Oxford, 1871). All translations of Aristotle, with the exception of the "Testimonia on Zeno," are those of W. D. Ross, *The Works of Aristotle*, 12 volumes (Oxford,

1931). The selection entitled "Testimonia on Zeno by Aristotle and Simplicius" is taken from H. D. P. Lee, *Zeno of Elea* (Cambridge University Press, 1936).

The selections of the Pre-Socratics themselves are usually those of Kathleen Freeman, *Ancilla to the Pre-Socratic Philosophers* (Harvard University Press, 1948), although in my interpretive essays I often use my own translations which are at variance with hers. I hope that the presence of the variance may give the reader a sense of the range of interpretations of the Greek. The Fragments of Anaximander, Anaximenes, and Leucippus, and selections of later secondary literature are taken from Philip Wheelwright, *The Pre-Socratics* (Odyssey Press, 1966). In each case the translation used is cited in a footnote.

Three final notes: I have offered at the back of the book a brief glossary of Greek terms which I considered so important, or in some cases so untranslatable, that it was better to leave them in their Greek form. I have also included a brief and by no means complete annotated bibliography.

Third, I often have occasion to refer to the authoritative work of Hermann Diels and Walther Kranz, *Die Fragmente Der Vorsokratiker* (Dublin/Zürich, Weidman, 1968). I shall abbreviate such references by the now standard (D.-K.).

Finally, because this book is directed in large measure to undergraduate audiences, I have, whenever possible, footnoted references to the English translations. This should in no way be taken as an affirmation that studying texts in the original language is no longer necessary; it is rather a grudging concession to one of the more deplorable aspects of contemporary education.

Contents

PREFACE   7

INTRODUCTION: THE QUESTION OF ORIGINS   15

1. MYTH AND (OR AS) PHILOSOPHY   29
     A. *The Epic of Gilgamesh*, 33
     B. Homer, 37
     C. Hesiod, 38
     D. Xenophanes, 44

II. PHILOSOPHY AND COSMOLOGY-
    THE MILESIANS   97
     A. Thales, 109
     B. Anaximander, 117
     C. Anaximens, 122

III. PHILOSOPHY AND MATHEMATICS—
    THE PYTHAGOREANS   127
     Pythagoras, 133

IV. THE BATTLE OF THE GIANTS   145
     Heraclitus—The Spokesman for Becoming, 160

V. THE BATTLE OF THE GIANTS   179
    Parmenides—The Spokesman for Being, 189

VI. CATCHING UP WITH ZENO   203
    Zeno, 224

VII. RESPONSES TO THE BATTLE OF THE GIANTS   237
    Empedocles, 224

VIII. RESPONSES TO THE BATTLE OF THE GIANTS   267
    Anaxagoras, 273

IX. THE ATOMISTS   285
    A. Leucippus, 294
    B. Democritus, 297

X. PHILOSOPHY AS RHETORIC—THE SOPHISTS   317
    A. Protagoras, 327
    B. Gorgias, 335

XI. THE NEW BEGINNING   343
    Socrates and Plato, 351

GLOSSARY OF GREEK TERMS   379
SUGGESTIONS FOR FURTHER READING   381

THE ORIGINS OF PHILOSOPHY

Introduction: The Question of Origins

For it is owing to their wonder that men both now begin and at first began to philosophize; they wondered originally at the obvious difficulties, then advanced little by little and stated difficulties about the greater matters, e.g. about the phenomena of the moon and those of the sun and of the stars, and about the genesis of the whole. And a man who is puzzled and wonders thinks himself ignorant (whence even a lover of myth is in a sense a lover of wisdom, for the myth is composed of wonders;) therefore, since they philosophized in order to escape from ignorance, evidently they were pursuing science in order to know, and not for any utilitarian end. . . .

. . . For all men begin, as we said, by wondering that things are as they are. . . .

—ARISTOTLE, *Metaphysica*, Book I,
Chap. 2, 982b 11-22, 983a 15.

ACCORDING to this saying of Aristotle, which he shares with his teacher, Plato,[1] philosophy begins for all men, no matter where or when they live, in essentially the same way, in what he called wonder or amazement that things are as they are. Whatever the meaning of this word "wonder" as used by Plato and Aristotle—and part of the intention of this book will be to work out its deeper meaning in terms of the philosophic thinking of the so-called Pre-Socratic philosophers—we might first be struck by the unhistorical character of this account of the beginning, the origin, of philosophy. For Aristotle does not suggest, nor does Plato, that only the historically first philosopher, traditionally con-

sidered to be Thales, began by wondering, and that subsequent generations of philosophers could replace this apparently humble beginning by
a more sophisticated one. No, he says that wonder is the beginning, or
origin, of philosophy for every man, no matter when or where he
lives.[2]

But this might seem a strange consideration with which to begin a
book on Pre-Socratic philosophy, since the vast majority of such works
do indeed make a historical claim as to the beginnings of philosophy by
saying who the first philosopher was—Thales, as most agree, Heraclitus
and Parmenides, as others would have it.[3] The point of such a claim,
no matter who the particular philosopher named as first, is that philosophy is of such a nature that its beginning is historically determinable.
Put in this way, it is easy to see that such a claim already assumes a
specific conception of what philosophy is; to be able to name the first
philosopher is to know in advance what philosophy is.

We are immediately faced, then, with two different although perhaps
not incompatible conceptions of the origins of philosophy, what we
might call the historical, or chronological, conception and what we can
call the ahistorical, or ontological, view. They are not necessarily incompatible because even if one holds an ontological view (for example,
that philosophy begins for each and every man in wonder), it is still
presumably true that there was a first man who began philosophizing
through wonder, and he would obviously deserve the title of first
philosopher. But from this standpoint, the historical fact that "X" was
the first determinable man who wondered does not affect the conception of philosophy under which he is so named. But if one does not hold
that the origin of philosophy is ahistorical—be it in wonder, the insight
into the unity of the mind with the whole of nature, or something else
—if, rather, the origins of philosophy are held to be historical in the
sense that a certain peculiar set of historical conditions determined that
philosophy began in a certain time and place with the utterances of a
certain man, then the particular things that he first said, and the particular prephilosophical conditions out of which his sayings arise,
become of decisive importance to an understanding of the nature of
philosophic thinking.

As indicated, the intention of this book is to defend the view articulated by Plato and Aristotle that philosophy begins again and again
for each one of us, and so also for the first philosopher, whoever he is,

in the experience of wonder. What that experience is shall be worked out more adequately in the interpretations of the wonderings of the Pre-Socratic philosophers. We shall not be able to definitively name the first philosopher. Accordingly, this book shall begin not with Thales, but with what are usually cited as prephilosophical works of literature—with *The Epic of Gilgamesh*, with Hesiod, and with Homer. This is done not to examine the prephilosophical conditions which gave rise to Thales, but to consider the philosophic issues present in those earlier works. But before doing so, it is best to set out the interpretation of the origins of philosophy against which we are contending.

To speak of the origins of philosophy, in whatever sense of the word one chooses, is already to have a certain conception of philosophy. For those who argue that the origins of philosophy are ontological rather than historical, this fact is explicit. To say that philosophy begins in wonder is itself to begin the speech about what philosophy is. Although this may be less obvious, it is no less true of a position that argues, to name the most dominant view, that philosophy arose with Thales out of the mythoreligious concerns of the earlier Greeks. To say this of philosophy is to claim to know both what philosophy is and from whence it came. Yet this consequence is often hidden and even denied by those who claim that one of its advantages is to help us understand what philosophy is. The suggestion is superficially appealing; in order to better understand what philosophy is, let us return to its historical beginnings, and indeed to the prephilosophical conditions which gave rise to philosophy. We shall presently elaborate this position in greater detail, but even this bare outline is sufficient to show that it is involved in a circle. To understand philosophy, we should return to its beginnings. Yet to be able to return to the historical beginnings of philosophy is to be able to name the first philosopher as well as his prephilosophical predecessors; but this is to claim to know what philosophy is.[4]

The circle becomes problematic only in so far as one gets involved in it unreflectively. As long as one realizes that the stipulation of the first philosopher presupposes a conception of philosophy, and so long as one is capable of offering an account of that conception on independent grounds, its application to the "first philosophers" can be penetrating and insightful, although never proof of the validity of one's conception. Plato and Aristotle, for example, both offer accounts of the nature of philosophy on independent grounds. In modern times, Hegel's *Lectures on the History of Philosophy*[5] represent perhaps the highest, most self-conscious achievement of this kind of enterprise. Hegel was indeed capable of offering his own account of the ontological origins of philosophy because he insisted upon an access to a transhistorical standard of truth, including the truth of what philosophy is.[6] Subsequent thinkers, although influenced knowingly or unknowingly by the historical character of Hegel's teaching but abandoning his optimism about access to an eternal, independent standard, have too often fallen prey to the circle set out above in such a way as to undercut their entire position. This is nowhere more obvious than in what is probably the most influential statement of the historical interpretation of the origins of philosophy in English, F. M. Cornford's *From Religion to Philosophy*.[7] There is no better way to lead into the interpretation of the Pre-Socratic philosophers than to set out in some detail our opposition to this famous and very persuasive account.

Cornford's fundamental thesis about the origin of philosophy is suggested in the title of the work and pervades nearly every page: Philosophy is a development out of the older religious myths of earlier Greek society. The movement from the mythoreligious formulations to the early but still naïve philosophic formulations is the movement from a basically emotional reaction to a set of issues to a more rational reaction to essentially the same issues. This movement corresponds to the movement from theogony and theology (the genesis and *logos* of the gods) to cosmogony and cosmology (the genesis and *logos* of the cosmos). In short, what makes Thales and Anaximander philosophical, but Hesiod and Homer prephilosophic, is that the former attempted nonmythic—and that is taken to mean "materialistic"—accounts of the world, whereas the latter depended on religious myth. "Rationality" is thus implicitly defined as materialistic explanation, or protoscience, and as in opposition to myth, which, it is implied, is at least nonrational. But in order both to let Cornford speak for himself and to avoid an unfair characterization of his position, we offer the following representative passages from his book. In the preface, in discussing the issue of *physis*, nature, in early Greek thought, he says,

I have called it [*physis*] the Datum of Philosophy, to mark that it was not invented by the philosophers, but derived from a representation which underlies all the shapes and symbols of religious thought.[8]

What has changed [in the movement from religion to philosophy] is, rather, man's attitude towards it (the Datum of Philosophy), which, from being active and emotional, has become intellectual and speculative. His earlier, emotional reaction gave birth to the symbols of myth, to objects of faith; his new procedure of critical analysis dissects it into concepts, from which it deduces various types of systematic theory.[9]

In the text itself he says,

This representation [of *physis* by Anaximander] was, moreover, of a religious character; it was taken over by philosophy from religion, not independently deduced from observation of the world and its natural processes.[10]

The Olympians had passed beyond the reach of human needs and the touch of human emotion; they had even left their provinces in Nature, and it was found out that the business of the world could go forward without them, just as it had been found out that the magnificent traffic of cloud and sunshine, and the daily circling of the heavens, could go on its appointed way without the impertinent aid of magical dances and incantation. The time had come for religion to give place to philosophy.[11]

Philosophy is the immediate successor of theology, and the conceptions held by philosophers of the relation between ultimate reality and the manifold sense world are governed by older religious conceptions of the relation between god and the human group or Nature.[12]

Now this view, especially as it is set out at length by Cornford, seems plausible and persuasive.[13] As suggested earlier, it has been accepted by nearly all English-speaking writers on the Pre-Socratics. To mention just a few of the more famous, Kirk and Raven, in their *The Pre-Socratic Philosophers*, say,

What gave these [Thales and the first Ionian philosophers] the title of philosopher was their abandonment of mytho-poeic forms of
thought, of personification and anthropomorphic theistic explanations, and their attempt to explain the seen world in terms of its
seen constituents.[14]

W. K. C. Guthrie, in *The Greek Philosophers from Thales to
Aristotle*, says,

His [Anaximander's] was an age when the supernatural was still
taken for granted, when the forces of nature were attributed to the
actions of anthropomorphic gods, a Zeus or a Poseidon, and the
origin of the universe had hitherto been sought in grotesque stories
about a sexual union between heaven and earth, conceived as vast
primeval deities, and their forcing apart by another gigantic spirit.
With Anaximander human reason asserted itself, and produced
what, right or wrong, was for the most part an account in purely
natural terms of the origin of the world and life.[15]

Even J. Burnet, who explicitly criticizes certain aspects of Cornford's
hypothesis, nevertheless says,

It was not till the traditional view of the world and the customary
rules of life had broken down, that the Greeks began to feel the
needs which philosophies of nature and of conduct seek to
satisfy.[16]

At this point, we might simply raise several problems, since the more
serious difficulties in Cornford's position emerge in his discussion of the
sources of early Greek myth and religion. To begin, we can note that his
position as so far stated presumes a conception of philosophy which is
by no means self-evident or easy to substantiate. It assumes, for example, that although philosophy somehow arises out of religion, it differs
from religion in that it abandons myth in favor of rational accounts of
the cosmos. But if this is so, what, for example, are we to make of the
philosophy of Plato, whom everyone agrees is a philosopher, yet whose
works are full of myths which function critically in his philosophy?

What of the easy insistence on the opposition between reason and myth? Must not such an opposition be justified? Is it altogether clear and uncontestable that a materialistic account of the structure or origin of the cosmos is more "rational" than a religious one? Must not *this* be defended *rationally*? Finally, nothing that Cornford mentions really substantiates his claim that philosophy *arises out of* religious myth. Rather, what it more plausibly shows is that the early religious myths and the sentences of Thales, Anaximander, and the other Pre-Socratics speak to the same issues in different ways. But no amount of confirmation of this parallel will ever show that philosophy *arises out of* religious myth. Cornford in fact vascillates between the latter claim and what is the more plausible view, that early philosophy and early religious myth are somewhat different ways of characterizing very similar issues. Cornford sets out this latter hypothesis by reasonably inquiring along the following lines. If religious myth is the source out of which philosophy arises, what is the source of religious myth itself? To this he offers the plausible but not self-evident suggestion that it has its source in the problems and concerns of man's practical life, with the elements—earth, air, fire, and water—with the way things happen to him (*Moira*), with problems of value and right (*Dike*), and, ultimately, in the structure of human society itself. Thus he says,

> The Gods have faded [by the time of Anaximander] and we are left with the elements from which Hesiod tells us that the gods arose. Seen against the background of the destined order, the life of the gods from first to last shows up as a mere episode. Nature—the living and self-moving stuff of all things that exist—and the primary forms in which her upspringing life is confined by the appointment of Destiny and Justice—these are older than the gods and they outlast them.[17]

> Here we touch at last the bedrock. Behind philosophy lay religion; behind religion, as we now see, lies social custom—the structure and institutions of the human group.[18]

From another point of view, which will be clear from what has gone before, philosophy rediscovers in the world that very scheme

of representation which had, by a necessary process, been pro-
jected into the world from the structure and institutions of society
in its earlier stages of development.[19]

Now there is an obvious, almost superficial, circle here which leads
into a more destructive one. If the way in which philosophy emerged out
of religion was by talking about the four elements (earth, air, water, and
fire), about *Dike* and *Moira* as structures of the world, rather than talking in the language of the gods of religious mythology, yet if religious
mythology was in fact a series of personifications of those four elements, of *Dike* and *Moira*, which are themselves embedded in the structure of early society and man's experience of the world, does this not
imply rather that religion arises out of a kind of primordial philosophy
than vice versa? This is an intriguing and genuinely thought-provoking
hypothesis. At very least Cornford's view suggests that religious myth as
it arose in early Greek society was a temporary aberration, an unfortunate representation of the genuine themes of early Greek society to
which the Ionian philosophers such as Thales and Anaximander
returned. Now, any truly religious man will see at once that such a view
presumes in advance the falseness of the religious standpoint. But Cornford's position hides what is for philosophy an even more fundamental
problem.

Cornford reasonably tries to trace the roots of early religion to the
structure of society itself. But it is possible to ask, as thoughtful men
have asked again and again throughout history, from what source does
the structure of society itself arise? Without insisting upon the rigor with
which Socrates claims to maintain an analogy between the city and the
soul in Plato's *Republic*, it is plausible to suggest that in some sense the
structure of society is the way it is because of the way men are. (This is
of course compatible with the converse, that men are influenced by the
society in which they live.) Even if one simply asserts that society arises
primitively because of man's need for mutual protection, then this
evidently inadequate account presumes that man is of a certain nature,
namely, sufficiently weaker than other creatures or natural forces as to
require mutual help. But this is to say that in one way or another the
structure of society originates in human nature. Now, if philosophy
arises out of the structure of primitive society, if, as Cornford suggests,
it gets its issues from that structure, then, given the origin of society in

human nature, it is fair to say that philosophy arises out of human nature itself. *The origin of philosophy then lies in the nature of being human.* Now, if human nature does not change through history, then it would follow that the origin of philosophy is also ahistorical, that philosophy originates again and again for men in essentially the same way. But this evidently implies some version of Aristotle's conception of the origin of philosophy as arising in wonder or, if not in wonder, in some other experience which can be shown to be *natural to human being*, part of man's nature. Only if one holds that human nature changes in history (not to be confused with the less controversial fact that individual men change in their lives) is it plausible to say, indeed does it become necessary to say, that the conditions which give rise to philosophy in one epoch are different from the conditions which precipitate or perpetuate philosophy in another.

Yet not even Cornford suggests that the Greeks held to a conception of a changing human nature. It is presently fashionable to insist that it was not until the nineteenth-century writings of such thinkers as Hegel, Marx, and Nietzsche that this idea, that not only individual human beings in the course of their lives but human nature itself changes in time, together with its consequential emphasis on history, came to be considered seriously, much less accepted as true. Suffice it to say that this decisive issue as to the nature of human being and its relation to history or time, an issue as alive today as in fact it was for the Greeks, is by no means decided. Therefore we can say this of Cornford's interpretation of the historical origins of philosophy in religious myth and ultimately in the structure of primitive society: It is plausible only on the basis of a conception of human nature as changing, or to use contemporary philosophical language, as historical or radically temporal. But (1) this hypothesis is radically un-Greek, untrue to the spirit of the greatest of the Greek thinkers, and therefore should not be imposed upon them without explicit justification; and (2) it is in any case a position which Cornford in no way defends or of which he even shows himself cognizant.[20]

All this shows Cornford's position to be circular. More importantly, it shows it to be unphilosophical in a sense of the term which I hope to show is at least as old as Thales, namely, that it is not aware of its origins; it does not exhibit self-knowledge. But surely what is needed in a study of the Pre-Socratic philosophers as originators of philosophy is that the study itself be philosophical. Philosophy has the peculiarity that nearly every philosophic speech, including this book, is in part about the nature of philosophy. In the criticism of Cornford's account we have suggested that according to an ancient tradition in philosophy itself that exhibition is superior, more genuinely philosophic, insofar as it is self-aware and, in particular, aware of its origins. Therefore it is especially necessary in a book about the origins of philosophy to begin with a reflection on man's concern with his origins and, in particular, on why it should be necessary or even relevant for philosophy to be origin-al, that is, aware of its origins in the several senses of what we have established to be that profoundly ambiguous term.

To begin, it is worth noting that an explicit concern with one's origins is by no means universal. The utterly dominant notion of "progress" which pervades contemporary culture often has as its consequence the view that, since we are always moving forward and toward the ever-brighter future, the past can be left behind, repudiated as something "over and done with," and in any case inferior to the present. We accordingly condemn those who remain committed to their origins as "dwelling in the past," "refusing to face the present (or future, or reality)," as "not changing with the times." This attitude is nowhere more prevalent than in the United States, where our self-image as still fundamentally a "frontier people" carries with it the frontier romanticization of leaving behind one's past for a new start in the "new world."[21] In professional philosophy, this attitude takes the following form: "Why study the history of philosophy, why especially study very ancient philosophy? Their thinking is extremely naïve, they solved few or no philosophic problems, and in any case, given the refinement in techniques of logical analysis and the general progress of the human intellect since those days, it is pointless to study the past since the source of the solution to philosophical problems lies in the present, in our own intellects and sophisticated logical techniques." As a consequence, it must not be forgotten that any effort, such as the present one, to investigate one's origins is necessarily a critique of one of the most dominant "world views" which inform our culture.

In the face of this it becomes necessary to consider why it is that we ought to and in fact do now and again turn to reflect upon our origins. Perhaps the first and most obvious response is that we ought to and do investigate the origins, both of ourselves and of other phenomena, because we seek knowledge, and we believe that knowledge of origins constitutes a very significant mode of knowledge. But this reasonably uncontroversial statement already raises two absolutely fundamental issues in Western thought which we hope to show were decisively established by the very Pre-Socratics we are about to study. The first issue has to do with the justification of the pursuit of knowledge itself. This can be stated descriptively—men do seek knowledge. As Aristotle put it in the opening line of the *Metaphysica*, "All men desire by nature to know."[22] If true, this complex utterance suggests that insofar as the reflection on origins is bound up with the pursuit of knowledge, it is literally part of human nature. But hidden in this statement is another issue which in this day of universal enlightenment and mass education may seem no issue at all, but certainly was for the Pre-Socratics, namely, *ought* man to pursue knowledge, or does such an enterprise constitute an act of *hybris* from which he should piously refrain, and in any case for which he is likely to be punished? The Judeo-Christian teaching about the fall of man is instructive in this regard, but such a view, without piety or clear pessimism, is still present today both theoretically in such theses of romanticism as the concept of the "noble savage," and practically in the anti-intellectualism that is always an aspect of romanticism and which is as strong as ever today. But second, the thesis that we seek origins in order to know presumes a view which is utterly decisive for the development of Western culture, namely, that the fundamental mode of knowledge, the deepest, most genuine knowledge, is knowledge of the *causes* of phenomena. The kernel of this view is present at least as early as Hesiod, and it was disputed at least as early as Pythagoras. Needless to say, it involves the interpretation of origins as causes, a conception which is by no means indisputable. Nevertheless, given the dominance of this interpretation, the decisive direction of which was set for Western culture by Aristotle in his famous doctrine of the four causes,[23] it is not difficult to note its profound consequences. One need only mention the conviction in psychology that the fundamental knowledge of man's psyche is knowledge of its causes, whether that causal explanation be stated in an elaborate metaphysic of id, ego, and superego or in the more somber language of stimulus-response theory. The significance of causal knowledge in the development of modern science testifies to the almost unquestioned acceptance of this view in that sphere; more generally, it is everywhere taken as the reasonable thing to do when one wants to attain knowledge of X, to investigate the causes of X, whether X be my soul, the molecular structure of water, or a malfunction in one's automobile. This dominant view presumes the validity of a certain interpretation of origins which in Pre-Socratic times was much more controversial, that is, less unreflectively accepted, than it is today. Finally, one can add the much too common view, which can only be interpreted as condescension, that it is worthwhile to seek origins, for example, that it is worthwhile to seek the origins of philosophy in Pre-Socratic thought, because in doing so we shall more easily avoid the mistakes of our less sophisticated predecessors.

But we should return to the view present in the remark of Aristotle quoted above that a dwelling upon or seeking out of our origins is literally natural for man, part of the nature of what it is to be human. This view, present in some Pre-Socratic thinkers but best worked out in the dialogues of Plato, can here perhaps most appropriately be discussed in the language of contemporary existentialism. It is that man is "temporal." To put this extremely complex view as succinctly as possible: What I am as a person, my unity or identity, is constituted at least in part by a relation between my past (what I have been and have done), my present (what I am and am doing), and my future (what I intend, aspire to, and more generally how I orient myself toward my future possibilities). If this view or anything like it is true, then even if we try to deny it, we *are* related to our origins, and from this it would seem to follow that if we wish to understand ourselves, we had better indeed reflect upon our origins and about the meaning of origins. But this, to repeat, presumes the desirability of self-knowledge. And indeed, it is Thales who first made explicit the significance of self-knowledge for man by saying that it is the most difficult of all things.[24]

The position that is defended in this book, then, is that the so-called Pre-Socratics are worth our thoughtful consideration not because they were the naïve origins of philosophy in the chronological sense, but because in their extant fragments is especially visible the atemporal, ontological origins of philosophy in something like the experience of wonder or the natural desire for knowledge and, ultimately, the origins of philosophy in human nature itself. To put this thesis in somewhat strong terms for the sake of emphasis and challenge: The origin of philosophy is human nature itself because philosophy is the culmination, the highest consequence, of what it is to be human. The beginning and the end, the origin and the *telos*, if not the same, are at least intimately connected.

NOTES: INTRODUCTION

1. *Cf.* Plato, *Theaetetus*, 155d.

2. Many modern philosophers have held a similar view. For the seventeenth-century philosopher Spinoza, the origin of philosophy was the insight into "the union existing between the mind and the whole of nature." *Works of Spinoza*, Vol. II, *On The Improvement of the Understanding*, trans. by R. H. M. Elwes (New York, Dover Publications, 1951), p. 6. *See also* Martin Heidegger, *What is Philosophy?* (New Haven, College and University Press, 1956), pp. 78 ff.

3. Martin Heidegger, *An Introduction to Metaphysics*, trans. by Ralph Manheim (New Haven, Conn., Yale University Press, 1959), pp. 82 ff. *See also* Alexandre Kojéve, *Essai d'une Histoire Raisonnée de la Philosophie Päienne*, (Gallimard, 1968), Tome I, p. 196.

4. *See* Kojéve, *ibid.*, p. 11. Stanley Rosen, "Thales: The Beginning of Philosophy," in *Essays in Philosophy* (University Park, the Pennsylvania State University Press, 1962), p. 25. George Seidel, O.S.B., *Martin Heidegger and the Pre-Socratics* (Lincoln, University of Nebraska Press, 1964), p. 18.

5. G. W. F. Hegel, *Lectures on the History of Philosophy*, trans. by E. S. Haldane, 3 Vols. (New York, Humanities Press, 1963).

6. *Cf.* G. W. F. Hegel, *The Phenomenology of Mind*, trans. by J. B. Baillie (New York, Macmillan Co., 1961).

7. F. M. Cornford, *From Religion to Philosophy* (New York, Harper Torchbooks, 1957).

8. *Ibid.*, p. 9.

9. *Ibid.*, p. 9.

10. *Ibid.*, p. 43.

11. *Ibid.*, p. 122.

12. *Ibid.*, p. 135.

13. Not to mention flattering; it makes the Pre-Socratics nearly primitives and suggests that our own "sophisticated" views represent immense progress.

14. G. S. Kirk and J. E. Raven, *The Pre-Socratic Philosophers* (Cambridge, England, Cambridge University Press, 1960), p. 72. *See also* p. 98.

15. W. K. C. Guthrie, *The Greek Philosophers from Thales to Aristotle* (New York, Harper Torchbooks, 1950), p. 29.

16. J. Burnet, *Early Greek Philosophy* (New York, Meridian Books, 1957), p. 1. *See* pages 13-14 for his criticism of Cornford, which is founded on Burnet's insistence on the atheistic character of what he significantly refers to as "Ionian science," or as he expresses it alternatively, the "complete break" with earlier religion. This view is itself not especially plausible and is hardly destructive of Cornford's hypothesis. And, in any case, as the quoted sentence testifies, Burnet does not entirely free himself from Cornford's view. For a view closer to my own, *see* M. Nahm, *Selections from Early Greek Philosophy* (New York, Appleton-Century-Crofts, 1964), pp. 17, 19, 21 *passim*.

17. Cornford, *op. cit.*, p. 39.

18. *Ibid.*, p. 54.

19. *Ibid.*, p. 126. *See also* pp. 19, 21, 43, 55 *passim*.

20. *Ibid.*, p. 45, for its undefended assumptions.

21. For an excellent account of this phenomenon, *see* John Anderson, *The Individual and the New World* (University Park, the Pennsylvania State University Press, 1955).

22. Aristotle, *Metaphysica*, 980a 20.

23. *Ibid.*, 983a 25-983b 1, *Physica*, 194b 15-195a 3.

24. Diogenes Laertius, *Lives of Eminent Philosophers*, trans. by R. D. Hicks, The Loeb Classical Library (New York, G. P. Putnam's Sons, 1935), Vol. I, pp. 36-37.

Myth and (or as) Philosophy

A S the discussion of Cornford's interpretation of the origins of philosophy indicated, one of the most plausible ways to distinguish between philosophy and whatever comes before philosophy is to interpret the former as an effort to give a quasiscientific or materialistic account of things—however naïve—and to call the latter myth, which offers an explanation of similar phenomena in terms of the gods, heroes, etc. Whenever this is done, one points of course to the great eighth-century B.C. epic poems of Homer, the *Iliad* and *Odyssey*, to Hesiod's *Theogony* and *Works and Days*, and occasionally to even earlier Babylonian and Sumerian epics, such as the *Epic of Gilgamesh*. Such an explanation begs the questions of, or at least does not penetrate the possibility of, the origin of both philosophy *and* myth in the very nature of man. Consequently, the relation between myth and philosophy is by no means clear; this relation itself becomes a philosophic *question*, and we can no longer speak in a facile way of philosophy "arising out of" myth. In the passage quoted at the beginning of the Introduction, Aristotle seems to well appreciate the complex character of this relation. For he emphasizes that "even a lover of myth is in a sense a lover of wisdom, for the myth is composed of wonders."[1] Aristotle recognizes that there is both a similarity and a difference between myth and philosophy, and so that their relation is problematic. Following Aristotle's guidance rather than Cornford's, we shall begin these reflections with such myth tellers as Homer, Hesiod, and the author(s) of Gilgamesh. But we shall do so with a special concern to discover what is "in a sense" philosophical about these works, and why we might consider them thus. Let us begin then with a general statement of what are the philosophic themes present in these works, and then go on to discuss each individual work in more detail. This scheme, then, will begin to set forth a conception of the nature of philosophy itself.

The first theme is a recognition of and reflection upon a twofold difference—between man and nature on the one hand, man and the divine on the other. From the beginning, it seems, men understood themselves as on the one hand distinctive, different from the other things in nature and from the divine, yet involved in a relationship with both and orienting their lives toward both. One the one hand, man sees himself as having a certain power or control over the world around him, control which can be exhibited by the ever-increasing *techne* of his hands and mind. Yet at the same time, we again and again come to the recognition that the world is not ours to master, that there are forces, dimensions to the world which operate outside of our control. It may be safely said that this latter recognition was held more firmly by the ancient Greek people than by men of our own time. It is easy to see that, given this view of the world, a hierarchy develops rather naturally, with the things of the world over which man can exhibit control as "below" man in dignity and worth, and those forces over which man cannot exert his power and to which he must submit as "higher" than man, or divine. This relation itself becomes immediately more complex when it is realized that what first and still strikes man as "divine" is often some aspect of nature. Nevertheless, present in all the works we are going to consider here is a conception of man's experience of the world which is so fundamental, so powerful, that it is in myriad ways still with us. This is a conception of man as "in the middle," between the things of nature on the one hand—and especially as they come to respond to man's efforts at control—and the divine on the other. Man lives his life largely in terms of the way he comports himself toward that which he recognizes as other than himself, and in the notions of nature and the divine we have two of the most pervasive and enduring modes of comportment available to man. Out of the recognition of the "inferior" status of the things of nature emerges man's propensity for mastery, and his general stance toward nature as one of exploitation, a stance the ambiguous fruits of which we are still realizing to this day. Out of his recognition of the superior, or "divine," status of other phenomena comes the necessity of submission, the very possibility of religion, the humility which acts as a temper to the *hybris* of the claim to mastery, and yet the insistence that however different and even superior the divine may be, it is still *ac-*

cessible in some way or another, whether by prayer, sacrifice, good behavior, or careful study. Perhaps most significant of all, out of these orientations comes a crucial aspect of man's understanding of himself as an intermediary creature, as such having a nature unique from other creatures, and as oriented toward the world of his experience in a way which is necessarily complex and ambiguous. It seems fair to say that out of this recognition of his status as superior to some things and inferior to others, that is, out of the recognition of the "ingredients" of his experience of mastery and submission, the mortal and the divine, emerges the possibility and the direction of morality, ethics, and man's comportment toward his fellowman.

One crucial aspect of man's conception of himself, present with remarkable explicitness at least as early as Gilgamesh, is *finitude* as that which decisively separates man from the divine. Man cannot be divine because he dies; human experience is thus fundamentally characterized, one may even say defined, by his finitude, and so by his special relation to time. But at the same time, man is finite in a special way, a way different, say, from the way in which a rock or an oak or an animal is finite. In particular, man is *aware* of his finitude, and the meaning which his life takes on, or the lack thereof, is intimately tied up with his attitude toward this recognition. Gilgamesh, Achilles, Odysseus, and Hesiod himself can be seen to exhibit some of the nuances of the way in which man, and man alone, self-consciously faces up to the fact of his mortality.

So whether man is different both from the divine and from nature, whether man is superior to some things and inferior to others, capable of mastering some but required to revere others, all this would seem to matter little unless man *knows* it. And so coprimordial with the sort of themes suggested is the issue of our *knowledge* of them. Yet strangely enough the very difference, or separation, of man from the divine and from nature is what makes our knowledge of them initially problematic. If we are different from the divine, different from nature, what is the nature of that access which we must already have to them which enables us to recognize that difference? This issue, in fact, gives rise to a network of issues centering in the question of knowledge of things other than oneself. Not surprisingly, because access to the divine seems both most fundamental and most problematic, these issues centered in these earlier writers, and especially in Hesiod and Xenophanes, around the nature and possibility of man's knowledge of the divine. Especially important to the development of Western thinking concerning knowledge were the responses given to questions such as these: Is complete, or genuine, knowledge of the cosmos, of both the mortal and the divine, possible? That is, is the world as a whole, including its beginnings, or origin (*arche*), through and through intelligible, or is human knowledge of the world limited by some primordial and unfathomable mystery? Is the pursuit of knowledge good, and so *ought* man to pursue knowledge? Does he do so at some great risk? To be sure, the responses given by these early writers to such questions as these are diverse and important. But what is at least as important, if not more so, was the fact that it was these issues and not others which were raised in the first place. It is the issues, even more than the specific answers, which are still with us today, and so which have had the most fundamental influence.

The way in which men first asked the questions they did and made the claims that they did to knowledge of the world tended to be in terms of juxtapositions of apparent opposites. This was eventually to be made an explicit and central part of the teachings of thinkers as diverse as Pythagoras, Heraclitus, and Empedocles, but this way of presenting the issues was present as early as the writers presently under discussion. In a way, the many "pairs" of opposites discussed can be seen as variations on one fundamental opposition, that between unity and multiplicity.

The issue can be put this way: As we look around us, what our senses first present us is a situation of remarkable and even bewildering multiplicity. There are many, many things—from hills, valleys, and rivers to acts of justice, piety, and treachery. In an account we give of the world and, in particular, of the origins of the world of our experience, are we to preserve the quality of multiplicity as primordial and unresolvable, or are we to suggest that this multiplicity is grounded in and arises out of a unity which, although less obvious, is nevertheless more fundamental? One of the most important nuances of this opposition is that between being and becoming, or alternatively between rest and motion, permanence and change.[2] Again, these themes become central and explicit in the controversy between such thinkers as Parmenides and Heraclitus, but their presence can already be appreciated in these early works of literature. Is the origin of the world fundamentally at rest, is it permanent, can it be called being? Or, from the beginning and at its fundament, is the whole in a state of becoming, of change and motion? To mention perhaps the most complex instance among the present writers, Hesiod's difficult response to the issue has been decisive not only to the development of later Pre-Socratic views, but to the sophisticated positions held by philosophers today. If one holds to the primacy of becoming, then the theme of genesis, of creativity, and so of Eros can be expected to arise at the very beginning of one's account, as it does with Hesiod. Such a view can naturally develop a conception of something like "progress" as itself a "natural" phenomenon. But if everything is in a state of radical becoming, change, flux, how does it become intelligible at all? Is not some primordial permanence or being required in order to explain the intelligibility of experience? The difficulty and complexity of these questions can be highlighted if we now introduce the political dimension of this issue, namely, the opposition between peace and war. In the political sphere, the most radical form of change, motion, or becoming is war, and the counterpart of unity, rest, permanence, and being would seem to be peace. To ask a question no less pertinent to our present-day situation than it was to Hesiod and Homer, if I want to hold to a world characterized fundamentally by multiplicity, by change, and so by the possibility of progress, must I not accept as a consequence the view that war is the fundamental condition existing among men, and peace at best a temporary imposition? Is "progress with peace" in the end even intelligible?

Let us turn in greater detail to the way in which these and later themes were treated by these early writings, and first to the oldest, the Sumerian *Epic of Gilgamesh*, which dates back to the second millennium B.C.

The Epic of Gilgamesh[3]

From the very beginning of the epic, it is made clear that Gilgamesh is a man, not a god. The single most important feature of that difference, for the story and certainly for Gilgamesh's view of himself, is that he is not immortal. But he is no ordinary man. Gilgamesh is an epic hero, destined to distinguish himself from more ordinary men by heroic deeds. As such, he stands as something of an ideal, a man indeed, but the kind of man whom we can and must aspire to be, the kind of man whom individual men succeed in emulating only in their most superb moments. But insofar as Gilgamesh represents a vision of what we might call the *telos* of man, it is made immediately clear that man, notwithstanding his mortality, has a nature, a being, which is unique indeed. In the Prologue we read,

> When the gods created Gilgamesh they gave him a perfect body. Shamash the glorious sun endowed him with beauty, Adad the god of the storm endowed him with courage, the great gods made his beauty perfect, surpassing all others. Two thirds they made him god and one third man.[4]

Insofar as man aspires to and becomes more than he usually is, he becomes "more than a man"; he participates in the divine. Man as an aspirer to unusual achievement is "part god" as the Prologue suggests of Gilgamesh. The *telos* of man, what he can be and is at his best, is "in the middle" between the mortal and the divine and, as such, participant in both. If man were at all times "merely mortal," he would be adequately accounted for as a biological specimen, no different in his ontological status from a rabbit or a lion. But such an account is always inadequate, that is, partial even when true, because man again and again aspires to and achieves more than could be expected of him as a biological specimen. Gilgamesh represents the achievement of this tendency in man, which nowadays is often called the transcendent character of human being. This aspect of man is represented in the epic by characterizing Gilgamesh as part god, part man. Indeed, the proportion even suggests man's propensity to aspire *more* toward the divine. In Enkidu, Gilgamesh's friend, we see presented the alternative possibility of man, that of inclining more toward the beasts. Enkidu is raised by beasts and early in his life behaves like one. Man lives between these two poles— the divine and the beasts.

But to characterize Gilgamesh as part man, part god, is already to have appreciated the difference between the mortal and the divine, to understand the world in terms of that utterly fundamental duality, and to understand human being as in the middle, that is, as participating in, mediating between, and referring to both. It is noteworthy that the epic thus begins with a characterization of Gilgamesh's, and so man's, *origins*, as ontological, and even teleological, that is, in terms of an account of man's nature which points toward what he *can* be. Only later do we learn who Gilgamesh's historical mother and father were.

But the initial exhilaration that might follow this recognition of man as a transcendent being is immediately tempered by the pervasive recognition that man is mortal, and so that what transcendence is his will always be finite. Gilgamesh's friend Enkidu first says, in a locution that gets repeated at several important junctures in the epic,

> The father of the gods has given you kingship, such is your destiny, everlasting life is not your destiny. Because of this do not be sad at heart, do not be grieved or oppressed.[5]

It can be said that this recognition is the chief motivation for Gilgamesh's achievements; it gives him that sense of urgency which demands that he take his life in his own hands and take that action which will lead him to become what he will become. In an extremely instructive passage, the god Shamash, who is immortal and consequently not motivated by the sense of urgency brought on by the recognition of finitude, wonders at Gilgamesh's impatience to go on the forest journey. Gilgamesh replies,

> O Shamash, hear me, hear me, Shamash, let my voice be heard. Here in the city man dies oppressed at heart, man perishes with despair in his heart. I have looked over the wall and I see the bodies floating on the river, and that will be my lot also. Indeed I know it is so, for whoever is tallest among men cannot reach the heavens, and the greatest cannot encompass the earth. Therefore I would enter that country: because I have not established my name stamped on brick as my destiny decreed, I will go to the country where the cedar is cut.[6]

Much later, when the goddess Siduri proposes to Gilgamesh the policy of "Eat, drink, and be merry," Gilgamesh replies,

> How can I be silent, how can I rest, when Enkidu whom I love is dust, and I too shall die and be laid in the earth for ever.[7]

We find here embodied an issue and a teaching as important today as it was for Gilgamesh. When we are in certain moods, the fact that we will die someday can strike us as rendering life and whatever aspirations we might have futile and even absurd. To this the teaching embodied in *The Epic of Gilgamesh* responds that it is precisely this recognition and the sense of urgency brought about by it which motivates us to act as we will, and so which enables our lives to take on what meaning they can. Far from being the *destruction* of meaning in life, our finitude constitutes one of the conditions for the very possibility of such meaning emerging.[8] This is very well brought out by the contrast between Gilgamesh and Utnapishtim, the only mortal to whom the gods ever granted eternal life. This apparent blessing did not enhance the quality of Utnapishtim's life. When Gilgamesh finally meets him he is disappointed:

> I look at you now, Utnapishtim, and your appearance is no different from mine; there is nothing strange in your features. I thought I should find you like a hero prepared for battle, but you lie here taking your ease on your back.[9]

Without the urgency of finitude, Utnapishtim achieves not noble deed after noble deed, but rather nothing. From this standpoint, it is not difficult to see why Gilgamesh should be encouraged on those occasions when he is reminded of his finitude,

> Because of this do not be sad at heart, do not be grieved or oppressed.[10]

Let us now turn to the issue discussed earlier—whether human experience of the world is characterized by a fundamental permanence or change, whether, that is, in its *origins* it is permanent or changing. Although Gilgamesh's nature as transcendent is the basic theme of the epic, insofar as the question becomes relevant to the story the epic itself is brief and unambiguous. In response to Gilgamesh's question about everlasting life, Utnapishtim replies,

> There is no permanence. Do we build a house to stand for ever, do we seal a contract to hold for all time? Do brothers divide an

inheritance to keep for ever, does the flood-time of rivers endure?
It is only the nymph of the dragon-fly who sheds her larva and sees
the sun in his glory. From the days of old there is no permanence.[11]

The claim to the priority of change to rest, of becoming to being, has
been established.

Homer's Iliad and Odyssey

It may be said that, taken together, the *Iliad* and *Odyssey* have as
their basic themes war (the Trojan war), wrath (the anger of Achilles
which the opening lines of the *Iliad* explicitly state as its theme), and
wandering (the journey of Odysseus from Troy to his home in Ithaca).
As such, one can plausibly say that Homer's epics continue to embody
the priority of becoming and change to permanence and being. What
Utnapishtim says to Gilgamesh is surely true of the experience of the
world presented in the *Iliad* and *Odyssey*: There is no permanence, not
for Achilles, not for Hector, not for Agamemnon, not for Odysseus, not
for the suitors of Penelope. If anything, their experience comes closer to
imitating the primal chaos out of which Hesiod says the world arises.
The war, of course, contributes to this, but war, wrath, and wandering
were not chosen as themes arbitrarily; they suggest an intimation of
what the fundamental condition of man is. But this lack of permanence
is accentuated in these epics by the fickleness of the gods, who might be
expected to be the representatives of permanence, stability, and being.
Their fickleness and quarrels perpetrate and continue the war. This is,
of course, what Xenophanes (and later Plato) criticizes so strongly in
Homer and Hesiod. The divine, which is to become in those writers who
defend permanence the *arche*, the principle and origin of what is depend-
able and permanent in the world, is in these epics the very *arche* of its
radical flux. It is Apollo's anger at the Greeks for their ill treatment of
one of his priests which precipitates the calamity with which the *Iliad*
opens; it is the anger of Poseidon at Odysseus which prolongs his
miseries on his long wandering homeward; indeed, it is often jealousies
and disputes among the gods themselves which precipitate and prolong
the war and the miseries of the heroes of Homer's epics. To be sure,

those heroes appeal to their gods for support, but certainly not as objective arbiters by which the war might justly be brought to an end. The gods are susceptible of propitiation and even bribery so that individual desires can be fulfilled. Thus the Homeric epic manifests a clear recognition of the distinction between the divine and the mortal, man as in thrall to forces beyond his control. But it is clear throughout that those superior forces are not superior by virtue of their rationality, goodness, or stability; they are superior by virtue of superior power which they employ with all the fickleness of the most irrational of humans. That vision of the world often presented today in the literature of the absurd, a world rendered absurd not only by the irrationality of human action but by the irrationality of those forces beyond our control and even by the structure of being itself, that vision is already strongly present in the Homeric epics.

Needless to say, there is much more of philosophical import present in these two magnificent epics. But adequate discussion would demand more detailed consideration of the entire works. Instead, let us move on to Hesiod's *Theogony*, where in a more succinct way, an equally remarkable conception of the structure of the world of human experience is presented.

Hesiod's Theogony and Works and Days

Let us begin the interpretation of Hesiod with a partial presentation of his account of the genesis of the gods in the form of a chart which we can use for easy reference (see page 39).

Surely the first issue of import is presented in the first clause of the genealogy: "First of all there came Chaos. . . ."[12] Now it has been shown to the satisfaction of most scholars that the word "Chaos" (*Xáos*) probably did not mean precisely the same thing as it does for us now. The most popular interpretation seems to be that as Hesiod employed it, it referred to the "gap" between earth and sky.[13] However, there is no interpretation of Hesiod's term "Chaos" which contradicts what is of central importance to Hesiod's account of the origins of the world: It was fundamentally unintelligible and inarticulable. First of all came Chaos; later the world becomes increasingly intelligible as it gets increasingly articulated, as earth and sky, day and

HESIOD'S THEOGONY

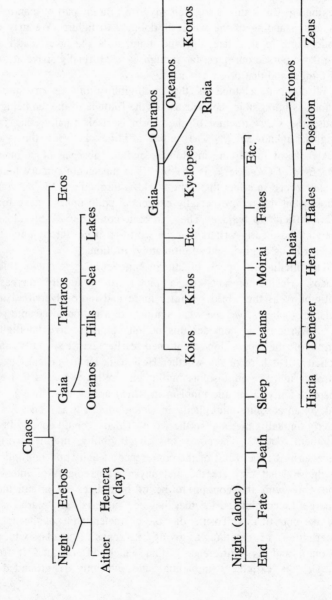

night, hills and lakes come to be. But the beginnings are radically unintelligible; that sense of the word "Chaos" is surely present from the beginning. But if this is so, then any effort on the part of man to come to an understanding of the whole is doomed to failure. We may come to understand, to articulate, day and night, hills and lakes, earth and sky, but if we pursue our quest far enough we shall finally arrive at the origin of things, and that origin is Chaos.

Wisdom, understood as the intelligibility of the structure of the whole, is impossible, not because of the finitude of human being but because the very structure of the world is itself finally, that is, in its origins, unknowable.[14] The initial affinities between this view, the fickleness of the divine in Homer, and the absence of permanence in *The Epic of Gilgamesh*, is striking. The nineteenth-century philosopher Hegel argued in effect that "the world is through and through rational." Subsequent thinkers, especially existential philosophers, have found this view difficult to believe. They, in fact, come remarkably close to the view of these early writers that the world is, if not through and through, at least in its origins, and so ultimately, irrational.

The intelligible aspects of human experience arise out of this primal Chaos. Hesiod presents us a picture of gradually increasing intelligibility as the world becomes more and more diversified into articulable segments; we see what amounts to a notion of cosmic progress. It is instructive to consider this notion of progressive intelligibility in terms of the opposition mentioned earlier between unity and multiplicity. It is hard to say whether Hesiod meant his primal Chaos as an absolute unity or an absolute multiplicity. What is true is that either an absolute unity, a cosmic monism in which not even a "two" was present, *or* an absolute multiplicity in which *nothing* was "one," would be utterly unintelligible, and so the word "Chaos" could equally be applied to them both.[15] Therefore any intelligibility in the world must necessarily be the result of the copresence of unity *and* multiplicity. We might say that they are the metaphysical ingredients of intelligibility, and only with the coming to be of both does an articulable world emerge. Later thinkers, whether they be "monists" or "pluralists," were to take note of this. To this day the characterization of the notion of a "definition" of something as giving its "genus" (that class with which it is one), and its "difference" (that which differentiates it from that class),[16] is extremely influential and evidently is grounded in the emergence of intelligibility out of the copresence of unity and multiplicity.

If we take it that "Chaos" was a "one" at least in the sense that "all there was was Chaos," then the world became increasingly intelligible as the multiplicity increased. Empedocles is later to suggest that this movement is cyclical, and that multiplicity, or what he calls "strife," will eventually increase to such a point that there will be no unity, or what he called "love," remaining, and the world will return to an unintelligible chaos. But such a cyclical view is not obviously present in Hesiod's *Theogony*. There, as indicated, we find a suggestion of progress, at least in the sense of an increasing intelligibility of the cosmos. In his account not of the gods, or cosmos, but of man, however, Hesiod seems considerably less optimistic. In the *Works and Days*, where he discusses the generations of men, we see if not a steady decline, at least a long-term downward trend in the quality of human beings. Is there at least a hint of an analogous situation in the *Theogony*? There is, and it becomes visible by more carefully considering the details of the conditions under which the increasing intelligibility of the cosmos comes about.

At what will seem to us appallingly regular intervals, the progressive articulation of the cosmos is purchased at the price of primal violence. Ouranos (sky) tries to force back the children of Gaia and himself, and so halt the progress of cosmic articulation. But Kronos (time), one of the sons of this mating, mutilates the father, Ouranos, thus paving the way for further articulation. Kronos in turn tries to halt the progressive development of the world, personified in his own children, and is forcibly overthrown by his son Zeus. Finally, Zeus too takes steps to halt any further development which might lessen his own hegemony. There are several points to be raised here. First and most basic, the suggestion is present that progressive articulation is accompanied by violence. Thus the opposition between war and peace must be raised as the political version of the earlier oppositions between unity and multiplicity, rest and motion, being and becoming. Hesiod's *Theogony* willingly accepts the metaphysical view that a world characterized by the necessary ingredients for progress—change, generation, multiplicity—will also be a world characterized by war. Hesiod does not even seem to entertain the possibility of avoiding this consequence. In our own time, the recognition that much of the impetus behind the

development of modern technology has been related to military purposes—to mention only the most obvious example—testifies to the fact
that we have still not resolved the problem.

Second, Ouranos, Kronos, and Zeus, each in his turn, tries to halt the
progress of the articulation, and so the intelligibility, of the cosmos.
There seems to be what amounts to a cosmic repulsion against articulation. That is, there is present in the world a resistance to articulation
which we can even call antiphilosophic; the pursuit of knowledge is not
unresisted, not welcomed by all forces of the cosmos. We see here the
origins of a conception of the world in which philosophy is considered,
as it was for the Greeks and for thinkers as recent as Nietzsche in the
nineteenth century, dangerous, a risk-taking enterprise.

Third, the progress that does occur, suggests the *Theogony*, is
achieved, perhaps paradoxically to our minds, through periodic recur-
rences of injustice. This evidently sets the stage for Anaximander's view
that the coming to be of intelligible entities out of *to apeiron*, "the indefinite," is an injustice, for which their death and return to the indefinite is a punishment, "according to the order of time."[17] But this
will be countered by Thales. The issue, which was indicated earlier and
is with us today, is thus set forth: Is knowledge, intelligibility, ar-
ticulateness, a fundamental good or evil? Or is it perhaps a double-
edged sword, dangerous, but best for man?

We might begin considering the ambiguity which the *Theogony*
preserves on this question by noting that to characterize the teaching of
the *Theogony* as that *all* progress was the result of violence would be a
gross overstatement. Some events in the development of the cosmos occur through love, through the acts of love whereby new "children" are
born to the likes of earth, and sky, and time. Evidently, then, progress
in the sense of increased articulation can come about both through love
and through strife, the very two opposites which Empedocles is later to
stipulate as the two origins of the cycle of the world.[18]

Indeed, Hesiod significantly makes Eros (love) be one of the very
first gods who come to be in the cosmic scheme of things. The appropriateness of this early coming to be is clear enough. Eros will henceforward serve as the generative, creative principle by which the subsequent development of the world will in significant measure come about.
But there is more to the primordial status of Eros than its being the
necessary symbol of creativity, significant though that may be. It testi-

fies as well to the presence even as early as Hesiod of the conviction that the erotic element was absolutely fundamental in the world and in the human psyche, a view which found its first and perhaps still greatest formulation in the dialogues of Plato[19] but is still evidently present for us in the theories of man developed as an outgrowth of Freudian psychology. And consistent both with Plato and with Freud, Hesiod indicates the ambiguous character of Eros itself, principle of creativity, most beautiful of the immortals, yet also the force which "breaks the limbs' strength, who in all gods, in all human beings, overpowers the intelligence in the breast, and all their shrewd planning."[20] In the hands of thinkers like Plato and Freud, this double-edged power of Eros, as the source of both the best and the worst for man and gods alike, becomes itself the source of two of the most profound examinations of human nature and human conduct.

But strangely enough, in the *Theogony*, love (Eros) is not the only or even the earliest principle of generation in the world. The opening line of the actual genesis of the world reads, "First of all there came Chaos, and after him came Gaia of the broad breast, to be the unshakable foundation of all the immortals who keep the crests of snowy Olympos, and Tartaros the foggy in the pit of the wide-wayed earth, and Eros, who is love, handsomest among all the immortals, who breaks the limbs' strength, who in all gods, in all human beings, overpowers the intelligence in the breast, and all their shrewd planning."[21] Chaos, Earth, Tartaros, and Eros itself "came to be," but not by the generative power of Eros since Eros itself was not yet born. This suggests a principle of generation or becoming prior not only to Eros but to Chaos itself, which "came to be" (*genet'*). Chaos, it seems, is not the *absolutely* fundamental source of the cosmos. That absolute origin would seem to be the apparently nonerotic generative principle by which Chaos "came to be." Could it be that thinkers such as the author(s) of *Gilgamesh*, Homer, and especially Hesiod, rather than twentieth-century existentialist philosophers, were the first to develop a conception of the world and of man which opted for the absolute priority of creativity, and so, if they had put it in such terms, that being *is* becoming?[22]

begins with the clear recognition of a difference between the mortal and

To conclude this discussion of Hesiod let us return to a theme which was developed in the discussion of *The Epic of Gilgamesh* and the Homeric epics. In both the *Theogony* and *Works and Days*, Hesiod the divine, and of the role of the Muses as the mediators between the divine and Hesiod.[23] Both the difference and the need for mediation are present here, and Hesiod's claim is to be the man blessed by the Muses to receive the divine word. But Hesiod shows his awareness of the greater complexity of this problem: If there is a difference between the mortal and the divine, how does man, a mortal, gain access to the divine and eternal? The poetic reference to the Muses does not solve the problem, since they themselves are divine, and the problem of access to the divine remains. Hesiod himself profoundly recognizes this when he has the Muses say, early in the *Theogony*, "You shepherds of the wilderness, poor fools, nothing but bellies, we know how to say many false things that seem like true sayings, but we know also how to speak the truth when we wish to."[24] Hesiod does not go on to tell us how, or whether, he knows that in what the Muses say to him they are lying or speaking the truth, and so the problem remains. It was necessary for a thinker to come along who pursued this issue more deeply and explicitly, even in terms of a criticism of Hesiod and Homer, and that thinker was Xenophanes.

Xenophanes

Although slightly inaccurate in terms of chronological order,[25] we shall now take up a consideration of Xenophanes in this first section because he responds so directly to the views of Homer and Hesiod on the problem of the divine. The first thing we note is that Xenophanes explicitly criticizes Homer and Hesiod, and by extension virtually all of Greek religion, because of their excessive anthropomorphism. Xenophanes rightly questions whether an adequate conception of the divine can be developed which makes the gods merely superpowerful, nonmortal humans. He thus begins his logos of the divine (theology) by the "negative way," insisting that the divine is "not at all like mortals in body or in mind."[26] But what he offers in its place is altogether remarkable, especially considering the strong assertion of the priority of becoming, multiplicity, and war in the earlier writings so far considered. For Xenophanes asserts a theological monism.[27] To this one god he ascribes changelessness, eternity, and rest.[28] Xenophanes' theology thus clearly exhibits the assertion, almost from the beginning, of the alternative to the account of the origins of things offered by Homer and Hesiod. The origin, the source, what is genuinely fundamental in the world, suggests Xenophanes, is eternal, one, and changeless. It is usually suggested that it was the later Pre-Socratics, Heraclitus and Parmenides, who were the outstanding spokesmen for the priority of flux and rest respectively. Whether or not this is true, it is now clear that such alternatives were available to man and being considered even before, according to the orthodox view, "philosophy" even began.

Even though Xenophanes explicitly denies that god is anthropomorphic, his is still a god characterized by intelligence, and so Xenophanes must indicate how god's "thought" differs from human thought. He does so in Fragments 24 and 25. "He sees as a whole, thinks as a whole, and hears as a whole." "But without toil he sets everything in motion, by the thought of his mind." Whereas for finite man, we see some things and with part of our minds, hear other things and with another part, think other things with another part, the divine does all as a whole. This is almost as instructive about Xenophanes' views of human awareness as it is of the divine. For it suggests that our finitude, the fact that we are not "one," changeless, and eternal means that all of our knowledge, be it the knowledge of our eyes, ears, or minds, will also be finite, that is, partial. There can be no complete knowledge for man, *because of his nature*. To have complete or perfect knowledge we would have to know with the intuitive, nonmediated completeness which Xenophanes ascribes to god as what differentiates his knowledge from our own.

It would seem to follow from the fact that god sees, thinks, and hears *as a whole*, that the activity of his mind is indistinguishable from his activity in the world. Therefore it is consistent to say, in words which remind one of the opening lines of Genesis, that god "sets everything in motion, by the thought of his mind." As a consequence of our lack of wholeness, human thought is disjuncted from the activity of man's body. Again, our incompleteness is what keeps our knowledge finite. But this disjunction is, consistently enough, overcome in the divine mind.

Yet, however different from Hesiod's and Homer's, Xenophanes' conception of the divine may be, indeed precisely because he preserves even more purely than they the *difference* between the human and the divine, he is still faced with the problem of the access for finite, incomplete man to the infinite whole of god. Xenophanes does not solve the problem but states it more explicitly.

> Truly the gods [*sic*] have not revealed to mortals all things from the beginning; but mortals by long seeking [in time] discover what is better.[29]

> And as for certain truth, no man has seen it, nor will there ever be a man who knows about the gods and about all the things I mention. For if he succeeds to the full in saying what is completely true, he himself is nevertheless unaware of it; and Opinion (seeming) is fixed by fate upon all things.[30]

> Let these things be stated as conjectural only, similar to the reality.[31]

Man is finite. Because he is so he cannot know the whole "from the beginning." But the pursuit of knowledge on man's part is still worthwhile because partial progress, progress interestingly enough in terms of an understanding of what is *better*, is possible. But it is always partial since, although man can be *aware* of the difference between the mortal and the divine or, to put this point in terms of the issue of knowing which Xenophanes suggests, although man can be aware of the difference between opinions and knowledge, he can never be clear *(saphes)* that his claim to knowledge, or access to the divine, is not really opinion. Man will never in principle *achieve* complete or adequate knowledge of the structure of the whole. He will always and necessarily be *on the way* toward knowledge, not hopelessly lost in the world of opinion but never quite certain when he has transcended opinion and achieved knowledge. The precariousness of human life and man's quest for knowledge, exhibited in Homer and Hesiod by the threat of divine violence, is still present in Xenophanes, but in the form of the finitude of human nature.

We have discussed these themes in terms of the early, so-called mythic writings of *The Epic of Gilgamesh*, Homer, Hesiod, and Xenophanes in order to call into question, that is, make worthy of question, the relation between myth and philosophy. In no sense was it intended to argue that the two were identical. But Homer, Hesiod, and the writers of *The Epic of Gilgamesh* were also poets, and Xenophanes, who so directly responded to them, wrote in verse as well. Therefore in discussing philosophic issues that arise in these poetic works we have also raised as worthy of question the relationship between philosophy and poetry, without in the least suggesting that they are identical. So far, we have seen that writers, poetic and mythic, have raised issues which seem to be philosophic, philosophic precisely because they raise questions, that is, wonder, about the origins of the world and of human being. Insofar as they do so, they themselves also reflect the question of the origin of philosophy in wonder. But this is all to say that our understanding of the very notion of origins, of wonder, and so of philosophy must be deepened as we turn to those Pre-Socratic thinkers who are more generally considered to be the "original" philosophers—Thales, Anaximander, and Anaximenes.

A. The Epic of Gilgamesh

The Epic of Gilgamesh* is a Sumerian epic poem which dates from the second millennium B.C. and is thus one of the oldest surviving works of literature. It cannot, of course, be traced to a single author but is rather part of the oral and written tradition of a whole people.

PROLOGUE

GILGAMESH KING IN URUK

O Gilgamesh, lord of Kullab, great is thy praise. This was the man to whom all things were known; this was the king who knew the countries of the world. He was wise, he saw mysteries and knew secret things, he brought us a tale of the days before the flood. He went on a long jour-

---

* From N. K. Sandars, *The Epic of Gilgamesh*.

ney, was weary, worn-out with labour, and returning engraved on a stone the whole story.

When the gods created Gilgamesh they gave him a perfect body. Shamash the glorious sun endowed him with beauty, Adad the god of the storm endowed him with courage, the great gods made his beauty perfect, surpassing all others. Two thirds they made him god and one third man.

In Uruk he built walls, a great rampart, and the temple of blessed Eanna for the god of the firmament Anu, and for Ishtar the goddess of love. Look at it still today: the outer wall where the cornice runs, it shines with the brilliance of copper; and the inner wall, it has no equal. Touch the threshold, it is ancient. Approach Eanna the dwelling of Ishtar, our lady of love and war, the like of which no latter-day king, no man alive can equal. Climb upon the wall of Uruk; walk along it, I say; regard the foundation terrace and examine the masonry: is it not burnt brick and good? The seven sages laid the foundations.

1. THE COMING OF ENKIDU

Gilgamesh went abroad in the world, but he met with none who could withstand his arms till he returned to Uruk. But the men of Uruk muttered in their houses, 'Gilgamesh sounds the tocsin for his amusement, his arrogance has no bounds by day or night. No son is left with his father, for Gilgamesh takes them all; yet the king should be a shepherd to his people. His lust leaves no virgin to her lover, neither the warrior's daughter nor the wife of the noble; yet this is the shepherd of the city, wise, comely, and resolute.'

The gods heard their lament, the gods of heaven cried to the Lord of Uruk, to Anu the god of Uruk: 'A goddess made him, strong as a savage bull, none can withstand his arms. No son is left with his father, for Gilgamesh takes them all; and is this the king, the shepherd of his people? His lust leaves no virgin to her lover, neither the warrior's daughter nor the wife of the noble.' When Anu had heard their lamentation the gods cried to Aruru, the goddess of creation, 'You made him, O Aruru, now create his equal; let it be as like him as his own reflection, his second self, stormy heart for stormy heart. Let them contend together and leave Uruk in quiet.'

So the goddess conceived an image in her mind, and it was of the stuff of Anu of the firmament. She dipped her hands in water and pinched off clay, she let it fall in the wilderness, and noble Enkidu was created. There was virtue in him of the god of war, of Ninurta himself. His body was rough, he had long hair like a woman's; it waved like the hair of Nisaba, the goddess of corn. His body was covered with matted hair like Samuqan's, the god of cattle. He was innocent of mankind; he knew nothing of the cultivated land.

Enkidu ate grass in the hills with the gazelle and jostled with wild beasts at the water-holes; he had joy of the water with the herds of wild game. But there was a trapper who met him one day face to face at the drinking-hole, for the wild game had entered his territory. On three days he met him face to face, and the trapper was frozen with fear. He went back to his house with the game that he had caught, and he was dumb, benumbed with terror. His face was altered like that of one who has made a long journey. With awe in his heart he spoke to his father: 'Father, there is a man, unlike any other, who comes down from the hills. He is the strongest in the world, he is like an immortal from heaven. He ranges over the hills with wild beasts and eats grass; he ranges through your land and comes down to the wells. I am afraid and dare not go near him. He fills in the pits which I dig and tears up my traps set for the game; he helps the beasts to escape and now they slip through my fingers.'

His father opened his mouth and said to the trapper, 'My son, in Uruk lives Gilgamesh; no one has ever prevailed against him, he is strong as a star from heaven. Go to Uruk, find Gilgamesh, extol the strength of this wild man. Ask him to give you a harlot from the temple of love, a child of pleasure; return with her, and let her woman's power overpower this man. When next he comes down to drink at the wells he will embrace her, and then the wild beasts will reject him.'

So the trapper set out on his journey to Uruk and addressed himself to Gilgamesh saying, 'A man unlike any other is roaming now in the pastures; he is as strong as a star from heaven and I am afraid to approach him. He helps the wild game to escape; he fills in my pits and pulls up my traps.' Gilgamesh said, 'Trapper, go back, take with you a harlot, a child of pleasure. At the drinking-hole he will embrace her and the game of the wilderness will surely reject him.'

Now the trapper returned, taking the harlot with him. After a three days' journey they came to the drinking-hole, and there they sat down; the harlot and the trapper sat facing one another and waited for the game to come. For the first day and for the second day the two sat waiting, but on the third day the herds came; they came down to drink and Enkidu was with them. The small wild creatures of the plains were glad of the water, and Enkidu with them, who ate grass with the gazelle and was born in the hills; and she saw him, the savage man, come from far-off in the hills. The trapper spoke to her: 'There he is. Now, woman, make your breasts bare, have no shame, do not delay but welcome his love. Let him see you naked, let him possess your body. When he comes near uncover yourself and lie with him; teach him, the savage man, your woman's art, for when his love is drawn to you the wild beasts that shared his life in the hills will reject him.'

She was not ashamed to take him, she made herself naked and welcomed his eagerness, she incited the savage to love and taught him the woman's art. For six days and seven nights they lay together, for Enkidu had forgotten his home in the hills; but when he was satisfied he went back to the wild beasts. Then, when the gazelle saw him, they bolted away; when the wild creatures saw him they fled. Enkidu would have followed, but his body was bound as though with a cord, his knees gave way when he started to run, his swiftness was gone. And now the wild creatures had all fled away; Enkidu was grown weak, for wisdom was in him, and the thoughts of a man were in his heart. So he returned and sat down at the woman's feet, and listened intently to what she said. 'You are wise, Enkidu, and now you have become like a god. Why do you want to run wild with the beasts in the hills? Come with me. I will take you to strong-walled Uruk, to the blessed temple of Ishtar and of Anu, of love and of heaven: there Gilgamesh lives, who is very strong, and like a wild bull he lords it over men.' . . .

2. THE FOREST JOURNEY

Enlil of the mountain, the father of the gods, had decreed the destiny of Gilgamesh. So Gilgamesh dreamed and Enkidu said, 'The meaning of the dream is this. The father of the gods has given you kingship, such is your destiny, everlasting life is not your destiny. Because of this do not be sad at heart, do not be grieved or oppressed. He has given you power to bind and to loose, to be the darkness and the light of mankind. He has given you unexampled supremacy over the people, victory in battle from which no fugitive returns, in forays and assaults from which there is no going back. But do not abuse this power, deal justly with your servants in the palace, deal justly before Shamash.'

The lord Gilgamesh turned his thoughts to the Country of the Living; on the Land of Cedars the Lord Gilgamesh reflected. He said to his servant Enkidu, 'I have not established my name stamped on brick as my destiny decreed; therefore I will go to the country where the cedar is felled. I will set up my name in the place where the names of famous men are written, and where no man's name is yet written I will raise a monument to the gods.'

The eyes of Enkidu were full of tears and his heart was sick. He sighed bitterly and Gilgamesh met his eye and said, 'My friend, why do you sigh so bitterly?' But Enkidu opened his mouth and said, 'I am weak, my arms have lost their strength, the cry of sorrow sticks in my throat. Why must you set your heart on this enterprise?' Gilgamesh answered Enkidu, 'Because of the evil that is in the land, we will go to the forest and destroy the evil; for in the forest lives Humbaba whose name is "Hugeness", a ferocious giant.' But Enkidu sighed bitterly and said, 'When I went with the wild beasts ranging through the wilderness I discovered the forest; its length is ten thousand leagues in every direction. Enlil has appointed Humbaba to guard it and armed him in sevenfold terrors, terrible to all flesh is Humbaba. When he roars it is like the torrent of the storm, his breath is like fire, and his jaws are death itself. He guards the cedars so well that when the wild heifer stirs in the forest, though she is sixty leagues distant, he hears her. What man would willingly walk into that country and explore its depths? I tell you, weakness overpowers whoever goes near it: it is not an equal struggle when one fights with Humbaba; he is a great warrior, Gilgamesh, the watchman of the forest never sleeps.'

Gilgamesh replied: 'Where is the man who can clamber to heaven? Only the gods live for ever with glorious Shamash, but as for us men, our days are numbered, our occupations are a breath of wind. How is this, already you are afraid! I will go first although I am your lord, and you may safely call out, "Forward, there is nothing to fear!" Then if I fall I leave behind me a name that endures; men will say of me, "Gilgamesh has fallen in fight with ferocious Humbaba." Long after the

child has been born in my house, they will say it, and remember.'
Enkidu spoke again to Gilgamesh, 'O my lord, if you will enter that
country, go first to the hero Shamash, tell the Sun God, for the land is
his. The country where the cedar is cut belongs to Shamash.'

Gilgamesh took up a kid, white without spot, and a brown one with
it; he held them against his breast, and he carried them into the presence
of the sun. He took in his hand his silver sceptre and he said to glorious
Shamash, 'I am going to that country, O Shamash, I am going; my
hands supplicate, so let it be well with my soul and bring me back to the
quay of Uruk. Grant, I beseech, your protection, and let the omen be
good.' Glorious Shamash answered, 'Gilgamesh, you are strong, but
what is the Country of the Living to you?'

'O Shamash, hear me, hear me, Shamash, let my voice be heard. Here
in the city man dies oppressed at heart, man perishes with despair in his
heart. I have looked over the wall and I see the bodies floating on the
river, and that will be my lot also. Indeed I know it is so, for whoever is
tallest among men cannot reach the heavens, and the greatest cannot encompass the earth. Therefore I would enter that country: because I have
not established my name stamped on brick as my destiny decreed, I will
go to the country where the cedar is cut. I will set up my name where the
names of famous men are written; and where no man's name is written I
will raise a monument to the gods.' The tears ran down his face and he
said, 'Alas, it is a long journey that I must take to the Land of Humbaba. If this enterprise is not to be accomplished, why did you move
me, Shamash, with the restless desire to perform it? How can I succeed
if you will not succour me? If I die in that country I will die without ran-
cour, but if I return I will make a glorious offering of gifts and of praise
to Shamash.'

So Shamash accepted the sacrifice of his tears; like the compas-
sionate man he showed him mercy. He appointed strong allies for
Gilgamesh, sons of one mother, and stationed them in the mountain
caves. The great winds he appointed: the north wind, the whirlwind, the
storm and the icy wind, the tempest and the scorching wind. Like
vipers, like dragons, like a scorching fire, like a serpent that freezes the
heart, a destroying flood and the lightnings' fork, such were they and
Gilgamesh rejoiced.

He went to the forge and said, 'I will give orders to the armourers;
they shall cast us our weapons while we watch them.' So they gave or-

ders to the armourers and the craftsmen sat down in conference. They went into the groves of the plain and cut willow and box-wood; they cast for them axes of nine score pounds, and great swords they cast with blades of six score pounds each one, with pommels and hilts of thirty pounds. They cast for Gilgamesh the axe 'Might of Heroes' and the bow of Anshan; and Gilgamesh was armed and Enkidu; and the weight of the arms they carried was thirty score pounds.

The people collected and the counsellors in the streets and in the market-place of Uruk; they came through the gate of seven bolts and Gilgamesh spoke to them in the market-place: 'I, Gilgamesh, go to see that creature of whom such things are spoken, the rumour of whose name fills the world. I will conquer him in his cedar wood and show the strength of the sons of Uruk, all the world shall know of it. I am committed to this enterprise: to climb the mountain, to cut down the cedar, and leave behind me an enduring name.' The counsellors of Uruk, the great market, answered him, 'Gilgamesh, you are young, your courage carries you too far, you cannot know what this enterprise means which you plan. We have heard that Humbaba is not like men who die, his weapons are such that none can stand against them; the forest stretches for ten thousand leagues in every direction; who would willingly go down to explore its depths? As for Humbaba, when he roars it is like the torrent of the storm, his breath is like fire and his jaws are death itself. Why do you crave to do this thing, Gilgamesh? It is no equal struggle when one fights with Humbaba.'

When he heard these words of the counsellors Gilgamesh looked at his friend and laughed, 'How shall I answer them; shall I say I am afraid of Humbaba, I will sit at home all the rest of my days?' Then Gilgamesh opened his mouth again and said to Enkidu, 'My friend, let us go to the Great Palace, to Egalmah, and stand before Ninsun the queen. Ninsun is wise with deep knowledge, she will give us counsel for the road we must go.' They took each other by the hand as they went to Egalmah, and they went to Ninsun the great queen. Gilgamesh approached, he entered the palace and spoke to Ninsun. 'Ninsun, will you listen to me; I have a long journey to go, to the Land of Humbaba, I must travel an unknown road and fight a strange battle. From the day I go until I return, till I reach the cedar forest and destroy the evil which Shamash abhors, pray for me to Shamash.' . . .

4. THE SEARCH FOR EVERLASTING LIFE

Bitterly Gilgamesh wept for his friend Enkidu; he wandered over the wilderness as a hunter, he roamed over the plains; in his bitterness he cried, 'How can I rest, how can I be at peace? Despair is in my heart. What my brother is now, that shall I be when I am dead. Because I am afraid of death I will go as best I can to find Utnapishtim whom they call the Faraway, for he has entered the assembly of the gods.' So Gilgamesh travelled over the wilderness, he wandered over the grasslands, a long journey, in search of Utnapishtim, whom the gods took after the deluge; and they set him to live in the land of Dilmun, in the garden of the sun; and to him alone of men they gave everlasting life.

At night when he came to the mountain passes Gilgamesh prayed: 'In these mountain passes long ago I saw lions, I was afraid and I lifted my eyes to the moon; I prayed and my prayers went up to the gods, so now, O moon god Sin, protect me.' When he had prayed he lay down to sleep, until he was woken from out of a dream. He saw the lions round him glorying in life; then he took his axe in his hand, he drew his sword from his belt, and he fell upon them like an arrow from the string, and struck and destroyed and scattered them.

So at length Gilgamesh came to that great mountain whose name is Mashu, the mountain which guards the rising and the setting sun. Its twin peaks are as high as the wall of heaven and its paps reach down to the underworld. At its gate the Scorpions stand guard, half man and half dragon; their glory is terrifying, their stare strikes death into men, their shimmering halo sweeps the mountains that guard the rising sun. When Gilgamesh saw them he shielded his eyes for the length of a moment only; then he took courage and approached. When they saw him so undismayed the Man-Scorpion called to his mate, 'This one who comes to us now is flesh of the gods.' The mate of the Man-Scorpion answered, 'Two thirds is god but one third is man.'

Then he called to the man Gilgamesh, he called to the child of the gods: 'Why have you come so great a journey; for what have you travelled so far, crossing the dangerous waters; tell me the reason for your coming?' Gilgamesh answered, 'For Enkidu; I loved him dearly, together we endured all kinds of hardships; on his account I have come, for the common lot of man has taken him. I have wept for him day and night, I would not give up his body for burial, I thought my friend would come back because of my weeping. Since he went, my life is nothing; that is why I have travelled here in search of Utnapishtim my father; for men say he has entered the assembly of the gods, and has found everlasting life. I have a desire to question him concerning the living and the dead.' The Man-Scorpion opened his mouth and said, speaking to Gilgamesh, 'No man born of woman has done what you have asked, no mortal man has gone into the mountain; the length of it is twelve leagues of darkness; in it there is no light, but the heart is oppressed with darkness. From the rising of the sun to the setting of the sun there is no light.' Gilgamesh said, 'Although I should go in sorrow and in pain, with sighing and with weeping, still I must go. Open the gate of the mountain.' And the Man-Scorpion said, 'Go, Gilgamesh, I permit you to pass through the mountain of Mashu and through the high ranges; may your feet carry you safely home. The gate of the mountain is open.'

When Gilgamesh heard this he did as the Man-Scorpion had said, he followed the sun's road to his rising, through the mountain. When he had gone one league the darkness became thick around him, for there was no light, he could see nothing ahead and nothing behind him. After two leagues the darkness was thick and there was no light, he could see nothing ahead and nothing behind him. After three leagues the darkness was thick, and there was no light, he could see nothing ahead and nothing behind him. After four leagues the darkness was thick and there was no light, he could see nothing ahead and nothing behind him. At the end of five leagues the darkness was thick and there was no light, he could see nothing ahead and nothing behind him. At the end of six leagues the darkness was thick and there was no light, he could see nothing ahead and nothing behind him. When he had gone seven leagues the darkness was thick and there was no light, he could see nothing ahead and nothing behind him. When he had gone eight leagues Gilgamesh gave a great cry, for the darkness was thick and he could see nothing ahead and nothing behind him. After nine leagues he felt the north wind on his face, but the darkness was thick and there was no light, he could see nothing ahead and nothing behind him. After ten leagues the end was near. After eleven leagues the dawn light appeared. At the end of twelve leagues the sun streamed out.

There was the garden of the gods; all round him stood bushes bearing gems. Seeing it he went down at once, for there was fruit of carnelian with the vine hanging from it, beautiful to look at; lapis lazuli leaves hung thick with fruit, sweet to see. For thorns and thistles there were haematite and rare stones, agate, and pearls from out of the sea. While Gilgamesh walked in the garden by the edge of the sea Shamash saw him, and he saw that he was dressed in the skins of animals and ate their flesh. He was distressed, and he spoke and said, 'No mortal man has gone this way before, nor will, as long as the winds drive over the sea.' And to Gilgamesh he said, 'You will never find the life for which you are searching.' Gilgamesh said to glorious Shamash, 'Now that I have toiled and strayed so far over the wilderness, am I to sleep, and let the earth cover my head for ever? Let my eyes see the sun until they are dazzled with looking. Although I am no better than a dead man, still let me see the light of the sun.'

Beside the sea she lives, the woman of the vine, the maker of wine; Siduri sits in the garden at the edge of the sea, with the golden bowl and the golden vats that the gods gave her. She is covered with a veil; and where she sits she sees Gilgamesh coming towards her, wearing skins, the flesh of the gods in his body, but despair in his heart, and his face like the face of one who has made a long journey. She looked, and as she scanned the distance she said in her own heart, 'Surely this is some felon; where is he going now?' And she barred her gate against him with the cross-bar and shot home the bolt. But Gilgamesh, hearing the sound of the bolt, threw up his head and lodged his foot in the gate; he called to her, 'Young woman, maker of wine, why do you bolt your door; what did you see that made you bar your gate? I will break in your door and burst in your gate, for I am Gilgamesh who seized and killed the Bull of Heaven, I killed the watchman of the cedar forest, I overthrew Humbaba who lived in the forest, and I killed the lions in the passes of the mountain.'

Then Siduri said to him, 'If you are that Gilgamesh who seized and killed the Bull of Heaven, who killed the watchman of the cedar forest, who overthrew Humbaba that lived in the forest, and killed the lions in the passes of the mountain, why are your cheeks so starved and why is your face so drawn? Why is despair in your heart and your face like the face of one who has made a long journey? Yes, why is your face burned from heat and cold, and why do you come here wandering over the pastures in search of the wind?'

Gilgamesh answered her, 'And why should not my cheeks be starved and my face drawn? Despair is in my heart and my face is the face of one who has made a long journey, it was burned with heat and with cold. Why should I not wander over the pastures in search of the wind? My friend, my younger brother, he who hunted the wild ass of the wilderness and the panther of the plains, my friend, my younger brother who seized and killed the Bull of Heaven and overthrew Humbaba in the cedar forest, my friend who was very dear to me and who endured dangers beside me, Enkidu my brother, whom I loved, the end of mortality has overtaken him. I wept for him seven days and nights till the worm fastened on him. Because of my brother I am afraid of death, because of my brother I stray through the wilderness and cannot rest. But now young woman, maker of wine, since I have seen your face do not let me see the face of death which I dread so much.'

She answered, 'Gilgamesh, where are you hurrying to? You will never find that life for which you are looking. When the gods created man they allotted to him death, but life they retained in their own keeping. As for you, Gilgamesh, fill your belly with good things; day and night, night and day, dance and be merry, feast and rejoice. Let your clothes be fresh, bathe yourself in water, cherish the little child that holds your hand, and make your wife happy in your embrace; for this too is the lot of man.'

But Gilgamesh said to Siduri, the young woman, 'How can I be silent, how can I rest, when Enkidu whom I love is dust, and I too shall die and be laid in the earth for ever.' He said again, 'Young woman, tell me now, which is the way to Utnapishtim, the son of Ubara-Tutu? What directions are there for the passage; give me, oh, give me directions. I will cross the Ocean if it is possible; if it is not I will wander still farther in the wilderness.' The wine-maker said to him, 'Gilgamesh, there is no crossing the Ocean; whoever has come, since the days of old, has not been able to pass that sea. The Sun in his glory crosses the Ocean, but who beside Shamash has ever crossed it? The place and the passage are difficult, and the waters of death are deep which flow between. Gilgamesh, how will you cross the Ocean? When you come to the waters of death what will you do? But Gilgamesh, down in the woods you will find Urshanabi, the ferryman of Utnapishtim; with him are the holy things, the things of stone. He is fashioning the serpent prow of the boat. Look at him well, and if it is possible, perhaps you will cross the waters with him; but if it is not possible, then you must go back.'

When Gilgamesh heard this he was seized with anger. He took his axe in his hand, and his sword from his belt, and like an arrow he sped down to the sea's edge. He shattered the stones in his anger, and he went into the wood and sat himself down, and Urshanabi saw the blade flashing, and he heard the axe, and Urshanabi said to him, 'Tell me, what is your name? I am Urshanabi, the ferryman of Utnapishtim the Faraway.' He replied to him, 'Gilgamesh is my name, I am from Uruk, from the house of Anu.' Then Urshanabi said to him, 'Why are your cheeks so starved and your face drawn? Why is despair in your heart and your face like the face of one who has made a long journey; yes, why is your face burned with heat and with cold, and why do you come here wandering over the pastures in search of the wind?'

Gilgamesh said to him, 'Why should not my cheeks be starved and my face drawn? Despair is in my heart, and my face is the face of one who has made a long journey. I was burned with heat and with cold. Why should I not wander over the pastures? My friend, my younger brother who seized and killed the Bull of Heaven, and overthrew Humbaba in the cedar forest, my friend who was very dear to me, and who endured dangers beside me, Enkidu my brother whom I loved, the end of mortality has overtaken him. I wept for him seven days and nights till the worm fastened on him. Because of my brother I am afraid of death, because of my brother I stray through the wilderness. His fate lies heavy upon me. How can I be silent, how can I rest? He is dust and I too shall die and be laid in the earth for ever. I am afraid of death, therefore, Urshanabi, tell me which is the road to Utnapishtim? If it is possible I will cross the waters of death; if not I will wander still farther through the wilderness.'

Urshanabi said to him, 'Gilgamesh, your own hands have prevented you from crossing the Ocean; when you destroyed the things of stone, you destroyed the safety of the boat.' Gilgamesh said, 'Why are you so angry with me, Urshanabi, for you yourself cross the sea by day and night, at all seasons you cross it?' Urshanabi replied. 'It was those very stones that brought me safely over. But now, go into the forest, Gilgamesh; with your axe cut poles, one hundred and twenty, cut them sixty cubits long, paint them with bitumen, set on them ferrules and bring them back.'

When Gilgamesh heard this he went into the forest, he cut poles one hundred and twenty; he cut them sixty cubits long, he painted them with bitumen, he set on them ferrules, and he brought them to Urshanabi.

Then they boarded the boat, Gilgamesh and Urshanabi together, launching it out on the waves of Ocean. For three days they ran on as it were a journey of a month and fifteen days, and at last Urshanabi brought the boat to the waters of death. Then Urshanabi said to Gilgamesh, 'Press on, take a pole and thrust it in, but do not let your hands touch the waters. Gilgamesh, take a second pole, take a third, take a fourth pole. Now, Gilgamesh, take a fifth, take a sixth and seventh pole. Gilgamesh, take an eighth, and ninth, a tenth pole. Gilgamesh, take an eleventh, take a twelfth pole.' After one hundred and twenty thrusts Gilgamesh had used the last pole. Then he stripped himself, he held up his arms for a mast and his covering for a sail. So Urshanabi the ferryman brought Gilgamesh to Utnapishtim, whom they call the Faraway, who lives in Dilmun at the place of the sun's transit, eastward of the mountain. To him alone of men the gods had given everlasting life.

Now Utnapishtim, where he lay at ease, looked into the distance and he said in his heart, musing to himself, 'Why does the boat sail here without tackle and mast; why are the sacred stones destroyed, and why does the master not sail the boat? That man who comes is none of mine; where I look I see a man whose body is covered with skins of beasts. Who is this who walks up the shore behind Urshanabi, for surely he is no man of mine?' So Utnapishtim looked at him and said, 'What is your name, you who come here wearing the skins of beasts, with your cheeks starved and your face drawn? Where are you hurrying to now? For what reason have you made this great journey, crossing the seas whose passage is difficult? Tell me the reason for your coming.'

He replied, 'Gilgamesh is my name. I am from Uruk, from the house of Anu.' Then Utnapishtim said to him, 'If you are Gilgamesh, why are your cheeks so starved and your face drawn? Why is despair in your heart and your face like the face of one who has made a long journey? Yes, why is your face burned with heat and cold; and why do you come here, wandering over the wilderness in search of the wind?'

Gilgamesh said to him, 'Why should not my cheeks be starved and my face drawn? Despair is in my heart and my face is the face of one who has made a long journey. It was burned with heat and with cold. Why should I not wander over the pastures? My friend, my younger brother who seized and killed the Bull of Heaven and overthrew Humbaba in the cedar forest, my friend who was very dear to me and endured dangers beside me, Enkidu, my brother whom I loved, the end of mortality has overtaken him. I wept for him seven days and nights till the worm fastened on him. Because of my brother I am afraid of death; because of my brother I stray through the wilderness. His fate lies heavy upon me. How can I be silent, how can I rest? He is dust and I shall die also and be laid in the earth for ever.' Again Gilgamesh said, speaking to Utnapishtim, 'It is to see Utnapishtim whom we call the Faraway that I have come this journey. For this I have wandered over the world, I have crossed many difficult ranges, I have crossed the seas, I have wearied myself with travelling; my joints are aching, and I have lost acquaintance with sleep which is sweet. My clothes were worn out before I came to the house of Siduri. I have killed the bear and hyena, the lion and panther, the tiger, the stag and the ibex, all sorts of wild game and the small creatures of the pastures. I ate their flesh and I wore their skins; and that was how I came to the gate of the young woman, the maker of wine, who barred her gate of pitch and bitumen against me. But from her I had news of the journey; so then I came to Urshanabi the ferryman, and with him I crossed over the waters of death. Oh, father Utnapishtim, you who have entered the assembly of the gods, I wish to question you concerning the living and the dead, how shall I find the life for which I am searching?'

Utnapishtim said, 'There is no permanence. Do we build a house to stand for ever, do we seal a contract to hold for all time? Do brothers divide an inheritance to keep for ever, does the flood-time of rivers endure? It is only the nymph of the dragon-fly who sheds her larva and sees the sun in his glory. From the days of old there is no permanence. The sleeping and the dead, how alike they are, they are like a painted death. What is there between the master and the servant when both have fulfilled their doom? When the Annunaki, the judges, come together, and Mammetun the mother of destinies, together they decree the fates of men. Life and death they allot but the day of death they do not disclose.'

Then Gilgamesh said to Utnapishtim the Faraway, 'I look at you now, Utnapishtim, and your appearance is no different from mine; there is nothing strange in your features. I thought I should find you like a hero prepared for battle, but you lie here taking your ease on your back. Tell me truly, how was it that you came to enter the company of the gods and to possess everlasting life?' Utnapishtim said to Gilgamesh, 'I will reveal to you a mystery, I will tell you a secret of the gods.' . . .

B. Homer

Homer is the great eighth-century B.C. Greek poet to whom is ascribed both the *Iliad* and *Odyssey*. Although today these two works are considered primarily as monumental works of literature, it should not be forgotten that for the ancient Greeks they carried very deep religious significance and could be appealed to almost as we might appeal to Biblical scripture. Like *The Epic of Gilgamesh*, these works were in good measure passed along through oral tradition; indeed, there even arose a group of men, about whom Plato writes in the *Ion*, who made the oral recitation of Homer their specialty. Not surprisingly, therefore, there is still some controversy as to whether Homer, supposedly a blind poet, was indeed a single man or simply the name for the whole of the tradition.

The selection which follows is taken from *The Odyssey*, Book V, "Hermes Is Speaking to Calypso," trans. by Alexander Pope, 1851.

"What moved this journey from my native sky,
A goddess asks, nor can a god deny:
Hear then the truth. By mighty Jove's command,
Unwilling have I trod this pleasing land;
For who, self-moved, with weary wing would sweep
Such length of ocean and unmeasured deep:
A world of waters! far from all the ways
Where men frequent, or sacred altars blaze?
But to Jove's will submission we must pay;
What power so great, to dare to disobey?   130
A man, he says, a man resides with thee,
Of all his kind most worn with misery;
The Greeks (whose arms for nine long years employ'd
Their force on Ilion, in the tenth destroy'd)
At length embarking in a luckless hour,
With conquest proud, incensed Minerva's power:
Hence on the guilty race her vengeance hurl'd,
With storms pursued them through the liquid world.
There all his vessels sunk beneath the wave!

There all his dear companions found their grave!   140
Saved from the jaws of death by Heaven's decree,
The tempest drove him to these shores and thee:
Him Jove now orders to his native lands
Straight to dismiss: so destiny commands:
Impatient Fate his near return attends,
And calls him to his country and his friends.''
   Ev'n to her inmost soul the goddess shook;
Then thus her anguish and her passion broke:
   "Ungracious gods! with spite and envy cursed!
Still to your own ethereal race the worst!   150
Ye envy mortal and immortal joy,
And love, the only sweet of life, destroy.
Did ever goddess by her charms engage
A favour'd mortal, and not feel your rage?
So when Aurora sought Orion's love,
Her joys disturb'd your blissful hours above,
Till, in Ortygia, Dian's winged dart
Had pierced the hapless hunter to the heart.
So when the covert of the thrice-ear'd field
Saw stately Ceres to her passion yield,   160
Scarce could Iäsion taste her heavenly charms,
But Jove's swift lightning scorch'd him in her arms.
And is it now my turn, ye mighty powers!
Am I the envy of your blissful bowers?
A man, an outcast to the storm and wave,
It was my crime to pity and to save;
When he who thunders rent his bark in twain,
And sunk his brave companions in the main.
Alone, abandon'd, in mid-ocean toss'd,
The sport of winds, and driven from every coast,   170
Hither this man of miseries I led,
Received the friendless, and the hungry fed;
Nay, promised—vainly promised!—to bestow
Immortal life, exempt from age and woe.
'Tis past: and Jove decrees he shall remove;
Gods as we are, we are but slaves to Jove.
Go then he may (he must, if he ordain,

Try all those dangers, all those deeps, again):
But never, never shall Calypso send
To toils like these her husband and her friend.   180
What ships have I, what sailors to convey,
What oars to cut the long laborious way?
Yet, I'll direct the safest means to go;
That last advice is all I can bestow."
    To her the power who bears the charming rod:
"Dismiss the man, nor irritate the god:
Prevent the rage of him who reigns above;
For what so dreadful as the wrath of Jove?"
    Thus having said, he cut the cleaving sky,
And in a moment vanish'd from her eye. . . .   190

    Four days were past, and now the work complete,
Shone the fifth morn, when from her sacred seat
The nymph dismiss'd him (odorous garments given)
And bath'd in fragrant oils that breath'd of heaven;
Then fill'd two goat-skins with her hands divine,
With water one, and one with sable wine:
Of every kind, provisions heaved aboard;
And the full decks with copious viands stored.   340
The goddess, last, a gentle breeze supplies,
To curl old Ocean, and to warm the skies.
    And now, rejoicing in the prosperous gales,
With beating heart Ulysses spreads his sails:
Placed at the helm he sat, and mark'd the skies,
Nor closed in sleep his ever-watchful eyes.
There view'd the Pleiads, and the Northern Team,
And great Orion's more refulgent beam,
To which, around the axle of the sky,
The Bear, revolving, points his golden eye: 350
Who shines exalted on th' ethereal plain,
Nor bathes his blazing-forehead in the main.
Far on the left those radiant fires to keep,
The nymph directed, as he sails the deep.
Full seventeen nights he cut the foamy way:
The distant land appear'd the following day:

Then swell'd to sight Phaeacia's dusky coast,
And woody mountains, half in vapours lost,
That lay before him, indistinct and vast,
Like a broad shield amid the watery waste.   360
    But him, thus voyaging the deeps below,
From far, on Solymè's aërial brow,
The king of ocean saw, and, seeing, burn'd;
(From Aethiopia's happy climes return'd:)
The raging monarch shook his azure head,
And thus in secret to his soul he said:
    "Heavens! how uncertain are the powers on high!
Is then reversed the sentence of the sky,
In one man's favour; while a distant guest
I shared secure the Aethiopian feast?   370
Behold, how near Phaeacia's land he draws!
The land, affix'd by Fate's eternal laws
To end his toils. Is then our anger vain?
No! if this sceptre yet commands the main."
    He spoke; and high the forky trident hurl'd,
Rolls clouds on clouds, and stirs the watery world,
At once the face of earth and sea deforms,
Swells all the winds, and rouses all the storms.
Down rush'd the night: east, west, together roar;
And south, and north, roll mountains to the shore;   380
Then shook the hero, to despair resign'd,
And question'd thus his yet unconquer'd mind:
    "Wretch that I am! what farther fates attend
This life of toils? and what my destined end?
Too well, alas! the island goddess knew,
On the black sea what perils should ensue.
New horrors now this destined head enclose,
Unfill'd is yet the measure of my woes;
With what a cloud the brows of heaven are crown'd!
What raging winds! what roaring waters round!   390
'Tis Jove himself the swelling tempest rears;
Death, present death, on every side appears.
Happy! thrice happy! who, in battle slain,
Press'd, in Atrides' cause, the Trojan plain!

Oh! had I died before that well-fought wall!
Had some distinguish'd day renown'd my fall
(Such as was that when showers of javelins fled
From conquering Troy around Achilles dead):
All Greece had paid me solemn funerals then,
And spread my glory with the sons of men.   400
A shameful fate now hides my hapless head,
Unwept, unnoted, and for ever dead!''
    A mighty wave rush'd o'er him as he spoke,
The raft it cover'd, and the mast it broke;
Swept from the deck, and from the rudder torn,
Far on the swelling surge the chief was borne;
While by the howling tempest rent in twain
Flew sail and sail-yards rattling o'er the main.
Long press'd, he heaved beneath the weighty wave,
Clogg'd by the cumbrous vest Calypso gave;   410
At length emerging, from his nostrils wide,
And gushing mouth, effused the briny tide;
Ev'n then, not mindless of his last retreat,
He seized the raft, and leap'd into his seat,
Strong with the fear of death. The rolling flood
Now here, now there, impel'd the floating wood.
As when a heap of gather'd thorns is cast
Now to, now fro, before th' autumnal blast;
Together clung, it rolls around the field;
So roll'd the float, and so its texture held: 420
And now the south, and now the north, bear sway,
And now the east the foamy floods obey,
And now the west-wind whirls it o'er the sea.
The wandering chief, with toils on toils oppress'd,
Leucothea saw, and pity touch'd her breast:
(Herself a mortal once, of Cadmus' strain,
But now an azure sister of the main.)
Swift as a sea-mew, springing from the flood,
All radiant on the raft the goddess stood: 430
Then thus address'd him: "Thou, whom Heaven decrees
To Neptune's wrath, stern tyrant of the seas,
(Unequal contest!) not his rage and power,

Great as he is, such virtue shall devour.
What I suggest, thy wisdom will perform:
Forsake thy float, and leave it to the storm;
Strip off thy garments; Neptune's fury brave
With naked strength, and plunge into the wave.
To reach Phaeacia all thy nerves extend,
There Fate decrees thy miseries shall end.
This heavenly scarf beneath thy bosom bind,   440
And live; give all thy terrors to the wind.
Soon as thy arms the happy shore shall gain,
Return the gift, and cast it in the main;
Observe my orders, and with heed obey,
Cast it far off, and turn thy eyes away.''
    With that, her hand the sacred veil bestows,
Then down the deeps she dived from whence she rose:
A moment snatch'd the shining form away,
And all was cover'd with the curling sea.

    Struck with amaze, yet still to doubt inclined,   450
He stands suspended, and explores his mind.
''What shall I do? Unhappy me! Who knows
But other gods intend me other woes?
Whoe'er thou art, I shall not blindly join
Thy pleaded reason, but consult with mine:
For scarce in ken appears that distant isle
Thy voice foretells me shall conclude my toil.
Thus then I judge; while yet the planks sustain
The wild waves' fury, here I fix'd remain;
But when their texture to the tempests yields,   460
I launch adventurous on the liquid fields,
Join to the help of gods the strength of man,
And take this method, since the best I can.'' . . .

C. Hesiod

Hesiod probably dates from around the end of the eighth or beginning of the seventh century B.C. and was thus a late Homeric contemporary. He came from Boeotia, an area of central Greece which later came to have a reputation, especially among Athenians, for the intellectual dullness of its inhabitants. Although much of the content of Hesiod's poems is indeed more rustic than is usually found in Homer, his works still stand, along with Homer's, as the source of much of Greek poetic tradition and of its religious tradition.

The first selection is from Hesiod's *Theogony*; the second selection is from his *Works and Days*.*

1. FROM THEOGONY

> Let us begin our singing
>   from the Helikonian Muses
> who possess the great and holy mountain
>   of Helikon
> and dance there on soft feet
>   by the dark blue water
> of spring, and by the altar
>   of the powerful son of Kronos;
> 5   who wash their tender bodies in the waters
>   of Permessos
> or Hippokrene, spring of the Horse,
>   or holy Olmeios,
> and on the high places of Helikon
>   have ordered their dances
> which are handsome and beguiling,
>   and light are the feet they move on.
> From there they rise, and put a veiling
>   of deep mist upon them,

* From Richmond Lattimore, *Hesiod*.

10 and walk in the night, singing
  in sweet voices, and celebrating
 Zeus, the holder of the aegis, and Hera,
  his lady
 of Argos, who treads on golden sandals,
  and singing also
 Athene the gray-eyed, daughter of Zeus
  of the aegis,
 Phoibos Apollo, and Artemis
  of the showering arrows,

15 Poseidon who encircles the earth in his arms
  and shakes it,
 stately Themis, and Aphrodite
  of the fluttering eyelids,
 Hebe of the golden wreath, beautiful Dione,
 Leto and Iapetos and devious-devising Kronos,
 Eos, the dawn, great Helios,
  and shining Selene,

20 Gaia, the earth, and great Okeanos,
  and dark Night,
 and all the holy rest of the everlasting
  immortals.
 And it was they who once taught Hesiod
  his splendid singing
 as he was shepherding his lambs
  on holy Helikon,
 and these were the first words of all
  the goddesses spoke to me,

25 the Muses of Olympia, daughters of Zeus
  of the aegis:
 "You shepherds of the wilderness, poor fools,
  nothing but bellies,
 we know how to say many false things
  that seem like true sayings,
 but we know also how to speak the truth
  when we wish to."
 So they spoke, these mistresses of words,
  daughters of great Zeus,

30   and they broke off and handed me a staff
             of strong-growing
        olive shoot, a wonderful thing;
             they breathed a voice into me,
        and power to sing the story of things
             of the future, and things past.
        They told me to sing the race
             of the blessed gods everlasting,
        but always to put themselves
             at the beginning and end of my singing.
35   But what is all this to me, the story
             of the oak or the boulder?

        Come you then, let us begin from the Muses,
             who by their singing
        delight the great mind of Zeus, their father,
             who lives on Olympos,
        as they tell of what is, and what is to be,
             and what was before now
        with harmonious voices, and the sound
             that comes sweet from their mouths
40   never falters, and all the mansion of Zeus
             the father
        of the deep thunder is joyful
             in the light voice of the goddesses
        that scatters through it, and the peaks
             of snowy Olympos re-echo
        and the homes of the immortals, and they
             in divine utterance
        sing first the glory of the majestic race
             of immortals
45   from its beginning, those born
             to wide Ouranos and Gaia,
        and the gods who were born to these in turn,
             the givers of blessings.
        Then next they sing of Zeus, the father
             of gods and of mortals,

and they begin this strain and end
   this strain singing of him,
how greatly he surpasses all gods,
   and in might is the strongest.

50   And then again the Olympian Muses,
     daughters of aegis-
bearing Zeus, delight his mind that dwells
   on Olympos
by singing the race of human kind,
   and the powerful Giants.
Mnemosyne, queen of the Eleutherian hills,
   bore them
in Pieria, when she had lain
   with the Kronian Father;

55   they bring forgetfulness of sorrows,
   and rest from anxieties.
For nine nights Zeus of the counsels
   lay with her, going
up into her sacred bed, far away
   from the other immortals.
But when it was a year,
   after the seasons' turning
and the months had waned away, and many days
   were accomplished,

60   she bore her nine daughters, concordant
   of heart, and singing
is all the thought that is in them,
   and no care troubles their spirits.
She bore them a little way off
   from the highest snowy summit
of Olympos; there are their shining
   dancing places, their handsome
houses, and the Graces and Desire live there
   beside them

65   in festivity; lovely is the voice
   that issues from their lips
as they sing of all the laws and all
   the gracious customs

of the immortals, and glorify them
　　with their sweet voices.
At that time, glorying in their power
　　of song, they went to Olympos
in immortal music, and all the black earth
　　re-echoed to them
70　as they sang, and the lovely beat
　　of their footsteps sprang beneath them
as they hastened to their father, to him
　　who is King in the heaven,
who holds in his own hands the thunder
　　and the flamy lightning,
who overpowered and put down
　　his father Kronos, and ordained
to the immortals all rights that are theirs,
　　and defined their stations.
75　　　All these things the Muses who have
　　their homes on Olympos
sang then, and they are nine daughters
　　whose father is great Zeus:
Kleio and Euterpe, Thaleia and Melpomene,
Terpsichore and Erato, Polymnia and Ourania,
with Kalliope, who of all holds
　　the highest position.
80　For it is she who attends
　　on the respected barons.
And when on one of these kingly nobles,
　　at the time of his birth,
the daughters of great Zeus cast their eyes
　　and bestow their favors,
upon his speech they make a distillation
　　of sweetness,
and from his mouth the words run blandishing,
　　and his people
85　all look in his direction as he judges
　　their cases
with straight decisions, and,
　　by an unfaltering declaration

can put a quick and expert end even
   to a great quarrel:
and that is why there are temperate barons,
   because for their people
who have gone astray in assembly these
   lightly turn back their actions

90   to the right direction, talking them over
   with gentle arguments.
As such a one walks through an assembly,
   the people adore him
like a god, with gentle respect;
   he stands out among all assembled.
Such is the holy gift the Muses
   give to humanity.
So it is from the Muses, and from Apollo
   of the far cast,

95   that there are men on earth who are poets,
   and players on the lyre.
The lords are from Zeus; but blessed
   is that one whom the Muses
love, for the voice of his mouth runs
   and is sweet, and even
when a man has sorrow fresh
   in the troublement of his spirit
and is struck to wonder over the grief
   in his heart, the singer,

100   the servant of the Muses singing
   the glories of ancient
men, and the blessed gods
   who have their homes on Olympos,
makes him presently forget his cares,
   he no longer remembers
sorrow, for the gifts of the goddesses
   soon turn his thoughts elsewhere.

Hail, then, children of Zeus:
   grant me lovely singing.

105   Now sound out the holy stock
            of the everlasting immortals
        who came into being out of Gaia
            and starry Ouranos
        and gloomy Night, whom Pontos, the salt sea,
            brought to maturity;
        and tell, how at the first the gods
            and the earth were begotten
        and rivers, and the boundless sea,
            raging in its swell,
110   the blazing stars, and the wide sky above all,
            tell of
        the gods, bestowers of blessings,
            who were begotten of all these,
        and how they divided their riches
            and distributed their privileges,
        and how they first took possession
            of many-folded Olympos,
        tell me all this, you Muses
            who have your homes on Olympos,
115   from the beginning, and tell who was first
            to come forth among them.
                First of all there came Chaos,
            and after him came
        Gaia of the broad breast,
            to be the unshakable foundation
        of all the immortals who keep the crests
            of snowy Olympos,
        and Tartaros the foggy in the pit
            of the wide-wayed earth,
120   and Eros, who is love, handsomest among all
            the immortals,
        who breaks the limbs' strength,
            who in all gods, in all human beings
        overpowers the intelligence in the breast,
            and all their shrewd planning.
        From Chaos was born Erebos, the dark,
            and black Night,

and from Night again Aither and Hemera,
    the day, were begotten,
125   for she lay in love with Erebos
    and conceived and bore these two.
But Gaia's first born was one
    who matched her every dimension,
Ouranos, the starry sky,
    to cover her all over,
to be an unshakable standing-place
    for the blessed immortals.
Then she brought forth the tall Hills,
    those wild haunts that are beloved
130   by the goddess Nymphs who live on the hills
    and in their forests.
Without any sweet act of love
    she produced the barren
sea, Pontos, seething in his fury of waves,
    and after this
she lay with Ouranos, and bore him
    deep-swirling Okeanos
the ocean-stream; and Koios, Krios,
    Hyperion, Iapetos,
135   and Theia too and Rheia, and Themis,
    and Mnemosyne,
Phoibe of the wreath of gold,
    and Tethys the lovely.
After these her youngest-born
    was devious-devising Kronos,
most terrible of her children;
    and he hated his strong father.
      She brought forth also the Kyklopes,
    whose hearts are proud and powerful,
140   Brontes and Steropes, and Arges
    of the violent spirit,
who made the thunder and gave it to Zeus,
    and fashioned the lightning.
These in all the rest of their shape
    were made like gods,

but they had only one eye set in the middle
    of their foreheads.
Kyklopes, wheel-eyed, was the name given them,
    by reason
145   of the single wheel-shaped eye
        that was set in their foreheads.
Strength and force, and contriving skills,
        were in all their labors.
        And still other children were born
        to Gaia and Ouranos,
three sons, big and powerful, so great
    they could never be told of,
Kottos, Briareos, and Gyes,
    overmastering children.
150   Each had a hundred intolerably strong arms
        bursting
out of his shoulders,
    and on the shoulders of each grew fifty
heads, above their massive bodies;
        irresistible
and staunch strength matched the appearance
    of their big bodies,
and of all children ever born
    to Gaia and Ouranos
155   these were the most terrible,
    and they hated their father
from the beginning, and every time each one
    was beginning
to come out, he would push them back again,
    deep inside Gaia,
and would not let them into the light,
    and Ouranos exulted
in his wicked work; but great Gaia
    groaned within for pressure
160   of pain; and then she thought of an evil,
    treacherous attack.
Presently creating the element of gray flint
she made of it a great sickle,

and explained it to her own children,
and spoke, in the disturbance of her heart,
    to encourage them:
"My sons, born to me of a criminal father,
    if you are willing

165   to obey me, we can punish your father
        for the brutal treatment
he put upon you, for he was first to think
    of shameful dealing."
        So she spoke, but fear took hold of all,
        nor did one of them
speak, but then great devious-devising Kronos
    took courage
and spoke in return,
    and gave his gracious mother an answer:

170   "My mother, I will promise to undertake
        to accomplish
this act, and for our father,
    him of the evil name, I care
nothing, for he was the first
    to think of shameful dealing."
        So he spoke, and giant Gaia
        rejoiced greatly in her heart
and took and hid him in a secret ambush,
    and put into his hands

175   the sickle, edged like teeth, and told him
        all her treachery.
And huge Ouranos came on
    bringing night with him, and desiring
love he embraced Gaia and lay over her
    stretched out
complete, and from his hiding place his son
    reached with his left hand
and seized him, and holding in his right
    the enormous sickle

180   with its long blade edged like teeth,
        he swung it sharply,
    and lopped the members of his own father,

and threw them behind him
to fall where they would,
   but they were not lost away when they were flung
from his hand, but all the bloody drops
   that went splashing from them
were taken in by Gaia, the earth,
   and with the turning of the seasons
185   she brought forth the powerful Furies
   and the tall Giants
shining in their armor
   and holding long spears in their hands;
and the nymphs they call, on boundless earth,
   the Nymphs of the Ash Trees.
But the members themselves, when Kronos
   had lopped them with the flint,
he threw from the mainland
   into the great wash of the sea water
190   and they drifted a great while
   on the open sea, and there spread
a circle of white foam
   from the immortal flesh, and in it
grew a girl, whose course first took her
   to holy Kythera,
and from there she afterward made her way
   to sea-washed Cyprus
and stepped ashore, a modest lovely Goddess,
   and about her
195   light and slender feet the grass grew,
   and the gods call her
Aphrodite, and men do too,
   and the aphro-foam-born
goddess, and garlanded Kythereia,
   because from the seafoam
she grew, and Kythereia because she had gone
   to Kythera,
and Kyprogeneia, because she came forth
   from wave-washed Cyprus,
200   and Philommedea, because she appeared

from *medea*, members.
And Eros went with her, and handsome Himeros
  attended her
when first she was born, and when she joined
  the immortal community,
and here is the privilege she was given
  and holds from the beginning,
and which is the part she plays among men
  and the gods immortal:

205   the whispering together of girls,
         the smiles and deceptions,
       the delight, and the sweetnesses of love,
         and the flattery.
           But their great father Ouranos,
         who himself begot them,
       bitterly gave to those others, his sons,
         the name of Titans,
       the Stretchers, for they stretched
         their power outrageously and accomplished

210   a monstrous thing, and they would some day
         be punished for it.

       But Night bore horrible Moros, and black Ker,
         End and Fate,
       and Death, and Sleep, and she bore also
         the brood of Dreams,
       she, dark Night, by herself,
         and had not been loved by any god,
       and then again she bore mocking Momos
         and painful Oizys,

215   and the Hesperides, who across
         the fabulous stream of the Ocean
       keep the golden apples
         and the fruit-bearing orchards,
       and she bore the destinies, the Moirai,
         and the cruelly never-forgetful
       Fates, Klotho, Lachesis, and Atropos,
         who at their birth

bestow upon mortals their portion
   of good and evil,
220   and these control the transgressions
   of both men and divinities,
and these goddesses never remit
   their dreaded anger
until whoever has done wrong
   gives them satisfaction.
And she, destructive Night, bore Nemesis,
   who gives much pain
to mortals; and afterward cheating Deception
   and loving Affection
225   and then malignant Old Age
   and overbearing Discord. . . .

Rheia, submissive in love to Kronos,
   bore glorious children,
Histia and Demeter,
   Hera of the golden sandals,
445   and strong Hades, who under the ground
   lives in his palace
and has a heart without pity;
   the deep-thunderous Earthshaker,
and Zeus of the counsels,
   who is the father of gods and of mortals,
and underneath whose thunder
   the whole wide earth shudders;
but, as each of these children
   came from the womb of its mother
460   to her knees, great Kronos swallowed it down,
   with the intention
that no other of the proud children
   of the line of Ouranos
should ever hold the king's position
   among the immortals.
For he had heard, from Gaia
   and from starry Ouranos,
that it had been ordained for him,

for all his great strength,
465   to be beaten by his son,
and through the designs of great Zeus.
Therefore he kept watch, and did not sleep,
but waited
for his children, and swallowed them,
and Rheia's sorrow was beyond forgetting.
But when she was about to bear Zeus,
the father of mortals
and gods, then Rheia went
and entreated her own dear parents,
470   and these were Gaia and starry Ouranos,
to think of some plan
by which, when she gave birth to her dear son,
the thing might not
be known, and the fury of revenge
be on devious-devising Kronos
the great, for his father,
and his own children whom he had swallowed.
They listened gladly
to their beloved daughter, and consented,
475   and explained to her
all that had been appointed to happen
concerning Kronos, who was King, and his son,
of the powerful
spirit, and sent her to Lyktos,
in the fertile countryside of Crete
at that time when she was to bring forth
the youngest of her children,
great Zeus; and the Earth, gigantic Gaia,
took him inside her
480   in wide Crete, there to keep him alive
and raise him.
There Earth arrived
through the running black night, carrying
him, and came first to Lyktos,
and holding him in her arms, hid him
in a cave in a cliff, deep in

under the secret places
of earth, in Mount Aigaion
which is covered with forest.

485 She wrapped a great stone in baby-clothes,
and this she presented
to the high lord, son of Ouranos,
who once ruled the immortals,
and he took it then in his hands
and crammed it down in his belly,
hard wretch, nor saw in his own mind
how there had been left him
instead of the stone a son,
invincible and unshakable

490 for the days to come, who soon by force
and his hands defeating him
must drive him from his title,
and then be lord over the immortals.
        And presently after this the shining limbs
and the power
of the lord, Zeus, grew great,
and with the years circling on
great Kronos, the devious-devising,
fooled by the resourceful

495 promptings of Gaia, once again
brought up his progeny.
First he vomited up the stone,
which last he had swallowed,
and this Zeus took and planted in place,
on earth of the wide ways,
at holy Pytho, in the hollow ravines
under Parnassos,

500 to be a portent and a wonder
to mortal men thereafter.
Then he set free from their dismal bonds
the brothers of his father,
the sons of Ouranos, whom his father
in his wild temper had enchained,
and they remembered, and knew gratitude

for the good he had done them,
and they gave him the thunder,
and the smoky bolt, and the flash

505   of the lightning, which Gaia the gigantic
had hidden till then.
With these to support him, he is lord
over immortals and mortals.

Iapetos took Klymene,
the light-stepping daughter of Ocean,
to be his wife, and mounted into the same bed
with her,

510   and she bore him a son, Atlas,
of the powerful spirit,
and she bore him high-vaunting Menoitios,
and Prometheus
of the intricate and twisting mind,
and Epimetheus
the gullible, who from the beginning
brought bad luck to men
who eat bread, for he first accepted
from Zeus the girl Zeus fashioned
and married her. . . .

2. FROM WORKS AND DAYS

Muses, who from Picria give glory through singing,
come to me, tell of Zeus, your own father,
sing his praises, through whose will
mortal men are named in speech or remain unspoken.
Men are renowned or remain unsung
as great Zeus wills it.

5   For lightly he makes strong,
and lightly brings strength to confusion,
lightly diminishes the great man,
uplifts the obscure one,
lightly the crooked man he straightens,

withers the proud man,
he, Zeus, of the towering thunders,
    whose house is highest.

Hear me, see me, Zeus: hearken:
    direct your decrees in righteousness.
10 To you, Perses, I would describe
    the true way of existence.

It was never true that there was only one kind
    of strife. There have always
been two on earth. There is one
    you could like when you understand her.
The other is hateful. The two Strifes
    have separate natures.
There is one Strife who builds up evil war,
    and slaughter.
15 She is harsh; no man loves her, but under compulsion
and by will of the immortals men
    promote this rough Strife.
But the other one was born
    the elder daughter of black Night.
The son of Kronos, who sits on high and
    dwells in the bright air,
set her in the roots of the earth and among men;
    she is far kinder.
20 She pushes the shiftless man to work,
    for all his laziness.
A man looks at his neighbor, who is rich:
    then he too
wants work; for the rich man presses on with
    his plowing and planting
and the ordering of his state.
    So the neighbor envies the neighbor
who presses on toward wealth. Such Strife
    is a good friend to mortals.
25 Then potter is potter's enemy, and
    craftsman is craftman's

rival; tramp is jealous of tramp,
and singer of singer.
So you, Perses, put all this firmly away
in your heart,
nor let that Strife who loves mischief
keep you from working
as you listen at the meeting place
to see what you can make of

30   the quarrels. The time comes short for litigations
and lawsuits,
too short, unless there is a year's living
laid away inside
for you, the stuff that the earth yields,
the pride of Demeter.
When you have got a full burden of that,
you can push your lawsuits,
scheming for other men's goods, yet you
shall not be given another chance

35   to do so. No, come, let us finally settle
our quarrel
with straight decisions, which are from Zeus,
and are the fairest.
Now once before we divided our inheritance,
but you seized
the greater part and made off with it,
gratifying those barons
who eat bribes, who are willing
to give out such a decision.

40   Fools all! who never learned
how much better than the whole the half is,
nor how much good there is
in living on mallow and asphodel.
For the gods have hidden and keep hidden
what could be men's livelihood. . . .

105   So there is no way to avoid what Zeus has intended.

Or if you will, I will outline it for you
    in a different story,
well and knowledgeably—store it up
    in your understanding—
the beginnings of things, which were the same for gods
    as for mortals.

In the beginning, the immortals
    who have their homes on Olympos
110   created the golden generation of mortal people.
These lived in Kronos' time, when he
    was the king in heaven.
They lived as if they were gods,
    their hearts free from all sorrow,
by themselves, and without hard work or pain;
    no miserable
old age came their way; their hands, their feet,
    did not alter.
115   They took their pleasure in festivals,
    and lived without troubles.
When they died, it was as if they fell asleep.
    All goods
were theirs. The fruitful grainland
    yielded its harvest to them
of its own accord; this was great and abundant,
    while they at their pleasure
quietly looked after their works,
    in the midst of good things
120   [prosperous in flocks, on friendly terms
    with the blessed immortals].

    Now that the earth has gathered over this generation,
these are called pure and blessed spirits;
    they live upon earth,
and are good, they watch over mortal men
    and defend them from evil;
they keep watch over lawsuits and hard dealings;
    they mantle

125   themselves in dark mist
                        and wander all over the country;
                     they bestow wealth; for this right
                        as of kings was given them.
                           Next after these the dwellers upon Olympos created
                     a second generation, of silver, far worse
                        than the other.
                     They were not like the golden ones either in shape
                        or spirit.
130   A child was a child for a hundred years,
                        looked after and playing
                     by his gracious mother, kept at home,
                        a complete booby.
                     But when it came time for them to grow up
                        and gain full measure,
                     they lived for only a poor short time;
                        by their own foolishness
                     they had troubles, for they were not able
                        to keep away from
135   reckless crime against each other,
                        nor would they worship
                     the gods, nor do sacrifice on the sacred altars
                        of the blessed ones,
                     which is the right thing among the customs of men,
                        and therefore
                     Zeus, son of Kronos, in anger engulfed them,
                        for they paid no due
                     honors to the blessed gods who live on Olympos.

140   But when the earth had gathered over this generation
                     also—and they too are called blessed spirits
                        by men, though under
                     the ground, and secondary, but still
                        they have their due worship—
                     then Zeus the father created the third generation
                        of mortals,
                     the age of bronze. They were not like
                        the generation of silver.

145   They came from ash spears. They were terrible
      and strong, and the ghastly
    action of Ares was theirs, and violence.
      They ate no bread,
    but maintained an indomitable and adamantine spirit.
    None could come near them; their strength was big,
      and from their shoulders
    the arms grew irresistible on their ponderous bodies.
150   The weapons of these men were bronze,
      of bronze their houses,
    and they worked as bronzesmiths. There was not yet
      any black iron.
    Yet even these, destroyed beneath the hands
      of each other,
    went down into the moldering domain of cold Hades;
    nameless; for all they were formidable black death
155   seized them, and they had to forsake
      the shining sunlight.

    Now when the earth had gathered over this generation
    also, Zeus, son of Kronos, created yet another
    fourth generation on the fertile earth,
      and these were better and nobler,
    the wonderful generation of hero-men, who are also
160   called half-gods, the generation before our own
      on this vast earth.
    But of these too, evil war and the terrible carnage
    took some; some by seven-gated Thebes
      in the land of Kadmos
    as they fought together over the flocks of Oidipous;
      others
    war had taken in ships over the great gulf
      of the sea,
165   where they also fought for the sake
      of lovely-haired Helen.
    There, for these, the end of death was misted
      about them.

But on others Zeus, son of Kronos, settled a living
    and a country
of their own, apart from human kind,
    at the end of the world.
And there they have their dwelling place,
    and hearts free of sorrow
in the islands of the blessed
    by the deep-swirling stream of the ocean,
prospering heroes, on whom in every year
    three times over
the fruitful grainland bestows its sweet yield.
    These live
far from the immortals, and Kronos
    is king among them.
For Zeus, father of gods and mortals,
    set him free from his bondage,
although the position and the glory still belong
    to the young gods.

After this, Zeus of the wide brows
    established yet one more
generation of men, the fifth, to be
    on the fertile earth.

And I wish that I were not any part
    of the fifth generation
of men, but had died before it came,
    or been born afterward.
For here now is the age of iron. Never by daytime
will there be an end to hard work and pain,
    nor in the night
to weariness, when the gods will send anxieties
    to trouble us.
Yet here also there shall be some good things
    mixed with the evils.
180   But Zeus will destroy this generation of mortals
    also,

in the time when children, as they are born,
    grow gray on the temples,
when the father no longer agrees with the children,
    nor children with their father,
when guest is no longer at one with host,
    nor companion to companion,
when your brother is no longer your friend,
    as he was in the old days.
185 Men will deprive their parents of all rights,
    as they grow old,
and people will mock them too,
    babbling bitter words against them,
harshly, and without shame in the sight of the gods;
    not even
to their aging parents will they give back
    what once was given.
Strong of hand, one man shall seek
    the city of another.
190 There will be no favor for the man
    who keeps his oath, for the righteous
and the good man, rather men shall give their praise
    to violence
and the doer of evil. Right will be in the arm.
    Shame will
not be. The vile man will crowd his better out,
    and attack him
with twisted accusations and swear an oath
    to his story.
195 The spirit of Envy, with grim face
    and screaming voice, who delights
in evil, will be the constant companion
    of wretched humanity,
and at last Nemesis and Aidos, Decency and Respect,
    shrouding
their bright forms in pale mantles, shall go
    from the wide-wayed
earth back on their way to Olympos,
    forsaking the whole race

200   of mortal men, and all that will be left by them
                        to mankind
                        will be wretched pain. And there shall be no defense
                        against evil. . . .

D. Xenophanes

Xenophanes of Colophon "flourished" around 530 B.C In classical scholarship, a man is said to "flourish" around his fortieth birthday, so we can suppose that Xenophanes was forty years of age around 530 B.C. He wrote poems for recitation in hexameters, and elegiacs. It is often said that he was the teacher of Parmenides, probably because of his emphasis on the unity of God. It is often debated whether he was really a "philosopher" or primarily a religious thinker.

XENOPHANES: FRAGMENT*

1.   For now, behold, the floor is clean, and so too the hands of all, and the cups. One (*attendant*) places woven garlands round our heads, another proffers sweet-scented myrrh in a saucer. The mixing-bowl stands there full of good cheer, and another wine is ready in the jar, a wine that promises never to betray us, honeyed, smelling of flowers. In our midst the frankincense gives forth its sacred perfume; and there is cold water, sweet and pure. Golden loaves lie to hand, and the lordly table is laden with cheese and with honey. The altar in the centre is decked with flowers all over, and song and revelry fill the mansion.

It is proper for men who are enjoying themselves first of all to praise God with decent stories and pure words. But when they have poured a libation and prayed for the power to do what is just—for thus to pray is our foremost need—it is no outrage to drink as much as will enable you to reach home without a guide, unless you are very old. But the man whom one must praise is he who after drinking expresses thoughts that are noble, as well as his memory (*and his endeavour*) concerning virtue allows, not treating of the battles of the Titans or of the Giants, fig-

---

* From Kathleen Freeman, *Ancilla to the Pre-Socratic Philosophers*.

ments of our predecessors, nor of violent civil war, in which tales there is nothing useful; but always to have respect for the gods, *that* is good.

2.   But if anyone were to win a victory with fleetness of foot, or fighting in the Pentathlon, where the precinct of Zeus lies between the springs of Pisa at Olympia, or in wrestling, or in virtue of the painful science of boxing, or in a dread kind of contest called Pancration: to the citizens he would be more glorious to look upon, and he would acquire a conspicuous seat of honour at competitions, and his maintenance would be provided out of the public stores by the City-State, as well as a gift for him to lay aside as treasure.

So too if he won a prize with his horses, he would obtain all these rewards, though not deserving of them as *I* am; for my craft (wisdom) is better than the strength of men or of horses. Yet opinion is altogether confused in this matter, and it is not right to prefer physical strength to noble Wisdom. For it is not the presence of a good boxer in the community, nor of one good at the Pentathlon or at wrestling, nor even of one who excels in fleetness of foot—which is highest in honour of all the feats of strength seen in men's athletic contests—it is not these that will give a City-State a better constitution. Small would be the enjoyment that a City-State would reap over the athletic victory of a citizen beside the banks of Pisa! These things do not enrich the treasure-chambers of the State.

3.   (*The men of Colophon*), having learnt useless forms of luxury from the Lydians, as long as they were free from hateful tyranny, used to go to the place of assembly wearing all-purple robes, not less than a thousand of them in all: haughty, adorned with well-dressed hair, steeped in the scent of skilfully-prepared unguents.

*   *   *

7.   Now again I shall pass to another theme, and shall show the way. . . .

   . . . And once, they say, passing by when a puppy was being beaten, he pitied it, and spoke as follows: 'Stop! Cease your beating, because this is really the soul of a man who was my friend: I recognised it as I heard it cry aloud.'

8.   By now, seven-and-sixty years have been tossing my care-filled heart over the land of Hellas. From my birth till then (*that is, till his exile*), there were twenty-five years to be added to these, if indeed I am able to tell correctly of these matters.

*   *   *

Hexameters

11.   Both Homer and Hesiod have attributed to the gods all things that are shameful and a reproach among mankind: theft, adultery, and mutual deception.

12.   They have narrated every possible wicked story of the gods: theft, adultery, and mutual deception.

*   *   *

14.   But mortals believe the gods to be created by birth, and to have their own (*mortals'*) raiment, voice and body.

15.   But if oxen (and horses) and lions had hands or could draw with hands and create works of art like those made by men, horses would draw pictures of gods like horses, and oxen of gods like oxen, and they would make the bodies (of their gods) in accordance with the form that each species itself possesses.

16.   Aethiopians have gods with snub noses and black hair, Thracians have gods with grey eyes and red hair.

*   *   *

18.   Truly the gods have not revealed to mortals all things from the beginning; but mortals by long seeking discover what is better.

19.   (*Xenophanes admired Thales for having predicted solar eclipses*).

*   *   *

21.   (*Of Simonides*). Skinflint.

*   *   *

23.   There is one god, among gods and men the greatest, not at all like mortals in body or in mind.

24.   He sees as a whole, thinks as a whole, and hears as a whole.

25.   But without toil he sets everything in motion, by the thought of his mind.

26.   And he always remains in the same place, not moving at all, nor is it fitting for him to change his position at different times.

27.   For everything comes from earth and everything goes back to earth at last.

28.   This is the upper limit of the earth that we see at our feet, in contact with the air; but the part beneath goes down to infinity.

29.   All things that come into being and grow are earth and water.

30.   The sea is the source of water, and the source of wind. For neither could (the force of the wind blowing outwards from within come into being) without the great main (sea), nor the streams of rivers, nor the showery water of the sky; but the mighty main is the begetter of clouds and winds and rivers.

31.   The sun rushing on its way above the earth and giving it warmth.

32.   And she whom they call Iris, she too is actually a cloud, purple and flame-red and yellow to behold.

33.   We all have our origin from earth and water.

34.   And as for certain truth, no man has seen it, nor will there ever be a man who knows about the gods and about all the things I mention. For if he succeeds to the full in saying what is completely true, he himself is nevertheless unaware of it; and Opinion (seeming) is fixed by fate upon all things.

35.   Let these things be stated as conjectural only, similar to the reality.

36.   All appearances which exist for mortals to look at. . . .

*   *   *

38.   If God had not created yellow honey, they would say that figs were far sweeter.

TESTIMONIA ON XENOPHANES BY DIOGENES LAERTIUS*

Xenophanes, a native of Colophon, the son of Dexius, or, according to Apollodorus, of Orthomenes, is praised by Timon, whose words at all events are:

Xenophanes, not over-proud, perverter of Homer, castigator.

He was banished from his native city and lived at Zancle in Sicily <and having joined the colony planted at Elea taught there>. He also lived in Catana. According to some he was no man's pupil, according to others he was a pupil of Boton of Athens, or, as some say, of Archelaus. Sotion makes him a contemporary of Anaximander. His writings are in epic metre, as well as elegiacs and iambics attacking Hesiod and Homer and denouncing what they said about the gods. Furthermore he used to recite his own poems. It is stated that he opposed the views of Thales and Pythagoras, and attacked Epimenides also. He lived to a very great age, as his own words somewhere testify:

*   From R. D. Hicks, *Lives of Eminent Philosophers*.

Seven and sixty are now the years that have been tossing my cares up and down the land of Greece; and there were then twenty and five years more from my birth up, if I know how to speak truly about these things.

He holds that there are four elements of existent things, and worlds unlimited in number but not overlapping <in time>. Clouds are formed when the vapour from the sun is carried upwards and lifts them into the surrounding air. The substance of God is spherical, in no way resembling man. He is all eye and all ear, but does not breathe; he is the totality of mind and thought, and is eternal. Xenophanes was the first to declare that everything which comes into being is doomed to perish, and that the soul is breath.

He also said that the mass of things falls short of thought; and again that our encounters with tyrants should be as few, or else as pleasant, as possible. When Empedocles remarked to him that it is impossible to find a wise man, "Naturally," he replied, "for it takes a wise man to recognize a wise man."

NOTES: 1

1. Aristotle, *Metaphysica*, Book I, Chap. 2, 982*b* 18.
2. I rather doubt that I could adequately defend the primordiality of the unity *vs.* multiplicity opposition to these other "nuances." What is fundamental depends upon the standpoint from which one asks the question.
3. For an excellent historical account of the Gilgamesh epic, *see* *The Epic of Gilgamesh*, trans. by N. K. Sanders (Baltimore, Penguin Books, 1960).
4. *Ibid.*, p. 59.
5. *Ibid.*, p. 68.
6. *Ibid.*, p. 70.
7. *Ibid.*, p. 99.
8. For important contemporary discussions of this issue *see* Martin Heidegger, *Being and Time*, trans. by John Macquarrie and Edward Robinson (New York, Harper and Row, 1962); Albert Camus, *The*

Myth of Sisyphus and Other Essays, trans. by Justin O'Brien (New York, Vintage Books, 1959).

9. *The Epic of Gilgamesh*, *op. cit.*, p. 104.

10. *Ibid.*, pp. 68, 115.

11. *Ibid.*, pp. 103-4.

12. Hesiod, *Theogony*, line 116.

13. The wide acceptance of this is curious since several lines *later* earth (Gaia) gives birth by herself to sky (Ouranos). *See* lines 126, 127. How could Chaos be the gap between earth and sky before earth and sky came to be?

14. This view is still present in modern philosophy. *See* John M. Anderson, "Truth, Process, and Creature in Heidegger's Thought," in Manfred Frings, ed., *Heidegger and the Quest for Truth* (Chicago, Quadrangle Books, 1968).

15. This point will be taken up more explicitly in our discussion of Empedocles.

16. For example, Aristotle's famous definition of man as the "rational animal."

17. Anaximander, Fragment 1 (D-K.).

18. *Cf.* Hesiod, *Works and Days*, lines 10-25.

19. *See* especially Plato's *Symposium, Phaedrus, Lysis*.

20. Hesiod, *Theogony*, lines 120-23.

21. *Ibid.*, lines 116-23.

22. *Cf.* Joseph Flay, "Hegel, Hesiod, and Xenophanes," in *Essays in Metaphysics* (University Park, The Pennsylvania State University Press, 1970).

23. Hesiod, *Works and Days*, lines 1-10; *Theogony*, lines 114-16.

24. Hesiod, *Theogony*, lines 26-29.

25. Xenophanes' *flourit* was 530 B.C., Thales' 585 B.C., Anaximander's 560 B.C., Anaximenes' 546 B.C.

26. Xenophanes, Fragment 23 (D.-K.)

27. *Ibid.* But note the ambiguity: "among gods and men the greatest. . . ."

28. *Ibid.*, Fragment 26.

29. *Ibid.*, Fragment 18.

30. *Ibid.*, Fragment 34.

31. *Ibid.*, Fragment 35.

Philosophy and Cosmology—
The Milesians

THE three great philosophers from Miletus—Thales, Anaximander, and Anaximenes—whose *flourits* are usually given as 585 B.C., 560 B.C., and 546 B.C. respectively, are almost universally considered to be the first philosophers. Although at the end of this section it will be argued that there is at least some point to this, it has already been argued that the justification usually given for this attribution, namely that they overcame the mythic formulations of earlier writers and replaced them with material or physical, that is, scientific, explanations of the cosmos, is utterly unsatisfactory. By way of leading into a discussion of these three philosophers, and especially now that their views have been presented, let us add a few points to the earlier discussion. By now it has been established that the easy separation of philosophy from myth, especially from the myths out of which philosophy is presumed to have arisen, is incoherent. At very least, these myths are *philosophical* myths. And is it obvious and uncontroversial that Thales' references to the quickness of *nous* or to the world as ensouled and full of daimons, or Anaximander's discussion of the retribution paid for coming-to-be, or Anaximenes' views about air as god, are devoid of reference to religious mythology? Yet even if we tentatively or partially accept the view that although the Greek myth-tellers were fundamentally *religious* thinkers, these Milesians were fundamentally scientists, this view contains more difficulties than insight. First of all, it presumes that philosophy, or at least philosophy as it originated with the Milesians, is indistinguishable from the first science, in particular from a kind of materialist physics.[1] Now, it may well be true that these first philosophers were also the first scientists; it does not therefore follow that the two are indistinguishable, much less that they deserve the auspicious title of the first philosophers by *virtue* of being the first scientists. Further, even if it is true that the enterprises of science and philosophy were not yet distinguished, which they almost certainly were not since Pythagoras was apparently the first to use the word "philosophy," the case remains the same. *We* have such a distinction, and on *that* basis what constitutes their early *scientific* thought need not be the same as what constitutes their philosophy. This point is made in an excellent way by Nietzsche in his *Philosophy in the Tragic Age of the Greeks*. In discussing Thales' principle of water as "the primal origin and the womb of all things,"[2] and so containing the thought "all things are one,"[3] he says,

> Had he [Thales] said, "Water turns into earth," we should have but a scientific hypothesis, a wrong one but difficult to disprove. But he went beyond scientific considerations. By presenting his unity-concept in the form of his water-hypothesis, Thales did not, it is true, overcome the low level of empiric insight prevalent in his time. What he did was to pass over its horizon. . . . What drove him to it was a metaphysical conviction which had its origin in a mystic intuition. We meet it in every philosophy, together with the ever-renewed attempts at a more suitable expression, this proposition that "all things are one."[4]

In short, if science is different from philosophy, today or yesterday, then what qualifies these men as scientists and what qualifies them as philosophers is not the same, and we solve nothing by saying that they were the first philosophers merely because they were the first scientists. Finally, if we do identify Milesian philosophy with Milesian science, then it follows, as an almost immediate consequence, that both their science and their philosophy are so naïve, so primitive as to hardly be worth consideration except perhaps as cultural antiques. Now although it seems true that as scientists the Milesian philosophers were naïve and primitive, they were not philosophically naïve. Let us therefore first consider Thales, not as a protoscientist, but as a philosopher.

Let us begin where Nietzsche does, with Thales' assertion that water is the *arche*, the principle, origin, or beginning of all things.[5] Before we even consider the specific choice of water, we should reflect upon the significance of the very claim that there *is* an *arche* of all things, and that it is accessible to (at least one) man. The "metaphysical conviction" of which Nietzsche spoke above is certainly present here. For Thales suggests nothing less than that beyond the multiplicity of things which our senses present us is something more fundamental, the origin, or principle, of that multiplicity. And that origin is a unity. Thales, even earlier than Xenophanes, thus argues in behalf of the priority of unity to multiplicity. What appears (multiplicity) is not all that there is nor even what is most fundamental. Behind appearances lies the origin of appearances in the unity of water. Do we not here witness the same conception of the world which gives rise to the philosophic issue today often referred to as "appearance *vs.* reality"? But further, this *arche*, this unity underlying the appearing multiplicity, this most fundamental of all things, is *intelligible*, articulable, accessible to man; it is water. Opposed to the teaching of *The Epic of Gilgamesh*, of Homer, of Hesiod, even of Xenophanes, Thales here asserts, to paraphrase Hegel, that "the world is through and through intelligible" to finite man. If Thales is right, not about water but about the presence and articulability of a unified *arche* of all things, then a complete philosophic speech, which gives a *logos* both of the *arche* and of the emergence of the subsequent multiplicity out of (and perhaps back into) the *arche*, is possible.[6] Wisdom, in the sense of knowledge of the structure of the whole, is possible for man, and from the beginning that wisdom is understood by and as reference to the origin of things and the articulability of that origin. Such optimism is nowhere to be found in the writers considered so far, and it will find its culmination in the philosophies of Hegel and Marx in the nineteenth century, and in our own time, but for very different reasons, in the optimism of certain representatives of analytic philosophy about "solving philosophical problems."

But Thales said that that origin was not absolute *Geist* or an adequate grammar, but water. Why water? Some may find Aristotle's rather professorial remarks about the necessity of liquid for life and the liquid quality of semen instructive, but we may do better to try to relate Thales' water principle to another statement attributed to him, that "Nous [mind] is quickest of all, for it runs through everything."[7] How is the whole and in particular the *arche* going to be accessible to the human psyche? By virtue of the nature of *nous* which is of such a quality as to "run through everything," that is, to be able to enter into and take on the form of that which is other than itself. Aristotle, in his work on the soul, is later to elaborate this conception of the nature and possibility of knowledge. For Aristotle, the soul takes on the form of that which it knows,[8] and it has no form of its own before it knows.[9] The mind, for both Thales and Aristotle, can know that which it is not because it is sufficiently "supple" to take on the form of other things. But perhaps a more appropriate metaphor than "supple" here would be to say that *nous* is sufficiently "fluid" to take on the form of other things. *Nous* thus imitates water, by being able to run through and take on the form of all things. Water is the *unity* behind appearances, but it is not a rigid and static unity. It is literally *fluid*, a unity which can incorporate all forms. There is thus an affinity between mind and the *arche* of things which makes it of all things especially accessible to *nous*. Wisdom is possible, knowledge of the origin or structure of the whole is possible for man because there is a remarkable affinity, a similarity in nature, of mind and the structure of the whole. Thales in one step thus bridges the gap which had seemed an insurmountable obstacle for the earlier writers in trying to account for man's access to the divine. For Thales, too, called water "god."[10]

Thales expressed this affinity between the knowing soul and the intelligible structure of the world in another way. He said that "the world is ensouled and full of daimons."[11] Why? Because embodied in this remark is the Thalenic conviction that the soul could not and does not know that which is radically other than it, resistant to its fluidity, as it were. What we come to know about the world is thus not what is utterly other than *nous*; we know rather the *intelligible aspect* of things, that which makes things akin in some way to the soul. The intelligibility of things other than *nous* to *nous* means that they must have this intelligible aspect, this affinity in nature with *nous*. It is for this reason that "the world is ensouled and full of daimons." To put it in terms of a principle which is at the absolute foundation both of that philosophical position which has come to be known as idealism and of "materialism" as well, "like knows like."

Further, it is in the light of the affinity between the knowing soul, the *arche* of all things, and what can be known about things (their intelligible or "daimonic" aspect) that we can understand why from the very beginning self-knowledge would be at the foundation of the philosophic enterprise and why "to know thyself" would be stated by Thales to be the most difficult of all things. Thanks to the affinity which Thales sets out, self-knowledge can never be adequate as the knowledge of one discrete "entity" in the world, reflected upon "introspectively" and apart from or distinct from all other things. Rather, genuine self-knowledge, which penetrates to the fluid, daimonic quality of the soul, always points beyond itself to knowledge of that which is other than it yet accessible to it, and ultimately to the *arche* of things of which the soul's fluidity is an imitation, or perhaps better put, a manifestation. Self-knowledge is thus the most difficult of all things because self-knowledge cannot and will not complete itself until it becomes knowledge of the structure of the whole, or wisdom. To put the point somewhat differently, the soul or self is not "what it is and not another thing," that is, a discrete entity definitely separable from other "things." Rather, the self, by virtue of the nature which it shares with the *arche* and with the intelligible structure of things, is always "more than" it is, always pointing beyond itself to that which it is not yet but can become. As Plato is later to put it using the language of Eros, the human psyche, as erotic, is incomplete of itself but desirous of, and so moving toward, completeness. Because the soul, according to the Greeks, is fundamentally *nous*, intellect, or reason, the ultimate or highest form of completeness is wisdom, or knowledge of the soul. Thus, to repeat a point made earlier, philosophy is a consequence of, that is, originates in, the nature of human being.

Self-knowledge is the most difficult of all things because it always points beyond itself to knowledge of the origin and structure of the whole. *Genuine* self-knowledge, then, always transcends or goes beyond the individual, historical self, a transcendence which we all know is immensely difficult. But this means that from the standpoint of genuine self-knowledge (which we can now virtually define as philosophy), the individual, historical self, its personal, historically determined desires and peculiarities, are not at issue. The individual self, from Thales' standpoint, *does not matter*. It is for this reason that Thales can say "there is no difference between life and death." The question of individual life and death is not what is at issue for Thalenic philosophy. What is at issue is rather that affinity of the soul with the *arche* and structure of the whole which does not die with the individual soul. The genuine concern of self-knowledge, then, is with what is deathless, or eternal. The same man who said that "there is no difference between life and death" can also say that "the soul is deathless" in the sense that the soul that genuinely knows itself transcends its temporality and gains access to that which it shares with the eternal *arche* and structure of the whole. As Plato was later to put it in the *Phaedo*, "philosophy is a preparation for death,"[12] not, as Socrates himself indicates, by concerning itself with what Martin Heidegger calls his "factical demise," but by orienting itself toward what is beyond death, that is, deathless, or eternal.

If this is plausible, then Thales is a genuine and not at all naïve philosopher because his thought embodies a profound reflection on or wondering about the fact that things are as they are and how they are as they are in such a way as to demonstrate that from the beginning that wondering which is philosophic wondering embodies a concern with the structure and origin of the whole and man's place in that whole as speaker of the speech about the whole. But such wondering is and can be by no means settled and uncontroversial. It is thus not surprising that before long, another man of the genius of Thales, Anaximander, arose to respond to Thales' *logos* with his own.

Anaximander

There are several outstanding accounts available of Anaximander's contributions as an early scientist. Most notable among these are Kirk and Raven's account in *The Pre-Socratic Philosophers*, and especially Charles Kahn's excellent book, *Anaximander and the Origins of Greek Cosmology*.[13] In either of these can be found remarkably thorough discussions of Anaximander's contributions to map making and measurement of the stars, the details of his complex cosmological views, the significance of his "evolutionary" theory of the development of man out of fishes, to name just a few of the relevant themes. It is certainly not the intention of this brief discussion to try to give even an abstract of what can be studied far more thoroughly in works such as these. But let us begin by reiterating that to cite, discuss, and even definitively understand Anaximander's scientific contributions is still not to understand why or whether he was a philosopher. And it is this issue upon which the following discussion will be a reflection.

Perhaps the initially most striking feature of Anaximander's thought, and the one which is most obviously a response to his apparent teacher, Thales, is his claim that the *arche* of all things, out of which, ultimately, all things arise, is not something so definite as water, but rather *to apeiron*, the indefinite, the boundless, or as Kahn suggests, "what can-not be passed over to the end."[14] There is much scholarly controversy over the exact meaning of *to apeiron*, whether it is to be understood as material, as space, as infinite, etc. But whatever the precise meaning of *to apeiron* for Anaximander, this much is clear; in responding to the de-mand that the understanding of the world and of man be understood in terms of an origin, even an origin which was a kind of unity, he returned to the view that the origin of man and the cosmos was fundamentally unintelligible, inarticulable. So consistent was Anaximander on this point that he referred to this *arche* only by "the negative way," by refer-ring to it as "the indefinite," that which cannot be de-fined, articulated as what it is. Gone from Anaximander is the optimism implied in Thales about the possibility of philosophy achieving a complete speech about the whole. The world, at its fundament, is unintelligible, resistant to ar-ticulation, and so we are not surprised that Anaximander rejoins Hesiod on the further point that what articulation and definition does occur will be paid for, because it constitutes an "injustice." The world that Anax-imander experiences is thus, like Hesiod's and Homer's, anti-philosophical, resistant to the enterprise or *telos* of philosophy. But Anaximander's own speech is then put in a strange position; his is a philosophic speech which sets out an antiphilosophic position, which argues that wisdom, the goal of philosophy, is in principle impossible, again *not* because of the finitude of man himself (which will become Plato's view), but because the origin of the world is itself finally unin-telligible. From Thales' view that "the world is through and through in-telligible," we return to "the world is at its fundament, and so ul-timately, unintelligible." If we replace "unintelligible" by "absurd," it is easy to see how this view forms the foundation of the popular version of contemporary existentialism.

Yet it is not the case that the articulated, de-finite things of our ex-perience simply and directly arise out of *to apeiron* and return to it. There is a kind of mediation present in Anaximander's view between the utterly inarticulable origin and the de-finable things of experience. That mediation principle is "the elements" (*stoicheion*) which turn out to be the primordial opposites, such as dry and wet, cold and hot, light and dark. It is these elemental opposites which are separated off or se-creted from *to apeiron* and which, in turn, presumably by their interac-tion and opposition, give rise to the individual things of the world. The

Introduction referred to the significance for man of understanding things in terms of opposites. For Anaximander, these opposites are the locus of a primordial *strife*, the consequence of which is the coming-to-be and the destruction of things which are. Thus notwithstanding Anaximander's agreement with Thales that the ultimate origin of things is one, changeless, eternal, and divine,[15] the *intelligible* source of the world is the fundamental strife, or tension between opposites. We can already begin to see an important pattern in the alternative ontological views of the priority of being or becoming which is still present in the spokesmen for those alternative views today. Those who argue that the origin of the world is a unity, changeless, being, tend to argue in turn that the world is in principle intelligible in its structure and origin. Those who hold to the priority of flux, of becoming, change and war, tend to argue in turn in behalf of the ultimate unintelligibility of that origin. But then the question arises of how that unintelligible origin is itself intelligible as unintelligible. How, if the origin really is unintelligible, can we even *say* this? Anaximander offers an interesting complication to this view by arguing that although the *ultimate* origin of things (*to apeiron*) is one, changeless, eternal, and divine, it is unintelligible; whereas what we may call the proximate origin of things (the elements), although intelligible or articulable, manifest the principles of change, opposition, and strife. But as most people, including his student, Anaximenes, have noted, it is by no means clear for Anaximander how the elements arise out of the *apeiron*, or even how exactly individual things arise out of the elements. The problem of access, to which Thales had responded by making intelligibility the affinity between the human and the divine, returns with Anaximander's assertion of an origin ultimately unintelligible.

There is an alternative interpretation of Anaximander's position which may enable him to avoid, at least in principle, this dilemma. Anaximander may be suggesting that the world is indeed intelligible, but intelligible *as* a mystery. We come to understand our world precisely insofar as we understand that its origins are inarticulable. This position, at the heart of all genuine mysticism, suggests that the appreciation of the mystery of the world is the most profound knowledge. A contemporary philosopher, Henry Bugbee, states this essentially Anaximandrian point:

As [Gabriel] Marcel would put it, our experience of the world involves us in a mystery which can be intelligible to us only as a mystery. The more we experience things in depth, the more we participate in a mystery intelligible to us only as such; and the more we understand our world to be an unknown world. Our true home is wilderness, even the world of everyday.[16]

But now Anaximander adds a decisive issue to his philosophical speech. For he adds that the passing away of things into the opposites is a *penalty* which we pay for the *injustice* of coming-to-be, or, alternatively, that the passing away of one opposite (say, the "hot" in winter) is a reparation for the injustice of its gaining dominance over the other opposite (the "cold" in summer), "according to the order of time."[17] Kahn argues persuasively in behalf of the latter interpretation;[18] but whichever of the interpretations we adopt, this point of Anaximander's remains: The coming to stand as dominant of one thing over the other is a cosmic injustice (*adikia*) for which penalty will have to be paid, and the penalty will be assessed by Time. Even by Kahn's view, individual things come to be by relation of the elements, and the elements arise originally out of the *apeiron*. Therefore, whatever the specific differences between Kahn's interpretation and that of Nietzsche which Kahn explicity criticizes,[19] the following assessment of Nietzsche's as to the philosophic significance of this teaching of Anaximander's remains as powerful as ever.

It may not be logical, but it certainly is human, to view now, together with Anaximander, all coming-to-be as though it were an illegitimate emancipation from eternal being, a wrong for which destruction is the only penance. Everything that has ever come-to-be again passes away, whether we think of human life, or of water, or of hot and cold. Wherever definite qualities are perceivable, we can prophesy, upon the basis of enormously extensive experience, the passing away of these qualities. Never, in other words, can a being which possesses definite qualities or consists of such be the origin or first principle of things. That which truly *is*, concludes Anaximander, cannot possess definite characteristics, or it would come-to-be and pass away like all the other things. In order that coming-to-be shall not cease, primal being must be indefinite. The immortality and everlastingness of primal being does not lie in its infinitude or its inexhaustability, but in the fact that it is devoid of definite qualities which would lead to its passing. Hence its name, "the indefinite."[20]

But perhaps even more fundamental than the deepening of the cosmic repulsion of articulation embodied in this view, and consequently the danger and even impiety of philosophy, is the more general conviction that the world is utterly pervaded by the essentially *moral* issue of injustice. Far from limiting the realm of "value" to the sphere of human conduct and suggesting that other aspects of the world are "beyond good and evil" or something which we can adequately explain while making "no value judgments," Anaximander offers us an ontology, literally an account of the being of things, in which the issue of value is at the fundament, absolutely unavoidable in an adequate account of things. Plato was later to express this ontological point by making the most fundamental of all his "Forms," that "Idea" which makes possible the intelligibility and the being of the other "Ideas," the "Idea of the Good."[21] It is the consensus of contemporary men, however, that the question of value is "relative," limited in any case to the social assessment of human experience. But there are those today who argue that our failure to maintain a concept of a standard of value at the origin of things has in large measure brought about the contemporary crisis of rationality known as "nihilism," the impossibility of defending any "value" as being rational itself.[22] Whatever we think about this, the point of Anaximander's teaching is that this issue is clearly at stake for him in his conviction that the very cycle of coming-to-be and passing away in which all de-finite things participate embodies the question of justice and injustice.

Finally, it is worthwhile to point to the profound philosophic significance of one aspect of Anaximander's cosmological theories: The oft-noted fact that Anaximander insisted upon the ordering of the sizes of the sun, moon, and stars not via empirical measurement but in terms of a mathematical ratio.[23] Embodied in this idea is precisely the idea most significantly developed by Anaximander's successor, Anaximenes, that the world may be able to be understood, finally, in quantitative, or mathematical, terms. But for the further development of this point, it is perhaps best to turn to the man who developed it so significantly, Anaximenes.

Anaximenes

In the view of many, Anaximenes' assertion that the *arche* of things is air seems a comedown from Anaximander's teaching on the necessary indefiniteness of the *arche*. We may begin by noting, however, that its ontological implication is the perfectly legitimate one of reasserting the intelligibility and articulability of the origin. The way again points toward the optimism of human wisdom, but Anaximenes develops this optimism further and in a direction which has been absolutely decisive for the development not only of science but of the Western conception of knowledge. For the ingenious thing about Anaximenes' *arche* of air, as most commentators seem to agree, is that from it he can account for the development of the other fundamental substances—earth, fire, and water—*out* of the origin through the processes of condensation and rarefication. Air rarefied becomes fire. Condensed, it becomes water; condensed still further, earth. Not only can Anaximenes offer us air as his *arche*, he can account in the most plausible way yet for the development of the multiplicity of other substances out of the original unity of air. But even more important, Anaximenes thus asserts that the difference between the original element, air, and the subsequent multiplicity of apparently qualitatively *different* things, is in fact quantitative; it is a question of the quantitatively measurable variations in the density or rarity of the primal being. Why is this so valuable? Because if knowledge of a thing can be expressed quantitatively, mathematically, it can be expressed exactly, with absolute certainty. It is no exaggeration to say that henceforward in Western thinking, the paradigm of genuine knowledge is the absolutely certain knowledge of mathematics. This standard of knowledge, present so clearly in Anaximenes, has in large measure been the impetus behind the almost astounding success of the sciences and, equally significant, of the near absolute dominance of the standard of "scientific knowledge" as in the end the only genuine or legitimate mode of knowledge.

But it is not only obviously material, tangible things that Anaximenes considers susceptible of quantitative explanation. Air—the *arche*, or origin of things—is, just as the *arche* was for Thales and Anaximander, divine. Thus all three thinkers decisively transform the conception of the divine from the anthropomorphic and usually whimsical gods of *The Epic of Gilgamesh*, Homer, and Hesiod into the impersonal principles of water, *to apeiron*, and air. As such, we can legitimately expect the world to "happen" not according to the whimsy of gods, but in a more ordered, predictable, and so intelligible way. We have seen Anaximenes extend this expectation to the hope of mathematical exactitude. But air, the divine, one *arche*, is not just the principle of material things. It is, in its form as breath, the principle of life (the Greek word for soul—*psyche*—has as its original meaning "breath"), and air is also the origin and fundamental makeup of the gods. Like Thales, Anaximenes argues for an affinity between the human and the divine and, consequently, in behalf of the accessibility of the divine, and so the whole, to man. But that affinity is for Anaximenes now quantitative. We all—the human, things, and the divine—share our origin in the quantitatively measurable manifestation of air. Not only can the origin and structure of the whole be known by man; it can be known quantitatively and so with absolute certainty! It is instructive that that has been our goal—as yet unattained—ever since.

The discussion of *The Epic of Gilgamesh*, Homer, and Hesiod showed that these works contain an intelligent, sophisticated treatment of philosophic themes. The discussion of Thales, Anaximander, and Anaximenes, however, referred to these thinkers as philosophers. There is a difference between a writer whose works contain philosophic themes and a writer whom we call a philosopher. The works of Dostoevski and Thomas Mann contain a multitude of philosophic issues, perhaps even as many as the works of A. J. Ayer and Jean-Paul Sartre. Yet we continue to refer to the former writers as novelists, not philosophers. Consequently, even though we have criticized the orthodox reasons for calling Thales the first philosopher, the language would seem to indicate the conviction that Thales is, after all, the first *philosopher* that we know of, although certainly not the first writer whose works contained philosophic themes. Why, then, might we call Thales, Anaximander, and Anaximenes the first *philosophers*, Hesiod and Homer poets, when it cannot be because of the mere presence of genuinely philosophical issues? Put differently, what is the difference between philosophy and poetry? Let us be struck by two things at once.

This very contemporary, very sophisticated, very complex, possibly unanswerable problem has arisen for us as a consequence of a consideration of these very ancient thinkers. Second, the very question of the difference between philosophy and poetry or myth is itself a philosophic question. We begin by finding ourselves involved in a circle.

The present hypothesis is that poetry is concerned primarily, although not exclusively, with the question of beauty, whereas philosophy is concerned primarily, but not exclusively, with the question of truth.[24] By "beauty" in its broadest sense, we mean a concern with the *manner* in which a thing is presented or, as Heidegger put it, its "happening."[25] The two concerns are in no way incompatible and usually—certainly in the case of the authors we have studied—overlap. The suggestion, in the context of this book, is this: Hesiod, Homer, and the authors of *The Epic of Gilgamesh* are poets because, although they present philosophical issues and seem concerned to speak the truth, their work exhibits a more fundamental concern with the *manner* in which that truth is revealed, that is, with the "happening" of the work, or beauty. Thales, Anaximander, Anaximenes, and even Xenophanes, on the other hand, are philosophers because, or insofar as, they exhibit a fundamental concern with the truth of what they say, even though, to be sure, they evidence a genuine concern with the manner of presentation, even to the point of writing in "poetical" style in the case in Xenophanes and Anaximander.

Thales, Anaximander, and Anaximenes

Thales, along with Anaximander and Anaximenes, are often referred to as the Milesian philosophers because they all came from Miletus, a seaport on the Aegean Sea in what is now southwestern Turkey. Thales flourished around 585 B.C. and was considered one of the famed Seven Sages. As the various anecdotes included in the selections suggest, he was apparently a man of widespread talents, who besides his philosophical speculations also predicted an eclipse and developed means of measuring the height of pyramids and the distance of ships at sea. In an apparent attempt to prove that thinkers could, if they wished, be successful businessmen, he once cornered the olive market!

Anaximander flourished around 560 B.C. and is often considered a student of Thales. In this case such an ascription seems plausible, although there was a tendency among early Greek historians to ascribe a teacher-student relationship to any two thinkers from the same location whose dates bear some proximity. Anaximander purportedly wrote one book, entitled *On Nature*, but this title was ascribed to nearly every Pre-Socratic treatise. As will be noted, only one fragment of this book remains, a situation which, unfortunately, is the rule rather than the exception when studying the works of Pre-Socratic philosophers. In addition to his philosophical contributions, he achieved renown as an astronomer and map maker.

Anaximenes flourished around 546 B.C. and, as in the earlier case, is considered the student of Anaximander. Little is known of him personally, and his thought is often considered inferior to Anaximander's—for the wrong reasons, as will be shown.

Almost none of their fragments remain and most of our knowledge of them comes from Greek and Roman writers as indicated in the "Testimonia" which constitute virtually the entire set of selections about them.

A. Thales

TESTIMONIA ON THALES BY DIOGENES LAERTIUS*

Herodotus, Duris, and Democritus are agreed that Thales was the son of Examyas and Cleobulina, and belonged to the Thelidae who are Phoenicians, and among the noblest of the descendants of Cadmus and Agenor. As Plato testifies, he was one of the Seven Sages. He was the first to receive the name of Sage, in the archonship of Damasias at Athens, when the term was applied to all the Seven Sages, as Demetrius of Phalerum mentions in his *List of Archons*. He was admitted to citizenship at Miletus when he came to that town along with Nileos, who had been expelled from Phoenicia. Most writers, however, represent him as a genuine Milesian and of a distinguished family.

After engaging in politics he became a student of nature. According to some he left nothing in writing; for the *Nautical Astronomy* attributed

---

* From R. D. Hicks, *Lives of Eminent Philosophers*.

to him is said to be by Phocus of Samos. Callimachus knows him as the
discoverer of the Ursa Minor; for he says in his *Iambics*:

> Who first of men the course made plain
> Of those small stars we call the Wain,
> Whereby Phoenicians sail the main.

But according to others he wrote nothing but two treatises, one *On the
Solstice* and one *On the Equinox*, regarding all other matters as in-
cognizable. He seems by some accounts to have been the first to study
astronomy, the first to predict eclipses of the sun and to fix the solstices;
so Eudemus in his *History of Astronomy*. It was this which gained for
him the admiration of Xenophanes and Herodotus and the notice of
Heraclitus and Democritus.

And some, including Choerilus the poet, declare that he was the first
to maintain the immortality of the soul. He was the first to determine
the sun's course from solstice to solstice, and according to some the first
to declare the size of the sun to be one seven hundred and twentieth part
of the solar circle, and the size of the moon to be the same fraction of
the lunar circle. He was the first to give the last day of the month the
name of Thirtieth, and the first, some say, to discuss physical problems.

Aristotle and Hippias affirm that, arguing from the magnet and from
amber, he attributed a soul or life even to inanimate objects. Pamphila
states that, having learnt geometry from the Egyptians, he was the first
to inscribe a right-angled triangle in a circle, whereupon he sacrificed an
ox. Others tell this tale of Pythagoras, amongst them Apollodorus the
arithmetician. (It was Pythagoras who developed to their furthest extent
the discoveries attributed by Callimachus in his *Iambics* to Euphorbus
the Phrygian, I mean "scalene triangles" and whatever else has to do
with theoretical geometry.)

Thales is also credited with having given excellent advice on political
matters. For instance, when Croesus sent to Miletus offering terms of
alliance, he frustrated the plan; and this proved the salvation of the city
when Cyrus obtained the victory. Heraclides makes Thales himself say
that he had always lived in solitude as a private individual and kept
aloof from State affairs. Some authorities say that he married and had a
son Cybisthus; others that he remained unmarried and adopted his
sister's son, and that when he was asked why he had no children of his

own he replied "because he loved children." The story is told that, when his mother tried to force him to marry, he replied it was too soon, and when she pressed him again later in life, he replied that it was too late. Hieronymus of Rhodes in the second book of his *Scattered Notes* relates that, in order to show how easy it is to grow rich, Thales, foreseeing that it would be a good season for olives, rented all the oil-mills and thus amassed a fortune.

His doctrine was that water is the universal primary substance, and that the world is animate and full of divinities. He is said to have discovered the seasons of the year and divided it into 365 days.

He had no instructor, except that he went to Egypt and spent some time with the priests there. Hieronymus informs us that he measured the height of the pyramids by the shadow they cast, taking the observation at the hour when our shadow is of the same length as ourselves. He lived, as Minyas relates, with Thrasybulus, the tyrant of Miletus.

The well-known story of the tripod found by the fishermen and sent by the people of Miletus to all the Wise Men in succession runs as follows. Certain Ionian youths having purchased of the Milesian fishermen their catch of fish, a dispute arose over the tripod which had formed part of the catch. Finally the Milesians referred the question to Delphi, and the god gave an oracle in this form:

Who shall possess the tripod? Thus replies
Apollo: "Whosoever is most wise."

Accordingly they give it to Thales, and he to another, and so on till it comes to Solon, who, with the remark that the god was the most wise, sent it off to Delphi. Callimachus in his *Iambics* has a different version of the story, which he took from Maeandrius of Miletus. It is that Bathycles, an Arcadian, left at his death a bowl with the solemn injunction that it "should be given to him who had done most good by his wisdom." So it was given to Thales, went the round of all the sages, and came back to Thales again. And he sent it to Apollo at Didyma, with this dedication, according to Callimachus:

Lord of the folk of Neleus' line,
Thales, of Greeks adjudged most wise,

Brings to thy Didymaean shrine
His offering, a twice-won prize.

But the prose inscription is:

Thales the Milesian, son of Examyas [dedicates this] to Delphinian Apollo after twice winning the prize from all the Greeks.

The bowl was carried from place to place by the son of Bathycles, whose name was Thyrion, so it is stated by Eleusis in his work *On Achilles*, and Alexo the Myndian in the ninth book of his *Legends*.

But Eudoxus of Cnidos and Euanthes of Miletus agree that a certain man who was a friend of Croesus received from the king a golden goblet in order to bestow it upon the wisest of the Greeks; this man gave it to Thales, and from him it passed to others and so to Chilon. . . .

Hermippus in his *Lives* refers to Thales the story which is told by some of Socrates, namely, that he used to say there were three blessings for which he was grateful to Fortune: "first, that I was born a human being and not one of the brutes; next, that I was born a man and not a woman; thirdly, a Greek and not a barbarian." It is said that once, when he was taken out of doors by an old woman in order that he might observe the stars, he fell into a ditch, and his cry for help drew from the old woman the retort, "How can you expect to know all about the heavens, Thales, when you cannot even see what is just before your feet?" Timon too knows him as an astronomer, and praises him in the *Silli* where he says:

Thales among the Seven the sage astronomer.

His writings are said by Lobon of Argos to have run to some two hundred lines. His statue is said to bear this inscription:

Pride of Miletus and Ionian lands,
Wisest astronomer, here Thales stands.

Of songs still sung these verses belong to him:

Many words do not declare an understanding heart.
Seek one sole wisdom.
Choose one sole good.
For thou wilt check the tongues of chatterers prating
    without end.

Here too are certain current apophthegms assigned to him:

Of all things that are, the most ancient is God, for he is
    uncreated.
The most beautiful is the universe, for it is God's workman-
    ship.
The greatest is space, for it holds all things.
The swiftest is mind, for it speeds everywhere.
The strongest, necessity, for it masters all.
The wisest, time, for it brings everything to light.

He held there was no difference between life and death. "Why then,"
said one, "do you not die?" "Because," said he, "there is no difference."
To the question which is older, day or night, he replied: "Night is the older by one day." Some one asked him whether a man could hide an evil
deed from the gods: "No," he replied, "nor yet an evil thought." To the
adulterer who inquired if he should deny the charge upon oath he
replied that perjury was no worse than adultery. Being asked what is
difficult, he replied, "To know oneself." "What is easy?" "To give advice to another." "What is most pleasant?" "Success." "What is the
divine?" "That which has neither beginning nor end." To the question
what was the strangest thing he had ever seen, his answer was, "An aged
tyrant." "How can one best bear adversity?" "If he should see his enemies in worse plight." "How shall we lead the best and most righteous
life?" "By refraining from doing what we blame in others." "What man
is happy?" "He who has a healthy body, a resourceful mind and a docile
nature." He tells us to remember friends, whether present or absent; not
to pride ourselves upon outward appearance, but to study to be
beautiful in character. "Shun ill-gotten gains," he says. "Let not idle
words prejudice thee against those who have shared thy confidence."
"Whatever provision thou hast made for thy parents, the same must
thou expect from thy children." He explained the overflow of the Nile

as due to the etesian winds which, blowing in the contrary direction, drove the waters upstream.

Apollodorus in his *Chronology* places his birth in the first year of the 35th Olympiad [640 B.C.]. He died at the age of 78 (or, according to Sosicrates, of 90 years); for he died in the 58th Olympiad, being contemporary with Croesus, whom he undertook to take across the Halys without building a bridge, by diverting the river. . . .

To him belongs the proverb "Know thyself," which Antisthenes in his *Successions of Philosophers* attributes to Phemonoë, though admitting that it was appropriated by Chilon. . . .

TESTIMONIA ON THALES BY ARISTOTLE*

. . . There is the anecdote of Thales the Milesian and his financial device, which involves a principle of universal application, but is attributed to him on account of his reputation for wisdom. He was reproached for his poverty, which was supposed to show that philosophy was of no use. According to the story, he knew by his skill in the stars while it was yet winter that there would be a great harvest of olives in the coming year; so, having a little money, he gave deposits for the use of all the olive-presses in Chios and Miletus, which he hired at a low price because no one bid against him. When the harvest-time came, and many were wanted all at once and of a sudden, he let them out at any rate which he pleased, and made a quantity of money. Thus he showed the world that philosophers can easily be rich if they like, but that their ambition is of another sort. (*Politics*, 1259a 5)

. . . Others say the earth rests upon water. This, indeed, is the oldest theory that has been preserved, and is attributed to Thales of Miletus. It was supposed to stay still because it floated like wood and other similar substances, which are so constituted as to rest upon water but not upon air. As if the same account had not to be given of the water which carries the earth as of the earth itself! It is not the nature of water, any more than of earth, to stay in mid-air: it must have something to rest upon. (*De Caelo*, 294a 29)

* From W. D. Ross, *The Works of Aristotle*.

Of the first philosophers, then, most thought the principles which were of the nature of matter were the only principles of all things. That of which all things that are consist, the first from which they come to be, the last into which they are resolved (the substance remaining, but changing in its modifications), this they say is the element and this the principle of things, and therefore they think nothing is either generated or destroyed, since this sort of entity is always conserved, as we say Socrates neither comes to be absolutely when he comes to be beautiful or musical, nor ceases to be when he loses these characteristics, because the substratum, Socrates himself, remains. Just so they say nothing else comes to be or ceases to be; for there must be some entity—either one or more than one—from which all other things come to be, it being conserved.

Yet they do not all agree as to the number and the nature of these principles. Thales, the founder of this type of philosophy, says the principle is water (for which reason he declared that the earth rests on water), getting the notion perhaps from seeing that the nutriment of all things is moist, and that heat itself is generated from the moist and kept alive by it (and that from which they come to be is a principle of all things). He got his notion from this fact, and from the fact that the seeds of all things have a moist nature, and that water is the origin of the nature of moist things.

Some think that even the ancients who lived long before the present generation, and first framed accounts of the gods, had a similar view of nature; for they made Ocean and Tethys the parents of creation, and described the oath of the gods as being by water, to which they give the name of Styx; for what is oldest is most honourable, and the most honourable thing is that by which one swears. It may perhaps be uncertain whether this opinion about nature is primitive and ancient, but Thales at any rate is said to have declared himself thus about the first cause. (*Metaphysica*, 983*b* 7)

Thales, too, to judge from what is recorded about him, seems to have held soul to be a motive force, since he said that the magnet has a soul in it because it moves the iron. (*De Anima*, 405*a* 20)

Certain thinkers say that soul is intermingled in the whole universe, and it is perhaps for that reason that Thales came to the opinion that all things are full of gods. (*De Anima*, 411*a* 7)

TESTIMONIA ON THALES BY HERODOTUS*

Thales, a man of Miletus, was originally of Phoenician descent. (*The Persian Wars* I. 170)

In the sixth year of the war [between the Medes and the Lydians], neither side having gained much of an advantage, it suddenly happened in the midst of battle that the day turned into night. The shift from day to night had been foretold to the Ionians by Thales of Miletus, who set as its limit the year in which it actually occurred. (I. 74)

Once when [King] Croessus was at a loss how to take his army across a river where there was no bridge, it is said that Thales, who was then serving with the army, switched the course of the river, causing it to flow behind the army instead of altogether in front of them. Here is how he did it. Going upstream he dug a deep channel in the shape of a crescent, thereby dividing the river and partly diverting it to the rear of the army, letting it return to its original course after passing the camp. The result was that both parts of the river were now shallow enough to be forded. (I. 75)

B. Anaximander

ANAXIMANDER: FRAGMENT**

1. The Unlimited is the first-principle of things that are. It is that from which the coming-to-be [of things and qualities] takes place, and it is that into which they return when they perish, by moral necessity, giving satisfaction to one another and making reparation for their injustice, according to the order of time.

** From Philip Wheelwright, *The Pre-Socratics*.

TESTIMONIA ON ANAXIMANDER BY ARISTOTLE

. . . Everything is either a source or derived from a source. But there cannot be a source of the infinite or limitless, for that would be a limit of it. Further, as it is a beginning, it is both uncreatable and indestructible. For there must be a point at which what has come to be reaches completion, and also a termination of all passing away. That is why, as we say, there is no principle of *this*, but it is this which is held to be the principle of other things, and to encompass all and to steer all, as those assert who do not recognize, alongside the infinite, other causes, such as Mind or Friendship. Further they identify it with the Divine, for it is 'deathless and imperishable' as Anaximander says, with the majority of the physicists. (*Physica*, 203*b* 6)

Nor (2) can the infinite body be one and simple, whether it is, as some hold, a thing over and above the elements (from which they generate the elements) or is not thus qualified.

(*a*) We must consider the former alternative; for there *are* some people who make this the infinite, and not air or water, in order that the other elements may not be annihilated by the element which is infinite. They have contrariety with each other—air is cold, water moist, fire hot; if one were infinite, the others by now would have ceased to be. As it is, they say, the infinite is different from them and is their source. (*Physica*, 204*b* 20)

. . . But there are some, Anaximander, for instance, among the ancients, who say that the earth keeps its place because of its indifference. Motion upward and downward and sideways were all, they thought, equally inappropriate to that which is set at the centre and indifferently related to every extreme point; and to move in contrary directions at the same time was impossible: so it must needs remain still. This view is ingenious but not true. (*De Caelo*, 295*b* 10)

TESTIMONIA ON ANAXIMANDER FROM
LATER GREEK SOURCES*

Anaximander, son of Praxiades, was a native of Miletus. He was the first inventor of the gnomon and, as Favorinus states in his *Miscellaneous History*, he set one up in Sparta for the purpose of determining the solstices and equinoxes. He also constructed instruments for marking the hours. He was the first to draw a map containing all the outlines of land and sea, and he constructed a global chart of the sky also. His exposition of his doctrine was made in the form of a summary which probably came into the hands of Apollodorus of Athens; that writer states in his *Chronology* that Anaximander was sixty-four years old in the second year of the fifty-eighth Olympiad [547-546 B.C.] and that he died soon after.

Anaximander held that while the parts undergo change the whole is unchangeable; that the earth, which is spherical, lies at the very center of things; and that the sun is as large as the earth and consists of purest fire. (Diogenes Laertius I. 1-2)

Anaximander of Miletus, son of Praxiades, successor and disciple of Thales, said that the "ultimate source and first principle" (*arche*) as well as the primary substance (*stoicheion*) is the [qualitatively] Unlimited; he was the first to apply this name to the ultimate source. He maintained that it is neither water nor any other of the so-called elements, but is of an altogether different nature from them, in that it is unlimited [i.e., is not limited to being just this or that]. From it there arose the universe and all the worlds within it. (Simplicius *Commentaria*, followed by the quotation of Fr. 1)

Evidently since he sees the four elements changing into one another he does not think it right to identify the underlying reality with any single one of them; it must be something distinct. Coming-to-be, he holds, does not involve any alteration of basic substance (*stoicheion*); it results from the separation of opposites which the eternal motion causes. (*ibid.*, preceded by the quotation of Fr. 1)

---

*   From Philip Wheelwright, *The Pre-Socratics*.

Anaximander's theory is that all change takes place by separation: that is to say, the opposites which are in the unlimited substratum are separated off from it. He was the first thinker to speak of the underlying reality as the "source and first principle" (*arche*). By the opposites he meant such [qualities] as hot and cold, dry and moist, etc. (*ibid.*)

Those who believed in an unlimited number of worlds, as Anaximander and his associates did, regarded them as coming-to-be and passing away throughout unlimited time. There are always some worlds in process of coming to be, others in process of passing away, they hold; such motion being eternal. (*ibid.*)

Anaximander, an associate of Thales, said that the earth is cylindrical in shape, its depth being one-third its breadth. And he said that at the beginning of the world there separated itself out from the eternal a something capable of producing heat and cold. It took the form of a flame, surrounding the air that surrounds the earth, like the bark of a tree. This sphere became broken into parts, each of which was a different circle; which is how the sun, moon and stars were generated. (Pseudo-Plutarch *Stromata*)

Anaximander held that the Unlimited is the first-principle and is eternal, without age, and that it encompasses all the worlds; moreover that it is in perpetual activity, and that out of its activity the worlds have originated.

He held that the earth is a body suspended in the sky, not resting on anything else but keeping its position because it is the same distance away from all [extremities]; that it is in the shape of a cylinder like a stone column with a curved top surface; and that it has two faces, the one of them being the surface on which we walk, the other opposite to it.

He further held that each of the heavenly bodies is a wheel of fire, surrounded by air, which separates it from the fire at the extremities. The air has little breathing holes somewhat like the holes in a flute, and through them the orbs are seen. When the hole of the [solar or lunar] orb gets clogged an eclipse occurs. The moon goes through its phases as its breathing hole gets successively opened and stopped up. The sun's wheel is twenty-seven times as large as that of the moon, and is situated higher, while the wheel of the stars is lower. (Hippolytus *Refutatio* I. 6)

Anaximander held that the stars are hoops of fire, compressed by air, and that they breathe out flames from little openings in the air. He said furthermore that the sun is as large as the earth, and that the wheel which carries it around and from which it breathes itself forth is twenty-seven times the size of the earth's wheel. When the sun is eclipsed, he said, it is because its breathing hole has gotten stopped up. (Aëtius)

Some of the early philosophers of nature declared that the sea is a remnant of the primal moisture. The upper part of that original moisture, they explain, was evaporated by the sun; out of it there came-to-be the winds, as well as the revolutions of the sun and moon, the causes of their revolutions being the vapors and exhalations which exist there in abundance. A small part of the moisture got left in the hollow places on the earth's surface and became the sea, which goes on diminishing in quantity as it is evaporated by the sun, and will eventually be dried up altogether. Theophrastus says that Anaximander and Diogenes [of Apollonia] held this view. (Alexander of Aphrodisias *Commentaria*)

Animals, according to Anaximander, came-to-be from vapors raised by the sun; and man came into being from an animal other than himself, namely the fish, which in early times he resembled. (Hippolytus, *loc. cit.*)

He says, too, that in earliest times men were generated from various kinds of animals. For whereas the other animals can quickly get food for themselves, the human infant requires careful feeding for a long while after birth; so that if he had originated suddenly he could not have preserved his own existence. (Pseudo-Plutarch *Stromata*)

TESTIMONIA ON ANAXIMANDER BY CICERO*

It was the opinion of Anaximander that the gods come into existence and perish, rising and setting at long intervals; and that there are countless worlds. (*De Natura Deorum* I. 25)

C. Anaximenes

ANAXIMENES: FRAGMENT**

1. As our souls, being air, hold us together, so breath and air embrace the entire universe.

TESTIMONIA ON ANAXIMENES BY ARISTOTLE

Anaximenes and Diogenes make air prior to water, and the most primary of the simple bodies. (*Metaphysica*, 984*a* 5)

Anaximenes and Anaxagoras and Democritus give the flatness of the earth as the cause of its staying still. Thus, they say, it does not cut, but covers like a lid, the air beneath it. This seems to be the way of flat-shaped bodies: for even the wind can scarcely move them because of their power of resistance. The same immobility, they say, is produced by the flatness of the surface which the earth presents to the air which underlies it; while the air, not having room enough to change its place because it is underneath the earth, stays there in a mass, like the water in the case of the water-clock. And they adduce an amount of evidence to prove that air, when cut off and at rest, can bear a considerable weight. (*De Caelo*, 294*b* 15)

---

* From Philip Wheelwright, *The Pre-Socratics*.
** From Philip Wheelwright, *The Pre-Socratics*.

TESTIMONIA ON ANAXIMENES FROM
LATER GREEK SOURCES*

Anaximenes, son of Eurystratus, a native of Miletus, was a disciple of Anaximander. He held that the first-principle is air, and that this is the unlimited. He denied that the stars pass under the earth, explaining that they travel around its periphery. He wrote in the Ionian dialect, in a plain style without affectation. Apollodorus says that he lived at the time of the taking of Sardis and died in the sixty-third Olympiad [528-525 B.C.]. (Diogenes Laertius II. 3)

He says that all things, even gods and daemons, come-to-be as products of air. (Hippolytus *Refutatio* I. 7)

Anaximenes of Miletus, son of Eurystratus, was an associate of Anaximander and agreed with him that the essence of things is one and unlimited; on the other hand he declared that it is not indeterminate but that it has the specific nature of air, which differs in rarity and density according to the kind of things into which it forms itself. Rarefied it becomes fire; condensed it becomes wind, then cloud, and as the condensation increases it becomes successively water, earth, and then stones. Everything else gets made out of these. (Simplicius *Commentaria*)

Or should we, as Anaximenes of old maintained, accept neither hot nor cold as real things but regard them rather as epiphenomena and temporary states which occur in any material thing when it undergoes certain inner alterations? For he said that cold is a thing's contraction and condensation, and that heat is its distension and rarefaction. (Plutarch *Moralia* 947F)

He held that when the air is of most even consistency it is imperceptible to the eye; it becomes visible as a result of cold or heat or moisture or being stirred up. It is always in motion, for if it were not there would be no changes. (Hippolytus, *loc. cit.*)

---

* From Philip Wheelwright, *The Pre-Socratics*.

Motion, according to Anaximenes, has existed forever. He adds that the earth came-to-be from a compression of the air; that it is very broad and rests on air. Sun, moon, and the other stars came-to-be as products of the earth. (Pseudo-Plutarch *Stromata*)

TESTIMONIA ON ANAXIMENES BY CICERO*

After Anaximander his disciple Anaximenes posited infinite air [as the first-principle] but held that the things which originate from it are finite—earth, water, fire, and out of them everything else. (*Academica* II. 37)

Anaximenes said that air is a god, that it is infinite and always in motion. As if air could be a god, or as if it could be an exception to the rule that everything must eventually perish! (*De Natura Deorum* I. 26)

TESTIMONIA ON ANAXIMENES BY ST. AUGUSTINE**

The successor to Anaximander was his disciple Anaximenes, who ascribed the causes of everything to infinite air. He neither denied nor ignored the existence of the gods; but instead of believing that the air had been created by them, he held on the contrary that they themselves were products of the air. (*Civitas Dei* VIII. 2)

Notes: II

1. A view presumed, for example, both by Burnet and Cornford despite their claimed differences. *See* F. M. Cornford, *From Religion to Philosophy* (New York, Harper Torchbooks, 1957) and J. Burnet, *Early Greek Philosophers* (New York, Meridian Books, 1957). For an excellent account of why this identification is impossible, *see* Stanley Rosen, "Thales, the Beginning of Philosophy," in *Essays in Philosophy* (University Park, The Pennsylvania State University Press,

** From Philip Wheelwright, *The Pre-Socratics*.

1962), pp. 23 ff. My interpretation of Thales owes much to this essay, which I believe is, to this day, one of the most insightful reflections on Thales available.

2. Friedrich Nietzsche, *Philosophy in the Tragic Age of the Greeks*, trans. by Marianne Cowan, Gateway Edition (Chicago, Henry Regnery Co., 1962), p. 38.

3. *Ibid.*, p. 39.

4. *Ibid.*

5. Diogenes Laertius, *Lives of Eminent Philosophers*, trans. by R. D. Hicks (The Loeb Classical Library and G. P. Putnam's Sons, 1925), Vol. 1, p. 27.

6. From which it follows that scientific theories such as allow for the prediction of eclipses, which presuppose the intelligibility of the world to man, become possible.

7. Diogenes Laertius, *op. cit.*, p. 35.

8. Aristotle, *De Anima*, 429*a* 15.

9. *Ibid.*, 429*a* 23.

10. Diogenes Laertius, *op. cit.*, p. 35.

11. *Ibid.*, p. 27.

12. Plato, *Phaedo*, 64a.

13. Kirk, G. S., and Raven, J. E., *The Pre-Socratic Philosophers* (Cambridge, *Art Criticism*, Vol. XXX (Winter, 1972), pp. 177-87. Charles Kahn, *Anaximander and the Origins of Greek Cosmology* (New York, Columbia University Press, 1960).

14. Kahn, *ibid.*, p. 232.

15. Aristotle, *Physics*, 203*b* 6

16. Henry Bugbee, *The Inward Morning* (New York, Collier Books, 1961), p. 83.

17. Anaximander, Fragment 1.

18. Kahn, *op. cit.*, p. 166 *passim*.

19. *Ibid.*, pp. 168, 194.

20. Nietzsche, *op. cit.*, pp. 46, 47.

21. Plato, *Republic*, 505a.

22. *Cf.* Stanley Rosen, *Nihilism: A Philosophical Essay* (New Haven, Conn., Yale University Press, 1969).

23. Hippolytus, *The Refutation of All Heresies*, I.6, cited in Diels-Kranz under Anaximander, A. 11.

24. For further discussion, *see* "Art and the Happening of Truth:

Reflections on the End of Philosophy,'' *The Journal of Aesthetics and Art Criticism*, Vol. (Winter, 1972), pp.

25. Martin Heidegger, ''The Origin of a Work of Art,'' trans. by A. Hofstadter in A. Hofstadter and R. Kuhns, eds., *Philosophies of Art and Beauty* (New York, Modern Library, 1964), pp. 649-701.

Philosophy and Mathematics—
The Pythagoreans

I T is at least as instructive about our own world view as it is about Pythagoras' views to note the almost universal agreement with which contemporary discussions of the Pythagoreans begin: Pythagoras' "religious mysticism" is bizarre. If that were his only contribution, he would be relegated to the status of a minor religious figure. What makes Pythagoras important, his real contribution, is his work in mathematics. What really puzzles us is not simply the fact that a great mathematician had strange religious views; many logical positivists today are Anglicans or Catholics. The sophisticated positivist, however, knows that his religious views have nothing whatsoever to do with his logical positivism. It is a segment of his life entirely divorced from, perhaps even contradictory to, his philosophical opinions. Pythagoras scandalizes us, rather, by insisting, and in many ways supporting the insistence, that his mathematical views are intimately tied up with his religious ones, indeed that they are mutually supportive! If we do not simply give in to our own prejudices by dismissing the Pythagorean religious views as peculiarities, however, and instead listen seriously to what Pythagoras tells us, we shall be challenged to consider mathematics not simply as an interesting and useful formal system but as a way of viewing, and experiencing, the world.

Pythagoras might be understood as taking the view of the structure of the world implicit in the teaching of Anaximenes, namely, that the differences between things, and so the being of each thing, are quantitatively measurable and determinable, and carrying this insight through to its logical conclusion: "All is number."[1] The world is not only through and through intelligible, or rational; it is through and through mathematical. This view is made more plausible still given the

127

extent to which the Pythagorean conception of number was geometric and even extended. As such, the essential nature of each object of our experience—and not just material objects either—can be determined with mathematical exactitude. Man is 250, justice 4, the "opportune time" 7. We need not agree with Pythagoras that the essence of man is 250 to appreciate the significance of his point. The difference between his view and the view that man can be adequately understood in terms of formulas expressing the neurological functions of the brain is primarily a measure of the greater complexity of modern science; it is not a fundamental change in outlook. Not only the essential nature of individual phenomena, but the relations among them, and so the structure of the whole, can hence be understood not in terms of material variation, but in terms of numerical relations. No one has expressed the significance of this point better than Hegel in his *Lectures on the History of Philosophy*:

> The first and altogether abstract determinations [of Greek philosophy] are found with Thales and the other Ionians; they grasped the universal in the form of a natural determination, as water and air. Progression must thus take place by leaving behind the merely natural determination; and we find that this is so with the Pythagoreans. They say that number is the substance or the essence of things; number is not sensuous, nor is it pure thought, but it is a non-sensuous object of sense.[2]

> We must acknowledge the grandeur of this idea of determining everything in the system of the heavenly spheres through number-relations which have a necessary connection amongst themselves, and have to be conceived of as thus necessarily related; it is a system of relations which must also form the basis and essence of what can be heard, or music. We have, comprehended here in thought, a system of the universe; the solar system is alone rational to us, for the other stars are devoid of interest.[3]

The necessary mathematical relations of all phenomena, and their essential nature as mathematical, implies that everything is related in a unified whole and even by nature akin. The "kinship of all living things," usually considered one of the more bizarre aspects of

Phythagoras' religious mysticism, is in fact a consistent consequence of his mathematization of the world.

Given this relatedness in a unified whole, based as it is on mathematical principles, it is not surprising that Pythagoras argues that *unity* is the fundamental *arche* out of which the world of our experience arises and in terms of which it is intelligible. For Greek mathematics, "one" was not simply or even at all "the first number." It was still the basis, the *arche*, of number and so, given Pythagoras' ontological views, of the world. The smallest "number" is the smallest collection of units, or two. Pythagoras thus clearly takes his ontological stand in behalf of the priority of unity to multiplicity, of the one to the many. To quote from Hegel again:

> The Pythagoreans say that the first simple Notion is unity *(monas)*; not the discrete, multifarious, arithmetic one, but identity as continuity and positivity, the entirely universal essence. They further say, according to Sextus (adv. Math. X. 260, 261): "All numbers come under the notion of the one; for duality is one duality and triplicity is equally a 'one,' but the number ten is the one chief number. This moved Pythagoras to assert unity as the principle of all things, because, through partaking of it, each is called one." That is to say, the pure contemplation of the implicit being of a thing is the one, the being like self; to all else it is not implicit, but a relationship to what is other.[4]

In the famous Pythagorean "table of opposites," we see presented what Pythagoras, or at any rate later Pythagoreans, believed to be the consequences of the priority of unity. Ranged on the side of unity on the table, it will be recalled, are odd, the limited, one, right, male, straight, light, good, and square; whereas ranged alongside of multiplicity are even, the unlimited, many, left, female, curved, darkness, evil, and oblong.[5] Without going into how these placements are made, it is possible to note a decisive consequence utterly consistent with Pythagoras' mathematization of the universe. In a direct response to the teaching of Anaximander, Pythagoras placed the "limited" on the side of the good, the unlimited on the side of the bad. The exact reverse of Anaximander's assertion that coming-to-be, articulation, is "injustice," Pythagoras asserts that the *indefinite* is evil. What is good is limitation in the sense of de-finition, articulation. The Pythagorean world, like the Anaximandrian, is also "through and through moral"; but it is a world where philosophy is justified and even completable.

If the intelligibility of the world is based upon its mathematical character, then we can also see implicit in Pythagoras a conception of reason, that "faculty" by which the world will become intelligible to man, as mathematical. In the Pythagorean world, to be reasonable is to know mathematics; the world is rational because it is mathematical, and man's rational knowledge of the world is his mathematical knowledge. To this day the Pythagorean conception of reason still prevails, with relatively slight variations. No better evidence for this could be offered than a famous remark of Galileo, the founder of modern science, the very modern science which so dominates contemporary man's experience of the world.

> Philosophy is written in the great book which is ever before our eyes—I mean the universe—but we cannot understand it if we do not first learn the language and grasp the symbols in which it is written. This book is written in the mathematical language, and the symbols are triangles, circles, and other geometrical figures, without whose help it is impossible to comprehend a single word of it; without which one wanders in vain through a dark labyrinth.[6]

But into this optimistic system a decisive difficulty arose, discovered, apparently, by Pythagoras himself. The difficulty arose, ironically, as a consequence of one of Pythagoras' most important discoveries, the Pythagorean Theorem. For consequent to his recognition that the square of the hypotenuse of a right triangle was equal to the sum of the squares of the two sides, Pythagoras began to wonder what the relationship was between the diagonal of the square formed by the right triangle (the hypotenuse) and one of the sides. Thus:

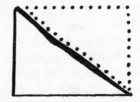

And what he discovered, on the basis of a mathematics based entirely on whole numbers, with no fractions as such or square roots, was that the relation could not be determined. Pythagoras had discovered incommensurable numbers. We can appreciate the profound disturbance that this must have caused if we remember that mathematics was not just a formal system but the ontological basis for the being and intelligibility of the world! If incommensurables really exist, then the claim that the world is through and through rational, that everything is related by a determinable mathematical relation, is made utterly precarious. Apparently, the reaction of the Pythagorean society was to keep this news a deep secret, and Hippasus, who later divulged the secret to outsiders was not only excommunicated from Pythagorean society but, if we can believe legend, punished by the gods by dying in a shipwreck. We have subsequently solved the problem posed by Pythagoras, and our optimism about the mathematization of the world has returned. But is it not instructive that those numbers which we do employ to express such relations as that of the diagonal to the side of a square are referred to as "irrational numbers"?

We may understand the consistency of Pythagoras' religious and mathematical views, and also make that transition ourselves, by a consideration of several important Pythagorean themes. The first has already been mentioned. The mathematical "kinship" of all things in terms of their essence as numerical and in terms of their numerical relations is expressed religiously in the doctrine of the kinship of all things and of the specific rules against the eating of flesh and taking of life consequent to it. Let us consider a specific aspect of Pythagorean religion—the doctrine of reincarnation. The essence of everything is number. But number is not the sort of thing that is born, dies, or even changes. "Six" was not born, will not die, and we can be as confident that "3 + 3" will equal "six" tomorrow as we are today. Number, that is, is eternal. Now the soul or life is given the nature of the one, or unity, by the Pythagoreans. Therefore, given the eternality of unity, it follows that the soul, whose essential nature is unity, is eternal. How, then, explain the apparent fact of death? The Pythagorean response is that death is really only the passing of the eternal soul from one body to another, or reincarnation.

A second way of understanding this consistency is to remember that it is not just the structure of the physical world but every aspect of human experience that is numerical in its essence. As such, and since number is eternal, and so divine, it is not surprising that the Pythagoreans should experience the presence of the divine in all things and comport themselves toward all things with religious reverence.

A third way is to take seriously the Pythagorean views about harmony. Pythagoras was the discoverer of the mathematical basis of harmony in music. If harmony in music was based upon the presence of ordered mathematical relations, and if similar mathematical relations pervade the entire cosmos and the world of our experience, then the entire world, ourselves included, must be involved in a harmony. The "music of the spheres" is thus the harmony among the heavenly bodies as they move through the cosmos. From such a view it is not surprising to find Pythagoreans endeavoring to preserve and express the harmony of all things by treating all things reverentially so far as possible.

Finally, and perhaps most important, is the following consideration. If the soul is in its essence one, or unity, and as such divine, then this means that what is divine in us and what we are in our *essence* is number. As such, our bodies are literally *irrelevant* to our essential nature. Hence the Pythagorean doctrine, expressed in Plato's *Phaedo*,[7] for example, that the soul is the prisoner of the body, and hence also the ease with which a Pythagorean could accept the notion of a soul almost casually leaving one body and moving on to another. But perhaps a far more enduring consequence of this view for Western man is that if the body is fundamentally irrelevant to what a person really is, if his real nature lies in his soul whose essence is in the realm of thought (mathematics), then it follows that the best life will be not a life which concerns itself with practical affairs, with the material and even monetary concerns of the everyday; the best life, the life most in accord with our nature, will be the theoretical or contemplative life. The famous Pythagorean parable about the superiority of the spectator to the vendors and contestants at an athletic contest is an expression of this. Pythagoras in a way first articulated, supported, and made a consistent part of his teaching the insistence that the theoretical or contemplative life, and so philosophy, was, first, a *way of life*, not just a pastime or occupation; second, a way of life which is most natural, that is, which origin-ates in our true nature as humans; and finally, a way of life which is the best life. Socrates, Plato, and Aristotle all believed this, and there are those among us who believe it still.

Pythagoras

Pythagoras of the island of Samos flourished around 530 B.C. He apparently traveled extensively and settled in the city of Crotona in southern Italy, where he founded a religious-philosophic order. His order was noteworthy for its intellectual accomplishments, which were many and varied, and also for the extent to which religion, philosophy, mathematical and other intellectual interests were combined into what amounted to a way of life. Pythagoras left no books because the order he founded was sworn to secrecy; the order also had the custom of attributing all important discoveries, no matter when or by whom, to Pythagoras himself. For these reasons, it is next to impossible to say with much confidence exactly what were Pythagoras' personal views and contributions. Nevertheless, both the famous Pythagorean Theorem and the discovery of incommensurables are generally attributed to Pythagoras himself.

TESTIMONIA ON PYTHAGORAS BY DIOGENES LAERTIUS*

Having now completed our account of the philosophy of Ionia starting with Thales, as well as of its chief representatives, let us proceed to examine the philosophy of Italy, which was started by Pythagoras, son of the gem-engraver Mnesarchus, and according to Hermippus, a Samian, or, according to Aristoxenus, a Tyrrhenian from one of those islands which the Athenians held after clearing them of their Tyrrhenian inhabitants. Some indeed say that he was descended through Euthyphro, Hippasus and Marmacus from Cleonymus, who was exiled from Phlius, and that, as Marmacus lived in Samos, so Pythagoras was called a Samian. From Samos he went, it is said, to Lesbos with an introduction to Pherecydes from his uncle Zoïlus. He had three silver flagons made and took them as presents to each of the priests of Egypt. He had brothers, of whom Eunomus was the elder and Tyrrhenus the second; he also had a slave, Zamolxis, who is worshipped, so says

---

* From R. D. Hicks, *Lives of Eminent Philosophers*.

Herodotus, by the Getans, as Cronos. He was a pupil, as already stated, of Pherecydes of Syros, after whose death he went to Samos to be the pupil of Hermodamas, Creophylus's descendant, a man already advanced in years. While still young, so eager was he for knowledge, he left his own country and had himself initiated into all the mysteries and rites not only of Greece but also of foreign countries. Now he was in Egypt when Polycrates sent him a letter of introduction to Amasis; he learnt the Egyptian language, so we learn from Antiphon in his book *On Men of Outstanding Merit*, and he also journeyed among the Chaldaeans and Magi. Then while in Crete he went down into the cave of Ida with Epimenides; he also entered the Egyptian sanctuaries, and was told their secret lore concerning the gods. After that he returned to Samos to find his country under the tyranny of Polycrates; so he sailed away to Croton in Italy, and there he laid down a constitution for the Italian Greeks, and he and his followers were held in great estimation; for, being nearly three hundred in number, so well did they govern the state that its constitution was in effect a true aristocracy (government by the best).

This is what Heraclides of Pontus tells us he used to say about himself: that he had once been Aethalides and was accounted to be Hermes' son, and Hermes told him he might choose any gift he liked except immortality; so he asked to retain through life and through death a memory of his experiences. Hence in life he could recall everything, and when he died he still kept the same memories. Afterwards in course of time his soul entered into Euphorbus and he was wounded by Menelaus. Now Euphorbus used to say that he had once been Aethalides and obtained this gift from Hermes, and then he told of the wanderings of his soul, how it migrated hither and thither, into how many plants and animals it had come, and all that it underwent in Hades, and all that the other souls there have to endure. When Euphorbus died, his soul passed into Hermotimus, and he also, wishing to authenticate the story, went up to the temple of Apollo at Branchidae, where he identified the shield which Menelaus, on his voyage home from Troy, had dedicated to Apollo, so he said; the shield being now so rotten through and through that the ivory facing only was left. When Hermotimus died, he became Pyrrhus, a fisherman of Delos, and again he remembered everything, how he was first Aethalides, then Euphorbus, then Hermotimus, and then Pyrrhus. But when Pyrrhus died, he became Pythagoras, and still remembered all the facts mentioned.

There are some who insist, absurdly enough, that Pythagoras left no writings whatever. At all events Heraclitus, the physicist, almost shouts in our ear, "Pythagoras, son of Mnesarchus, practised inquiry beyond all other men, and in this selection of his writings made himself a wisdom of his own, showing much learning but poor workmanship." The occasion of this remark was the opening words of Pythagoras's treatise *On Nature*, namely, "Nay, I swear by the air I breathe, I swear by the water I drink, I will never suffer censure on account of this work." Pythagoras in fact wrote three books, *On Education, On Statesmanship,* and *On Nature.* But the book which passes as the work of Pythagoras is by Lysis of Tarentum, a Pythagorean, who fled to Thebes and taught Epaminondas. Heraclides, the son of Serapion, in his *Epitome of Sotion,* says that he also wrote a poem *On the Universe,* and secondly the *Sacred Poem* which begins:

> Young men, come reverence in quietude
> All these my words;

thirdly *On the Soul,* fourthly *Of Piety,* fifthly *Helothales the Father of Epicharmus of Cos,* sixthly *Croton,* and other works as well. The same authority says that the poem *On the Mysteries* was written by Hippasus to defame Pythagoras, and that many others written by Aston of Croton were ascribed to Pythagoras. Aristoxenus says that Pythagoras got most of his moral doctrines from the Delphic priestess Themistoclea. According to Ion of Chios in his *Triagmi* he ascribed some poems of his own making to Orpheus. They further attribute to him the *Scopiads* which begins thus:

> Be not shameless, before any man.

Sosicrates in his *Successions of Philosophers* says that, when Leon the tyrant of Phlius asked him who he was, he said, "A philosopher," and that he compared life to the Great Games, where some went to compete for the prize and others went with wares to sell, but the best as spectators; for similarly, in life, some grow up with servile natures, greedy for fame and gain, but the philosopher seeks for truth. Thus much for this part of the subject.

The contents in general of the aforesaid three treatises of Pythagoras are as follows. He forbids us to pray for ourselves, because we do not know what will help us. Drinking he calls, in a word, a snare, and he discountenances all excess, saying that no one should go beyond due proportion either in drinking or in eating. Of sexual indulgence, too, he says, "Keep to the winter for sexual pleasures, in summer abstain; they are less harmful in autumn and spring, but they are always harmful and not conducive to health." Asked once when a man should consort with a woman, he replied, "When you want to lose what strength you have."

He divides man's life into four quarters thus: "Twenty years a boy, twenty years a youth, twenty years a young man, twenty years an old man; and these four periods correspond to the four seasons, the boy to spring, the youth to summer, the young man to autumn, and the old man to winter," meaning by youth one not yet grown up and by a young man a man of mature age. According to Timaeus, he was the first to say, "Friends have all things in common" and "Friendship is equality"; indeed, his disciples did put all their possessions into one common stock. For five whole years they had to keep silence, merely listening to his discourses without seeing him, until they passed an examination, and thenceforward they were admitted to his house and allowed to see him. They would never use coffins of cypress, because the sceptre of Zeus was made from it, so we are informed by Hermippus in his second book *On Pythagoras*.

Indeed, his bearing is said to have been most dignified, and his disciples held the opinion about him that he was Apollo come down from the far north. There is a story that once, when he was disrobed, his thigh was seen to be of gold; and when he crossed the river Nessus, quite a number of people said they heard it welcome him. According to Timaeus in the tenth book of his *History*, he remarked that the consorts of men bore divine names, being called first Virgins, then Brides, and then Mothers. He it was who brought geometry to perfection, while it was Moeris who first discovered the beginnings of the elements of geometry: Anticlides in his second book *On Alexander* affirms this, and further that Pythagoras spent most of his time upon the arithmetical aspect of geometry; he also discovered the musical intervals on the monochord. Nor did he neglect even medicine. We are told by

Apollodorus the calculator that he offered a sacrifice of oxen on finding that in a right-angled triangle the square on the hypotenuse is equal to the squares on the sides containing the right angle. And there is an epigram running as follows:

> What time Pythagoras that famed figure found,
> For which the noble offering he brought.

He is also said to have been the first to diet athletes on meat, trying first with Eurymenes—so we learn from Favorinus in the third book of his *Memorabilia*—whereas in former times they had trained on dried figs, on butter, and even on wheatmeal, as we are told by the same Favorinus in the eighth book of his *Miscellaneous History*. Some say it was a certain trainer named Pythagoras who instituted this diet, and not our Pythagoras, who forbade even the killing, let alone the eating, of animals which share with us the privilege of having a soul. This was the excuse put forward; but his real reason for forbidding animal diet was to practise people and accustom them to simplicity of life, so that they could live on things easily procurable, spreading their tables with un-cooked foods and drinking pure water only, for this was the way to a healthy body and a keen mind. Of course the only altar at which he wor-shipped was that of Apollo the Giver of Life, behind the Altar of Horns at Delos, for thereon were placed flour and meal and cakes, without the use of fire, and there was no animal victim, as we are told by Aristotle in his *Constitution of Delos*.

He was the first, they say, to declare that the soul, bound now in this creature, now in that, thus goes on a round ordained of necessity. He too, according to Aristoxenus the musician, was the first to introduce weights and measures into Greece. It was he who first declared that the Evening and Morning Stars are the same, as Parmenides maintains. So greatly was he admired that his disciples used to be called "prophets to declare the voice of God," besides which he himself says in a written work that "after two hundred and seven years in Hades he has returned to the land of the living." Thus it was that they remained his staunch adherents, and men came to hear his words from afar, among them Lucanians, Peucetians, Messapians and Romans.

Down to the time of Philolaus it was not possible to acquire knowledge of any Pythagorean doctrine, and Philolaus alone brought out those three celebrated books which Plato sent a hundred minas to purchase. Not less than six hundred persons went to his evening lectures; and those who were privileged to see him wrote to their friends congratulating themselves on a great piece of good fortune. Moreover, the Metapontines named his house the Temple of Demeter and his porch the Museum, so we learn from Favorinus in his *Miscellaneous History*. And the rest of the Pythagoreans used to say that not all his doctrines were for all men to hear, our authority for this being Aristoxenus in the tenth book of his *Rules of Pedagogy*, where we are also told that one of the school, Xenophilus by name, asked by some one how he could best educate his son, replied, "By making him the citizen of a well-governed state." Throughout Italy Pythagoras made many into good men and true, men too of note like the lawgivers Zaleucus and Charondas; for he had a great gift for friendship, and especially, when he found his own watchwords adopted by anyone, he would immediately take to that man and make a friend of him.

The following were his watchwords or precepts: don't stir the fire with a knife, don't step over the beam of a balance, don't sit down on your bushel, don't eat your heart, don't help a man off with a load but help him on, always roll your bed-clothes up, don't put God's image on the circle of a ring, don't leave the pan's imprint on the ashes, don't wipe up a mess with a torch, don't commit a nuisance towards the sun, don't walk the highway, don't shake hands too eagerly, don't have swallows under your own roof, don't keep birds with hooked claws, don't make water on nor stand upon your nail- and hair-trimmings, turn the sharp blade away, when you go abroad don't turn round at the frontier.

This is what they meant. Don't stir the fire with a knife: don't stir the passions or the swelling pride of the great. Don't step over the beam of a balance: don't overstep the bounds of equity and justice. Don't sit down on your bushel: have the same care of to-day and the future, a bushel being the day's ration. By not eating your heart he meant not wasting your life in troubles and pains. By saying do not turn round when you go abroad, he meant to advise those who are departing this life not to set their hearts' desire on living nor to be too much attracted by the pleasures of this life. The explanations of the rest are similar and would take too long to set out.

Above all, he forbade as food red mullet and blacktail, and he enjoined abstinence from the hearts of animals and from beans, and sometimes, according to Aristotle, even from paunch and gurnard. Some say that he contented himself with just some honey or a honeycomb or bread, never touching wine in the daytime, and greens boiled or raw for dainties, and fish but rarely. His robe was white and spotless, his quilts of white wool, for linen had not yet reached those parts. He was never known to over-eat, to behave loosely, or to be drunk. He would avoid laughter and all pandering to tastes such as insulting jests and vulgar tales. He would punish neither slave nor free man in anger. Admonition he used to call "setting right." He used to practise divination by sounds or voices and by auguries, never by burnt-offerings, beyond frankincense. The offerings he made were always inanimate; though some say that he would offer cocks, sucking goats and porkers, as they are called, but lambs never. However, Aristoxenus has it that he consented to the eating of all other animals, and only abstained from ploughing oxen and rams.

The same authority, as we have seen, asserts that Pythagoras took his doctrines from the Delphic priestess Themistoclea. Hieronymus, however, says that, when he had descended into Hades, he saw the soul of Hesiod bound fast to a brazen pillar and gibbering, and the soul of Homer hung on a tree with serpents writhing about it, this being their punishment for what they had said about the gods; he also saw under torture those who would not remain faithful to their wives. This, says our authority, is why he was honoured by the people of Croton. Aristippus of Cyrene affirms in his work *On the Physicists* that he was named Pythagoras because he uttered the truth as infallibly as did the Pythian oracle. . . .

Pythagoras met his death in this wise. As he sat one day among his acquaintances at the house of Milo, it chanced that the house was set ablaze out of jealousy by one of the people who were not accounted worthy of admittance to his presence, though some say it was the work of the inhabitants of Croton anxious to safeguard themselves against the setting-up of a tyranny. Pythagoras was caught as he tried to escape; he got as far as a certain field of beans, where he stopped, saying he would be captured rather than cross it, and be killed rather than prate about his doctrines; and so his pursuers cut his throat. . . .

TESTIMONIA ON PYTHAGORAS BY PLATO

. . . What do you mean, Socrates?

I will tell you, he said. The lovers of knowledge are conscious that their souls when philosophy receives them, are simply fastened and glued to their bodies: the soul is only able to view existence through the bars of a prison, and not in her own nature; she is wallowing in the mire of all ignorance; and philosophy, seeing the terrible nature of her confinement, and that the captive through desire is led to conspire in her own captivity (for the lovers of knowledge are aware that this was the original state of the soul, and that when she was in this state philosophy received and gently counselled her, and wanted to release her, pointing out to her that the eye is full of deceit, and also the ear and the other senses, and persuading her to retire from them in all but the necessary use of them, and to be gathered up and collected into herself, and to trust only to herself and her own intuitions of absolute existence, and mistrust that which comes to her through others and is subject to vicissitude)—philosophy shows her that this is visible and tangible, but that what she sees in her own nature is intellectual and invisible. And the soul of the true philosopher thinks that she ought not to resist this deliverance, and therefore abstains from pleasures and desires and pains and fears, as far as she is able; reflecting that when a man has great joys or sorrows or fears or desires, he suffers from them, not the sort of evil which might be anticipated—as for example, the loss of his health or property which he has sacrificed to his lusts—but he has suffered an evil greater far, which is the greatest and worst of all evils, and one of which he never thinks. . . . (*Phaedo*, 82-83)

TESTIMONIA ON PYTHAGORAS BY ARISTOTLE

Contemporaneously with these philosophers and before them, the so-called Pythagoreans, who were the first to take up mathematics, not only advanced this study, but also having been brought up in it they thought its principles were the principles of all things. Since of these principles numbers are by nature the first, and in numbers they seemed to see many resemblances to the things that exist and come into be-

ing—more than in fire and earth and water (such and such a modifica-
tion of numbers being justice, another being soul and reason, another
being opportunity—and similarly almost all other things being
numerically expressible); since, again, they saw that the modifications
and the ratios of the musical scales were expressible in numbers;—since, then, all other things seemed in their whole nature to be
modelled on numbers, and numbers seemed to be the first things in the
whole of nature, they supposed the elements of numbers to be the elements of all things, and the whole heaven to be a musical scale and a
number. And all the properties of numbers and scales which they could
show to agree with the attributes and parts and the whole arrangement
of the heavens, they collected and fitted into their scheme; and if there
was a gap anywhere, they readily made additions so as to make their
whole theory coherent. E. g. as the number 10 is thought to be perfect
and to comprise the whole nature of numbers, they say that the bodies
which move through the heavens are ten, but as the visible bodies are
only nine, to meet this they invent a tenth—the 'counter-earth'. We
have discussed these matters more exactly elsewhere. (*De Caelo*, ii. 13)

But the object of our review is that we may learn from these
philosophers also what they suppose to be the principles and how these
fall under the causes we have named. Evidently, then, these thinkers also consider that number is the principle both as matter for things and as
forming both their modifications and their permanent states, and hold
that the elements of number are the even and the odd, and that of these
the latter is limited, and the former unlimited; and that the One proceeds from both of these (for it is both even and odd), and number from
the One; and that the whole heaven, as has been said, is numbers.

Other members of this same school say there are ten principles,
which they arrange in two columns of cognates—limited and unlimited,
odd and even, one and plurality, right and left, male and female, resting
and moving, straight and curved, light and darkness, good and bad,
square and oblong. In this way Alcmaeon of Croton seems also to have
conceived the matter, and either he got this view from them or they got
it from him; for he expressed himself similarly to them. For he says
most human affairs go in pairs, meaning not definite contrarieties such
as the Pythagoreans speak of, but any chance contrarieties, e. g. white
and black, sweet and bitter, good and bad, great and small. He threw

out indefinite suggestions about the other contrarieties, but the Pythagoreans declared both how many and which their contrarieties are. (*Metaphysica*, 985*b* 23)

. . . Again, the Pythagoreans, because they saw many attributes of numbers belonging to sensible bodies, supposed real things to be numbers—not separable numbers, however, but numbers of which real things consist. But why? Because the attributes of numbers are present in a musical scale and in the heavens and in many other things. (*Metaphysica*, 1090*a* 20)

. . . And the Pythagoreans, also, believe in one kind of number—the mathematical; only they say it is not separate but sensible substances are formed out of it. For they construct the whole universe out of numbers—only not numbers consisting of abstract units; they suppose the units to have spatial magnitude. But how the first 1 was constructed so as to have magnitude, they seem unable to say. (*Metaphysica*, 1080*b* 16)

. . . All who have touched on this kind of science in a way worth considering have formulated views about the infinite, and indeed, to a man, make it a principle of things.

(I) Some, as the Pythagoreans and Plato, make the infinite a principle in the sense of a self-subsistent substance, and not as a mere attribute of some other thing. Only the Pythagoreans place the infinite among the objects of sense (they do not regard number as separable from these), and assert that what is outside the heaven is infinite. Plato, on the other hand, holds that there is no body outside (the Forms are not outside, because they are nowhere), yet that the infinite is present not only in the objects of sense but in the Forms also.

Further, the Pythagoreans identify the infinite with the even. For this, they say, when it is cut off and shut in by the odd, provides things with the element of infinity. An indication of this is what happens with numbers. If the gnomons are placed round the one, and without the one, in the one construction the figure that results is always different, in the other it is always the same. But Plato has two infinites, the Great and the Small. (*Physica*, 203*a* 1)

. . . A magnitude if divisible one way is a line, if two ways a surface, and if three a body. Beyond these there is no other magnitude, because the three dimensions are all that there are, and that which is divisible in three directions is divisible in all. For, as the Pythagoreans say, the world and all that is in it is determined by the number three, since beginning and middle and end give the number of an 'all', and the number they give is the triad. And so, having taken these three from nature as (so to speak) laws of it, we make further use of the number three in the worship of the Gods. . . . (*De Caelo*, 268*a* 8)

. . . But the Italian philosophers known as Pythagoreans take the contrary view. At the centre, they say, is fire, and the earth is one of the stars, creating night and day by its circular motion about the centre. They further construct another earth in opposition to ours to which they give the name counter-earth. In all this they are not seeking for theories and causes to account for observed facts, but rather forcing their observations and trying to accommodate them to certain theories and opinions of their own. But there are many others who would agree that it is wrong to give the earth the central position, looking for confirmation rather to theory than to the facts of observation. Their view is that the most precious place befits the most precious thing: but fire, they say, is more precious than earth, and the limit than the intermediate, and the circumference and the centre are limits. Reasoning on this basis they take the view that it is not earth that lies at the centre of the sphere, but rather fire. The Pythagoreans have a further reason. They hold that the most important part of the world, which is the centre, should be most strictly guarded, and name it, or rather the fire which occupies that place, the 'Guard-house of Zeus', as if the word 'centre' were quite unequivocal, and the centre of the mathematical figure were always the same with that of the thing or the natural centre. (*De Caelo*, 293*a* 20)

Its supporters say that the soul is a kind of harmony, for (a) harmony is a blend or composition of contraries and (b) the body is compounded out of contraries. (*De Anima*, 407*b* 28)

Notes: III

1. See *The Pre-Socratics*, Philip Wheelwright, ed. (New York, Odyssey Press, 1966), p. 203.

2. G. F. Hegel, *Lectures on the History of Philosophy*, trans. by E. S. Haldane (New York, Humanities Press, 1963), Vol. 1, p. 170.

3. *Ibid.*, p. 230.

4. *Ibid.*, pp. 212, 213.

5. For an account of how these relations are worked out, *see* J. M. Robinson, *An Introduction to Early Greek Philosophy* (Boston, Houghton Mifflin Co., 1968), pp. 63-87.

6. Galileo: *Opera Complete di Galileo Galilei* (Firenze, 1842), IV, 171. Quoted in E. A. Burtt, *Metaphysical Foundations of Modern Science* (Anchor Books, 1954), p. 75; and in Robinson, *op. cit.*, p. 69.

7. Plato, *Phaedo*, 62a *passim*.

The Battle of the Giants: I

ACCORDING to a view set forth by the seventeenth-century philosopher, Benedict de Spinoza, the beginning of philosophy is the insight into the unity of the mind with the whole of nature.[1] In the course of his own philosophic thinking Spinoza works out in detail his interpretation of the meaning of this view. But without even attempting to accurately characterize Spinoza's meaning, it is possible to apply this penetrating insight to many of the Pre-Socratic philosophers so far studied. Certainly Spinoza's statement is appropriate to Thales' remarks on the affinity of *nous*, "everything," and primal water. It applies as well to Anaximenes' insistence on the qualitative affinity of the soul and air, and so ultimately of all things, and to Pythagoras' considerations concerning the "kinship" of the soul to the structure of the whole through mathematics. As we shall subsequently see, it is explicitly appropriate to Parmenides' famous thesis that "thinking and being are the same".[2] But there is perhaps no one of the Pre-Socratics to whose position this conception of the origin of philosophy is so central as it is to Heraclitus. The present discussion shall interpret the Heraclitean fragments as an effort to respond to and adequately work out precisely this conception of the origin of philosophy, and of the relation between man and nature, or the structure of the whole. The following "arrangement" of the fragments is thus an original interpretation of the coherent philosophical position that they contain. In the text of the fragments themselves is a more standard arrangement so as not to bias the reader's own reading of the fragments in favor of this interpretation.

If the beginning of philosophy is the insight into the unity of the mind with the whole of nature, then it would not be surprising, especially for philosophers in the tradition of Thales, if this insight itself began by a consideration of or wonder about "the mind," or in Greek terms, the soul or self. Several of Heraclitus' fragments do refer to this beginning, and for the purposes of the present interpretation they constitute the beginning, in the sense of the *arche*, of Heraclitus' thinking. Thus Fragment 101 reads simply "I searched into myself." From the time of Thales' insistence on the importance and difficulty of self-knowledge to the present, this concern with self-knowledge has been crucial to the thinking of the greatest Western philosophers. In Heraclitus' simple fragment we can find that he too begins and is sustained in his philosophizing with this most fundamental of concerns. But with his characteristic terseness and power, Heraclitus goes on both to deepen and make more complex the enterprise of coming to self-knowledge. From the standpoint of my interpretation, the next Heraclitean fragment would be number 116: "All men have the capacity to know themselves and to act with *sophrosyne*."[3]* We can note first Heraclitus' assertion that self-knowledge, and so philosophy, is *available* as a possibility to all men. Subsequent fragments express Heraclitus' disappointment and disdain that so few men take up this possibility.[4] Nevertheless, he here indicates that it *is* a possibility for all men; the capacity for self-knowledge is thus from the beginning asserted to be part of man's nature (*physis*), even if it is rarely realized. To put the point in more traditional philosophic language, philosophy is a *telos* for human being, or as put more strongly in the Introduction, philosophy is the culmination of what it means to be human. Heraclitus reminds us forcefully how difficult that *telos* is of achievement; but as we shall see, the difficulty is understandable.

Aphoristic writing such as Heraclitus' depends on the power of carefully chosen words to penetrate to some fundamental meaning. We must therefore be struck that Heraclitus in this fragment chooses to associate self-knowledge or the beginning of philosophy with the almost forgotten Greek virtue of *sophrosyne*. These two concepts, self-knowledge and *sophrosyne*, would not have been put in the same fragment if Heraclitus did not want us to think about the fact of their con-

---

* The use of a different and more literal translation here than in the selections is intentional. Part of the difficulty in understanding Pre-Socratic fragments is their own ambiguity. We shall often henceforward employ alternative translations of fragments to suggest both the range of possible translations and the difference that variations can make.

nection and what that connection might be. Plato, for one, thought about that connection so deeply that he devoted a dialogue, the *Charmides*, to its consideration. At least one of the nuances of the virtue of *sophrosyne* as the Greeks understood it was that of self-control as knowing one's place, knowing one's limitations, and not aspiring for that which it is not given to man to be. And this meant especially, not striving to be a god. Pindar regularly issues this injunction in his odes, and Greek tragedy is replete with accounts of the consequences for men who forget their *sophrosyne* and do strive to be gods; they become instead tragic heroes. Socrates and Plato, on the other hand, are rather ambiguous in their adherence to this conception of *sophrosyne*, but Aristotle virtually sounds the bugle for modern man by denying explicitly that man should be *sophron* in this sense; we should strive to be "as much like the divine as possible."[5] We can already see the beginnings of what we might call this philosophic heresy in Heraclitus. Self-knowledge means at least in part knowing one's limits, and so not presuming to attain to the divine. This is one sense of the relation between self-knowledge and *sophrosyne*, and to be sure, Heraclitus seems well aware of its practical consequences, as for example in Fragment 43: "To extinguish *hybris* [arrogance or pride] is more needful than to extinguish a fire." Yet as we shall see, Heraclitus also, perhaps more than any other Pre-Socratic philosopher, claims an access to what he calls the divine and at the same time a close kinship between man and the divine which makes that access possible. But the impetus toward that access is accompanied by that very propensity for *hybris* which *sophrosyne* as knowledge of one's limits is meant to control. Explicitly, *philosophic* access to the divine, for Heraclitus as for Socrates, Plato, and Aristotle, takes the form of wisdom, or knowledge of the structure of the whole. Heraclitus demonstrates his appreciation of the tension between these two concepts, a tension which has come to be closely associated with his thought, by placing them together in a striking way. Fragment 112 reads: "To be *sophron* [to act with *sophrosyne—sophronein*] is the greatest virtue, and wisdom is to speak and act the truth, paying heed to the nature of things." So far we have: Self-knowledge is the beginning of the philosophic quest; but self-knowledge means, at least in part, knowledge of one's limits and, in particular, of what separates or distinguishes man from the divine. But this knowledge and the action consequent to it is *sophrosyne*. Yet knowledge of the truth "according to nature," knowledge of the relation between the mortal and the divine, is wisdom. *Sophrosyne*, it seems, is the middle term between self-knowledge and wisdom or knowledge of the divine. It is also necessary to note that wisdom, as Heraclitus understands it, is evidently not simply "epistemic" or "theoretical" knowledge. Wisdom is "to speak and act the truth, paying heed to the nature of things." Truth is not simply the content of propositions uttered. It is also a way of life. Self-knowledge seems to point beyond itself, to knowledge first of one's limits, or *sophrosyne*, and consequently to knowledge of the relation between man and the divine, or knowledge of the structure of the whole, or wisdom. But it points as well to a way of life, an *acting* according to the truth of the nature of things. But we are getting ahead of ourselves. We should step back a moment and note that it is not surprising that most men fail in what increasingly appears as the infinitely complex and difficult achievement of self-knowledge. Nevertheless, Heraclitus castigates us for this failure. To quote Fragments 17 and 89:

> For many men—those who encounter such things—do not understand them, and do not grasp them after they have learnt; but to themselves they seem (to understand).

> To those who are awake, there is one ordered universe common (to all) whereas in sleep each man turns away (from the world) to one of his own.[6]

Because the movement from self-knowledge to *sophrosyne* to wisdom is so difficult, let us retrace it more slowly by drawing in other relevant fragments. Let us turn first to those fragments which seem to deal exclusively with the nature of the soul, or self-knowledge.

One of Heraclitus' favorite metaphors is that of fire to express the sense both of flux and of liveliness. Not surprisingly, therefore, the soul too, as the principle of life, is associated with the liveliness and flux of fire through the image of dryness. Yet also characteristic of Heraclitus' concern with opposites, the soul arises out of the opposite of fire, that which is moist. There is even a hint, though undeveloped, that in this case at least the return to origins, or the moist, would be destructive rather than beneficial to the soul, yet enjoyable. The following fragments encapsulate this view:

Souls are vaporized from what is moist.[7]

Soul is the vaporization out of which everything else is composed; moreover, it is the least corporeal of things and is in ceaseless flux, for the moving world can only be known by what is in motion.[8]

A dry soul is the wisest and best.[9]

Souls take pleasure in becoming moist.[10]

It is death to souls to become water, and it is death to water to become earth. Conversely, water comes into being out of earth, and souls out of water.[11]

From this view of the soul there follows a series of more practical, or, as the existentialists say, "ontic" consequences which Heraclitus sets out in fragments too numerous to quote or discuss.[12]

Needless to say, the attempt to treat of the soul taken by itself, and in terms of the fundamental metaphor of fire, is hardly the stuff of which great philosophy is made. Far more suggestive are the following two fragments, however:

The soul has a *logos*, which increases itself.[13]

A man's character is his *daimon*.[14]

Fragment 115 informs us that, notwithstanding the evident inadequacy of the previous account, the soul does have a *logos*; there is an adequate account to be given of the soul, if we can only gain access to it. But it also informs us that this *logos* is peculiar. It is not static, stated once and for all time, but rather "increases itself." The soul is thus a peculiar entity, if it be an entity at all, for apparently it is of a nature as to be constantly changing, and changing in such a way as to *increase* itself. If we take this view seriously, it suggests that for Heraclitus, although philosophic speech about the soul is possible, it is a speech which will not end but continue as long as the soul itself exists. Suffice it to say that from Plato, through the nineteenth-century philosophies of Hegel and Marx, to such contemporary philosophers as Heidegger and Wittgenstein, philosophers have been trying to complete the speech about the soul or else agreeing with Heraclitus that it cannot be done.

Heraclitus himself elaborates on the unending character of the *logos* of the soul in the second fragment quoted, Fragment 119. According to the teaching of Socrates in Plato's *Symposium*, which he claims to have learned from Diotima, a priestess, a *daimon* is a "spirit" who occupies a position in the middle between the mortal and the divine, and occupying this intermediate position it is able to bridge the gap between the mortal and the divine, and so have access to both.[15] If man's character is his *daimon*, then Heraclitus would seem to agree with Socrates that there is something about man which is more than man, something which enables him to gain access to the divine. Man is daimonic. The direction in which the *logos* of the soul "increases" seems to be indicated by this fragment. The *logos* of the soul must be unending because it points to a *logos* of the daimonic, or that which is in between the mortal and the divine. But an adequate *logos* of that which is *in between* the mortal and the divine must include as well a *logos* of the divine. To give a complete *logos* of the soul is to give a complete *logos* of the structure of the whole, and for reasons which Heraclitus presently makes clear, such a speech must be unending.

But we again are moving ahead too fast and must retrace our steps more cautiously with the aid of Heraclitus' fragments. What the fragments so far have established is that any attempt to give an account of the soul in its own terms, independent of anything other than soul, will be necessarily inadequate. The soul, strange as it seems, "is more than what it is"; it points or is oriented beyond itself. Heraclitus makes this explicit in Fragment 45: "You could not discover the limits of soul, even if you traveled by every path; such is the depths of its logos."

The effort to give a *logos* of the soul necessarily leads beyond the soul to that which is other than the soul. That is why the earlier attempts to account for the soul in its own terms failed. This means, however, that what *appears* to be the case is not so. What *appears*, what appears even to the behaviorists of our own day, is that the soul or self is an entity unto itself; it "is what it is and not another thing." Henceforward in

Heraclitus' search, and he will remind us of this at all subsequent levels of the investigation, he will be seeking what is hidden, what is precisely *not* apparent. I submit that it is in the light of the daimonic nature of the soul, then, that we must understand Heraclitus' emphasis on the hidden character of the *logos* he is seeking in such fragments as these:

> Unless you expect the unexpected, you will never find it. For it is hard to discover and difficult.[16]

> A hidden harmony is better than an apparent one.[17]

> Nature loves to hide.[18]

> The lord whose oracle is at Delphi neither speaks nor conceals, but gives a sign.[19]

The effort to attain self-knowledge, to give a *logos* of the soul and to act out that *logos* by going beyond the soul, might take several directions. Heraclitus offers three as possibilities. The *logos* might move from a *logos* of the individual soul to a *logos* of the relations between men, that is, to the level of mankind; second, it might move to a *logos* of the physical cosmos. Finally, and decisively, it might move toward a *logos* of the divine. We have already intimated the ultimacy of the third way.

The *logos* of man's relation to his fellowman has two central themes. The first is the commonality among men of the capacity for thinking, which both grounds the earlier assertion regarding the commonality of self-knowledge and points toward the universality of the *Logos*. The second, not surprisingly, centers around political things. The conservative-sounding appeal that Heraclitus makes to the need to respect and even revere the law is what contemporary existentialist thinkers might call an "ontic" manifestation of the "ontological" call which Heraclitus issues to pay heed to the *Logos*. Heraclitus again insists that if there is a difference between the realm of human encounter and the realm of the divine, between the ontic and the ontological, there is nonetheless a symmetry between them. The ontic realm is a reflection or imitation of the ontological; ontological or philosophical obedience to the *Logos* must be reflected in ontic or political respect for the law of the city. In this day of the reverence not of the law but of civil disobedience, we may be disinclined to accept Heraclitus' specific recommendations; we might nevertheless pay heed to his recommendation that, whatever our specific political views, they be a reflection of, and so grounded in, an ontology, a philosophic conception of the relation between man and the most fundamental things. The greatest danger of the present age might well be not that we disagree with Heraclitus' reverence for the law, but that we may forget the need of grounding our political views even in a conception of human nature, much less a relation of man to the most fundamental things, the divine, or Being. It is in the light of considerations such as these that such fragments as the following should be reflected upon:

Thinking is common to all.[20]

Speaking with intelligence men should base their strength on that which is common to all, as the city on the law, and even more strongly. For all human laws are nourished by one, which is divine. For it governs as far as it will, and is sufficient for all and is more than they.[21]

The people should fight for their law as for their city wall.[22]

Law involves obeying the counsel of one.[23]

However demanding of reflection such considerations may be, they are evidently insufficient as a *logos* of the soul, since even in articulating them Heraclitus forces us to refer beyond them to that which grounds them, the *Logos*, which as has no doubt been obvious for a long time, is the *telos* of all Heraclitus' thought.

Heraclitus' cosmological fragments center on the notion of fire as the fundamental element in the cosmos, out of which other things arise. It is of course possible that Heraclitus meant these literally, in which case, as physical explanations, they can hardly compare with the latest results of quantum physics and should perhaps not be dwelled upon too long. But it is also possible and even consistent with this that Heraclitus meant them to be taken as metaphors which, not unlike the Thalenic fragments concerning the affinity of water, *nous*, and the daimonic character of the cosmos, asserts most fundamentally the *accessibility* to human thinking of the structure, or *arche*, of the physical cosmos. Thanks to the participation both of the soul and of the cosmos in the liveliness and flux of fire, man's speech about the whole can include and must include a speech about the cosmos. To put the point differently, because man's soul is not complete unto itself but oriented toward that which it is not, and because man dwells—lives, breathes, and has his being—in the cosmos, self-knowledge must include knowledge of the cosmos—even if the cosmos turns out to be not literally composed of fire. "So deep is its *logos*."[24] Today, the physicist, unless he happens to be an Einstein or a Heisenberg, may consider his investigations into physics to be distinct and even divorced from his own nature as a man. Men like Einstein and Heisenberg believe differently. The genuine significance of such apparently "naïve" fragments as the following is to indicate Heraclitus' agreement with these titans of contemporary physics that speech about the cosmos, or what we today call physics, must be understood as grounded in and indeed part of the speech about human being.

There is exchange of all things for fire and of fire for all things, as there is of wares for gold and of gold for wares.[25]

This cosmos, which is the same for all, has not been made by any god or man, but it always has been, is, and will be, an ever-living fire, kindling itself by regular measures and going out by regular measures.[26]

The transformations of fire: first, sea; and of sea half becomes earth and half the lightning flash. . . .[27]

. . . When earth has melted into sea, the resultant amount is the same as there had been before sea became hardened into earth.[28]

Fire lives in the death of earth, air in the death of fire, water in the death of air, and earth in the death of water.[29]

But as Heraclitus' famous Fragment 119 has already intimated, an adequate *logos* of the soul can be given neither by incorporating an ac-

count of human encounter nor by including an account of man's orientation toward the cosmos. Heraclitus does not say, as thinkers from
Aristotle to Marx have subsequently said, "Man is a political animal."
Nor does he assert a materialist atomism such as maintained by Democritus or Leucippus or present-day philosophers who argue that man is
a machine and thereby nothing but a cog in the machine of the cosmos.
Instead, Heraclitus says, "Man's character is his *daimon*," and in so
saying asserts that man's most fundamental stake rests in his orientation
toward the divine.

But what Heraclitus calls the divine is as far as possible from the utterly anthropomorphic, fickle, even irrational gods of the Homeric epics
and Hesiod's *Theogony*. Like Xenophanes before him, Heraclitus
castigates traditional Greek theology for its complete misconstrual of
the true nature of the divine. Fragment 14, for example, reads: "Night
walkers, magicians, bacchantes, revelers, and participants in the
mysteries! What are regarded as mysteries among men are unholy rit-
uals." And Fragment 5 reads: "They pray to images, much as if they
were to talk to houses; for they do not know what gods and heroes
are."[30]

Heraclitus' "positive theology" begins with fragments which call our
attention to the difficulty and yet the genuine possibility of man's access
to the divine. This concern is understandable in the light of the interpretation offered here, that the movement toward the divine is grounded
in an origin-al concern with self-knowledge. From this standpoint the
initial issue of "theology" will naturally be man's access or relation to
the divine. The possibility but difficulty of access is first indicated by
Fragment 93: "The lord whose oracle is at Delphi neither speaks nor
conceals, but gives a sign." The difference between the human and the
divine, and perhaps the ultimate finitude of human understanding, is indicated by Fragment 78: "Human nature (*ethos*) has no real understanding; but the divine does." But even though human being *by itself* is inadequate of understanding, man can gain understanding by virtue of his participation in that which is more than human, as the fragment on the daimonic has indicated. According to Sextus Empiricus,
Heraclitus argued that man is not himself rational, but that we become
intelligent by virtue of our participation in "that which encompasses
us."[31] Again, it must be noted that such a view would only be possible
if man is of such a nature as to be *encompassed*, to consciously comport

himself toward "the encompassing." But in the light of this, it is necessary to ask next, what is that which encompasses us by participation in which we gain what insight is ours? Fragment 72 both reasserts the difficulty of access and names the encompassing: "Although intimately connected with the *Logos*, men keep setting themselves against it."

The origin, or *arche*, of the intelligibility of all things, and so the *arche* of man's self-knowledge as that creature who stands in participation with that which he is not, Heraclitus calls the *Logos*. And now this famous spokesman for eternal flux, to whom is often ascribed the dictum that "everything flows," this lover of strife and contention says something that astounds. He asserts of the *Logos* that which is usually ascribed to his supposedly philosophic polar-opposite, Parmenides. He says that the *arche* of things is *one*. Fragments 32, 41, and 50 read successively:

> Wisdom is one and unique; it is unwilling and yet willing to be called by the name of Zeus.

> Wisdom is one—to know the intelligence by which all things are steered by all things.

> Listening not to me but to the *Logos*, it is wise to agree that all things are one.

The "hidden harmony" that is better or stronger than the "apparent one"[32] is that all things are gathered together into one. The one is the *Logos*. The "apparent harmony" is the flux and multiplicity with which our senses present us, the senses which we can now well understand are "bad witnesses for barbarian souls." Is it any wonder that an *arche* so apparently different from what is apparent should be difficult to comprehend?

> Although this *Logos* is eternally valid, yet men are unable to understand it—not only before hearing it, but even after they have heard it for the first time. That is to say, although all things come to pass in accordance with the *Logos*, men seem to be quite without any experience of it—at least if they are judged in the light

of such words and deeds as I am here setting forth. My own method is to distinguish each thing according to its nature, and to specify how it behaves; other men on the contrary are as neglectful of what they do when awake as they are when asleep.[33]

We should let ourselves be guided by what is common to all. Yet although the *Logos* is common to all, most men live as if each had a private intelligence of his own.[34]

But can it be that ours is a world in which the origin of things is the exact contradictory of what appears? What kind of relation or access to the *Logos* could man have if that *Logos* is simply the opposite of what his experience reveals? We have already seen the implausibility of this in our discussion of Heraclitus' political views in Fragment 114. The ontic or political realm must be a reflection, not the contradictory, of the ontological realm of the *Logos*. Evidently, then, we have not adequately comprehended the nature of the *Logos* when we note only that it is one. We must pay more heed to the assertion that it *gathers* things together in one. The *Logos*, it seems, although a unity, is a moving or flowing unity. The *Logos*, in fact, is the unification in intelligibility of the principle of flux itself. Everything indeed *is* in flux, including the *Logos* itself. We can add to the fragments already quoted which express this Heraclitus' famous river fragments, 91 and 12, which express this flowing of all things: "You cannot step twice into the same river, for other waters and yet others go ever flowing on."[35]

The political version of this principle is expressed in the famous and disturbing Fragment 53: "War is father of all and king of all; some it shows forth as gods, and others as men, some as freemen, others as slave."[36] Again, what is especially worthy of thought here is that Heraclitus believes that this follows as a political consequence of his ontological doctrine of flux, and so he faces up to it. The Introduction cited contemporary efforts to maintain a doctrine of radical progress and yet political peace, and the difficulty of keeping such a *Weltanschauung* coherent. Heraclitus, far from being the disdainer of logic and reason that Nietzsche portrays,[37] is a model for us of the demand to make our political and philosophical views, our ontics and our ontology, coherent.

Yet none of the fragments expressing the doctrine of flux, either ontological, political, or cosmological, suggests that the world is *merely* eternal flux. Heraclitus is not Hesiod. The *arche* of the world is a *Logos*, not a chaos. The flux of things, that is to say, must be an *ordered* flux, and this *ordered* movement is the heart of the *Logos*. The order is the intelligibility of the "dialectic" between opposites, or what Heraclitus calls the *harmony* of opposites. Many fragments attest to this famous aspect of Heraclitus' *Logos*.

> The bones connected by joints are at once a unitary whole and not a unitary whole. To be in agreement is to differ; the concordant is the discordant. From out of all the many particulars comes oneness, and out of oneness come all the many particulars.[38]

> People do not understand how that which is at variance with itself agrees with itself. There is a harmony in the bending back, as in the cases of the bow and the lyre.[39]

> Into the sames rivers we do and do not step.[40]

> Cool things become warm, the warm grows cool; the moist dries, the parched becomes moist.[41]

> Opposition brings concord. Out of discord comes the fairest harmony.[42]

What at first may appear as paradox is in fact the intelligible order of the emergence of things out of their opposites, and of the harmony brought about by the placing together of discordant or opposite elements. The decisive point for our purposes in Heraclitus' *Logos* is this: The world, and, most of all, man's experience of the world, of himself, of his fellowman, of the physical cosmos, of the divine, is gathered together into an intelligible order called the *Logos*. But the *Logos* itself is not a static principle of the flow of becoming. That view remains for Plato to articulate. Heraclitus' *Logos* is itself flowing according to its own order. Man in particular is a central participant in what we can now call the rhythm of becoming which is the *Logos*. It is now necessary to return to the issue of the exact nature of our access to this *Logos*.

Evidently in a world the *arche*, or origin, of which, however intelligible, is not stationary but itself in flux, the mode of knowledge of the *arche* is not going to be that of gazing upon or contemplating an object which is stationary and changeless. That conception of knowledge was set out in detail by Plato in his discussions of the Ideas, or Forms. It is this conception of knowledge which makes possible the notion of *theoretical* knowledge, and which gives us the model of the unbiased observer who *sees* the principles of intelligibility of that which he is investigating.[43] But to gain access to a *Logos* which is itself moving, Heraclitus needs a conception of knowledge which will reflect the necessity of *moving along at a rate commensurate with and true to the movement of the* Logos *itself*. He finds this in the notion of *attunement*. Man gains access to the *Logos* insofar as he affirms and participates in its movement rather than resisting it. "Although intimately connected with the *Logos*, men keep setting themselves against it."[44] This means that knowledge of the origin of things, and so also, because of the intimate connection between the *Logos* and all things, self-knowledge, knowledge of political things, and knowledge of the cosmos—all this knowledge will be much more than what we might call "epistemic" knowledge, the ability to utter the correct set of true propositions about the cosmos. What Heraclitus presents us with is a knowledge more akin to the knowledge spoken of by the Old Testament writer when he says, "And Jacob knew his wife,"[45] than the conception exhibited by a twentieth-century scientist. For Heraclitus, the self-knowledge which is in fact *sophrosyne* and which leads ineluctably to knowledge of the cosmos is a *participation* in the world "according to the nature of things"; it is *a way of living*, of comporting oneself toward things in such a way as to truly affirm one's belonging to the coursing of the world. It is a conception of knowledge present today in the writings of certain European existential philosophers such as Heidegger, Marcel, and Buber—a conception of knowledge in no way naïve or primitive, but a genuine possibility for man as much today as in Heraclitus' time.

Let us close this interpretation of Heraclitus with a consideration of what is one of the most decisive problems that Heraclitus left for human thought. We have argued that one of Heraclitus' most significant contributions was the exhibition of the necessary link between the ontic and the ontological, the apparent and the hidden harmony, between beings and Being. However closely Heraclitus does preserve that link, there is one realm, an utterly decisive one, in which this symmetry would seem to break down. For there are fragments that suggest that the movement from the "apparent harmony," the everyday world, to the "hidden harmony" of the divine *Logos* is the movement from the realm of reasonably clear-cut "values" to a world "beyond good and evil." Fragments 82 and 83, and most decisively 102, read respectively:

> The most handsome ape is ugly compared with the human race. (The wisest man will appear an ape in relation to God, both in wisdom and beauty, and everything else.)

> To god all things are beautiful, good, and just; men, on the other hand, deem some things unjust and others just.

Such a view easily generates a propensity for relativism as exhibited by such fragments as 61, 9, 37, and 58. But the most critical consequence of such a view is this. Precisely on the basis of a conception of access to the origins, or ontological realm, which is an *activity*, a way of life, and not merely theoretical knowledge—precisely, that is, when one's access to Being must be lived out—what is to happen when men discover that that realm, and so that *mode of activity*, is "beyond good and evil"? What is then to prevent men who believe they have achieved that realm from *acting* "beyond good and evil"? Or again, if the *arche* of things is beyond good and evil, if "value," that is, is grounded only in the custom of the *local* "apparent harmony" in which one finds oneself and not in the *arche* itself, is there, finally, any real justification of any value, including even the value of the truth of Heraclitus' view itself? These problems were not overcome in Heraclitus' time, and they have not yet been overcome; they are part of the phenomenon of what is today called nihilism—possibly the most critical problem of our time. One of the most important responses to this situation was formulated by Plato in his discussion of the Ideas in the dialogues. But not before the intervention of one of the true giants of the history of thought—Parmenides of Elea.

Heraclitus—The Spokesman for Becoming

Heraclitus of Ephesus, on the coast of Asia Minor, flourished around 500 B.C. As the selections make clear, legend has it that he was a rather arrogant and aristocratic person, and his peculiar writing style— aphoristic, obscure, and replete with apparent contradictions—is often attributed to his deliberate desire to obscure his views from "the many." He is usually considered, along with Parmenides, as one of the two giants of Pre-Socratic philosophy; the usual reason for this is that they are almost invariably presented as polar opposites—that Heraclitus espoused a doctrine of radical change, while Parmenides advocated one of radical permanence. This traditional interpretation will be called into question.

HERACLITUS: FRAGMENTS*

1. The Law** *(of the universe)* is as here explained; but men are always incapable of understanding it, both before they hear it, and when they have heard it for the first time. For though all things come into being in accordance with this Law, men seem as if they had never met with it, when they meet with words *(theories)* and actions *(processes)* such as I expound, separating each thing according to its nature and explaining how it is made. As for the rest of mankind, they are unaware of what they are doing after they wake, just as they forget what they did while asleep.

2. Therefore one must follow (the universal Law, namely) that which is common *(to all)*. But although the Law is universal, the majority live as if they had understanding peculiar to themselves.

3. *(On the size of the sun)*: the breadth of a man's foot.

4. If happiness lay in bodily pleasures, we would call oxen happy when they find vetch to eat.

---

* From Kathleen Freeman, *Ancilla to the Pre-Socratic Philosophers*.

** Logos, the intelligible Law of the universe, and its reasoned statement by Heraclitus.

5.   They purify themselves by staining themselves with other blood, as if one were to step into mud in order to wash off mud. But a man would be thought mad if any of his fellow-men should perceive him acting thus. Moreover, they talk to these statues (*of theirs*) as if one were to hold conversation with houses, in his ignorance of the nature of both gods and heroes.

6.   The sun is new each day.

7.   If all existing things turned to smoke, the nose would be the discriminating organ.

8.   That which is in opposition is in concert, and from things that differ comes the most beautiful harmony.

9.   Donkeys prefer chaff to gold.

10.   Joints: whole and not whole, connected-separate, consonant-dissonant.

11.   Every creature is driven to pasture with a blow.

12.   Anhalation (*vaporisation*). Those who step into the same river have different waters flowing ever upon them. (Souls also are vaporised from what is wet).

13.   Do not revel in mud. (*Swine enjoy mud rather than pure water*).

14.   Night-ramblers, magicians, Bacchants, Maenads, Mystics: the rites accepted by mankind in the Mysteries are an unholy performance.

15.   If it were not in honour of Dionysus that they conducted the procession and sang the hymn to the male organ (*the phallic hymn*), their activity would be completely shameless. But Hades is the same as Dionysus, in whose honour they rave and perform the Bacchic revels.

16.   How could anyone hide from that which never sets?

17. For many men—those who encounter such things—do not understand them, and do not grasp them after they have learnt; but to themselves they seem *(to understand)*.

18. If one does not hope, one will not find the unhoped-for, since there is no trail leading to it and no path.

19. Men who do not know how to listen or how to speak.

20. When they are born, they are willing to live and accept their fate *(death)*; and they leave behind children to become victims of fate.

21. All that we see when we have wakened is death; all that we see while slumbering is sleep.

22. Those who seek gold dig much earth and find little.

23. They would not know the name of Right, if these things *(i.e. the opposite)* did not exist.

24. Gods and men honour those slain in war.

25. The greater the fate *(death)*, the greater the reward.

26. In the night, a man kindles a light because his sight is quenched; while living, he approximates to a dead man during sleep; while awake, he approximates to one who sleeps.

27. There await men after they are dead things which they do not expect or imagine.

28. The most wise-seeming man knows, *(that is)*, preserves, only what seems; furthermore, retribution will seize the fabricators of lies and the *(false)* witnesses.

29.   The best men choose one thing rather than all else: everlasting fame among mortal men.* The majority are satisfied, like well-fed cattle.

30.   This ordered universe (*cosmos*), which is the same for all, was not created by any one of the gods or of mankind, but it was ever and is and shall be ever-living Fire, kindled in measure and quenched in measure.

31.   The changes of fire: first, sea; and of sea, half is earth and half fiery water-spout . . . Earth is liquified into sea, and retains its measure according to the same Law as existed before it became earth.

32.   That which alone is wise is one; it is willing and unwilling to be called by the name of Zeus.

33.   To obey the will of one man is also Law (*political law, Nomos*).

34.   Not understanding, although they have heard, they are like the deaf. The proverb bears witness to them: 'Present yet absent.'

35.   Men who love wisdom must be inquirers into very many things indeed.

36.   To souls, it is death to become water; to water, it is death to become earth. From earth comes water, and from water, soul.

37.   Pigs wash themselves in mud, birds in dust or ashes.

38.   (*Thales was the first to study astronomy*).

39.   In Priênê was born Bias son of Teutamos, whose fame (*or, 'worth'*) is greater than that of the rest.

40.   Much learning does not teach one to have intelligence; for it would have taught Hesiod and Pythagoras, and again, Xenophanes and Hecataeus.

* Or: 'rather than things mortal'.

41.   That which is wise is one: to understand the purpose which steers all things through all things.

42.   Homer deserves to be flung out of the contests and given a beating; and also Archilochus.

43.   One should quench arrogance rather than a conflagration.

44.   The people should fight for the Law (*Nomos*) as if for their city-wall.

45.   You could not in your going find the ends of the soul, though you travelled the whole way: so deep is its Law (*Logos*).

46.   Conceit: the sacred disease (*i.e. epilepsy*).

47.   Let us not conjecture at random about the greatest things.

48.   The bow is called Life, but its work is death.

49.   One man to me is (*worth*) ten thousand, if he is the best.

49a.   In the same river, we both step and do not step, we are and we are not.

50.   When you have listened, not to me but to the Law (*Logos*), it is wise to agree that all things are one.

51.   They do not understand how that which differs with itself is in agreement: harmony consists of opposing tension, like that of the bow and the lyre.

52.   Time is a child playing a game of draughts; the kingship is in the hands of a child.

53.   War is both king of all and father of all, and it has revealed some as gods, others as men; some it has made slaves, others free.

54.   The hidden harmony is stronger (*or*, 'better') than the visible.

55.   Those things of which there is sight, hearing, knowledge: these are what I honour most.

56.   Men are deceived over the recognition of visible things, in the same way as Homer, who was the wisest of all the Hellenes; for he too was deceived by boys killing lice, who said: 'What we saw and grasped, that we leave behind; but what we did not see and did not grasp, that we bring.'

57.   Hesiod is the teacher of very many, he who did not understand day and night: for they are one.

58.   For instance, physicians, who cut and burn, demand payment of a fee, though undeserving, since they produce the same (*pains as the disease*).

59.   For the fuller's screw, the way, straight and crooked, is one and the same.

60.   The way up and down is one and the same.

61.   Sea water is the purest and most polluted: for fish, it is drinkable and life-giving; for men, not drinkable and destructive.

62.   Immortals are mortal, mortals are immortal: (*each*) lives the death of the other, and dies their life.

63.   When he (*God?*) is there, they (*the souls in Hades*) arise and become watchful guardians of the living and the dead.

64.   The thunder-bolt (*i.e. Fire*) steers the universe.

65.   Need and satiety.

66.   Fire, having come upon them, will judge and seize upon (condemn) all things.

67.   God is day-night, winter-summer, war-peace, satiety-famine. But he changes like (fire), which when it mingles with the smoke of incense, is named according to each man's pleasure.

*   *   *

70.   Children's toys (*i.e. men's conjectures*).

71.   (*One must remember also*) the man who forgets which way the road leads.

72.   The Law (*Logos*): though men associate with it most closely, yet they are separated from it, and those things which they encounter daily seem to them strange.

73.   We must not act and speak like men asleep.

74.   (*We must not act like*) children of our parents.

75.   Those who sleep are workers and share in the activities going on in the universe.

76.   Fire lives the death of earth, and air lives the death of fire; water lives the death of air, earth that of water.

77.   It is delight, or rather death, to souls to become wet . . . We live their (*the souls'*) death, and they (*the souls*) live our death.

78.   Human nature has no power of understanding; but the divine nature has it.

79.   Man is called childish compared with divinity, just as a boy compared with a man.

80.   One should know that war is general (*universal*) and jurisdiction is strife, and everything comes about by way of strife and necessity.

81.   (*On Pythagoras*). Original chief of wranglers.

82.   (*The most handsome ape is ugly compared with the human race*).*

83.   (*The wisest man will appear an ape in relation to God, both in wisdom and beauty and everything else*).*

84a.   It rests from change. (*Elemental Fire in the human body*).

84b.   It is a weariness to the same (*elements forming the human body*) to toil and to obey.

85.   It is hard to fight against impulse; whatever it wishes, it buys at the expense of the soul.

86.   (*Most of what is divine*) escapes recognition through unbelief.

87.   A foolish man is apt to be in a flutter at every word (*or, 'theory': Logos*).

88.   And what is in us is the same thing: living and dead, awake and sleeping, as well as young and old; for the latter (*of each pair of opposites*) having changed becomes the former, and this again having changed becomes the latter.

89.   To those who are awake, there is one ordered universe common (*to all*), whereas in sleep each man turns away (*from this world*) to one of his own.

90.   There is an exchange: all things for Fire and Fire for all things, like goods for gold and gold for goods.

* Paraphrases in Plato, *Hippias Maior*.

91.   It is not possible to step twice into the same river. (*It is impossible to touch the same mortal substance twice, but through the rapidity of change*) they scatter and again combine (*or rather, not even 'again' or 'later', but the combination and separation are simultaneous*) and approach and separate.*

92.   The Sibyl with raving mouth uttering her unlaughing, unadorned, unincensed words reaches out over a thousand years with her voice, through the (*inspiration of the*) god.

93.   The lord whose oracle is that at Delphi neither speaks nor conceals, but indicates.

94.   The sun will not transgress his measures; otherwise the Furies, ministers of Justice, will find him out.

95.   It is better to hide ignorance (*though this is hard in relaxation and over wine*).

96.   Corpses are more worthy to be thrown out than dung.

97.   Dogs bark at those whom they do not recognise.

98.   Souls have the sense of smell in Hades.

99.   If there were no sun, so far as depended on the other stars it would be night.

100.   (*The sun is in charge of the seasonal changes, and*) the Hours (Seasons) that bring all things.

101.   I searched into myself.

101a.   The eyes are more exact witnesses than the ears.

---

*   Phrases of Heraclitus quoted in Aristotle, *Metaphysics*.

102.   To God, all things are beautiful, good and just; but men have assumed some things to be unjust, others just.

103.   Beginning and end are general in the circumference of the circle.

104.   What intelligence or understanding have they? They believe the people's bards, and use as their teacher the populace, not knowing that 'the majority are bad, and the good are few'.

105.   Homer was an astrologer.

106.   (*Heraclitus reproached Hesiod for regarding some days as bad and others as good*). Hesiod was unaware that the nature of every day is one.

107.   The eyes and ears are bad witnesses for men if they have barbarian souls.

108.   Of all those whose discourse I have heard, none arrives at the realisation that that which is wise is set apart from all things.

109.   *See* 95.

110.   It is not better for men to obtain all that they wish.

111.   Disease makes health pleasant and good, hunger satisfaction, weariness rest.

112.   Moderation is the greatest virtue, and wisdom is to speak the truth and to act according to nature, paying heed (*thereto*).

113.   The thinking faculty is common to all.

114.   If we speak with intelligence, we must base our strength on that which is common to all, as the city on the Law (*Nomos*), and even more strongly. For all human laws are nourished by one, which is divine. For it governs as far as it will, and is sufficient for all, and more than enough.

115.   The soul has its own Law (*Logos*), which increases itself (*i.e. grows according to its needs*).

116.   All men have the capacity of knowing themselves and acting with moderation.

117.   A man, when he gets drunk, is led stumbling along by an immature boy, not knowing where he is going, having his soul wet.

118.   A dry (desiccated) soul is the wisest and best.

119.   Character for man is destiny.

120.   The limits of morning and evening are the Bear and, opposite the Bear, the boundary-mark of Zeus god of the clear sky.

121.   The Ephesians would do well to hang themselves, every adult man, and bequeath their City-State to adolescents, since they have expelled Hermodôrus, the most valuable man among them, saying: 'Let us not have even one valuable man; but if we do, let him go elsewhere and live among others.'

122.   (*Word for*) Approximation.

123.   Nature likes to hide.

124.   The fairest universe is but a dust-heap piled up at random.

125.   The 'mixed drink' (*Kykeôn: mixture of wine, grated cheese and barley-meal*) also separates if it is not stirred.

125a. May wealth not fail you, men of Ephesus, so that you may be convicted of your wickedness!

126.   Cold things grow hot, hot things grow cold, the wet dries, the parched is moistened.

Doubtful and spurious fragments

126a. According to the law of the seasons, the number Seven is combined in the moon, separated in the constellations of the Bear, the signs of immortal Memory.

126b. One thing increases in one way, another in another, in relation to what it lacks.

127. (*To the Egyptians*): 'If they are gods, why do you lament them? If you lament them, you must no longer regard them as gods.'

128. They (*the Hellenes*) pray to statues of the gods, that do not hear them, as if they heard, and do not give, just as they cannot ask.

129. Pythagoras, son of Mnêsarchus, practised research most of all men, and making extracts from these treatises he compiled a wisdom of his own, an accumulation of learning, a harmful craft.

130. It is not proper to be so comic that you yourself appear comic.

131. Conceit is the regress (*hindrance*) of progress.

132. Positions of honour enslave gods and men.

133. Bad men are the adversaries of the true.

134. Education is another sun to those who are educated.

135. The shortest way to fame is to become good.

136. Souls of men slain in battle are purer than those who die of disease.

137. Utterly decreed by Fate.

TESTIMONIA ON HERACLITUS BY DIOGENES LAERTIUS*

Heraclitus, son of Bloson or, according to some, of Heracon, was a native of Ephesus. He flourished in the 69th Olympiad. He was lofty-minded beyond all other men, and over-weening, as is clear from his book in which he says: "Much learning does not teach understanding; else would it have taught Hesiod and Pythagoras, or, again, Xenophanes and Hecataeus." For "this one thing is wisdom, to understand thought, as that which guides all the world everywhere." And he used to say that "Homer deserved to be chased out of the lists and beaten with rods, and Archilochus likewise."

Again he would say: "There is more need to extinguish insolence than an outbreak of fire," and "The people must fight for the law as for city-walls." He attacks the Ephesians, too, for banishing his friend Hermodorus: he says: "The Ephesians would do well to end their lives, every grown man of them, and leave the city to beardless boys, for that they have driven out Hermodorus, the worthiest man among them, saying, 'We will have none who is worthiest among us; or if there be any such, let him go elsewhere and consort with others.' " And when he was requested by them to make laws, he scorned the request because the state was already in the grip of a bad constitution. He would retire to the temple of Artemis and play at knuckle-bones with the boys; and when the Ephesians stood round him and looked on, "Why, you rascals," he said, "are you astonished? Is it not better to do this than to take part in your civil life?"

Finally, he became a hater of his kind and wandered on the mountains, and there he continued to live, making his diet of grass and herbs. However, when this gave him dropsy, he made his way back to the city and put this riddle to the physicians, whether they were competent to create a drought after heavy rain. They could make nothing of this, whereupon he buried himself in a cowshed, expecting that the noxious damp humour would be drawn out of him by the warmth of the manure. But, as even this was of no avail, he died at the age of sixty.

There is a piece of my own about him as follows:

* From R. D. Hicks, *Lives of Eminent Philosophers*.

Often have I wondered how it came about that Heraclitus endured to live in this miserable fashion and then to die. For a fell disease flooded his body with water, quenched the light in his eyes and brought on darkness.

Hermippus, too, says that he asked the doctors whether anyone could by emptying the intestines draw off the moisture; and when they said it was impossible, he put himself in the sun and bade his servants plaster him over with cow-dung. Being thus stretched and prone, he died the next day and was buried in the market-place. Neanthes of Cyzicus states that, being unable to tear off the dung, he remained as he was and, being unrecognizable when so transformed, he was devoured by dogs.

He was exceptional from his boyhood; for when a youth he used to say that he knew nothing, although when he was grown up he claimed that he knew everything. He was nobody's pupil, but he declared that he "inquired of himself," and learned everything from himself. Some, however, had said that he had been a pupil of Xenophanes, as we learn from Sotion, who also tells us that Ariston in his book *On Heraclitus* declares that he was cured of the dropsy and died of another disease. And Hippobotus has the same story.

As to the work which passes as his, it is a continuous treatise *On Nature*, but is divided into three discourses, one on the universe, another on politics, and a third on theology. This book he deposited in the temple of Artemis and, according to some, he deliberately made it the more obscure in order that none but adepts should approach it, and lest familiarity should breed contempt. Of our philosopher Timon gives a sketch in these words:

> In their midst uprose shrill, cuckoo-like, a mob-reviler, riddling Heraclitus.

Theophrastus puts it down to melancholy that some parts of his work are half-finished, while other parts make a strange medley. . . .

TESTIMONIA ON HERACLITUS BY PLATO

. . . SOCRATES: My good friend, I have discovered a hive of wisdom.

HERMOGENES: Of what nature?

SOCRATES: Well, rather ridiculous, and yet plausible.

HERMOGENES: How plausible?

SOCRATES: I fancy to myself Heraclitus repeating wise traditions of antiquity as old as the days of Cronus and Rhea, and of which Homer also spoke.

HERMOGENES: How do you mean?

SOCRATES: Heraclitus is supposed to say that all things are in motion and nothing at rest; he compares them to the stream of a river, and says that you cannot go into the same water twice.

HERMOGENES: That is true.

SOCRATES: Well, then, how can we avoid inferring that he who gave the names of Cronus and Rhea to the ancestors of the gods agreed pretty much in the doctrine of Heraclitus? Is the giving of the names of streams to both of them purely accidental? Compare the line in which Homer, and, as I believe, Hesiod also, tells of 'Oceanus, the origin of gods, and mother Tethys.' And again, Orpheus says that 'The fair river of Oceanus was the first to marry, and he espoused his sister Tethys, who was his mother's daughter.' You see that this is a remarkable coincidence, and all in the direction of Heraclitus. . . . (*Cratylus*, 402)

. . . Here, then, let us approach nearer, as the advocate of Protagoras desires, and give the truth of the universal flux a ring: is the theory sound or not? at any rate, no small war is raging about this way, and there are many combatants.

Theod. No small war, indeed, for in Ionia the sect makes rapid strides; the disciples of Heraclitus are most energetic upholders of the doctrine.

Soc. Then we are the more bound, my dear Theodorus, to examine the question from the beginning as set forth by themselves.

Theod. Certainly we are. About these speculations of Heraclitus, which, as you say, are as old as Homer, or even older still, the Ephesians themselves, who profess to know them, are downright mad, and you cannot talk with them about them. For, in accordance with their text-books, they are always in motion; but as for dwelling upon an argument or a question, and quietly asking and answering in turn, they are absolutely without the power of doing this; or rather, they have no particle of rest in them, and they are in a state of negation of rest which no words can express. If you ask any of them a question, he will produce, as from a quiver, sayings brief and dark, and shoot them at you; and if you inquire the reason of what he has said, you will be hit by some other new fangled word, and will make no way with any of them, nor they with one another; for their great care is, not to allow of any settled principle either in their arguments or in their minds, conceiving, as I imagine, that this would be stationary; and they are at war with the stationary, which they would like, if they could, to banish utterly. . . . (*Theaetetus*, 178-180).

TESTIMONIA ON HERACLITUS BY ARISTOTLE

. . . Others again, with Empedocles of Acragas and Heraclitus of Ephesus, believe that there is alteration in the destructive process, which takes now this direction, now that, and continues without end. (*De Caelo*, 279*b* 16)

For it is impossible for anyone to believe the same thing to be and not to be, as some think Heraclitus says. (*Metaphysica*, 1005*b* 24)

. . . The supporters of the ideal theory were led to it because on the question about the truth of things they accepted the Heraclitean sayings which describe all sensible things as ever passing away, so that if knowledge or thought is to have an object, there must be some other and permanent entities, apart from those which are sensible; for there could be no knowledge of things which were in a state of flux. (*Metaphysica*, 1078*b* 13)

Notes: IV

1. Benedict de Spinoza, *On the Improvement of the Understanding*, in *The Chief Works of Benedict de Spinoza*, trans. by R. H. M. Elwes (New York, Dover Publications, 1951), Vol. II, p. 6.

2. Parmenides, Fragment 3 (D-K).

3. *Sophronein: Sophrosyne* is usually translated as "temperance," "moderation," or "self-control." But for both Heraclitus and for Plato in the *Charmides*, these translations are inadequate.

4. *See* Fragments 1, 2, 17, 34, 40, 72, 86, 104, 108.

5. Aristotle, *Nicomachean Ethics*, Book 10, Chap. 7, 1177b 25-1178a 1.

6. Consider also, in broader contexts, Fragments 1, 2, 27, 34, 40, 56, 73, 78, 86, 108.

7. Heraclitus, Fragment 12.

8. Cited in *The Pre-Socratics*, Philip Wheelwright, ed. (Odyssey Press, 1966), p. 72, no. 43.

9. Heraclitus, Fragment 118.

10. *Ibid.*, Fragment 77. *Cf.* Fragment 117.

11. *Ibid.*, Fragment 36.

12. *See* Fragments 29, 34, 35, 40, 43, 47, 49, 55, 73, 85, 95, 96, 98, 101a, 107, 110.

13. Fragment 115.

14. Fragment 119.

15. Plato, *Symposium*, 202e-203b.

16. Heraclitus, Fragment 18.

17. *Ibid.*, Fragment 54.

18. *Ibid.*, Fragment 123.

19. *Ibid.*, Fragment 93. The German philosopher Martin Heidegger has argued again and again in behalf of the etymology of the Greek word for truth, *aleitheia*, as "unhiddenness." Such an interpretation fits in well with the present one. The truth, the speaking and acting of which is wisdom, must be brought forth from its hiddenness to un-hiddenness *(a-leitheia)* in the speaking and acting.

20. *Ibid.*, Fragment 113.

21. *Ibid.*, Fragment 114.

22. *Ibid.*, Fragment 44.

23. *Ibid.*, Fragment 33.

24. *Ibid.*, Fragment 45.

25. *Ibid.*, Fragment 90.

26. *Ibid.*, Fragment 30.

27. *Ibid.*, Fragment 31.

28. *Ibid.*, Fragment 31 (continued).

29. *Ibid.*, Fragment 76. *See also* Fragments 3, 6, 64, 99, 120, 124.

30. *See also* Fragments 27, 15, 5 (continued), 92.

31. Sextus Empiricus, *Against the Logicians*, I, 126-34.

32. Heraclitus, Fragment 54.

33. *Ibid.*, Fragment 1.

34. *Ibid.*, Fragment 2.

35. *See* Plato, *Cratylus*, 401E-402A: Everything flows and nothing abides.

36. *See also* Fragment 80; and Aristotle, *Eudemian Ethics*, 124a 20, 25.

37. Friedrich Nietzsche, *Philosophy in the Tragic Age of the Greeks*, trans. by Marianne Cowan, Gateway Edition (Chicago, Henry Regnery Co., 1962), p. 52.

38. Heraclitus, Fragment 10.

39. *Ibid.*, Fragment 51.

40. *Ibid.*, Fragment 49a.

41. *Ibid.*, Fragment 126. *See also* Fragments 36, 49a.

42. *Ibid.*, Fragment 8. *See also* Fragments 49, 60, 62, 67, 88, 111.

43. The two Greek words for the Forms, *eidos* and *idea*, as well as the root of the word "theoretical," are all formed from Greek words for seeing.

44. Heraclitus, Fragment 72.

45. Genesis 29. *See also* Ruth 4.

The Battle of the Giants: II

H ERACLITUS and Parmenides are generally considered to be the two most important of the Pre-Socratic philosophers, and Parmenides especially is credited with an immense influence on the whole history of philosophy. Yet this seems strange in the light of the orthodox interpretation of Parmenides' thought, which attributes to him a view which nearly no Western man believes today; nor has it been at all influential in the development of Western thought, indeed which is considered rather ludicrous: that all motion, change, and multiplicity are illusory. To elaborate on the orthodox interpretation: Heraclitus and Parmenides are the polar opposites of Pre-Socratic philosophy. Heraclitus was the spokesman for a world of radical flux in which all permanence was illusory and in which even the *Logos* by which things became intelligible was itself in flux. The multiplicity, change, and motion with which our senses present us is the fundamental reality; we can thus trust our senses as the vehicle by which we gain access to the fundamentally real. Parmenides, on the other hand, is the spokesman for the absolute unity, changelessness, and motionlessness of existence. Whereas Heraclitus had trusted his senses, Parmenides defends a conception of reason understood as rigorous logic. If the results of our logical reasoning conflict with the testimony of the senses, we must simply repudiate sense experience as illusory. But Parmenides' reasoning tells him that "what is" cannot come to be or pass away, cannot change, cannot move; it is one, changeless, motionless, eternal. Therefore the world with which our senses present us is illusory; thus the general view, at least among English-speaking scholars.[1]

Yet no less influential a thinker than Martin Heidegger has been so bold as to say, "Actually Heraclitus, to whom is ascribed the doctrine of becoming as diametrically opposed to Parmenides' doctrine of being, says the same as Parmenides."[2] In a certain very qualified way, we shall defend the view set forth by Heidegger, although for very different reasons than his own. His view is a necessary corrective to what seems to be the overstated opposition between these thinkers held by the traditional position. But perhaps more importantly, Heidegger's interpretation comes closer to exemplifying the kind of interpretation which is set out in the Preface. It is true to say that the traditional interpretation arises from a desire to be "historically accurate," that is, to say as exactly as possible from the evidence of the fragments what those two men, Heraclitus and Parmenides, *actually believed*. As suggested in the Preface, the trouble with this procedure is that since it is fundamentally historical and only secondarily philosophical, it is bound to develop a view of primarily historical and not philosophical interest. The consensus concerning Heidegger's interpretations, on the other hand, seems to be that they shed relatively little light on the historical views in question but are most valuable for understanding Heidegger's own philosophy. Let us consider these thinkers first and foremost for the philosophic significance of their positions, not, certainly, for our own thinking, but for man's understanding of himself.

Parmenides, as mentioned, is usually considered the father of rationalism, the first great spokesman for the view that we must trust to the results of our reasoning, even if that means distrusting the evidence of our senses. To an extent this is surely true. What complicates this view is that this father of rationalism began his great argument for rationalism not with a defense of deductive logic but with a poem about a youth driven by horses and maidens to a goddess who reveals to him the Truth. Now other great rationalists, even Greek ones, have not felt the necessity of such a prologue. Euclid did not preface his mathematical writings with such a myth, Archimedes did not preface his discovery of the lever with such a poetic flight, nor did Aristotle begin his treatises *Physica* and *Metaphysica* in such a way. Yet Parmenides did. Consequently, to discover more accurately the sense in which Parmenides really can be called "the father of rationalism," we shall have to investigate with special care the philosophic significance of the Proem of his great poem.

Strangely enough, we do get a presentation in the Proem, not of deductive logic but of a conception of philosophy as a journey, a quest, or path, a conception which has had profound significance from Socrates to Heidegger.[3] The youth is presented not as sitting at home and having a revelation, but as having this revelation as a culmination of a journey, or quest, not unlike the epic quests of heroes such as Odysseus. As Plato was later to draw out by an analysis of the word itself, *philosophia* is a pursuit, not a condition, and the philosopher is one best or most fundamentally understood as a *searcher*, not an already wise man. As Alex Mourelatos points out with great penetration, this metaphor of the journey, or path, introduced in the Proem, is not abandoned in the later sections. *Thinking* is itself conceived as a path, error as "going astray," and even the two "ways," "it is" and "it is not" are presented not as concepts which are "conceivable or inconceivable" but as *paths for thought* which can be completed or not.[4] As Mourelatos points out, Parmenides in fact *shares* this conception of philosophy as a search with Heraclitus, who distinguished his own enterprise ("I searched into myself") from the "much-learning" *(polumathie)* of "sages" such as Homer, Hesiod, Xenophanes, and Pythagoras.[5]

But the journey, or quest, of philosophy is a special one indeed. For one thing, it is a journey very much bound up with the erotic. The horses (themselves an erotic symbol) which lead the youth are driven by *maidens*, and they lead him to a *goddess* who reveals to him the truth, not unlike the way the priestess Diotima reveals the mysteries of love to Socrates.[6] The erotic symbolism is indicative of the deeper nature of the erotic which, as Plato is later to elucidate, is intimately bound up with the theme of the quest: eros as incompleteness and the impetus toward the overcoming of that incompleteness. The incompleteness which the youth's journey is meant to overcome is the lack of wisdom or lack of the truth. The erotic desire for the wholeness of wisdom becomes in Plato virtually definitive of the philosophic life. We can see that such a conception of philosophy is already nascent in Parmenides. Moreover, and again similarly to the way Plato is later to deal with the theme, Parmenides chooses to elicit the erotic nature of the pursuit of wisdom not primarily by the rigorous argument of which he is obviously capable, but by the more dramatic "existential" presentation of the Proem and the Platonic dialogues. It is as if both Parmenides and Plato believe that although rigorous and even abstract argument are of great importance in philosophy, there are other aspects, and in particular the nature of the philosophic life itself, which are best presented in more concrete and even dramatic terms. Parmenides is indeed a rationalist; he does not thereby suggest that philosophy be reduced to logic.

Next, the youth's journey from the ignorance of opinion (*doxa*) to the revelation of truth is presented as the movement from darkness to light.[7] We have remarked on the significance of this metaphor before; it is intimately bound up with the decisive metaphor for knowing of "seeing," and is easily related to the notion of truth as unhiddenness (*a-leitheia*). Although there were difficulties with this metaphor for Heraclitus, Parmenides' insistence that Being, the real object, or *telos*, of thought, is changeless and eternal will become the paradigm for that conception of the process of knowing in which seeing becomes the most appropriate metaphor.

The passage from darkness to light which the youth takes, indeed the very gates of day and night, are guarded by Justice (*Dike*), whom the maidens persuade to open the gates and allow the youth to pass. The road to knowledge is guarded by justice; the question of value, of good and evil, justice and injustice, is bound up with the very nature of the pursuit of knowledge. Stated differently, all knowledge includes the issue of value; there is no such thing for Parmenides as a "value-free science." Genuine *knowledge* of something must include knowledge of its value. Evidently such a view stands in very strong contrast to the positivism of the twentieth century which considers itself the latest descendant of the tradition of "rationalism" which supposedly began with Parmenides. Ironically, on this point at least, Parmenides would seem to have more in common with his supposed antithesis, Heraclitus, than with the latest representatives of the tradition he fathered. Moreover, least of all is the philosophic pursuit itself "value free"; it is presided over and approved by Justice. Philosophy and the pursuit of knowledge, suggests Parmenides against Anaximander, are good. Man's quest for knowledge is in accordance with his own nature and the nature of the whole.

There are many indications in the Proem that we must understand the youth's journey of revelation as utterly extraordinary, "*un-heimlichkeit*" as the Germans say, not at all an ordinary everyday event. We are told, in an obvious reference to Odysseus, that the journey takes the youth "through all towns,"[8] and that the path he takes is "far from the trodden path of men."[9] The very fact that it is pictured as the kind of journey it is testifies again to its extraordinary character.

Plato in his dialogues sets out in considerable detail the problem of the difference between opinion and knowledge.[10] Most men are satisfied with and live their lives according to opinion (*doxa*), usually the received opinion, laws, and customs, of the cities in which they live. Some men at least have *true opinion* (orthodoxy) and live their lives accordingly. A very few men are dissatisfied even with true opinion; they want to ground, or "anchor," that opinion with knowledge. Such men are philosophers. We again see the germ both of the distinction between knowledge and opinion (the two last sections of Parmenides' poem are called "Truth" and "Opinion") and of the rarity of the movement toward knowledge. The youth in question is a participant in no ordinary journey; the life of philosophy is not simply one of the many "choices" available to men as they decide from day to day how to conduct their lives.

Perhaps the most obvious way in which the journey is extraordinary is this: It requires the intervention and constant support of the divine. It is a goddess who reveals the truth to the youth, not one of Parmenides' supposed teachers, Xenophanes or Ameinias. He is led to this revelation by obviously divine maidens, and it is granted by persuading Justice. Now there are several nuances to the association of the revelation of truth and the philosophic pursuit with the divine. The first we have already discussed at length as the theme arose in earlier thinkers. Man now and again finds himself related to, oriented toward, that which he is inclined to call the divine. This is part of the human situation, and any adequate account of that situation must come to terms with such a relationship. More specifically in the case of Parmenides, it is precisely in terms of the philosophic quest, precisely in terms of man's occasional access to truth, that the issue of his relation to the divine comes to the fore. Man's taking the path of philosophy, and quite especially his occasional attainment of truth, is not something entirely within his control, not a question simply of his "willpower." Truth and philosophy itself come to us rather, as Gabriel Marcel might put it, as a gift, albeit a gift for which we must long and rigorously make ourselves worthy. To cite again the work of a man both profoundly influenced by Parmenides and himself a profound influence on Western culture—Plato was later to put this Parmenidean point in terms of his famous phrase, "divine madness."[11] The point, again, is a metaphorical one. Man's access to truth, although requiring rigorous preparation of his own, is never quite his own affair. Truths, as we are still wont to say in more secular fashion, "come to us."

The movement from the issues of the Proem to those of "Truth" can perhaps fruitfully be made by reference to two more themes of the Proem, the portrayal of truth as "well-rounded,"[12] and the emphasis both in the Proem and elsewhere on the relation between truth and *Persuasion*.[13] Truth is "well-rounded." Later in "Truth," Being is itself characterized as "like a well-rounded sphere."[14] Further, the goddess says of the rigorous argument of "Truth," "It is all the same to me from what point I begin, for I shall return again to this same point."[15] Truth, Being, and their *logos* are all thus characterized as akin by virtue of their being in some sense rounded or circular. By putting these three references together, we can say this. Any interpretation of Being, of truth, and of the thought which gains access to the truth about Being in Parmenides, must take account of this triadic affinity. Such will be our task in our interpretation of "Truth."

Second, the association of truth with persuasion, and also perhaps the oft-repeated reference to bonds or limits,[16] points toward the necessity of the rigorous argument of the section on "Truth." Thinkers previous to Parmenides, even Heraclitus, had seemed content to *utter* their truths. Parmenides suggests in the Proem that such is not enough. Truth must be united to persuasion or, as Parmenides puts it, persuasion (*peitho*) must "attend upon truth." What does this mean? It means, of course, that Parmenides felt the need that his truths be defended. In the past, the claim that one's truths had the imprimatur of "the divine" was often considered sufficient. By pointedly characterizing his truth as having its source in the divine yet demanding more, Parmenides shatters the appeal to the divine as adequate justification, and with that step he sends off philosophy and religion in two decisively different directions. For the additional "persuasion" that Parmenides presented was rigorous argument, and that has been the hallmark of philosophy ever since.[17]

Fragment B2, considered the opening lines of "Truth," presents us with two paths, which later are apparently expanded to three. It is important, in the literal translation that follows, to remember that these are presented as paths, or routes, not concepts. A literal translation of B2 runs:[18]

Come now, and I shall tell you, and do you listen and preserve the account, what routes of search alone there are for thinking [knowing]: the One, that "it is" (or "that—— is——")[19] and that it is not possible that it is not (or "that——be not——"), is the course of Persuasion, for she attends upon truth: the other, that it is not (or "that——is not——") and that it is right that it is not (or "that——be not——") this I point to you as being a path from which no tidings ever come; for you could neither come to know that which is not (or "is not——") (for it cannot be completed), nor could you single it out.

Later, a third possible path seems to be indicated, from which the goddess also restrains us, that of mortals

carried along as deaf as they are blind, amazed, uncritical hordes, by whom To Be and Not To Be are regarded as the same and not the same, and (*for whom*) in everything there is a way of opposing stress.[20]

Mourelatos argues persuasively in his book[21] that this apparent third way dissolves into a special case of the second. For it amounts to asserting that what is not is and that what is, is not. It is also quite evidently related to the "Way of Opinion" which constitutes the last part of Parmenides' poem. But what is especially important to understand is that these two are paths of inquiry, not "concepts." Thus when the goddess restrains us from the negative path, she is restraining us not from a "concept" which is "inconceivable" or "unintelligible"—for example, from "nothingness" or "non-being," but from a path of inquiry the pursuit of which would be pointless, indeed never-ending.[22]

Thinking, then, is to be understood as a path.[23] The goddess encourages us down one path, discourages us from the other. The path on which she encourages us might be understood as beginning as a path of "affirmative predication" ("——is——") as the path to genuine knowledge. But evidently, the further down that path we get, the more it becomes concrete, and soon Parmenides is talking not just about the propositional form "——is——" or "it is," but about Being. Being, or "what is," is characterized, and defended logically, as one, ungenerated and imperishable, unchanging, motionless, and finite, "like a well-

rounded sphere." The arguments in behalf of each attribute are not difficult to follow, although the significance of Being being "finite" is a
subject of scholarly controversy. Many scholars take it in the literal
sense of "physically finite." This generates not only the problem of
what is then "outside" of the sphere of Being, but more fundamentally it
presumes that "Being" is "what is" in the sense of the materially existent things of the world. And if this is so, then Parmenides, in saying
that "what is," or Being, is changeless, motionless, ungenerated and imperishable, one and finite, can only be understood as ascribing these
characteristics to the physical world, and so as condemning all the corresponding attributes, movement, change, multiplicity, etc., as illusory.
And if he believes this, why should we twentieth-century philosophers
study him seriously?

Let me begin an alternative interpretation by suggesting that the
"finitude" in question is the finiteness of "de-finition." That is, Being is
finite in the sense that it has *intelligible* boundaries, or again, that it is
capable of articulation. To put it most simply, Being is finite means
most fundamentally, Being is de-finable, Being is intelligible and articulable. But the very mention of the issue of the intelligibility of Being
reminds us of several of the most controversial sentences in Parmenides' poem, to a consideration of which we can now turn. They are
precisely those fragments alluded to earlier which suggest that Being
stands in intimate relation with truth and with thinking.

Fragment B3 reads, "Thinking and Being are the same," or alternatively and more widely accepted, "For the same thing can be
thought as can be." In Fragment B8 we read, "Thinking and that for the
sake of which thinking is, is the same. For you will not find thinking
without Being, in regard to which it is uttered." Finally and to repeat,
we are told of "well-rounded truth," that Being is "like a well-rounded
sphere," and that the *logos* itself is somehow circular.

Now the above quoted lines cannot be made intelligible both with a
conception of Being as having the characteristics of unity, etc., which
Parmenides ascribes to it, and with a conception of Being as "what exists"—that is, the material things of the world. But there is an interpretation which makes Parmenides coherent. It also makes him considerably less naïve. And, in any case, it is an interpretation which
points to the genuine significance and even the truth of Parmenides'
poem.

Whatever Being is or, alternatively, whatever "what is" is, it must be of such a nature as to be "the same" as, or for, thinking. As elaborated in Fragment B8, Being must be such as to be always present when thinking occurs, and indeed to be that "for the sake of which" thinking is. In traditional philosophic language, we could say that Being must be such as to be the "immanent *telos*" of thinking.

Now the things of the material world, to say the least, hardly measure up to such requirements. This alone is sufficient to conclude that Being, or what is, cannot simply mean "that which exists," much less "body," or the "material plenum of the world" as Burnet has suggested.[24] What then is it? We can fruitfully begin by reminding ourselves of Plato's suggestion that Parmenides was his "philosophic father." The Ideas or Forms which are discussed in the dialogues, whatever their very complex nature, have at least this quality, that they are the *intelligible aspect* of things, that which we "come to know" when and insofar as we know "phenomena." We indeed find the roots of this view in Parmenides' poem. Being, as that which is the same as, or for, thinking, as that which is the ever-present "for the sake of which" of thinking, is that which is *intelligible* to thinking, that which has that *affinity* with thinking which Parmenides as well as the other Pre-Socratics seem to agree is essential to the nature and possibility of knowledge. Thus Being is the intelligible, knowable aspect of things, or, as the Greeks can say in their marvelously literal language, "the what it is" (*to ti estin*) of things, that intelligible "entity" which has the affinity by nature with *nous*—namely, that it is "intellectual"—which makes knowledge possible. It is thus Being as the *intelligibility* of things which is one whole, changeless, eternal, not created or destroyed, and of course, finite in the sense of de-finite. Thus Parmenides is not denying that *things* change, come to be, perish, and move. He is denying that the principle(s) of intelligibility by which they are *understood* do so.[25] From this standpoint, the "well-roundedness" of truth, of Being, and of the thought which, articulating them, is the same as them (*logos*) can be understood in precisely the sense suggested by Mourelatos. Being, truth, and the philosophic speech of men like Parmenides, are "perspectively neutral,"[26] that is, accessible and intelligible in principle to all men at all times, no matter where they may be in space or in history. This conception of the "permanence" of the objects of knowledge, suffice it to say, is at the very foundation of the Western conception of science, of knowledge generally, and of truth. It receives its most serious challenge from the position present in Heraclitus and the Greek sophists, but popularized especially today through such nineteenth- and twentieth-century thinkers as Marx, Nietzsche, and Heidegger, as "historicism," the view that truths, human nature, and even Being "change in history."

Evidently the view attributed to Parmenides has immense difficulties. The problem of how Being, so understood, can be a "unity" while at the same time being the source of intelligibility for a multiplicity of phenomena, the problem of the precise nature of the relationship between existent things and the Being by which they are intelligible, such problems have occupied defenders of this view from Plato and Aristotle to contemporary philosophy. But they are difficulties born not of Parmenides' naïveté but of his greatness, for he in many ways articulates a view of experience so complex and challenging yet so plausible that we today still think it worthwhile to reflect upon its still unsolved difficulties.

One of the most important of these difficulties is very much present in Parmenides, and we shall conclude the discussion of "Truth" with a consideration of this difficulty. Parmenides argues for the affinity or "sameness" of thought (and therefore speech—*logos*) and Being. Being, he insists, is changeless, eternal, one, ungenerated, imperishable, and finite. It is not at all obvious that these qualities adhere to thought. More needs to be said about the relation between the *psyche* who thinks and speaks, and Being, whose access he seeks and sometimes precariously achieves. We could say that the problem of the relation between the dramatic myth of the Proem and the "deduction" of "Truth" is really that of the erotic (that is incomplete but striving) *psyche* and the permanently present objects of intelligibility. Heraclitus responded to this issue by making the *Logos* which was the *arche* of things itself in motion like the *psyche*. For him, the intelligibility of even asserting this relation as permanently true in a world where *everything*, including the *arche*, changes, becomes a decisive problem. From this standpoint, Parmenides sees the necessity of the permanence and changelessness of the *arche* and origin of things, the objects of thought, or Being. But then, to repeat, how are we to account for the access of the moving *psyche* to changeless Being? One might speculate that the "deduction" of Truth is itself an effort to "halt" speech or thought, to offer, that is, a mode of speech—what we today call logic—which is changeless, permanent, and "perspectively neutral." But Parmenides' own recognition of the inadequacy of this is testified by the presence of the Proem, which suggests that such access must in the end be accounted for by the intervention or mediation of the daimonic between Being and the human *psyche*. Not surprisingly, it is this direction which Parmenides' "son," Plato, took in his own efforts to respond to the same issue.[27]

The "Way of Opinion" which concludes Parmenides' poem always offers difficulties of interpretation since it seems contrary to the spirit and intention of the earlier sections. We shall close the discussion of Parmenides by briefly outlining three compatible interpretations of the general significance of the "Way of Seeming." Parmenides himself virtually tells us the first. Even though it is deceptive and untrustworthy, the goddess reveals this path of Parmenides so that "no intellect of mortal man may outstrip you."[28] It is important, as it were, to know well the position to which the truth is opposed and which, perhaps, is the most serious rival to "truth." To this Burnet adds the suggestion that the "Way of Seeming" is in fact a version of the Pythagoreanism to which Parmenides had himself earlier held, perhaps under the tutelage of the Pythagorean, Ameinias.[29] Finally, Mourelatos in his book works out in persuasive detail the extent to which the "Way of Opinion" is ironic; it shows how the putative "third" way in fact dissolves, even in spite of itself, into the unfruitful second way which it is supposedly a way to avoid.[30] In any case, the central significance of the "Way of Opinion" is fairly uncontroversial. Opinion is distinguished from knowledge as deceptive and unacceptable for thought. Henceforward this view will be at the very core of Western philosophy.

Parmenides—The Spokesman for Being

Parmenides of Elea, in Italy, supposedly flourished around 475 B.C. This date makes plausible the account in Plato's *Parmenides* that Parmenides and Zeno visited Athens when Parmenides was an old man and Socrates very young. But it conflicts with the date given by the third-century A.D. historian Diogenes Laertius as 500 B.C. Fortunately, we have a significant segment of Parmenides' famous untitled poem, which is divided into three parts: the Prologue (or Proem), the Way of Truth, and the Way of Opinion (or Way of Seeming). He, along with

Heraclitus, exerted a decisive influence on Plato and indeed the whole of Western philosophy.

PARMENIDES: FRAGMENT*

1. The mares which carry me conveyed me as far as my desire reached, when the goddesses who were driving had set me on the famous highway which bears a man who has knowledge through all the cities. Along this way I was carried; for by this way the exceedingly intelligent mares bore me, drawing the chariot, and the maidens directed the way. The axle in the naves gave forth a pipe-like sound as it glowed (for it was driven round by the two whirling circles (*wheels*) at each end) whenever the maidens, daughters of the Sun, having left the Palace of Night, hastened their driving towards the light, having pushed back their veils from their heads with their hands.

There (*in the Palace of Night*) are the gates of the paths of Night and Day, and they are enclosed with a lintel above and a stone threshold below. The gates themselves are filled with great folding doors; and of these Justice, mighty to punish, has the interchangeable keys. The maidens, skilfully cajoling her with soft words, persuaded her to push back the bolted bar without delay from the gates; and these, flung open, revealed a wide gaping space, having swung their jambs, richly-wrought in bronze, reciprocally in their sockets. This way, then, straight through them went the maidens, driving chariot and mares along the carriage-road.

And the goddess received me kindly, and took my right hand in hers, and thus she spoke and addressed me:

Young man, companion of immortal charioteers, who comest by the help of the steeds which bring thee to our dwelling: welcome!—since no evil fate has despatched thee on thy journey by this road (for truly it is far from the path trodden by mankind); no, it is divine command and Right. Thou shalt inquire into everything: both the motionless heart of well-rounded Truth, and also the opinions of mortals, in which there is no true reliability. But nevertheless thou shalt learn these things

* From Kathleen Freeman, *Ancilla to the Pre-Socratic Philosophers*.

(*opinions*) also—how one should go through all the things-that-seem, without exception, and test them.

2. Come, I will tell you—and you must accept my word when you have heard it—the ways of inquiry which alone are to be thought: the one that IT IS, and it is not possible for IT NOT TO BE, is the way of credibility, for it follows Truth; the other, that IT IS NOT and that IT is bound NOT TO BE: this I tell you is a path that cannot be explored; for you could neither recognise that which is not, nor express it.

3. For it is the same thing to think and to be.

4. Observe nevertheless how things absent are securely present to the mind; for it will not sever Being from its connection with Being, whether it is scattered everywhere utterly throughout the universe, or whether it is collected together.

5. It is all the same to me from what point I begin, for I shall return again to this same point.

6. One should both say and think that Being Is; for To Be is possible, and Nothingness is not possible. This I command you to consider; for from the latter way of search first of all I debar you. But next I debar you from that way along which wander mortals knowing nothing, two-headed,* for perplexity in their bosoms steers their intelligence astray, and they are carried along as deaf as they are blind, amazed, uncritical hordes, by whom To Be and Not To Be are regarded as the same and not the same, and (*for whom*) in everything there is a way of opposing stress.**

7., 8. For this (*view*) can never predominate, that That Which Is Not exists. You must debar your thought from this way of search, not let ordinary experience in its variety force you along this way, (*namely, that of allowing*) the eye, sightless as it is, and the ear, full of sound, and the

---

* *i.e.*, 'in two minds'.

** Heraclitus, Frg. 8.

tongue, to rule; but (*you must*) judge by means of the Reason (*Logos*) the much-contested proof which is expounded by me.

There is only one other description of the way remaining, (*namely*), that (*What Is*) Is. To this way there are very many sign-posts: that Being has no coming-into-being and no destruction, for it is whole of limb, without motion, and without end. And it never Was, nor Will Be, because it Is now, a Whole all together, One, continuous; for what creation of it will you look for? How, whence (*could it have*) sprung? Nor shall I allow you to speak or think of it as springing from Not-Being; for it is neither expressible nor thinkable that What-Is-Not Is. Also, what necessity impelled it, if it did spring from Nothing, to be produced later or earlier? Thus it must Be absolutely, or not at all. Nor will the force of credibility ever admit that anything should come into being, beside Being itself, out of Not-Being. So far as that is concerned, Justice has never released (*Being*) in its fetters and set it free either to come into being or to perish, but holds it fast. The decision on these matters depends on the following: IT IS, or IT IS NOT. It is therefore decided—as is inevitable—(*that one must*) ignore the one way as unthinkable and inexpressible (for it is no true way) and take the other as the way of Being and Reality. How could Being perish? How could it come into being? If it came into being, it Is Not; and so too if it is about-to-be at some future time. Thus Coming-into-Being is quenched, and Destruction also into the unseen.*

Nor is Being divisible, since it is all alike. Nor is there anything (*here or*) there which could prevent it from holding together, nor any lesser thing, but all is full of Being. Therefore it is altogether continuous; for Being is close to Being.

But it is motionless in the limits of mighty bonds, without beginning, without cease, since Becoming and Destruction have been driven very far away, and true conviction has rejected them. And remaining the same in the same place, it rests by itself and thus remains there fixed; for powerful Necessity holds it in the bonds of a Limit, which constrains it round about, because it is decreed by divine law that Being shall not be without boundary. For it is not lacking; but if it were (*spatially infinite*), it would be lacking everything.**

* 'Beyond perception'; also 'never-ending'.

** Reading and meaning doubtful. Diels-Kranz: 'if it lacked Limit, it would fall short of being a Whole', but without any certainty.

To think is the same as the thought that It Is; for you will not find
thinking with Being, in (*regard to*) which there is an expression. For
nothing else either is or shall be except Being, since Fate has tied it down
to be a whole and motionless; therefore all things that mortals have
established, believing in their truth, are just a name: Becoming and
Perishing, Being and Not-Being, and Change of position, and alteration of
bright color.

But since there is a (*spatial*) Limit, it is complete on every side, like
the mass of a well-rounded sphere, equally balanced from its centre in
every direction; for it is not bound to be at all either greater or less in
this direction or that; nor is there Not-Being which could check it from
reaching to the same point, nor is it possible for Being to be more in this
direction, less in that, than Being, because it is an inviolate whole. For,
in all directions equal to itself, it reaches its limits uniformly.

At this point I cease my reliable theory (*Logos*) and thought, concerning Truth; from here onwards you must learn the opinions of mortals, listening to the deceptive order of my words.

They have established (*the custom of*) naming two forms, one of
which ought not to be (*mentioned*): that is where they have gone astray.
They have distinguished them as opposite in form, and have marked
them off from another by giving them different signs: on one side the
flaming fire in the heavens, mild, very light (*in weight*), the same as itself in every direction, and not the same as the other. This (*other*) also is
by itself and opposite: dark Night, a dense and heavy body. This world-
order I describe to you throughout as it appears with all its phenomena,
in order that no intellect of mortal men may outstrip you.*

9.   But since all things are named Light and Night, and names have
been given to each class of things according to the power of one or the
other (*Light or Night*), everything is full equally of Light and invisible
Night, as both are equal, because to neither of them belongs any share
(of the other).**

---

* Or, reading 'in order that no mortal may outstrip you in intelligence.'

** Kranz takes ἐπεί with the previous line, and translates: 'For nothing is possible
which does not come under either of the two' (*i.e.*, everything belongs to one or other
of the two categories Light and Night).

10.   You shall know the nature of the heavens, and all the signs in the heavens, and the destructive works of the pure bright torch of the sun, and whence they came into being. And you shall learn of the wandering works of the round-faced moon, and its nature; and you shall know also the surrounding heaven, whence it sprang and how Necessity brought and constrained it to hold the limits of the stars.

11.   *(I will describe)* how earth and sun and moon, and the aether common to all, and the Milky Way in the heavens, and outermost Olympus, and the hot power of the stars, hastened to come into being.

12.   For the narrower rings were filled with unmixed Fire, and those next to them with Night, but between *(these)* rushes the portion of Flame. And in the centre of these is the goddess who guides everything; for throughout she rules over cruel Birth and Mating, sending the female to mate with the male, and conversely again the male with the female.

13.   First of all the gods she devised Love.

14.   *(The moon)*: Shining by night with a light not her own, wandering round the earth.

15.   *(The moon)*: Always gazing towards the rays of the sun.

15a.   *(Earth)*: Rooted in water.

16.   For according to the mixture of much-wandering limbs which each man has, so is the mind which is associated with mankind: for it is the same thing which thinks, namely the constitution of the limbs in men, all and individually; for it is excess which takes Thought.

17.   On the right, boys, on the left, girls . . . *(in the womb)*.

18.   When a woman and a man mix the seeds of Love together, the power *(of the seeds)* which shapes *(the embryo)* in the veins out of different blood can mould well-constituted bodies only if it preserves proportion. For if the powers war *(with each other)* when the seed is mixed,

and do not make a unity in the body formed by the mixture, they will terribly harass the growing (*embryo*) through the twofold seed of the (*two*) sexes.

19.   Thus, therefore, according to opinion, were these things created, and are now, and shall hereafter from henceforth grow and then come to an end. And for these things men have established a name as a distinguishing mark for each. . . .

TESTIMONIA ON PARMENIDES BY PLATO

. . . I had almost forgotten the opposite doctrine, Theodorus,

"That is alone unmoved which is named the universe."

This is the language of Parmenides, Melissus, and their followers, who stoutly maintain that all being is one and self-contained, and has no place in which to move. What shall we say, friend, to all these people; for, advancing step by step, we have imperceptibly got between the combatants, and, unless we can protect our retreat, we shall pay the penalty of our rashness—like the players in the palaestra who are caught upon the line, and are dragged different ways by the two parties. Therefore I think that we had better begin by considering those whom we first accosted, "the river-gods," and, if we find any truth in them, we will pull ourselves over to their side, and try to get away from the others. But if the partisans of "the whole" appear to speak more truly, we will fly off from the party which would move the immovable to them. And if we find that neither of them have anything reasonable to say, we shall be in a ridiculous position, having ourselves to assert our own poor opinion and reject that of ancient and famous men. . . .

Soc. My reason is that I have a kind of reverence; not so much for Melissus and the others, who say that "all is one and at rest," as for the great leader himself, Parmenides, venerable and awful, as in Homeric language he may be called; him I should be ashamed to approach in a spirit unworthy of him. I met him when he was an old man, and I was a mere youth, and he appeared to me to have a glorious depth of mind.

And I am afraid that we may not understand his language, and may fall short even more of his meaning; and I fear above all that the nature of knowledge, which is the main subject of our discussion, may be thrust out of sight by the unbidden guests who will come pouring in upon us, if they are permitted; besides, the question which we are now stirring is of immense extent, and will be treated unfairly if only considered by the way; or if treated adequately and at length, will put into the shade the question of science. But neither of these things ought to be allowed, and I must, if I can, by the midwives' art, try to deliver Theaetetus of his conceptions about knowledge. . . . (*Theaetetus*, 180-81, 183-84)

TESTIMONIA ON PARMENIDES BY ARISTOTLE

All thinkers then agree in making the contraries principles, both those who describe the All as one and unmoved (for even Parmenides treats hot and cold as principles under the names of fire and earth) and those too who use the rare and the dense. (*Physica*, 188a 18)

Hence Parmenides must be thought to have spoken better than Melissus. The latter says that the whole is infinite, but the former describes it as limited, 'equally balanced from the middle'. (*Physica*, 207a 15)

Parmenides seems to fasten on that which is one in definition, Melissus on that which is one in matter, for which reason the former says that it is limited, the latter that it is unlimited. (*Metaphysica*, 986b 19)

Of those who said the universe was one, then, none succeeded in discovering a course of this sort, except perhaps Parmenides, and he only inasmuch as he supposes that there is not only one but also in some sense two courses. (*Metaphysica*, 984b 2)

TESTIMONIA ON PARMENIDES FROM
LATER GREEK SOURCES*

Parmenides, son of Pyres and a native of Elea, was a pupil of Xenophanes. But although he listened to Xenophanes' teachings Parmenides was no follower of his. According to Sotion's account he also associated with Ameinias the Pythagorean, who although poor was a most worthy man. After the death of Ameinias, whose teachings were more to his taste, Parmenides, who was of good family and quite wealthy, built him a shrine. It was Ameinias and not Xenophanes who led him to adopt the peaceful life of a student.

Parmenides was the first to declare that the earth is spherical and is situated at the center. He maintained that there are two elements, fire and earth, the one playing the role of craftsman, the other of material. The coming-to-be of man he explained as originating from the sun. Heat and cold he regarded as more basic than the sun, and indeed as the basic constituents of everything. Soul and mind he held to be identical. He divided philosophy into two parts, the one dealing with truth, the other with opinion.

He flourished in the sixty-ninth Olympiad [504-500 B.C.]. It is said that he was the first to discover the identity of Hesperus and Phosphorus [the evening and morning appearances of the planet Venus]: at least so Favorinus says in the fifth book of his *Memorabilia*, although some others attribute the discovery to Pythagoras. On the authority of Speusippus in his treatise *On Philosophers* it is said that Parmenides held a legislative office in his native city. According to Favorinus in his *Miscellaneous History* Parmenides was the first to use the "Achilles and the Tortoise" argument. (Diogenes Laertius IX. 3)

Declaring that the All is eternal and yet undertaking to explain the coming-to-be of things, Parmenides tries to work out his views in a double manner. From the standpoint of truth he postulates that the All is one, ungenerated, and in the form of a sphere; while in terms of popular opinion he explains the generation of phenomena by two first-

---

* From Philip Wheelwright, *The Pre-Socratics*.

principles, fire and earth, the latter being identified with matter, the former with cause and agent. (Theophrastus, *Physical Opinions*)

In the first book of his *Physical Opinions* Theophrastus summarizes Parmenides' view as follows: Whatever is other than being is not-being; not-being is nothing whatever; therefore being is one. (Simplicius, *Commentaria*)

Parmenides holds that the All is one and eternal, without beginning, and spherical in shape. However, he does not escape the opinion of the many, for he speaks of fire and earth as first-principles, earth being the material and fire the active cause. He declares that the world will come to an end, but he does not say how. The All is eternal, he says, without beginning, spherical, homogeneous, independent of place, unchanging, and limited. (Hippolytus, *Refutatio*)

Parmenides taught that there are "crowns," or concentric orbits,—one of rarefied matter, another of dense, and others containing various mixtures of light [rare] and dark [dense]. A solid wall, he said, forms the periphery, and under it is a crown of fire; the innermost center of all the crowns is solid, and is immediately surrounded by a ring of fire. Of the mixed crowns the one that is nearest the center is the source of motion and generation; this is what he has described as "the goddess who steers and who holds the keys"; he characterizes her as Justice and as Necessity. (Aëtius)

On the whole Parmenides has said nothing definite about sensation, except that rational awareness exists according as one or other of the two basic elements is in excess. For according as the hot or the cold predominates so does the understanding come-to-be [and diminish]. A better and purer understanding is derived from the hot; but it, too, requires a certain proportion. [Fr. 18 is quoted.]

Since he holds that thinking and perceiving are the same, it follows that remembering and forgetting also come about as a result of the mixture. He does not explain, however, what happens if the elements [the hot and the cold] enter into the mixture in equal amounts—i.e., whether or not thinking will then occur, and what its disposition will then be. (Theophrastus, *De Sensu* I. 3)

He says it is owing to its complete lack of fire that a corpse does not perceive light, heat, and sound; that it does, however, perceive cold and silence and similar qualities. In general, he holds, all being involves a certain degree of knowing. (*ibid.*, I. 4)

TESTIMONIA ON PARMENIDES BY CICERO*

Parmenides devised the theory that there is a sort of contrivance like a "crown," as he called it,—an orb of light with continuous heat, arching the sky. He spoke of this as a god. . . . Moreover he raised war, discord, desire, and other such transient things to the status of gods. (*De Natura Deorum* I. 28)

Notes: V

1. There is, of course, room for much disagreement as to the precise interpretation of Parmenides, especially concerning the sophistication of his "logic." Even Nietzsche falls prey to this interpretation. *See* especially Friedrich Nietzsche, *Philosophy in the Tragic Age of the Greeks*, trans. by Marianne Cowan, Gateway Edition (Chicago, Henry Regnery Co., 1962), pp. 78-80.
2. Martin Heidegger, *Introduction to Metaphysics*, trans. by Ralph Manheim (New York, Doubleday Anchor Books, 1961), p. 83.
3. This theme has been superbly worked out in detail by Alex Mourelatos, *The Route of Parmenides* (New Haven, Conn., Yale University Press, 1970). *See* especially pp. 40, 46.
4. *Ibid.*, pp. 40, 46, 47, 71 *passim*.
5. *Ibid.*, p. 68.
6. Plato, *Symposium*, 210 ff.
7. Parmenides, Fragment B1, lines 8-12 (D-K).
8. *Ibid.*, Fragment B1, line 3.
9. *Ibid.*, Fragment B1, line 27.

* From Philip Wheelwright, *The Pre-Socratics*.

10. Plato's *Meno* is an especially instructive dialogue in this regard. See also *Theaetetus*.

11. Plato, *Phaedrus*, 244a *passim*.

12. Parmenides, Fragment B1, line 29.

13. *Ibid.*, Fragment B1, line 16; Fragment B2, line 5.

14. *Ibid.*, Fragment B8, line 43.

15. *Ibid.*, Fragment B5.

16. *Ibid.*, Fragments B1, lines 5-10; Fragment 8, lines 10-18, lines 26, 30, 49.

17. *See* Mourelatos, *op. cit.*, pp. 218-19.

18. I follow closely the translation of Mourelatos, *op. cit.*, p. 55.

19. *See* Mourelatos, *op cit.*, pp. 51 ff.

20. Parmenides, Fragment 6.

21. Mourelatos, *op. cit.*, pp. 91 ff.

22. Mourelatos' explanation of this is ingenious, and so it is quoted at length: "But the journey to what-is-not is one which heads for everywhere and nowhere. Where do I go if I am told to go to 'not Ithica'? Where do I go if I set my bearings on the 'non-Cimmerians'? It is fated to be a journey of *plane*, of regress and wandering. Here we see how intimately Parmenides' argument depends on the models in terms of which he understands the philosopher's radically new concept of cognition, inquiry, and predication." (Mourelatos, *op. cit.*, p. 78.)

23. A conception developed by Martin Heidegger in such works as *Feldweg* (Field-path), *Holzwege* (Timber-tracks), *Unterwegs zur Sprache* (On the Way Toward Language).

24. J. Burnet, *Early Greek Philosophy* (New York, Meridian Books, 1957), pp. 178, 179.

25. This, of course, involves making the famous distinction between "being and existence" which it is often said "could not" have been made before Plato. I am arguing that making it is the only way to make Parmenides coherent.

It might seem that there is one piece of almost insurmountable evidence against my interpretation. That is the fact that Zeno, Parmenides' student, presented argument after argument against motion, plurality, and the other aspects of our visible world which Parmenides denied to Being. This would seem to suggest that both Parmenides and Zeno thought that these qualities simply did not exist. But again, all that need be concluded is that Being, the object of intelligibility, does not participate in these qualities. This is in fact the way the young Socrates interprets it in Plato's *Parmenides*, 129a-130a.

26. Mourelatos, *op. cit.* p. 129.

27. *See* Plato, *Symposium* and *Phaedrus*.

28. Parmenides, Fragment B8.

29. Burnet, *op. cit.*, pp. 184, 196.

30. Mourelatos, *op cit.*, pp. 222-63.

Catching Up with Zeno

T HE passage of time inexorably brings about the destruction of historical evidence: some by human design or accident, much by natural deterioration.* Of all such destruction none is more lamentable than the loss of the bulk of the writings of the Pre-Socratic philosophers. For it was through them that Western science and philosophy came into being: geometry, physics, ethics, and metaphysics all had their origin in the thought of this very small group of men. Our evidence about the Pre-Socratics is so meager that any contemporary account must be considered at best as a "likely story." Zeno of Elea (c. 490 B.C.-c. 430 B.C.) shares with most other Pre-Socratics the fate of having his writings completely destroyed. Further, the evidence we have about his life and thought is widely scattered and most of it in the works of thinkers who were unsympathetic to his thought. Hence what follows is tentative, pending (we may hope) the discovery of more evidence. But what is clear even from our very limited evidence is that Zeno was an enormously impressive thinker and his influence may have been decisive in such areas as logic, mathematics, and philosophy.

Of his life we know little. He apparently lived in Elea, was an associate of Parmenides, was a forceful and popular teacher, visited Athens (where it is said that Pericles heard him lecture), was involved in politics, and died a heroic death under torture.

Of his thought the most certain thing we know about him is that he composed a number of paradoxes. Interest in these paradoxes has waxed and waned over the course of the centuries, but there was probably no time in which that interest was greater than now. The twentieth century has been unique in the number of men who have investigated the

* This introduction section is by Howard De Long.

paradoxes. However, most of the effort has been in resolving the paradoxes, or showing that another resolution is inadequate, or proposing a new interpretation. Relatively little sustained effort has been made toward understanding the *purposes* for which the paradoxes were invented and the social environment from which they came. Without a serious attempt at understanding these things it is unlikely that a tenable interpretation of the paradoxes will be produced.

The Purposes of the Paradoxes

The vast majority of commentators have judged Zeno to be either a frivolous inventor of sophisms or, contrariwise, a serious disciple of Parmenides intent on proving the validity of the master's doctrine. Both these views contain an element of truth but neither is satisfactory. By examining them, however, we can come to a more adequate interpretation of Zeno.

Let us first consider whether Zeno was a mere inventor of frivolous conundrums, or riddles. He was not, but this is not to deny that he invented conundrums, or riddles. "Tell me, Protagoras," he is reported to have said to the famous sophist, "does a single grain of millet or the ten thousandth part of a grain make any sound when it falls?" Zeno then shows how the obvious answer to this question leads into difficulties. Plato characterizes sophistry as something which "teaches you nothing about the nature of things; you only learn how to fool people with subtleties and equivocations. It is no better than tripping somebody up or taking his chair away as he is about to sit down" (*Euthydemus,* 278B). Zeno was not a sophist in this sense because of the peculiar nature of his paradoxes. They are through and through philosophical. We look in vain for a comparable poser of riddles which are of interest to philosophers. Perhaps the person who comes closest in modern times is Lewis Carroll who invented a number of philosophical paradoxes, one which takes as its beginning the setting of one of Zeno's paradoxes. Both *Alice in Wonderland* and *Through the Looking Glass* also elicit philosophical interest.[1]

A parallel can perhaps be drawn with the writings of the contemporary thinker J. L. Austin. His philosophical writings are so devoted to words and their various interrelations that both admirers and detractors have said he is just a philologist. The logician Willard Van Orman Quine has rightly objected to this by saying that Austin's work is philosophical, in particular, that "Austin was philosophical in choosing what idioms to analyze."[2] Similarly, Zeno was not a mere inventor of paradoxes—he was philosophical in his choice of paradoxes, and a study of them does teach us something "about the nature of things."

But in rejecting the view that Zeno is not a mere inventor of riddles we must remember he was at least that. There is an essential element of playfulness and even competitiveness to Zeno's paradoxes, an element which does not exclude seriousness of purpose. According to the *Alcibiades* (a dialogue attributed to Plato) Zeno was highly paid for his teaching. What was that teaching? Apparently it was how to refute people by the use of the *reductio ad absurdum* method. This would be very useful to politicians, lawyers, and sophists—especially if their opponents did not understand the method. Plato's *Phaedrus,* perhaps the earliest reference we have to Zeno, tells us that Zeno "has an art of speaking by which he makes the same things appear to his hearers like and unlike, one and many, at rest and in motion" (*Phaedrus* 261D). The "appear to his hearers" is there because Plato didn't believe that Zeno was sincere; rather, it seemed that Zeno could make things appear as he wanted.

Zeno, in short, excelled in contentious argument. His popularity apparently depended on a spirit akin to that of those who wanted to get Socrates and Protagoras together (as described in Plato's *Protagoras*). Most of that audience was uninterested in the philosophical outcome but just wanted to see how the game was played and who won. Philosophical conversation was both an exhibition and a contest: It was a sport through and through. The case of J. L. Austin again comes to mind. He was an immensely interesting, controversial, and entertaining person to see doing linguistic philosophy—especially when he had a philosophical opponent to verbally duel. But that does not mean he had no serious purpose. Zeno's fame is an indication that there were sportive, controversial, and entertainment aspects to the man, but he should not be understood merely that way.

Now let us consider whether Zeno was a serious disciple of Parmenides whose sole or principal object was to produce arguments proving the truth of the master's doctrine. The earliest and certainly the most extensive account we have of Zeno's purposes is given in the opening paragraphs of Plato's *Parmenides*. There Socrates claims that Zeno's intention is to give an argument for Parmenides' belief that the All is One, using the indirect method of showing there is no plurality. Since Parmenides maintains the One, and Zeno asserts no plurality, Socrates says that their positions "really . . . are saying much the same" (128B). Unfortunately many scholars have taken this to mean that Zeno is a loyal disciple of Parmenides' *simpliciter*. Yet Zeno immediately states that Socrates did "not fully apprehend the true motive" of his book. Zeno agrees that all the arguments in his book are toward proving that a plurality does not exist; but he adds that this is incidental. The book is only a kind of defense of Parmenides because it attacks those who make fun of Parmenides' arguments by showing that the assumption of a plurality "appears to be still more ridiculous than the hypothesis of the being of the One." (A genuine defense would of course require that he prove Parmenides right.) Zeno then states that his treatise was inspired by "the pugnacity of a young [man]" and not by "the ambition of an older man"—meaning, presumably, the search for the truth of the matter. Socrates accepts Zeno's qualifications of Socrates' own account.

Hence Zeno must not be thought of as someone whose purpose is to establish a thesis. In fact no positive doctrine whatsoever is ascribed to him. His purpose was to demolish viewpoints. If the views were widely believed, or maintained by a famous philosopher or by a famous school, so much the better for his sport. According to Plutarch, Zeno "treated of natural philosophy in the same manner as Parmenides did, but had also perfected himself in an art of his own for refuting and silencing opponents in argument; as Timon of Philius describes it—

"Also the two-edge tongue of mighty Zeno, who,
Say what one would, could argue it untrue. . . .[3]

Since Timon was an extreme skeptic, it is hardly likely that he would have said this if Zeno maintained Parmenides' positive doctrine. Further, Simplicius reports that in one argument Zeno does away with the One and allows for the existence of plurality.

This point of view is supported by the earlier quoted passage in the *Phaedrus* (261D) where Zeno is portrayed as being able to make "the same things appear to his hearers as like and unlike, one and many, at rest and in motion." A loyal disciple of Parmenides would not have to make things appear to be unlike, many, and in motion. On the contrary.

The relationship between Parmenides and Zeno is a much more subtle one than is indicated by the word "disciple." An analogy will make it clear. Suppose a fideist has a younger associate who is an atheist. To the great mass of ordinary believers the atheist might be understood as a disciple since they both reject the widely held belief in the reasonableness of believing in God. Yet neither the fideist nor the atheist would identify with the other's position since the fideist believes in God and the atheist does not. Hence their common rejection of the majority view is only incidental. What they do have in common is a social status, namely, being widely ridiculed or thought wrong by the majority. To many people the difference between, say, Kierkegaard or Unamuno on one side, and Hume or Russell on the other side, is moot.

Similarly what Parmenides and Zeno had in common was a common social status. Parmenides maintained an initially absurd view that only the One exists. Zeno maintained paradoxes, say, that the same things were both one and many. From the point of view of the majority these views come to *pretty* much the same thing. But if we are careful we can see that it was Zeno's purpose to refute the majority's view of plurality, *not* to argue for the One. As Seneca remarks: "If I believe Parmenides there is nothing left but the One; if I believe Zeno, not even the One is left." In fact, Seneca tells us that Zeno, in contrast to Parmenides, maintained that "nothing exists" (Letter 88).

Zeno, then, probably had three purposes in the invention of the paradoxes. First, there is a delight in puzzles and paradoxes for their own sake. Like many of the puzzles of Lewis Carroll, Zeno's paradoxes are interesting in themselves even if no attention is paid to their philosophical significance. Furthermore, this delight may be heightened by making them part of an exhibition, and the exhibition may be made exciting by incorporating the paradoxes in a verbal context.

Second, the paradoxes gave concrete evidence of his ability to make things appear like and unlike, at rest and in motion, etc., on the basis of plausible premises and arguments. This ability depended on the enormous logical power of the *reductio ad absurdum* mode of argument. It was probably the secrets of this mode of argument which formed the content of his teaching.

Third, the paradoxes were meant to show the uncanny difficulty or even impossibility of coming up with a coherent view of very simple everyday components of our experience. For example, Zeno's arguments pose difficulties whether one holds that space is continuous or atomic. In this regard, then, Zeno's purpose is through and through skeptical.

The Paradoxes

We may now turn to a brief description and explanation of the paradoxes. For each paradox two or three interpretations and resolutions are presented. We do not have enough evidence to know which, if any, of these interpretations would apply to the paradoxes as originally formulated. However, as we shall see, perhaps this very ambiguity is what allows them to possess such great philosophic interest for us today. In any case, what follows is not meant to suggest that the paradoxes are either easy to interpret or easy to resolve. Rather by illustrating a variety of philosophical interpretations and resolutions a *start* may be made toward appreciating the truly great difficulty in giving a comprehensive and adequate account of them. For our purposes they will be divided into four groups accordingly as they concern motion, plurality, place, or sound.

Paradoxes of Motion

These paradoxes are the most famous and have perhaps received more careful attention than the others. There are four paradoxes of motion: the Dichotomy, the Achilles, the Arrow, and the Stadium. The first and third deny motion altogether, the second and fourth assume motion and show the assumption leads to absurdities.

The Dichotomy. The argument is that motion is impossible because for anything to move from one place to another it must first go halfway, but before going halfway it must go a quarter way, but before going a quarter way it must go an eighth way, and so on *ad infinitum*. Since one cannot exhaust an infinity in a finite time, motion cannot occur.

To understand the paradox more clearly let us consider the following diagram:

AG	F	E	D	C
...$(1/2)^4$	$(1/2)^3$		$(1/2)^2$	1/2

Interpretation A. Suppose the difficulty is how it is possible to do an infinite number of things in a finite time. Each of the tasks takes a finite amount of time and thus (it apparently seemed) that all of them would take an infinite time. However, we now know this need not be the case. If it takes 1 hour to go from A to B, 1/2 hour to go from A to C, 1/4 (= $(1/2^2)$ hour to go from A to D, etc., then the amount of time is not infinite. In particular,

$$1/2 + (1/2)^2 + (1/2)^3 + \ldots = 1.$$

as can now be proven by many a schoolboy. However, the ancient Greeks had great difficulty in dealing with limits—in part due to a clumsy notation. (Our notation derives from the Indians and Arabs. To get some idea of the difficulty facing the Greeks, try dealing with infinite series in Roman numerals.) Even geometry—the first developed science in ancient Greece—was in a rapid state of flux in Zeno's time. Hence, it can hardly be expected that he would have understood even simple infinite series or that his hearers wouldn't be puzzled by them.

Interpretation B. Suppose the difficulty is how one can exhaust an infinite sequence from the "open" end. We might then deny that the mathematical model that we have created to describe the situation is physically significant for arbitrarily small distances. Thus, although a mathematical line is infinitely divisible, a physical distance might not be. In this regard it would be similar to concepts which apply to human affairs. For example, a person can take a 3-mile walk or a walk around the block, but one cannot take a hundredth of an inch walk. To be sure one can move a hundredth of an inch, but that movement is not a walk.[4] It may be that physical distance itself has a lower limit below which it doesn't make sense to talk about movement. If so, then the paradox under this interpretation is resolved.

Interpretation C. Suppose the difficulty is to determine the first task.

We can then with perfect consistency deny there is a first task. Some infinite mathematical sequences have a first element and no last element (such as the positive integers: 1, 2, 3 . . .), some have a last element but no first element (such as the negative integers: . . . -3, -2, -1), and some have neither a first nor a last element (such as the integers: . . . -3, -2, -1, 0, 1, 2, 3 . . .). There is today no particular difficulty in dealing with such sequences. However, be it noted that even St. Thomas Aquinas—with a much richer and longer philosophical heritage than Zeno—did not conceive of the possibility of an infinite sequence with no first element.

THE ACHILLES. This paradox is Zeno's most famous and goes as follows: Achilles, born of a goddess and the fastest of human runners, cannot even catch a tortoise, the slowest of moving creatures. For suppose we have a race in which the tortoise is given a lead. However fast Achilles runs to reach the point where the tortoise was, he must take some time to do it. In that time the tortoise will move forward some (smaller) distance. This argument may now be repeated *ad infinitum*. Hence Achilles may get closer and closer to the tortoise, but he cannot catch the tortoise.

Again a diagram might be helpful. Let T_0 be the time of the start of the race and let's assume that Achilles is running twice as fast as the tortoise.

Time	Course
T_0	A T ·
	O 1 2
T_1	A T ·
	O 1 1½ 2
T ½	A T
	O 1 1½ 1¾ 2
·	·
·	·
·	·

Of course the difficulty in the Achilles argument might be susceptible to the kinds of resolutions proposed in Interpretations A and B of the Dichotomy. But there are other possibilities.

Interpretation A. Suppose the difficulty is how we are to use our reason to understand motion once it is assumed, as this paradox assumes for the sake of argument, that motion exists. We might answer that motion can't be understood by reason and if we try to so understand motion then Zeno's argument is correct! Hence what the paradox proves is not that motion doesn't exist, but rather that we are incapable of understanding motion by reason alone. What we need is an intuition or some direct experience, as when we close and open our hand. Reason, in short, is not a proper mode to knowledge of motion.

Interpretation B. Suppose the difficulty is in the comparison of infinite sets, and in particular with the assumption that the whole is greater than the part. To see this, consider that for each point on the line that Achilles is at, the tortoise is also at a point and yet the distance Achilles travels is greater than the distance the tortoise travels. The problem and its solution may be made clearer by considering the following diagram.

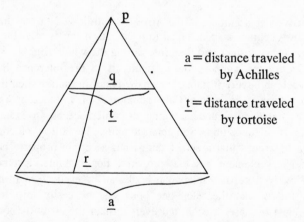

a = distance traveled
    by Achilles

t = distance traveled
    by tortoise

Now it is clear that to each point on *a* there corresponds a unique point on *t*, and vice versa. This can be easily seen by drawing straight lines through *p* which cross both *t* and *a*. Any point on line *t* (say, *q*) corresponds to a unique point (say, *r*) on line *a*, and vice versa. Hence if motion exists, the whole is not greater than the part. This difficulty may be resolved by denying that the whole is greater than the part for infinite sets. Such a possibility is now well known owing to the creation of set theory by Georg Cantor. For example, we can easily see that there are as many even positive integers as there are positive integers:

The comparisons of the sizes of infinite sets was exploited by Cantor into a beautiful and elaborate theory, but the bare fact that infinite sets may have subsets of equal size was known by many men before him including Plutarch (46-120), Proclus (410-485), Adam of Balsham (fl. 1130), Robert Halkot (d. 1349), Galileo (1564-1642), Leibniz (1646-1716), Bernard Balzano (1781-1848) and Janos Bolyai (1802-1860). In fact, as we shall see, there is further evidence that Zeno himself might have known that the whole is not necessarily greater than the part when infinite sets are involved.

THE ARROW. The argument of the Arrow is as follows: at every instant a flying arrow occupies a space equal to itself, but if this is true, the arrow is at rest at every instant and therefore during the whole flight.

Interpretation A. Suppose the difficulty is in the inference that because at each and every instance the arrow is not in motion then it is not in motion during the whole time composed of instances. We may resolve the paradox by understanding this inference as an example of the fallacy of composition. Someone commits the fallacy of composition when he argues that a set of things has a certain property because each and every element has that property. For example, just because each and every page of a telephone book can be easily torn in half, it does not follow that the telephone book can be easily torn in half. Similarly, just because at each and every instant the arrow is not moving, it doesn't follow that the arrow doesn't move over the whole time interval.

Interpretation B. Suppose the difficulty of the argument is the assumption that the flying arrow cannot move in a place where it is, nor in a place where it is not, and hence cannot move. We may get around the difficulty by showing that this premise is false if an *interval* of time is involved or, contrarywise, if only an instant of time is involved the conclusion does not follow (fallacy of composition).

THE STADIUM. This paradox is the most difficult to reconstruct because the texts are both cryptic and corrupt. However, it probably is something like the following:

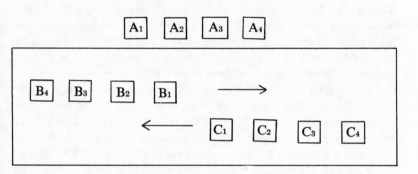

Imagine three sets of equal-sized bodies. The first set (A_1, A_2, A_3, A_4) is stationary. The second set (B_1, B_2, B_3, B_4) is moving from one end of a stadium toward the other, and the third (C_1, C_2, C_3, C_4) is moving at an equal velocity in the opposite direction. Assume they continue moving until the following situation is reached:

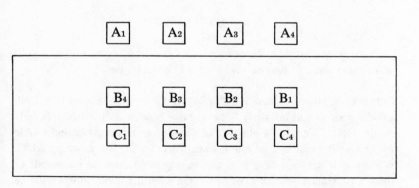

B_1 reaches its point opposite A_4 at the same time C_1 reaches its point opposite A_1. But C_1 passes all the B's whereas B_1 passes only half the A's. Since each requires an equal time passing each body, the time (that is, the time required for B_1 to pass two A's) is equal to double the time (that is, the time required for C_1 to pass four B's).

Interpretation A. Suppose the difficulty concerns relative motion. Hence there is a false premise, namely that "each requires an equal time passing each body." Although the B's and C's are moving with identical velocities relative to the A's, it is not true that their velocity relative to each other is the same as their velocities relative to the A's. Thus if the B's and C's are moving at 10 miles an hour *relative* to the A's, they are moving at 20 miles an hour relative to each other.

Interpretation B. Suppose the difficulty concerns the fact that at each and every instant the position of B_1 relative to the A's corresponds to a unique position of C_1 relative to the B's. Yet one distance is twice the other. Hence the whole distance is equal to its half, and since the velocities are the same, a similar argument holds for time. The solution under such an interpretation would consist in pointing out that there is no paradox in saying the time equals its double if what is meant is that to each and every instant of each time there corresponds a unique instant of the other. But from this we can't conclude that the time intervals are equal, any more than we can say any two finite lines are equal in length because every point in one corresponds to a point of the other (see Interpretation B of the Achilles).

Paradoxes of Plurality

Zeno composed a large number of arguments against plurality of which only three or four survive. We will consider two.[5]

FIRST ARGUMENT. If there is a plurality of things, then things will be both infinitely small and infinitely large. On one hand, they must be infinitely small since if we have a plurality of units each unit must be indivisible (otherwise it would not be a unit since it has parts). But anything which is indivisible may not have size, and having no size (= no magnitude or thickness or mass) cannot exist at all. On the other hand, things must be infinitely big since each thing will have a certain size and hence parts, and those parts also parts, *ad infinitum*. If we add an infinite number of parts together, we naturally get something infinite in size.

Interpretation A. Suppose the difficulty is how something can be a unit and still have parts, that is, how something can be both one and many. One way around this difficulty is to consider something whose parts are not of like character with the whole. Thus a molecule of water is the unit of water. Yet it has parts but they are not water but the gases hydrogen and oxygen. Hence a molecule of water is both one (unit of water) and many (parts of hydrogen and oxygen).[6]

Interpretation B. Suppose the difficulty consists in the necessity of getting an infinite-sized object from the addition of an infinite number of finite-sized objects. But this is not necessary as we have already seen in Interpretation A of the Dichotomy.

SECOND ARGUMENT. If there are a plurality of things then there are exactly as many as there are—neither more nor less. But then there will be a finite number of them. There will also be an infinite number since between any two things there must be another thing. And so the plurality of things is both finite and infinite.

Interpretation A. Suppose the difficulty consists in the question of whether or not infinite sets exist. Then we may get around Zeno's argument by pointing out some clear examples of infinite sets, as for instance the set of all positive integers. By Cantor's set theory we know there are different sizes of infinite sets which can be compared. Hence it doesn't follow that if in a plurality of things there are exactly as many things as there are then there must be a finite number of them.

Interpretation B. Suppose the difficulty is in the assumption that between any two existing things there must be another existing thing. Interpreting Zeno to be talking about the continuum, we may agree with the conclusion and deny that there is anything paradoxical about it. After all, between any two real numbers there is another real number but this fact, although perhaps an occasion for wonder, is not paradoxical.

Paradox of Place

This paradox concerns the following problem: If everything that exists, exists in a place, then the place itself has to have a place and so on *ad infinitum*.

Interpretation A. Suppose the difficulty concerns the infinite regress. We may then deny that a place has to be in another place. Instead we could allow a place to be in itself.

Interpretation B. Suppose the difficulty concerns the assumption that everything that exists, exists in a place. We can easily deny it. For example, numbers exist without existing in a place.

Paradox of Sound: The Millet Seed

Since a single millet seed makes no sound when it is falling, the bushel of millet makes no sound when it falls; or contrarywise, since the bushel of millet makes a sound when it falls, so does the single millet seed.

Interpretation A. Suppose the difficulty consists in the question of why we do not hear the sound of a single falling millet seed. We may easily escape the paradoxical consequences by asserting that sound has a threshold and the "sound" of a single falling millet seed is below that threshold.

Interpretation B. Suppose the difficulty of the paradox depends on the fallacy of composition. Perhaps our hearing has no threshold and the individual millets make no sound. It does not follow that all of them together would make no sound. Conversely, if a bushel of millet makes a sound when falling, it doesn't follow that the individual grains do (fallacy of division).

Such then is our summary of the paradoxes. The purpose of giving each several interpretations is not to show how easy it is to resolve the paradoxes. On the contrary, the purpose is to indicate that any adequate treatment of them must recognize the vagueness and ambiguity of the problems involved. The "interpretations" were meant to serve as some indication of this ambiguity and the various arguments that may be given to get around the paradoxes as so interpreted. Furthermore, even given a fairly definite interpretation, the resolutions are not as easy as the above discussion might seem to indicate. For example, the question of whether it is possible to do an infinite number of things in a finite time is still much debated. Even an adequate treatment of the most trivial of Zeno's paradoxes—the millet seed—would require a background in the philosophies of Leibniz and Berkeley as well as some knowledge of modern psychology and physics.

Zeno's Skepticism and His Contemporary Value

But is it right to give these paradoxes interpretations which Zeno may not have intended? We can get some kind of insight into this question by considering an analogous problem in artistic interpretation.

One of the greatest sculptures of ancient Greece that has come down to us is the Winged Victory of Samothrace. This judgment is nearly universal in spite of the fact that the ravages of time have been severe—the head is missing, so are the arms, much of the remaining marble is chipped, and all the paint is gone. Yet, if we reflect, it may be that the ravages of time have added immeasurably to the artistic value we find there. It is hard to imagine that, if the head and arms were restored, the color brought back, and in general the statue returned to its original finished condition, it would be an artistic improvement. It may be that in this case the ravages of time have brought about a result that for us is artistically superior to what the artist originally produced. The sculptor, so to say, had a helper in the accidents of history, and this helper greatly improved the original product.

The case of Zeno may be analogous. Of course, for purposes of historical reconstruction we would want all the evidence we could get about the man, his works, and his cultural environment. However, if Zeno's main purpose was to produce philosophical *aporia,* then the fragmentary and cryptic texts, the obscure references to him by writers familiar with him or his writings, the uncertainties concerning what problems the several paradoxes were meant to illustrate, or at whom they might be aimed—all these things may have turned out to serve his purposes better than would have been the case if his full writings had survived intact.

In particular, it *may* be that Zeno's paradoxes as originally stated were merely philosophical puzzles, that is, intellectual difficulties whose subject matter is such that they deserve the adjective "philosophical" and yet are also of such a character that once their solution is found, all interest in them ceases. It is in this way that Gilbert Ryle understands Zeno's work; indeed he believes the Achilles paradox "deserves to rank as the paradigm of a philosophical puzzle." He suggests that "Zeno's argument seems to prove one thing, namely that the chase cannot end, but really proves, perfectly validly, a different and undisturbing conclusion. . . ."[7]

If it is true that Zeno's intention was to produce philosophical puzzles, then it is also true (despite Ryle) that the accidents of history have been such that the evidence remaining allows us to understand him as intending to produce philosophical problems. Unlike philosophical problems (such as the mind-body problem or the problem of free will), philosophical puzzles can be dealt with "in virtual ignorance of the content of science and in virtual innocence of the depths of artistic, moral and religious experience."[8] Furthermore, they do not call for philosophical synthesis, and it is perfectly possible for them to be adequately dealt with within the context of the concepts and distinctions from ordinary life.

Although it may be that producing philosophical puzzles was Zeno's intention, there is nothing we know about him or his paradoxes which makes this view more plausible than that which has him intending to produce philosophical problems. In any case, however, the end result of Zeno's labors plus the ravages of time is a set of philosophical *problems*. And it is consistent with everything we know to consider his principal purpose to be the production of philosophical *aporia*.

Hence, the true heirs of Zeno are not the scholars and historians who try diligently on completely inadequate evidence to reconstruct exactly what the historical Zeno really meant. Rather they are those who, in many times and places, have taken the bare framework of the paradoxes as they have come down to us and then exploited their rich ambiguity to show that there is an interpretation of them such that, for the *Weltanschauung* of that time and place, philosophical problems inhere in Zeno's paradoxes, after all the philosophical puzzles have been solved.

Professor Adolf Grünbaum's difficult text, *Modern Science and Zeno's Paradoxes*, states in its introduction that this "book deals with those versions of Zeno's paradoxes of motion and of extension which may be thought to pose intellectual difficulties for modern mathematical physics. The comprehensive philosophical and scientific treatment of the paradoxes which I am aiming to provide here disregards altogether the question of their historical authenticity and of Zeno's own intentions in propounding them."[9] Ironically, it may be that Grünbaum is a true heir of Zeno just because he disregards the question of historical authenticity. In any case, their value for us comes mainly by ignoring questions of history and seeing if the paradoxes cannot be the skeleton on which we embody (by some interpretation or other) the flesh of a profound contemporary philosophical problem. Hence the student of Zeno should read him to discover new problems and *not* merely try to find an interpretation for which we have an already formulated answer.

Influence

The correct determination of the influence of Zeno is almost as difficult—and certainly almost as controversial—as the correct treatment of his paradoxes. The evidence is fragmentary and a case could be made that his influence is almost nil. The contrary case—namely, that his influence has been enormous—appears more plausible. We will explore some of the rationale behind this view by considering the subject of Zeno's influence under three headings: logic, mathematics, and philosophy.

Logic

Zeno may have had a decisive influence in the creation of logic by Aristotle. Ancient Athens of Aristotle's time provided a bewildering variety of viewpoints, many of them derived from the Pre-Socratic philosophers. In order to analyze and/or refute these viewpoints Aristotle devised a set of principles which he could use to divide good from bad arguments. Since Aristotle thought of some of Zeno's arguments as being especially difficult, it may be they were influential in providing the motivation to state logical principles. For example, Aristotle states that the most certain of all principles is that "the same attribute cannot at the same time belong and not belong to the same subject and in the same respect" (*Metaphysica,* 1000b 18ff.). He uses this principle in his refutation of the Achilles paradox when he argues that in one sense—that is, potentially—infinity belongs to a line and in another—that is, actually—it does not.

It is even more probable that Zeno influenced Aristotle's formulation of the *reductio ad absurdum* argument. A *reductio ad absurdum* argument is one where a false or self-contradictory conclusion is derived from a premise. The premise is thereby shown to be false. It is possible that the first self-conscious use of this type of argument was in Pythagorean mathematics where it was used to show the incommensurability of a side of a square and its diagonal. Zeno may have adapted it to philosophy—at any rate, we know of no one who used it in philosophy earlier than he.

Zeno probably had even greater influence in the development of the other main ancient logical school, namely, Stoic logic. For Zeno almost certainly inspired some of the work of the Megarians who were a decisive influence in Stoic logic. The Megarians were very much interested in paradoxes (such as the Liar paradox), and it was the Stoic logicians who first formulated *modus tollens,* a form of argument closely related to the *reductio ad absurdum.*

In short, Zeno may have had a crucial influence on the development of logic by providing abundant evidence that we mis-argue, and by providing examples of a very powerful logical tool—the *reductio ad absurdum* argument.

Mathematics

In mathematics we have no direct evidence that Zeno was influential, but the indirect evidence is substantial, or rather, the postulation of Zeno's influence helps explain a number of otherwise very puzzling facts. The puzzling facts have to do with the nature of Greek mathematics, specifically Euclid's *Elements.* Euclid does not explain his purpose, but there is evidence to suggest that his purpose was to base both arithmetic and cosmology on geometry. Euclid's book starts out with twenty-three definitions of his key terms, five postulates concerning specifically geometric assumptions, and five common notions concerning more general assumptions. From these he derives a large number of theorems.

One of the questions which we can ask about this most famous example of the axiomatic method is what governed the choice of axioms, that is, the postulates and common notions. No doubt there were several factors, but one possibility is generally overlooked, namely, there is no necessity to have as an axiom something which no one questions—that is, that which "goes without saying." Hence, since no one in ancient Greece thought to question that a line has two sides or that closed figures have insides and outsides, such assumptions didn't have to be stated (until the nineteenth century when these questions arose). Furthermore, by Aristotle's account (and one which we today accept) axioms cannot be proved on the pain of circularity or infinite regress, that is, any proof of an axiom would require additional axioms, and proofs of these axioms further axioms, etc., until we get circular reasoning or an infinite regress. Thus, Euclid's axioms for the most part consisted of propositions which were considered true by the vast majority but had been questioned by a few.

If so, Zeno and Euclid are closely connected. For if Zeno's arguments against Parmenidean critics were correct, most of Euclid's axioms would be doubtful. For example, Euclid's first three postulates are as follows:

1. To draw a straight line from any point to any point.
2. To produce a finite straight line continuously in a straight line.
3. To describe a circle with any center and distance.

All three are questionable if Zeno's arguments against motion are valid. In fact, Euclid's conceptual system very much depends on *moving* mathematical objects. Thus Euclid's fourth common notion states:

4. Things which coincide with one another are equal to one another.

As Euclid's use of this common notion makes clear, he meant that, for example, one triangle could be moved and placed on another. Or again, Zeno's Stadium paradox concludes that the time is equal to its double, something which is inconsistent with Euclid's fifth common notion: The whole is greater than the part. Further, the theory of proportion elaborated in the *Elements* also seems aimed at avoiding some of Zeno's errors.[10]

Hence we may conclude that it is probable that Euclid's motivation in both the choice of axioms and his methods was partly to be rid of pests like Zeno who maintained absurdities which couldn't be refuted. Of course, there is no direct evidence that Zeno and Euclid are thus connected, but in the absence of such a connection it becomes much more difficult to explain Euclid's motivation as well as the remarkable way in which his axioms and methods can be easily understood as countering Zeno.

Since Euclid's time a great deal of time and effort has gone into solving certain mathematical problems which are connected with Zeno's paradoxes: the problems of continuity, the infinite, the infinitesimal, the limit of a sequence. The men who made mathematical progress in these areas—Cauchy, Dedekind, Weierstrass, Cantor—all were no doubt aware of Zeno's arguments. Nevertheless the degree to which Zeno was directly or indirectly influential in their work is hard to assess—it may have been insignificant. Yet it is hard to believe that they were not at least trying to counter Zeno-type arguments in their work.[11]

Philosophy

In philosophy, Zeno's skeptical use of dialectic probably had a decisive influence on both Gorgias and Socrates. For example, Gorgias maintained that if a thing is, it must be either one or many. Either possibility Gorgias thought could be reduced to an absurdity. This argument is very Zeno-like, as are several others by Gorgias. As for Socrates, he often uses the method of starting from an interlocutor's assumptions and showing by a series of questions and answers that absurd consequences follow. This method, called dialectic, was invented by Zeno (according to Aristotle). Of course, Socrates, unlike Zeno, possessed some positive doctrine, but the critical method of examining widely held opinions and showing difficulties was shared by both. In fact, it is probable that Zeno's dialectic was the inspiration for the Socratic belief in the philosophic power of negative thinking. The fact that Plato has a young Socrates meeting Zeno lends some weight to this conjecture. Of course, Socrates went beyond Zeno in using dialectic as a method of self-criticism.

Beyond Plato, Zeno's influence is remarkable. The number and quality of thinkers who would have to be discussed in any adequate history of Zeno's influence is impressive. And they are far from all being mathematicians or logicians. Here is a partial list: Democritus, Archimedes, St. Augustine, Roger Bacon, Galileo, Descartes, Hobbes, Pierre Bayle, Leibniz, Newton, Berkeley, Hume, Kant, Hegel, John Stuart Mill, Engels, Tolstoi, William James, C. S. Pierce, Josiah Royce, C. D. Broad, Whitehead, Bergson, Bertrand Russell, Sartre. (Of course, there are many, many lesser names.)

It is far from the case that most of these men thought highly of Zeno.

Nevertheless, Zeno's admirers are sometimes extravagant in their views, and they are not all in the same philosophical camp. For example, Hegel states that Zeno's "dialectic of matter" had never been refuted and that his paradoxes were as important as Kant's antinomies (which is high praise for Hegel). Now consider Bertrand Russell's comments: "In this capricious world, nothing is more capricious than posthumous fame. One of the most notable examples of posterity's lack of judgment is the Eleatic Zeno. This man . . . invented four arguments, all immeasurably subtle and profound, to prove that motion is impossible. . . . Zeno was concerned . . . with the problems of the infinitesimal, the infinite, and continuity. To state clearly the difficulties involved was to accomplish perhaps the hardest part of the philosopher's task. This was done by Zeno. From him to our own day, the finest intellects of each generation in turn attacked the problems, but achieved, broadly speaking, nothing."[12]

Zeno's paradoxes may be appreciated from still another point of view. For when read by a person of poetic sensibilities the predominant effect may be the production of an uncanny feeling—a kind of simultaneous horror and fascination with the infinite and in general with the fragility of our knowledge. Freud once made a study of the uncanny and suggested (without mentioning Zeno) that the writer who produces an uncanny feeling "pretends to move in the world of common reality" but then "takes advantage, as it were, of our supposedly surmounted superstitiousness; he deceives us into thinking that he is giving us the sober truth, and then after all oversteps the bounds of possibility. We react to his inventions as we should have reacted to real experiences; by the time we have seen through his trick it is already too late and the author has achieved his object; but it must be added that his success is not unalloyed. We retain a feeling of dissatisfaction, a kind of grudge against the attempted deceit. . . ."[13] This kind of grudge reaction to Zeno is common, both now and in antiquity. But it should be added that in the case of uncanny effects with respect to philosophical issues the effect may be reversed and we hold the "grudge" not against the writer, but against the so-called common reality. It is thus that the great Argentine writer Jorge Luis Borges reacts to Zeno. Consider his haunting words: "Art—always—requires visible unrealities. Let it suffice for me to mention one: the metaphorical or numerous or carefully accidental diction of the interlocutors in a drama . . . Let us admit what all idealists admit: the hallucinatory nature of the world. Let us do what no idealist has done: seek unrealities which confirm that nature. We shall find them, I believe, in the antinomies of Kant and in the dialectic of Zeno.''[14] For the poetic mind, then, the road from Zeno to Plato's dialogues is a short one. In Zeno, we not only have a person committed to following an argument wheresoever it leads, we have a philosopher who disturbs our firm belief in "common reality," and who thereby helps create that sense of wonder which both Plato and Aristotle saw as the true origin of philosophy.

ZENO

Zeno of Elea flourished around 450 B.C. He was supposedly the student and favorite of Parmenides. His method of arguing against such positions as the belief in motion and plurality was to show that absurd consequences follow from such beliefs. It is often held that such argument was meant as an attack on those detractors of Parmenides who supposedly pointed out absurd consequences of the master's view. Zeno as much as said, "Look what absurd consequences follow from the *denial* of Parmenides' thesis." But this, as the companion essay in this chapter by Howard DeLong shows, is a complex issue.

TESTIMONIA ON ZENO BY PLATO

. . . He told us that Pythodorus had described to him the appearance of Parmenides and Zeno; they came to Athens, he said, at the great Panathenaea; the former was, at the time of his visit, about sixty-five years old, very white with age, but well favored. Zeno was nearly forty years of age, of a noble figure and fair aspect; and in the days of his youth he was reported to have been beloved of Parmenides. He said that they lodged with Pythodorus in the Ceramicus, outside the wall, whither Socrates and others came to see them; they wanted to hear some writings of Zeno, which had been brought to Athens by them for the first time. He said that Socrates was then very young, and that Zeno read them to him in the absence of Parmenides, and had nearly finished when Pythodorus entered, and with him Parmenides and Aristoteles who was afterward one of the Thirty; there was not much more to hear, and Pythodorus had heard Zeno repeat them before.

When the recitation was completed, Socrates requested that the first hypothesis of the first discourse might be read over again, and this having been done, he said: What do you mean, Zeno? Is your argument that the existence of many necessarily involves like and unlike, and that this is impossible, for neither can the like be unlike, nor the unlike like; is that your position? Just that, said Zeno. And if the unlike cannot be like, or the like unlike, then neither can the many exist, for that would involve an impossibility. Is the design of your argument throughout to disprove the existence of the many? and is each of your treatises intended to furnish a separate proof of this, there being as many proofs in all as you have composed arguments, of the non-existence of the many? Is that your meaning, or have I misunderstood you?

No, said Zeno; you have quite understood the general drift of the treatise.

I see, Parmenides, said Socrates, that Zeno is your second self in his writings too; he puts what you say in another way, and half deceives us into believing that he is saying what is new. For you, in your compositions, say that the all is one, and of this you adduce excellent proofs; and he, on the other hand, says that the many is naught, and gives many great and convincing evidences of this. To deceive the world, as you have done, by saying the same thing in different ways, one of you affirming the one and the other denying the many, is a strain of art beyond the reach of most of us.

Yes, Socrates, said Zeno. But although you are as keen as a Spartan hound in pursuing the track, you do not quite apprehend the true motive of the performance, which is not really such an artificial piece of work as you imagine; there was no intention of concealment effecting any grand result—that was a mere accident. For the truth is, that these writings of mine were meant to protect the arguments of Parmenides against those who ridicule him, and urge the many ridiculous and contradictory results which were supposed to follow from the assertion of the one. My answer is addressed to the partisans of the many, and intended to show that greater or more ridiculous consequences follow from their hypothesis of the existence of the many if carried out, than from the hypothesis of the existence of the one. A love of controversy led me to write the book in the days of my youth, and some one stole the writings, and I had therefore no choice about the publication of them; the motive, however, of writing, was not the ambition of an old man, but the pugnacity of a young one. This you do not seem to see, Socrates; though in other respects, as I was saying, your notion is a very just one.

That I understand, said Socrates, and quite accept your account. But tell me, Zeno, do you not further think that there is an idea of likeness in the abstract, and another idea of unlikeness, which is the opposite of likeness, and that in these two, you and I and all other things to which we apply the term many, participate; and that the things which participate in likeness are in that degree and manner like; and that those which participate in unlikeness are in that degree unlike, or both like and unlike in the degree in which they participate in both? And all things may partake of both opposites, and be like and unlike to themselves, by reason of this participation. Even in that there is nothing wonderful. But if a person could prove the absolute like to become unlike, or the absolute unlike to become like, that, in my opinion, would be a real wonder; not, however, if the things which partake of the ideas experience likeness and unlikeness—there is nothing extraordinary in this. Nor, again, if a person were to show that all is one by partaking of one, and that the same is many by partaking of many, would that be very wonderful? But if he were to show me that the absolute many was one, or the absolute one many, I should be truly amazed. And I should say the same of other things. I should be surprised to hear that the genera and species had opposite qualities in themselves; but if a person wanted to prove of me that I was many and also one, there would be no marvel in that. When he wanted to show that I was many he would say that I have a right and a left side, and a front and a back, and an upper and a lower half, for I cannot deny that I partake of multitude; when, on the other hand, he wants to prove that I am one, he will say, that we who are here assembled are seven, and that I am one and partake of the one, and in saying both he speaks truly. Of if a person shows that the same wood and stones and the like, being many are also one, we admit that he shows the existence of the one and many, but he does not show that the many are one or the one many; he is uttering not a wonder but a truism. If, however, as I was suggesting just now, we were to make an abstraction, I mean of like, unlike, one, many, rest, motion, and similar ideas, and then to show that these in their abstract form admit of admixture and separation, I should greatly wonder at that. This part of the argument appears to be treated by you, Zeno, in a very spirited manner; nevertheless, as I was saying, I should be far more amazed if any one found in the ideas themselves which are conceptions, the same puzzle and entanglement which you have shown to exist in visible objects.

While Socrates was saying this, Pythodorus thought that Parmenides and Zeno were not altogether pleased at the successive steps of the argument; but still they gave the closest attention, and often looked at one another, and smiled as if in admiration of him. When he had finished, Parmenides expressed these feelings in the following words:— . . . (*Parmenides,* 127-130)

SOCRATES: Do you tell me, instead, what are plaintiff and defendant doing in a law-court—are they not contending?

PHAEDRUS: Exactly.

Soc. About the just and unjust—that is the matter in dispute?

Phaedr. Yes.

Soc. And a professor of the art will make the same thing appear to the same persons to be at one time just and at another time unjust, if he has a mind?

Phaedr. Exactly.

Soc. And when he speaks in the assembly, he will make the same things seem good to the city at one time, and at another time the reverse of good?

Phaedr. That is true.

Soc. Have we not heard of the Eleatic Palamedes (Zeno), who has an art of speaking which makes the same things appear to his hearers like and unlike, one and many, at rest and in motion too?

Phaedr. Very true.

Soc. The art of disputation, then, is not confined to the courts and the assembly, but is one and the same in every use of language; this is that art, if such an art there be, which finds a likeness of everything to which a likeness can be found, and draws into the light of day the likenesses and disguises which are used by others? . . . (*Phaedrus,* 261)

TESTIMONIA ON ZENO BY ARISTOTLE AND SIMPLICIUS*

The Four Arguments on Motion

I. The Dichotomy

There are four arguments of Zeno about motion which give trouble to those who try to solve the problems they involve. The first says that motion is impossible, because an object in motion must reach the half-way point before it gets to the end. This we have discussed above. sc. *Phys. Z.* 2. 233 *a* 21. Hence Zeno's argument makes a false assumption when it asserts that it is impossible to traverse an infinite number of positions or to make an infinite number of contacts one by one in a finite time. For there are two senses in which length and time and, generally, any continuum are called infinite, namely either in respect of divisibility or of extension. So while it is impossible to make an infinite number of contacts in a finite time where the infinite is a quantitative infinite, yet it is possible where the infinite is an infinite in respect of division; for the time itself is also infinite in this respect. And so we find that it is possible to traverse an infinite number of positions in a time in this sense infinite, not finite; and to make an infinite number of contacts because its moments are in this sense infinite, not finite. (*Physica* 239*b* 14; Diels, A. 25).

The first argument is the following: If there is motion, then a moving object must in a finite time complete an infinite number of positions, but since this is impossible there is no motion. He proves his hypothesis thus: An object in motion must move through a certain distance; but since every distance is infinitely divisible the moving object must first traverse half the distance through which it is moving, and then the whole distance; but before it traverses the whole of the half distance, it must traverse half of the half, and again half of this half. If then these halves are infinite in number, because it is always possible to halve any given length, and if it is impossible to traverse an infinite number of positions in a finite time—this Zeno assumed as self-evident; and Aristotle has previously referred to his argument when he speaks of it being impossible to traverse an infinite number of positions or to make

* From H. D. P. Lee, *Zeno of Elea*.

an infinite number of contacts in a finite time—anyhow, to resume, every magnitude has an infinite number of subdivisions, and therefore it is impossible to traverse any magnitude in a finite time. (Simplicius, 1013.4, *ad* 239*b* 10)

Zeno's argument is the following: If there is motion, it is possible in a finite time to traverse an infinite number of positions, making an infinite number of contacts one by one; but this is impossible, and therefore there is no motion. His hypothesis he proved by means of the infinite divisibility of magnitude. For if every magnitude is infinitely divisible, it will be made up of an infinite number of parts, and so a body, moving through and traversing a distance of given magnitude, will move through and complete an infinite number of positions and make an infinite number of contacts in a finite time, that is, in the time it takes to move through the whole finite distance. He says "to make an infinite number of contacts one by one", because it might seem that a body traversed an infinite number of positions by passing *over* them without making *contact* with each. In this way he proves the hypothesis. The minor premiss, which says "but it is impossible (1) to traverse an infinite number of positions or (2) to make an infinite number of contacts in a finite time", he proves (1) from the interminability of the infinite and (2) from the impossibility of making an infinite number of contacts in a finite time, if the moving object makes contact with the successive parts of the distance in question at successive moments of time; for he said that it is impossible to make contact with each member of an infinite collection because the person making the contacts is as it were counting, and it is impossible to count infinite collections. (Simplicius, 947.5, *ad* 233 *a* 21)

The same method should be adopted in replying to those who put Zeno's puzzle, and claim that in traversing any distance we must first traverse the half of it, that these subdivisions are infinite, and that it is impossible to complete an infinite number of distances: or, as some, who put the puzzle in a different form, claim, that in the course of its motion the moving body must, as it reaches each half-way point, count the half of this half, so that when it has moved through the whole distance it has counted an infinite number—which is admittedly impossible. (Aristotle, *Physica*, 263a 5)

The argument of Zeno, to which he now refers, was as follows: If there is motion there will be something which has traversed an infinite number of positions in a finite time; for, since the process of dichotomy can continue infinitely, in every continuum there will be an infinite number of halves owing to every part of it having a half. A body therefore which has moved over a finite distance will have traversed an infinite number of halves in a finite time, that is, in the time which it took to traverse the finite distance in question. He then goes on to assume the opposite of the consequence that follows from his hypothesis, i.e. he assumes that it is impossible to get to the end of an infinite number of positions in a finite time, because it is impossible absolutely to exhaust any infinite collection, and so does away with the reality of motion. So Zeno argued: but some, Aristotle says, put the puzzle in a different way, as follows: 'If there is motion, since there is an infinite number of halves in any continuum, a body moving through a continuum should be able to count each of these halves as it comes to it. But if this is so, then when the moving body has traversed the finite magnitude in question, the counter will have counted an infinite number of halves. If therefore it is impossible to count an infinite number, then any premiss from which this follows as conclusion must be impossible; but the premiss from which it followed was the supposition that motion is real.' (Simplicius, 1289.5, *ad* 263*a* 5)

II. The Achilles

The second is the so-called Achilles. This is that the slower runner will never be overtaken by the swiftest, since the pursuer must first reach the point from which the pursued started, and so the slower must always be ahead. This argument is essentially the same as that depending on dichotomy, but differs in that the successively given lengths are not divided into halves. The conclusion of the argument is that the slowest runner is not overtaken, but it proceeds on the same lines as the dichotomy argument (for in both, by dividing the distance in a given way, we conclude that the goal is not reached: only in the Achilles a dramatic effect is produced by saying that not even the swiftest will be successful in its pursuit of the slowest) and so the solution of it must be the same. (Aristotle, *Physica,* 239*b* 14; Diels, A 26.)

This argument also bases its attempted proof on infinite divisibility but is arranged differently. It runs as follows: If there is movement the slowest will never be overtaken by the swiftest: but this is impossible: therefore there is no motion. . . . (1014.9) The argument is called the Achilles because of the introduction into it of Achilles, who, the argument says, cannot possibly overtake the tortoise he is pursuing. For the overtaker must, before he overtakes the pursued, first come to the point from which the pursued started. But during the time taken by the pursuer to reach this point, the pursued advances a certain distance; even if this distance is less than that covered by the pursuer, because the pursued is the slower of the two, yet none the less it does advance, for it is not at rest. And again during the time which the pursuer takes to cover this distance which the pursued has advanced, the pursued again covers a certain distance which is proportionately smaller than the last, according as its speed is slower than that of the pursuer. And so, during every period of time in which the pursuer is covering the distance which the pursued moving at its lower relative speed has already advanced, the pursued advances a yet further distance; for even though this distance decreases at each step, yet, since the pursued is also definitely in motion, it does advance some positive distance. And so by taking distances decreasing in a given proportion *ad infinitum* because of the infinite divisibility of magnitudes, we arrive at the conclusion that not only will Hector never be overtaken by Achilles, but not even the tortoise. (Simplicius, 1013.31, *ad loc.*)

III. The Arrow

The third is that just given above, that the flying arrow is at rest. This conclusion follows from the assumption that time is composed of instants; for if this is not granted the conclusion cannot be inferred. (Aristotle, *Physica,* 239*b* 30)

Zeno's argument is fallacious. For if, he says, everything is either at rest or in motion, but nothing is in motion when it occupies a space equal to itself, and what is in flight is always at any given instant occupying a space equal to itself, then the flying arrow is motionless. But this is false, for time is not composed of indivisible instants any more than any other magnitude is composed of indivisibles. (Aristotle, *Physica*, 239*b* 5)

The flying missile is at rest during its flight, if everything must either be in motion or at rest, but an object in flight always occupies a space equal to itself. But what always occupies a space equal to itself is not in motion, it is therefore at rest. (Simplicius, 1015.19, *ad* 239*b* 30)

Zeno's argument after making the preliminary assumptions that everything when it occupies a space equal to itself is either in motion or at rest, that nothing is in motion in the instant, and that an object in flight occupies at each instant a space equal to itself, seems to infer as follows: The flying missile occupies a space equal to itself at each instant, and so during the whole time of its flight: what occupies a space equal to itself at an instant is not in motion, since nothing is in motion at an instant: but what is not in motion is at rest, since everything is either in motion or at rest: therefore the flying missile, while it is in flight, is at rest during the whole time of its flight. (Simplicius, 1011.19, *ad* 239*b* 5)

IV. The Stadium

The fourth is the one about the two rows of equal bodies which move past each other in a stadium with equal velocities in opposite directions, the one row originally stretching from the goal <to the middle-point> of the stadium, the other from the middle-point <to the starting post>. This, he thinks, involves the conclusion that half a given time is equal to its double <i.e. the whole time>. The fallacy lies in assuming that a body takes an equal time to pass with equal velocity a body that is in motion and a body of equal size at rest, an assumption which is false. For example, let *AA* be the stationary bodies of equal size, let *BB* be the bodies, equal in number and size to the *A*s, stretching from the middle-point <of the stadium to the starting post>, and *CC* those stretching from the goal <to the middlepoint>, being equal in number and size to the *A*s, and moving with a velocity equal to that of the *B*s. Then it follows that, as *B*s and Cs move past each other, the first B reaches the last C at the same time as the first C reaches the last B. And it follows that the first C has passed all the Bs, the first B half that number of bodies <viz. two As>: and so the first B has taken only half the time <that the first C has taken>, since each takes an equal time in passing each body. And it follows that at the same moment the first B has passed all the Cs: for the first C and the first B will arrive simultaneously at the opposite end As, since both take an equal time passing the As. This then is his argument, and it rests on the above-mentioned fallacy. (Aristotle, *Physica*, 239b 33)

Place

Further if <place> is itself an existent, where will it be? For Zeno's difficulty demands some explanation: for if everything that exists has a place, it is clear that place too will have a place and so on *ad infinitum*. (Aristotle, *Physica*, 209a 23; Diels, A 24)

Plurality

In his book, in which many arguments are put forward, he shows in each that a man who says that there is a plurality is stating something self-contradictory. One of these arguments is that in which he shows that, if there is a plurality, things are both large and small, so large as to be infinite in magnitude, so small as to have no magnitude at all. And in this argument he shows that what has neither magnitude nor thickness nor mass does not exist at all. For, he argues, if it were added to something else, it would not increase its size; for a null magnitude is incapable, when added, of yielding an increase in magnitude. And thus it follows that what was added was nothing. But if, when it is subtracted from another thing, that thing is no less; and again, if, when it is added to another thing, that thing does not increase, it is evident that both what was added and what was subtracted were nothing. (Simplicius, 139.5; Diels, fr. 2)

The infinity of magnitude he showed previously by the same process of reasoning. For, having first shown that "if what is had not magnitude, it would not exist at all", he proceeds: "But, if it is, then each one must necessarily have some magnitude and thickness and must be at a certain distance from another. And the same reasoning holds good of the one beyond: for it also will have magnitude and there will be a successor to it. It is the same to say this once and to say it always: for no such part will be the last nor out of relation to another. So, if there is a plurality, they must be both small and large. So small as to have no magnitude, so large as to be infinite." (Simplicius, 140.34; Diels, fr.1)

There is no need to labour the point; for such an argument is to be found in Zeno's own book. For in his proof that, if there is plurality, the same things are both finite and infinite, Zeno writes the following words: "If things are a plurality, they must be just as many as they are, and neither more nor less. But, if they are as many as they are, they will be finite in number. If things are a plurality, they will be infinite in number. For there will always be others between any of them, and again between these yet others. And so things are infinite in number." Thus he demonstrates numerical infinity by means of the argument from dichotomy. (Simplicius, 140.27; Diels, fr. 3)

THE MILLET SEED

By this means he solves the conundrum which Zeno the Eleatic asked Protagoras the sophist. "Tell me, Protagoras," he said, "does a single grain of millet or the ten thousandth part of a grain make any sound when it falls?" And when Protogoras said it did not, "Then", asked Zeno, "does a bushel of millet make any sound when it falls or not?" Protagoras answered that it did, whereupon Zeno replied, "But surely there is some ratio between a bushel of millet and a single grain or even the ten thousandth part of a grain"; and when this was admitted, "But then surely", Zeno said, "the ratios of the corresponding sounds to each other will be the same: for as the bodies which make the sounds are to one another, so will the sounds be to one another. And if this is so, and if the bushel of millet makes a sound, then the single grain of millet and the ten thousandth part of a grain will make a sound." This was the way Zeno used to put his questions. (Simplicius, 1108.18, *ad loc.*)

Notes: VI

1. In Western culture Zeno had no real rivals as a composer of paradoxes, but perhaps Hui Shih represents a parallel in Chinese culture. For example, he stated that "if a stick one foot long is cut in half every day, it will still have something left after ten thousand generations." This is closely related to one of Zeno's paradoxes. The reader who is interested in exploring this and other parallels in Chinese and Indian culture should consult Joseph Needham, *Science and Civilization in China* (Cambridge, England, Cambridge University Press, 1954, 1959), Vols. II, III.

2. W. V. O. Quine, "J. L. Austin, Comment," *Journal of Philosophy,* 62 (1965), p. 509.

3. Plutarch, *The Lives of the Noble Grecians and Romans,* trans. by John Dryden and rev. by Arthur Hugh Clough (New York, Modern Library, no date), p. 185. Notice that Plutarch, like Plato before him, does not merely identify the positions of Parmenides and Zeno but suggests further a strong skeptical aspect to Zeno's thought.

4. For more on this point, *see* R. G. Collingwood, *The Idea of Nature* (New York, Oxford University Press, 1945) pp. 17 ff.

5. My statement of the first and second arguments against plurality has been influenced by Professor Vlastos' fine article on Zeno in *The Encyclopedia of Philosophy,* Paul Edwards, ed. (New York, Macmillan, 1967). Nevertheless, the overall interpretation of Zeno's paradoxes is quite different from his.

6. For more on this point, *see* Collingwood, *loc. cit.*

7. Gilbert Ryle, *Dilemmas* (Cambridge, England, Cambridge University Press, 1964), p. 37.

8. Abraham Kaplan, review of *Dilemmas, Philosophical Review,* 64 (1955), pp. 644-46. My comments here and in the next two paragraphs have been influenced by Kaplan.

9. Adolph Grünbaum, *Modern Science and Zeno's Paradoxes* (Middletown, Conn., Wesleyan University Press, 1967), p. 4.

10. For more discussion on these topics, *see* Howard DeLong, *A Profile of Mathematical Logic* (Reading, Mass., Addison-Wesley Publishing Co., 1970); Karl R. Popper, *Conjectures and Refutations: The Growth of Scientific Knowledge* (London, Routledge and Kegan Paul,

1963); Arpód Szabó, "Greek Dialectic and Euclid's Axiomatics," in Imre Lakatos, ed., *Problems in the Philosophy of Mathematics: Proceedings of the International Colloquium in the Philosophy of Science* (London, 1965; Amsterdam, North-Holland, 1967) Vol. 1; Imre Tóth, "Non-Euclidean Geometry Before Euclid," *Scientific American*, 221, No. 5 (November, 1969), pp. 87-98.

11. This introduction to Zeno has taken the orthodox view that the work of these men is beyond reasonable doubt. As is well known, a small group of logicians and mathematicians—the so-called finitists and intuitionists—reject part of the work of these men. For an example, an article which rejects the analysis of "Dedekind, Cantor or Weierstrass" via a consideration of Zeno's paradoxes, *see* Sadeo Shiraishi, "The Structure of the Continuity of Psychological Experiences and the Physical World," *The Science of Thought* (Tokyo), 1 (1954), pp. 12-24.

12. Bertrand Russell, *Mysticism and Logic* (Garden City, N. Y., Doubleday Anchor Books, 1957), pp. 76-77.

13. Sigmund Freud, "The 'Uncanny,' " in Sigmund Freud, *Studies in Parapsychology*, Philip Rieff, ed. (New York, Collier Books, 1963), pp. 57-58.

14. Jorge Luis Borges, *Labyrinths*, D. A. Yates and J. E. Inby, eds. (New York, New Directions, 1964), pp. 207-8.

Responses to the Battle of the Giants: I

AFTER the *gigantomachia*, the battle of the giants, between Parmenides and Heraclitus, it is not surprising that successive philosophers, especially Empedocles, Anaxagoras, and the atomists Leucippus and Democritus, would to a certain extent think in response to the issues left by these two great thinkers. That at least is the almost universal consensus of interpreters of these later philosophers.

Empedocles was evidently convinced by Parmenides and his Eleatic followers that Being could not change, and especially that Being could not participate in the processes of coming to be and passing away. At the same time, he evidently appreciated the difficulty discussed earlier as to how a conception of Being as permanent and changeless could be made intelligible as the *arche*, the origin of the phenomenal world of change and multiplicity. But to note and respond to this difficulty is already to differ in an important way from Parmenides; for Parmenides had already decisively changed the conception of the origin of things away from the view that the origin is the primordial stuff or material out of which things arise. Accordingly Parmenides, by drawing the intimate connection that he did between Being, truth, and thought, offered a conception of origins of a very different sort. For him, the origin of things was literally the ontological origin, that is, an account of the *being* of things; and the *being* of things was tantamount to what they are *intelligible* as, that by and through which they are intelligible as what they are. Empedocles, almost in anticipation of the later Aristotelian criticism of Plato's Forms, implies that such an account of origins is insufficient, that we still need an account of the material origins of things as well. But he accepted from Parmenides the conviction that even the material origins, if they be genuine origins, have the basic constitution of Parmenides' Being; they must be changeless and eternal. From this

237

standpoint, the problem of participation—how the changing things of the world can participate in, be grounded in, a changeless and permanent Being—does indeed arise in an acute way. Empedocles' response is to argue not against the changelessness and eternality of the origin but against its radical unity. Being is not one, but heterogeneous, not only in number but, as we shall presently see, in genus or kind. The material origins of things are in fact four: earth, air, fire, and water, presented at first mythically as Zeus, Hera, Aidoneus, and Nestis. Each of them bear the qualities requisite to Parmenidean Being. Each of them is one, changeless, eternal. The changing things of the world are then various mixtures of the four elements, and their passing away is their dissolution into the four elements again. To explain this, Empedocles employs the rather appropriate analogy of the painter who mixes his paints in various ways in order to paint the various figures. The "elements" remain the same, but their combinations produce different things. We can see here clearly the conviction, which we saw first in Anaximenes, that quantitative explanations can be given of qualitative differences. But Empedocles has added an important subtlety. Starting with four *qualitatively* different elements, or *archai,* a quantitative account of the myriad things of the world can be given in terms of combinations of the four elements. We thus move a step closer toward the framework of modern science: a certain relatively small number of qualitatively different "elements" "mixed" together in indefinitely many ways to get the actual objects of our experience. This movement, we shall see, will take another important step in the philosophy of Anaxagoras.

But the very appropriateness of the painter analogy raises an issue which Empedocles raises explicitly, and which may in fact be his single most important contribution to Western philosophy. The various paints are mixed together to form a picture by a painter. How do the four elements come to be mixed so as to produce the myriad objects of experience? To use Aristotelian and indeed contemporary language, what is the *cause* of the elements being mixed together? With this question, Empedocles sees the necessity of still another dimension in our understanding of the origin of things, what Aristotle is later to call the efficient cause. The elements come to be mixed together, Empedocles suggests, thanks to the contending influence of two contrary but equally primordial forces at work in the cosmos, Love (*Philotes*) and Strife

(*Neikos*). Love is the principle of union, the force which leads things to come together into one, Strife the principle of disunion, the force which tends to separate things into an increasing multiplicity. These two "elements" are equiprimordial with the four elements earth, air, fire, and water. But they are qualitatively heterogeneous to those elements in that they serve a very different function, that of setting in motion by their mutual opposition the processes of combination and dissolution of the four elements which bring about the coming to be and passing away of the things of the world.

In Empedocles' view, the opposition of Love and Strife as they combine and dissolve the elements gives rise to a cyclical view of the cosmos, and so at least implicitly, a cyclical view of history. The two poles of this cycle are the situations in which one or the other of the two forces are totally dominant to the exclusion of the other—what we might call the Age of Love and the Age of Strife. Intermittent between them are two periods which include elements both of Love and of Strife, one moving out of the Age of Love as an increasing element of Strife enters the cosmos, the other moving out of the Age of Strife as an increasing element of Love enters. A diagram should make this clear:

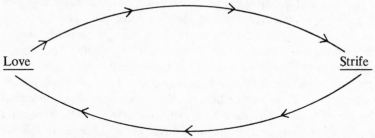

The Age of Love Empedocles characterizes as a literal version of the sphere of Parmenides' Being.[1] It is a complete mixture or union of all the elements into one. Adequate discussion of the Age of Strife does not survive in Empedocles' fragments, but what little we have,[2] as well as Aristotle's comments in the *Metaphysica*,[3] suggest that during this age the four elements are totally separated from each other into four homogeneous masses.[4] There is still some controversy about whether our present age is in the transition from Love to Strife or from Strife to Love.[5] In any case, it is significant that Empedocles makes explicit a conception of history which to this day is a very real alternative for men thinking about the course of events. The view of a cyclical movement in history lacks either the happy optimism of a linear conception of history as "progress" toward the eventual perfection of man or the profound pessimism of a conception of history, also linear, as the decline and fall of man.[6] To be sure, Empedocles does have an account of the evolution of man into his present form, one of his contributions which points directly to contemporary evolutionary theory. But unlike the present theory of evolution, which fits in most naturally with a linear view of progress, Empedocles' evolutionary theory clearly falls within the cycle of history. The evolution of man, from disunited limbs, to "whole natured forms," to an age of random conglomerations of limbs and bodies, to our present situation, repeats itself as the cycle of the cosmos repeats itself. Thus even the notion of "natural selection" implicit in his theory cannot give rise to an optimism about the increasing superiority of the species, because of its place in the cycle of the cosmos.

It can be shown by a detailed consideration of Empedocles' fragments that all four evolutionary stages occur during one of the two transitional stages of the cosmic cycle—either when Love is gaining ascendancy or when Strife is gradually becoming dominant.[7] This in itself is instructive, for it points to a very significant issue for the possibility of intelligibility and articulation. Let us consider first the impossibility of any significant "intelligibility" in the two polar stages of Love and Strife. In the Age of Love everything is brought together into a homogeneous mass. Indeed, there is no longer "everything" but simply a one. But such a radical monism is in fact radically unintelligible and, in the end, indistinguishable from an utter chaos. For since there is only "a one," there could neither be any other thing from which to distinguish the one, nor could there be a distinguishable "mind" who could know it. The radical homogeneity of the Age of Love teaches us that intelligibility is impossible without the presence of some element of multiplicity. There must be at least a "two"—two entities intelligibly distinct from each other—and quite probably a "three," an *intelligent* entity which *knows* the intelligible difference between the one and the two, and so binds them together. Even if, as seems to be the case with Hegel's notion of Absolute Geist, there is really only the one in its different aspects, or "moments," it remains the case that those "moments" must be intelligibly distinct—Absolute Geist as itself, as the world, and as itself knowing itself.

The converse point can be made if we consider the situation in an

Age of Strife somewhat more radical than the one Empedocles apparently presents us. His Age of Strife is apparently one in which the world is resolved into its four elemental constituents—earth, air, fire, and water—all separated one from the other. As Aristotle and others saw, such a conception is not really devoid of all evidence of the unifying power of "Love," since in fact four *unities*—earth, air, fire, and water—are intelligible. The genuine alternative to the complete unity of the Age of Love would be an Age of Strife understood as an age of utter disunity, complete multiplicity and change, such that *nothing* is identifiable as a single thing, that is, the usual notion of utter chaos. Such a state where there was complete disunity and no unity, where *nothing* is intelligible as an *entity*, would be, as said earlier, indistinguishable from the age of radical homogeneity. This in turn teaches us that the possibility of intelligibility requires the presence of unity; for intelligibility to occur, a thing must be identifiable *as* what it is, a single thing. The possibility of intelligibility thus requires the co-presence and the interaction of unity and multiplicity. There can be neither a radical monism nor a radical pluralism.[8] This is of course a version of, indeed an introduction into, the famous metaphysical problem of the one and the many which occupies modern logicians and philosophers as much as it occupied Plato. Empedocles raises it in an especially visible way by presenting us with an *intelligible* cosmic cycle which, strangely enough, could only be *known* as such in two of its four periods, precisely the two periods which are marked by the "intermixing" of unity and multiplicity, of Love and Strife.

There are a multitude of other issues raised by Empedocles' fragments, and we will close by briefly discussing just a few more. One surely is the emphasis that Empedocles places on the primordiality of Love in the cosmos and for man. Continuing a tradition which we saw begin with Hesiod, Empedocles interprets Love not simply as a psychological event happening now and again between individual human beings, but as a primordial force in the cosmos of which human "love" is one of the manifestations. With important modifications, the notion that Love is a multidimensional force, at least in human being, of which only one of the manifestations is human personal, or romantic, love, is a position maintained by probably the three greatest accounts of love ever offered—those of Plato,[9] Judeo-Christianity, and Freud. Under a different name, it can be found in such diverse places as Spinoza's conception of God, or Nature, as power of activity,[10] in Nietzsche's notion of Will to Power,[11] and in Heidegger's more recent discussion of what he calls Care.[12]

Empedocles' famous experiment with the *Klepsydra* is noteworthy in conjunction with his cautious appeal to the evidence of the senses in man's quest for knowledge.[13] Although not in the least arguing in a strong empiricist vein that knowledge comes *only* or even primarily from the senses, Empedocles would seem to qualify the utter pessimism about the trustworthiness of the senses that many find implicit in Parmenides' teaching. Sensory evidence is for Empedocles important in man's coming to know his world, and Empedocles demonstrates its function in such "protoscientific" experiments as the *Klepsydra* experiment regarding respiration. Again, what is most significant here is not the question of the rigor of his use of a scientific method—which is not very rigorous at all—but rather the raising of this *kind of investigation* and kind of thinking as a path to knowledge.[14] Empedocles, as it were, legitimizes both the cautious appeal to the senses and the use of something like experiment which subsequently have become so integral to that mode of knowledge which has become the dominant and indeed paradigm mode of knowledge in our civilization, scientific knowledge.

Empedocles also makes at least implicit reference to two themes which we have again and again seen raised by the Pre-Socratic philosophers—the issue of the relation between man and the divine and the question of the accessibility of the objects of knowledge to human consciousness. The first problem, it will be recalled, is that of the recognition on the one hand of the presence in the world of forces superior to and more primordial than man—the divine—and yet the *recognition* of that presence and difference, and so the at-least-partial accessibility to the divine, by man. Empedocles' response to this issue is not a new one even in his own time, nor a particularly adequate one. But it prefigures his response to the second issue which is indeed an important one. For Empedocles makes the gods themselves spring from the same primordial elements—earth, air, fire, and water—as does man and all the entities of the world of experience.[15] Empedocles thus accounts for the access to the divine by man thanks to the accessibility of our common origins.

But that makes utterly opaque the real *difference* between the divine and mortal and involves Empedocles as well in what we today would call the heresy of making the gods subject to an origin not only more primordial than themselves but an origin which they share with mortal man. Nevertheless, this prefigures Empedocles' response to the second issue as to how human consciousness can come to know the objects of knowledge. Whereas Parmenides, on our interpretation, by his close association of Being, thought, and truth, at least strongly implied what we now call the *ideality* of thought, Being, and truth, Empedocles employs the principle of "like knows like" in a very different way. He makes consciousness, or thought itself, material; it is the "blood round the heart."[16] We do not have to agree either with the location or the precise chemical makeup of Empedocles' suggested account of thought to appreciate its profound significance as a response to the problem of how human "thought" knows "things." It is the basic thesis of materialism, and whether couched in terms of the flow of blood or the movement of electrons through our nervous system, it represents one of the most tempting versions of the "like knows like" principle available to man. We can know "things" because ultimately we are qualitatively of the same "stuff" as things.

Like the Pythagoreans before him, Empedocles gives this view religious significance, at least in the sphere of living objects, through his doctrine of reincarnation. Our fundamental kinship with all living things is asserted through the reincarnation doctrine and the various rules of abstinence, many of which are similar to the Pythagorean ones. Empedocles himself recalls being "boy, girl, plant, bird, and dumb sea-fish."[17] A possible hint at the opaque difference between the mortal and the divine is given by the possibility of escaping from the cycle of rebirth. Empedocles apparently understood himself as on the verge of such an escape, and so characterized himself as "an immortal god."[18] Is the difference between the gods and men simply that gods are men who have escaped the cycle of rebirth?

In any case, perhaps the central importance of the religious teaching presented in Empedocles' *Purifications* is that it exhibits once again, as in the case of Pythagoras, the view that a strongly philosophic, mathematical, and, we may now even say, scientific concern was compatible, at least in the eyes of Empedocles, with a strong religious conviction and a religious way of life.[19]

Empedocles

Empedocles of Acragas, in Sicily, flourished around 450 B.C. He wrote two poems, or books, one given the title *On Nature*, the other called *Purifications* which is of a more religious, mystical nature. The view of the world that he set out in *On Nature* was apparently quite influential on the development of early Greek medicine, and, according to Diogenes Laertius, Empedocles was himself a famous and, given some examples of his cures, rather astounding doctor.

Empedocles: Fragment*

A. *On Nature*

1. Pausanias, but you must listen, son of wise Anchites!

2. For limited are the means of grasping (*i.e. the organs of sense-perception*) which are scattered throughout their limbs, and many are the miseries that press in and blunt the thoughts. And having looked at (*only*) a small part of existence during their lives, doomed to perish swiftly like smoke they are carried aloft and wafted away, believing only that upon which as individuals they chance to hit as they wander in all directions; but every man preens himself on having found the Whole: so little are these things to be seen by men or to be heard, or to be comprehended by the mind! But you, since you have come here into retirement, shall learn—not more than mortal intellect can attain.

3. But, ye gods, avert from my tongue the madness of those men, and guide forth from my reverent lips a pure stream! I beseech thee also, much-wooed white-armed maiden Muse, convey (*to me*) such knowledge as divine law allows us creatures of a day to hear, driving the well-harnessed car from (*the realm of*) Piety!**

---

* From Kathleen Freeman, *Ancilla to the Pre-Socratic Philosophers*.

** Others translate: 'Muse of such things as it is lawful for mortals to hear, escort me from the realms of Piety, driving my well-harnessed car!

Here there is probably a gap, where Empedocles takes up his address to Pausanias again.

Nor shall the flowers of honour paid to fame by mortals force you at least to accept them on condition that you rashly say more than is holy—and are thereupon enthroned on the heights of wisdom!

But come, observe with every means, to see by which way each thing is clear, and do not hold any (*percept of*) sight higher in credibility than (*those*) according to hearing, nor (*set*) the loud-sounding hearing above the evidence of the tongue (*taste*); nor refuse credence at all to any of the other limbs where there exists a path for perception, but use whatever way of perception makes each thing clear.

4.   But it is of great concern to the lower orders to mistrust the powerful; however, as the trustworthy evidence of my Muse commands, grasp (*these things*), when my reasoned argument has been sifted in your innermost heart!

5.   To protect it within your silent bosom.

6.   Hear, first, the four roots of things: bright Zeus, and life-bearing Hera, and Aidôneus, and Nêstis who causes a mortal spring of moisture to flow with her tears.

7.   (*The Elements*): uncreated.

8.   And I shall tell you another thing: there is no creation of substance in any one of mortal existences, nor any end in execrable death, but only mixing and exchange of what has been mixed; and the name 'substance' (*Physis, 'nature'*) is applied to them by mankind.

9.   But men, when these (*the Elements*) have been mixed in the form of a man and come into the light, or in the form of a species of wild animals, or plants, or birds, then say that this has 'come into being' and when they separate, this men call sad fate (*death*). The terms that Right demands they do not use; but through custom I myself also apply these names.

10.   Death the Avenger.

11.   Fools!—for they have no long-sighted thoughts, since they imagine

that what previously did not exist comes into being, or that a thing dies and is utterly destroyed.

12.   From what in no wise exists, it is impossible for anything to come into being; and for Being to perish completely is incapable of fulfilment and unthinkable; for it will always be there, wherever anyone may place it on any occasion.

13.   Nor is there any part of the Whole that is empty or overfull.

14.   No part of the Whole is empty; so whence could anything additional come?

15.   A wise man would not conjecture such things in his heart, namely, that so long as they are alive (which they call Life), they exist, and experience bad and good fortune; but that before mortals were combined (*out of the Elements*) and after they were dissolved, they are nothing at all.

16.   (*Love and Hate*): As they were formerly, so also will they be, and never, I think, shall infinite Time be emptied of these two.

17.   I shall tell of a double (*process*): at one time it increased so as to be a single One out of Many; at another time again it grew apart so as to be Many out of One. There is a double creation of mortals and a double decline: the union of all things causes the birth and destruction of the one (*race of mortals*), the other is reared as the elements grow apart, and then flies asunder. And these (*elements*) never cease their continuous exchange, sometimes uniting under the influence of Love, so that all become One, at other times again each moving apart through the hostile force of Hate. Thus in so far as they have the power to grow into One out of Many, and again, when the One grows apart and Many are formed, in this sense they come into being and have no stable life; but in so far as they never cease their continuous exchange, in this sense they remain always unmoved (*unaltered*) as they follow the cyclic process.

But come, listen to my discourse! For be assured, learning will increase your understanding. As I said before, revealing the aims of my discourse, I shall tell you of a double process. At one time it increased so as to be a single One out of Many; at another time it grew apart so as to be Many out of One—Fire and Water and Earth and the boundless height of Air, and also execrable Hate apart from these, of equal weight in all directions, and Love in their midst, their equal in length and breadth. Observe her with your mind, and do not sit with wondering eyes! She it is who is believed to be implanted in mortal limbs also; through her they think friendly thoughts and perform harmonious actions, calling her Joy and Aphrodite. No mortal man has perceived her as she moves in and out among them. But *you* must listen to the undeceitful progress of my argument.

All these (*Elements*) are equal and of the same age in their creation; but each presides over its own office, and each has its own character, and they prevail in turn in the course of Time. And besides these, nothing else comes into being, nor does anything cease. For if they had been perishing continuously, they would Be no more; and what could increase the Whole? And whence could it have come? In what direction could it perish, since nothing is empty of these things? No, but these things alone exist, and running through one another they become different things at different times, and are ever continuously the same.

18.   Love (*Philia*).*

19.   Adhesive Love (*Philotês*).*

20.   This process is clearly to be seen throughout the mass of mortal limbs: sometimes through Love all the limbs which the body has as its lot come together into One, in the prime of flourishing life; at another time again, sundered by evil feuds, they wander severally by the breakers of the shore of life. Likewise too with shrub-plants and fish in their watery dwelling, and beasts with mountain lairs and diver-birds that travel on wings.

21.   But come, observe the following witness to my previous discourse, lest in my former statements there was any substance of which the form was missing. Observe the sun, bright to see and hot everywhere, and all

---

* Empedocles probably used *Philotês*, not *Philia*; both words mean Love in the widest sense, not merely *Eros*.

the immortal things (*heavenly bodies*) drenched with its heat and brilliant light; and (*observe*) the rain, dark and chill over everything; and from the Earth issue forth things based on the soil and solid. But in (*the reign of*) Wrath they are all different in form and separate, while in (*the reign of*) Love they come together and long for one another. For from these (*Elements*) come all things that were and are and will be; and trees spring up, and men and women, and beasts and birds and water-nurtured fish, and even the long-lived gods who are highest in honour. For these (*Elements*) alone exist, but by running through one another they become different; to such a degree does mixing change them.

22.   For all these things—beaming Sun and Earth and Heaven and Sea—are connected in harmony with their own parts: all those (*parts*) which have been sundered from them and exist in mortal limbs. Similarly all those things which are more suitable for mixture are made like one another and united in affection by Aphrodite. But those things which differ most from one another in origin and mixture and the forms in which they are moulded are completely unaccustomed to combine, and are very baneful because of the commands of Hate, in that Hate has wrought their origin.

23.   As when painters decorate temple-offerings with colours—men who, following their intelligence, are well-skilled in their craft—these, when they take many-coloured pigments in their hands, and have mixed them in a harmony, taking more of some, less of another, create from them forms like to all things, making trees and men and women and animals and birds and fish nurtured in water, and even long-lived gods, who are highest in honour; so let not Deception compel your mind (*to believe*) that there is any other source for mortals, as many as are to be seen existing in countless numbers. But know this for certain, since you have the account from a divinity.*

24.   . . . Touching on summit after summit, not to follow a single path of discourse to the end.

25.   For what is right can well be uttered even twice.

* The Muse.

26.   In turn they get the upper hand in the revolving cycle, and perish into one another and increase in the turn appointed by Fate. For they alone exist, but running through one another they become men and the tribes of other animals, sometimes uniting under the influence of Love into one ordered Whole, at other times again each moving apart through the hostile force of Hate, until growing together into the Whole which is One, they are quelled. Thus in so far as they have the power to grow into One out of Many, and again, when the One grows apart and Many are formed, in this sense they come into being and have no stable life; but in so far as they never cease their continuous exchange, in this sense they remain always unmoved (*unaltered*) as they follow the cyclic process.

27.   (*The Sphere under the dominion of Love*): Therein are articulated neither the swift limbs of the sun, nor the shaggy might of Earth, nor the sea: so firmly is it (*the Whole*) fixed in a close-set secrecy, a rounded Sphere enjoying a circular solitude.*

27a.   There is no strife nor unseemly war in his limbs.

28.   But he (*God*) is equal in all directions to himself and altogether eternal, a rounded Sphere enjoying a circular solitude.

29.   For there do not start two branches from his back; (*he has*) no feet, no swift knees, no organs of reproduction; but he was a Sphere, and in all directions equal to himself.

30.   But when great Hate had been nourished in its limbs, and had rushed up into honour, when the time was fulfilled which, alternating, is fixed for them (*Love and Hate*) by a broad oath . . .

31.   For all the limbs of the god trembled in succession.

32.   The joint connects two things.

*   *   *

* *i.e.*, content with these conditions, self-sufficient.

35.   But I will go back to the path of song which I formerly laid down, drawing one argument from another: that (*path which shows how*) when Hate has reached the bottommost abyss of the eddy, and when Love reaches the middle of the whirl, then in it (*the whirl*) all these things come together so as to be One—not all at once, but voluntarily uniting, some from one quarter, others from another. And as they mixed, there poured forth countless races of mortals. But many things stand unmixed side by side with the things mixing—all those which Hate (*still*) aloft* checked, since it had not yet faultlessly** withdrawn from the Whole to the outermost limits of the circle, but was remaining in some places, and in other places departing from the limbs (*of the Sphere*). But in so far as it went on quietly streaming out, to the same extent there was entering a benevolent immortal inrush of faultless Love. And swiftly those things became mortal which previously had experienced immortality, and things formerly unmixed became mixed, changing their paths. And as they mixed, there poured forth countless races of mortals, equipped with forms of every sort, a marvel to behold.

36.   As they came together, Hate returned to the outermost (*bound*).

37.   (*Fire increases Fire*), Earth increases its own substance, Aether (*increases*) Aether.

38.   Come now, I will first tell you of (the sun) the beginning, (*the Elements*) from which all the things we now look upon came forth into view: Earth, and the sea with many waves, and damp Air, and the Titan Aether which clasps the circle all round.

39.   If the depths of the Earth were unlimited, and also the vast Aether, a doctrine which has foolishly issued forth off the tongues of many, and has been spread abroad out of their mouths, since they have seen only a little of the Whole . . .

* * *

* *i.e.*, not yet fallen to the bottom.
** *i.e.*, 'completely', so that no fault could be found with the mixture.

41.   But (*the sun*) collected in a ball travels round the great sky.

42.   (*The moon*) cuts off his (*the sun's*) rays, whenever she goes below him, and she throws a shadow on as much of the Earth as is the breadth of the bright-eyed moon.

* * *

45.   There whirls round the Earth a circular borrowed light.

* * *

48.   It is the Earth that makes night by coming in the way of the (*sun's*) rays.

* * *

52.   Many fires burn below the surface (*of the Earth*).

* * *

55.   Sea, the sweat of Earth.

* * *

57.   On it (*Earth*) many foreheads without necks sprang forth, and arms wandered unattached, bereft of shoulders, and eyes strayed about alone, needing brows.

58.   Limbs wandered alone.

59.   But as the one divinity became more and more mingled with the other (*i.e. Love and Hate*), these things fell together as each chanced, and many other things in addition to these were continuously produced.

60.   Creatures with rolling gait and innumerable hands.

61.   Many creatures were created with a face and breast on both sides; offspring of cattle with the fronts of men, and again there arose offspring of men with heads of cattle; and (*creatures made of elements*) mixed in part from men, in part of female sex, furnished with hairy limbs.

62.   Come now, hear how the Fire as it was separated sent up the night-produced shoots of men and much-lamenting women; for my tale is not wide of the mark nor ill-formed. At first, undifferentiated shapes of earth arose, having a share of both elements Water and Heat. These the Fire sent up, wishing to reach its like, but they did not yet exhibit a lovely body with limbs, nor the voice and organ such as is proper to men.

*   *   *

64.   Upon him comes Desire also, reminding him through sight.

65.   And they (*male and female seed*) were poured into the pure parts. Some of it forms women, (*namely*) that which has encountered Cold, (*and conversely that which encounters Hot produces males*).

*   *   *

67.   For in the warmer part the stomach (*i.e. the womb*) is productive of the male, and for this reason men are swarthy and more powerfully built and more shaggy.

*   *   *

71.   But if your belief concerning these matters was at all lacking—how from the mixture of Water, Earth, Aether and Sun (*Fire*) there came into being the forms and colours of mortal things in such numbers as now exist fitted together by Aphrodite . . .

*   *   *

96. But the Earth obligingly in its broad vessels received two parts out of the eight of shining Nêstis, four of Hephaestus. And these became the white bones fitted together by the cementing of Harmony, divinely originated.

* * *

98. The Earth, having been finally moored in the harbours of Love, joined with these in about equal proportions: with Hephaestus, with moisture, and with all-shining Aether, either a little more (*of Earth*) or a little less to their more. And from these came blood and the forms of other flesh.

* * *

100. The way everything breathes in and out is as follows: all (*creatures*) have tubes of flesh, empty of blood, which extend over the surface of the body; and at the mouths of these tubes the outermost surface of the skin is perforated with frequent pores, so as to keep in the blood while a free way is cut for the passage of the air. Thus, when the thin blood flows back from here, the air, bubbling, rushes in in a mighty wave; and when the blood leaps up (*to the surface*), there is an expiration of air. As when a girl, playing with a water-catcher* of shining brass—when, having placed the mouth of the pipe on her well-shaped hand she dips the vessel into the yielding substance of silvery water, still the volume of air pressing from inside on the many holes keeps out the water, until she uncovers the condensed stream (*of air*). Then at once when the air flows out, the water flows in in an equal quantity. Similarly, when water occupies the depths of the brazen vessel, and the opening or passage is stopped by the human flesh (*hand*), and the air outside, striving to get in, checks the water, by controlling the surface at the entrance of the noisy strainer [the base of the water-catcher, pierced with holes through which the liquid enters] until she lets go with her hand: then again, in exactly the opposite way from what happened

---

* *Klepsydra*: not here the water-clock, but a domestic vessel for picking up small quantities of liquid out of a larger vessel. See Hugh Last. *Class. Q.* XVIII (1924), pp. 169 *sqq.* for description and illustration.

before, as the air rushes in, the water flows out in equal volume. Similarly when the thin blood, rushing through the limbs, flows back into the interior, straightway a stream of air flows in with a rush; and when the blood flows up again, again there is a breathing-out in equal volume.

* * *

103.   Thus all (*creatures*) have intelligence, by the will of Fortune.

* * *

105.   (*The heart*) nourished in the seas of blood which courses in two opposite directions: this is the place where is found for the most part what men call Thought; for the blood round the heart is Thought in mankind.

106.   The intelligence of Man grows towards the material that is present.

107.   For from these (*Elements*) are all things fitted and fixed together, and by means of these do men think, and feel pleasure and sorrow.

108.   In so far as their natures have changed (*during the day*), so does it befall men to think changed thoughts (*in their dreams*).

109.   We see Earth by means of Earth, Water by means of Water, divine Air by means of Air, and destructive Fire by means of Fire; Affection by means of Affection, Hate by means of baneful Hate.

* * *

110.   If you press them (*these truths?*) deep into your firm mind, and contemplate them with good will and a studious care that is pure, these things will all assuredly remain with you throughout your life; and you will obtain many other things from them; for these things of themselves cause each (*element*) to increase in the character, according to the way

of each man's nature. But if you intend to grasp after different things such as dwell among men in countless numbers and blunt their thoughts, miserable (*trifles*), certainly these things will quickly desert you in the course of time, longing to return to their own original kind. For all things, be assured, have intelligence and a portion of Thought.

111.   You shall learn all the drugs that exist as a defence against illness and old age; for you alone will I accomplish all this. You shall check the force of the unwearying winds which rush upon the earth with their blasts and lay waste the cultivated fields. And again, if you wish, you shall conduct the breezes back again. You shall create a seasonable dryness after the dark rain for mankind, and again you shall create after summer drought the streams that nourish the trees and [which will flow in the sky].* And you shall bring out of Hades a dead man restored to strength.

B. KATHARMOI (PURIFICATIONS)

112.   Friends, who dwell in the great town on the city's heights, looking down on yellow Acragas, you who are occupied with good deeds, who are harbours (*of refuge*) treating foreigners with respect, and who are unacquainted with wickedness: greeting! I go about among you as an immortal god, no longer a mortal, held in honour by all, as I seem (*to them to deserve*), crowned with fillets and flowing garlands. When I come to them in their flourishing towns, to men and women, I am honoured; and they follow me in thousands, to inquire where is the path of advantage, some desiring oracles, while others ask to hear a word of healing for their manifold diseases, since they have long been pierced with cruel pains.

113.   But why do I lay stress on these things, as if I were achieving something great in that I surpass mortal men who are liable to many forms of destruction?

114.   Friends, I know that Truth is present in the story that I shall tell;

* Reading corrupt.

but it is actually very difficult for men, and the impact of conviction on their minds is unwelcome.

115.   There is an oracle of Necessity, an ancient decree of the gods, eternal, sealed fast with broad oaths, that when one of the divine spirits whose portion is long life sinfully stains his own limbs with bloodshed, and following Hate has sworn a false oath—these must wander for thrice ten thousand seasons far from the company of the blessed, being born throughout the period into all kinds of mortal shapes, which exchange one hard way of life for another. For the mighty Air chases them into the Sea, and the Sea spews them forth on to the dry land, and the Earth (*drives them*) towards the rays of the blazing Sun; and the Sun hurls them into the eddies of the Aether. One (*Element*) receives them from the other, and all loathe them. Of this number am I too now, a fugitive from heaven and a wanderer, because I trusted in raging Hate.

116.   (*The Grace*) loathes intolerable Necessity.

117.   For by now I have been born as boy, girl, plant, bird, and dumb sea-fish.

118.   I wept and wailed when I saw the unfamiliar land (*at birth*).

* * *

124.   Alas, oh wretched race of mortals, direly unblessed! Such are the conflicts and groanings from which you have been born!

* * *

128.   And for them there was no god Ares, nor Battle-Din, nor Zeus the King, nor Cronos nor Poseidon, but only Cypris the Queen. These men sought to please her with pious gifts—with painted animals and perfumes of cunningly-devised smell, with sacrifice of unmixed myrrh and of fragrant incense, and by casting libations of yellow honey on the ground. And the altar was not drenched with the unmixed blood of bulls, but this was the greatest pollution among men, to devour the goodly limbs (*of animals*) whose life they had reft from them.

129.   There was living among them a man of surpassing knowledge, who had acquired the extremest wealth of the intellect, one expert in every kind of skilled activity. For whenever he reached out with his whole intellect, he easily discerned each one of existing things, in ten and even twenty lifetimes of mankind.

130.   And all creatures, both animals and birds, were tame and gentle towards men, and friendliness glowed between them.

131.   If for the sake of any mortal, immortal Muse, it has pleased thee that my poetic endeavours should be of concern to thee, now once again, in answer to my prayer, stand beside me, Calliopeia, as I expound a good theory concerning the blessed gods!

132.   Happy is he who has acquired the riches of divine thoughts, but wretched the man in whose mind dwells an obscure opinion about the gods!

133.   It is not possible to bring God near within reach of our eyes, nor to grasp him with our hands, by which route the broadest road of Persuasion runs into the human mind.

134.   For he is not equipped with a human head on his body, nor from his back do two branches start; (*he has*) no feet, no swift knees, no hairy genital organs; but he is Mind, holy and ineffable, and only Mind, which darts through the whole universe with its swift thoughts.

135.   But that which is lawful for all extends continuously through the broad-ruling Air and through the boundless Light.*

136.   Will ye not cease from this harsh-sounding slaughter? Do you not see that you are devouring one another in the thoughtlessness of your minds?

* Divine law as opposed to human law; said to refer in particular to the art of prohibition of animal-slaughter.

137.   The father having lifted up the son slaughters him with a prayer, in his great folly. But they are troubled* at sacrificing one who begs for mercy. But he, on the other hand, deaf to (the victim's) cries, slaughters him in his halls and prepares the evil feast. Likewise son takes father, and children their mother, and tearing out the life, eat the flesh of their own kin.

*   *   *

139.   (Hymn of repentance for sins of diet): 'Alas that a pitiless day did not destroy me before I planned evil deeds of eating with my lips!'

140.   Keep entirely away from laurel-leaves!

141.   Wretches, utter wretches, keep your hands off beans!

142.   Him will the roofed palace of aegis-bearing Zeus never receive, nor yet the roof of Hades and of the piteous voice.**

*   *   *

146.   And at the last they become seers, and bards, and physicians, and princes among earth-dwelling men, from which (state) they blossom forth as gods highest in honour.

147.   Sharing the hearth of the other immortals, sharing the same table, freed from the lot of human griefs, indestructible.

*   *   *

TESTIMONIA ON EMPEDOCLES BY DIOGENES LAERTIUS***

---

*   Diels takes 'they' as 'the attendants at the sacrifice'.
**   An uncertain restoration by Diels of a passage quoted for grammatical reasons, from Herculanean MSS.
***   From R. D. Hicks Lives of Eminent Philosophers.

[Empedocles] was a pupil of Pythagoras, adding that, having been convicted at that time of stealing his discourses, he was, like Plato, excluded from taking part in the discussions of the school; and further, that Empedocles himself mentions Pythagoras in the lines:

> And there lived among them a man of superhuman knowledge, who verily possessed the greatest wealth of wisdom.

Others say that it is to Parmenides that he is here referring.

Neanthes states that down to the time of Philolaus and Empedocles all Pythagoreans were admitted to the discussions. But when Empedocles himself made them public property by his poem, they made a law that they should not be imparted to any poet. He says the same thing also happened to Plato, for he too was excommunicated. But which of the Pythagoreans it was who had Empedocles for a pupil he did not say. For the epistle commonly attributed to Telauges and the statement that Empedocles was the pupil of both Hippasus and Brontinus he held to be unworthy of credence.

Theophrastus affirms that he was an admirer of Parmenides and imitated him in his verses, for Parmenides too had published his treatise *On Nature* in verse. But Hermippus's account is that he was an admirer not so much of Parmenides as of Xenophanes, with whom in fact he lived and whose writing of poetry he imitated, and that his meeting with the Pythagoreans was subsequent. Alcidamas tells us in his treatise on *Physics* that Zeno and Empedocles were pupils of Parmenides about the same time, that afterwards they left him, and that, while Zeno framed his own system, Empedocles became the pupil of Anaxagoras and Pythagoras, emulating the latter in dignity of life and bearing, and the former in his physical investigations.

Aristotle in his *Sophist* calls Empedocles the inventor of rhetoric as Zeno of dialectic. In his treatise *On Poets* he says that Empedocles was of Homer's school and powerful in diction, being great in metaphors and in the use of all other poetical devices . . .

Satyrus in his *Lives* says that he was also a physician and an excellent orator: at all events Gorgias of Leontini, a man pre-eminent in oratory and the author of a treatise on the art, had been his pupil. . . .

. . . Thus Heraclides, after telling the story of the woman in a trance, how that Empedocles became famous because he had sent away the dead woman alive, goes on to say that he was offering a sacrifice close to the field of Peisianax. Some of his friends had been invited to the sacrifice, including Pausanias. Then, after the feast, the remainder of the company dispersed and retired to rest, some under the trees in the adjoining field, others wherever they chose, while Empedocles himself remained on the spot where he had reclined at table. At daybreak all got up, and he was the only one missing. A search was made, and they questioned the servants, who said they did not know where he was. Thereupon someone said that in the middle of the night he heard an exceedingly loud voice calling Empedocles. Then he got up and beheld a light in the heavens and a glitter of lamps, but nothing else. His hearers were amazed at what had occurred, and Pausanias came down and sent people to search for him. But later he bade them take no further trouble, for things beyond expectation had happened to him, and it was their duty to sacrifice to him since he was now a god.

Hermippus tells us that Empedocles cured Panthea, a woman of Agrigentum, who had been given up by the physicians, and this was why he was offering sacrifice, and that those invited were about eighty in number. Hippobotus, again, asserts that, when he got up, he set out on his way to Etna; then, when he had reached it, he plunged into the fiery craters and disappeared, his intention being to confirm the report that he had become a god. . . .

TESTIMONIA ON EMPEDOCLES BY ARISTOTLE

So much, then, for those who posit one cause such as we mentioned; but the same is true if one supposes more of these, as Empedocles says the matter of things is four bodies. For he too is confronted by consequences some of which are the same as have been mentioned, while others are peculiar to him. For we see these bodies produced from one another, which implies that the same body does not always remain fire or earth (we have spoken about this in our works on nature); and regarding the cause of movement and the question whether we must posit one or two, he must be thought to have spoken neither correctly nor altogether plausibly. And in general, change of quality is necessarily done away with for those who speak thus, for on their view cold will not come from hot nor hot from cold. For if it did there would be something

that accepted the contraries themselves, and there would be some one
entity that became fire and water, which Empedocles denies. (*Metaphysica*, 989*a* 19)

But some advocate four (elements) from the start, *e.g.*, Empedocles:
yet he too draws them together so as to reduce them to the two, for he
opposes all the others to Fire. (*De Generatione et corruptione*, 330*b* 19)

Empedocles, then, in contrast with his predecessors, was the first to
introduce the dividing of this cause, not positing one source of movement, but different and contrary sources. Again, he was the first to
speak of four material elements; yet he does not *use* four, but treats
them as two only; he treats fire by itself, and its opposites—earth, air,
and water—as one kind of thing. We may learn this by study of his
verses. (*Metaphysica*, 985*a* 29)

If then it is possible that at any time nothing should be in motion, this
must come about in one of two ways: either in the manner described by
Anaxagoras, who says that all things were together and at rest for an infinite period of time, and that then Mind introduced motion and
separated them; or in the manner described by Empedocles, according
to whom the universe is alternately in motion and at rest—in motion,
when Love is making the one out of many, or Strife is making many out
of one, and at rest in the intermediate periods of time—his account
being as follows:

> 'Since One hath learned to spring from Manifold,
> And one disjoined makes Manifold arise,
> Thus they Become, nor stable is their life:
> But since their motion must alternate be,
> Thus have they ever Rest upon their round':

for we must suppose that he means by this that they alternate from the
one motion to the other. (*Physica*, 250*b* 22)

. . . For if we were to follow out the view of Empedocles, and interpret it according to its meaning and not to its lisping expression, we
should find that friendship is the cause of good things, and strife of bad.

Therefore, if we said that Empedocles in a sense both mentions, and is the first to mention, the bad and the good as principles, we should perhaps be right, since the cause of all goods is the good itself. (*Metaphysica*, 985a 4)

Empedocles also has a paradoxical view; for he identifies the good with love, but this is a principle both as mover (for it brings things together) and as matter (for it is part of the mixture). Now even if it happens that the same thing is a principle both as matter and as mover, still the being, at least, of the two is not the same. In which respect then is love a principle? It is paradoxical also that strife should be imperishable; the nature of his "evil" is just strife. (*Metaphysica*, 1075b 1)

. . . Even the man whom one might suppose to speak most consistently—Empedocles—even he has made the same mistake; for he maintains that strife is a principle that causes *destruction*, but even strife would seem no less to *produce* everything, except the One; for all things excepting God proceed from strife. At least he says:—

From which all that was and is and will be hereafter—
Trees, and men and women, took their growth,
And beasts and birds and water-nourished fish,
And long-aged gods.

The implication is evident even apart from these words; for if strife had not been present in things, all things would have been one, according to him; for when they have come together, 'then strife stood outermost.' Hence it also follows on his theory that God most blessed is less wise than all others; for he does not know all the elements; for he has in him no strife, and knowledge is of the like by the like. 'For by earth,' he says,

we see earth, by water water,
By ether godlike ether, by fire wasting fire,
Love by love, and strife by gloomy strife.

But—and this is the point we started from—this at least is evident, that on his theory it follows that strife is as much the cause of existence as of destruction. (*Metaphysica*, 1000a 25)

. . . And Empedocles, though he uses the causes to a greater extent than this, neither does so sufficiently nor attains consistency in their use. At least, in many cases he makes love segregate things, and strife aggregate them. For whenever the universe is dissolved into its elements by strife, fire is aggregated into one, and so is each of the other elements; but whenever again under the influence of love they come together into one, the parts must again be segregated out of each element. (*Metaphysica*, 985a 21)

. . . But there is no sense in starting generation from an original state in which bodies are separated and in movement. Hence Empedocles begins after the process rules by Love: for he could not have constructed the heaven by building it up out of bodies in separation, making them to combine by the power of Love, since our world has its constituent elements in separation, and therefore presupposes a previous state of unity and combination. (*De Caelo*, 301a 14)

Empedocles, as well as others, expresses the opposite view that like aims at like. (*Nicomachean Ethics*, 1155b 7)

It is equally absurd to suppose that anything has been explained by calling the sea 'the sweat of the earth', like Empedocles. Metaphors are poetical and so that expression of his may satisfy the requirements of a poem, but as a scientific theory it is unsatisfactory. (*Meteorologica*, 375a 24)

Empedocles is wrong in adding that growth in plants is to be explained, the downward rooting by the natural tendency of earth to travel downwards, and the upward branching by the similar natural tendency of fire to travel upwards. For he misinterprets up and down; up and down are not for all things what they are for the whole Cosmos. . . . (*De Anima*, 415b 27)

Life is found in animals and plants; but while in animals it is clearly manifest, in plants it is hidden and less evident. But before we can assert the presence of life in plants, a long inquiry must be held as to whether plants possess a soul and a distinguishing capacity for desire and pleasure and pain. Now Anaxagoras and Empedocles say that they are influenced by desire; they also assert that they have sensation and sadness and pleasure. Anaxagoras declared that plants are animals and feel joy and sadness, deducing this from the bending of their foliage; while Empedocles held the opinion that sex has a place in their composition. (*De Plantis,* 815a 10)

. . . The view of Plato in thus holding that plants have sensation and desire was marvellous enough; but Anaxagoras and Democritus and Empedocles declared that they possessed intellect and intelligence. These views we must repudiate as unsound and pursue a sane statement of the case. (*De Plantis,* 815b 15)

Notes: VII

1. Empedocles, Fragments 27, 28 (D-K).
2. *Ibid.,* Fragments 17, 26.
3. Aristotle, *Metaphysica,* 985a 23 ff.
4. For a thorough discussion of this, *see* G. S. Kirk and J. E. Raven, *The Pre-Socratic Philosophers* (Cambridge, England, Cambridge University Press, 1960), p. 327 ff., 345 ff.
5. *Cf.* J. Burnet, *Early Greek Philosophers* (New York, Meridan Books, 1957), p. 234 *passim*; Kirk and Raven, *op. cit.,* pp. 339, 340; Eduard Zeller, *Die Philosophie der Griechen, dargestellt von Dr. Eduard Zeller,* Erster Theil, Fünfte Auflage (Leipzig, 1892), pp. 758 ff.
6. *Cf.* the discussion of the Eternal Return in Friedrich Nietzsche, *Thus Spake Zarathustra,* (New York, Viking Press, 1954), Books III and IV. The recognition of the Eternal Return of the Same at first causes Zarathustra nausea, later joy.
7. *Cf.* Kirk and Raven, *op. cit.,* pp. 336 ff.
8. Although a superficial reading of Parmenides and Heraclitus may suggest that they represent these respective views, I hope I have disspelled such a misconception.
9. The modifications are nicely indicated by noting that in Plato's *Symposium* it is Eryximachus, not Socrates, who most nearly presents the Empedoclean view.
10. Benedict de Spinoza, *Ethics,* in *The Chief Works of Benedict*

de Spinoza, trans. by R. H. M. Elwes (New York, Dover Publications, 1951), Vol. II, Part I, p. 74, proposition XXXIV, *passim.*

11. Friedrich Nietzsche, *The Will to Power,* trans. by Walter Kaufmann and R. J. Hollingdale, (New York, Random House, 1967).

12. Martin Heidegger, *Being and Time,* trans. by John Macquarrie and Edward Robinson, (New York, Harper and Row, 1962), pp. 225 ff.

13. Empedocles, Fragments 100, 3 (D-K).

14. It is instructive to note that few contemporary experiments include accounts of the "well-shaped hand" of the laboratory assistant as she conducts her experiment! Perhaps ours is the loss.

15. Empedocles, Fragment 21.

16. *Ibid.,* Fragment 105.

17. *Ibid.,* Fragment 117.

18. *Ibid.,* Fragment 112.

19. Although there is often thought to be an incompatibility between the immortality of the soul presented in the *Purifications* and the nonimmortality strongly implied by the materiality of the soul presented in *On Nature. Cf.* Kirk and Raven, *op. cit.,* pp. 355 ff.

Responses to the Battle of the Giants: II

LIKE his contemporary Empedocles', Anaxagoras' thought seems in many ways intended as a response to the problem presented to philosophy by the confrontation of Heraclitus and Parmenides. Assuming on the one hand what Parmenides seemed to have shown, namely, that Being, if it is to be intelligible as the *arche,* or origin of what is, must be changeless and eternal, how can we nevertheless account for the coming to be of the manifold world of human experience? Heraclitus had shown that any acceptable account of the hidden origin of things must be able to show that it is an account of *our* world, a world of change, multiplicity, coming to be, and passing away. Parmenides had argued that no account of coming to be, change, and multiplicity could be acceptable which argued for a coming to be *ex nihilo.* What is cannot come to be from what is not. Being, therefore, as the *arche* of the intelligibility of the world, must be changeless and eternal.

We have seen that Empedocles responded to this problematic by arguing that Being, although indeed changeless and eternal, was heterogeneous in a twofold way, in genus—the material *arche* and the "efficient" *arche* of Love-Strife—and in number—the material *archai* of earth, air, fire, and water. By the quantitative variety in the combinations of the four elements coupled with the causal agency of the Love-Strife oppositions, Empedocles proposed an intelligible account of the world.

To Anaxagoras, it would seem, such an account still dissolved into an unacceptable creation *ex nihilo.*[1] As he puts it in Fragment 10, "How can hair come from not-hair, and flesh from not-flesh?" Parmenides had been convincing in his denial of such a possibility. What *would* be acceptable, however, would be that hair might come to *appear* as hair, to be intelligible and visible as hair, out of something in which the hair was present but hidden. An explanation of coming to be and passing away, of change and multiplicity, which still paid heed to Parmenides, could be given which argued that the "coming to be" of, say, hair or bone was in fact the emergence into unhiddenness of that which was formerly present but hidden. Such an explanation would also pay heed to the Greek experience of truth as *a-leitheia*, unhiddenness. One alternative, then, would have been for Anaxagoras to endeavor an exhaustive catalogue of all the things which appear to "change into" anything else. Evidently such an attempt would be hopelessly long and doomed to incompleteness. Much more "economical" and appropriate to the emergence of new possibilities would be to say that somehow everything is present in everything, and that a thing—hair or bone—appears as what it is according to what dominates in it. This is the position that Anaxagoras adopted: "There is a portion (*moira*) of everything in everything."² Such a view evidently offers an account of how something "comes to be" bone or hair without having to assert that it came to be bone or hair from what is genuinely *not* bone or hair. If there is a portion of everything in everything, then whether an entity is called hair or bone, whether it appears as hair or bone or anything else, depends on what "portions" predominate, and the change, say, of lamb chops to human flesh, would be explained by an alteration from a predominance of lamb chop portions to a predominance of human flesh portions. Moreover, these "portions" are infinitely divisible. No matter how far you divide them, you will continue to get nothing but the qualitatively homogeneous portions. Thus, it seems, no sooner had Zeno, in defense of Parmenides, repudiated Parmenides' critics on the grounds that the dissenters end up in what is now called a "vicious regress" than a thinker by no means antagonistic to Parmenides asserts a view which apparently finds the notion of an infinite regress not "vicious" but quite acceptable, indeed, a part of an account of the way things are. To repeat, such a view is based not on a creation *ex nihilo* but on the view which we have seen present in Greek thought from the very beginning that an account of appearances cannot be given simply in terms of appearances, that appearances are grounded in an *arche,* or origin, which, though present in appearances, is hidden to the senses but accessible to thought.

There are, however, problems in Anaxagoras' account as so far offered, perhaps the most obvious of which is how one can make intelligible the dominance of one portion over the other, such that the world comes to contain the multitude of apparently different entities that it exhibits. To use a somewhat blatant example, if there is a portion of everything in everything, how is it yogurt bears so little apparent resemblance to the shield of Achilles? To this problem Anaxagoras responds with his doctrine of "seeds," or as later writers referred to them, homoeomeries. Yogurt is different from Achilles' shield for a reason very congenial to students of modern chemistry: Yogurt is made up of yogurt "seeds," and Achilles' shield is made up, for the most part, of bronze "seeds," and bronze seeds and yogurt seeds are very different. More than that, yogurt is made up of yogurt seeds alone and nothing else, bronze of bronze seeds and nothing else, and so on. Thus we have an account of the heterogeneity of substances remarkably similar to modern molecular theory. Water is made up of water molecules, wood of wood molecules, and so on. This seems an eminently plausible account of the nature of and differences among various substances, indeed a most remarkable forerunner to modern theory.

But does not Anaxagoras' doctrine of "seeds" flatly contradict the doctrine of portions? How can it be both that there is "a portion of everything in everything" and also that everything is made up of its own "seeds" alone? If there is no resolution to this apparently blatant contradiction, Anaxagoras can hardly be taken seriously as a genuinely important and great thinker. But a resolution is at hand.

It seems that Anaxagoras is here developing further the very significant insight of earlier Pre-Socratic thinkers that it may be possible to explain qualitative heterogeneity in terms of the quantitative arrangement of some homogeneous substance. "There is a portion of everything in everything"; that is, it seems, a rather complex and sophisticated return to those earlier thinkers such as Thales, Anaximander, and Anaximenes who espoused a single *arche*, or primal substance, as an explanatory principle. Anaxagoras is of course closer to Anaximander. The *arche* is not one of the many discrete substances; it rather somehow contains a "portion" of them all. According to the way these portions get arranged, that is, according to which portions come to dominate in any given instance, there develops a "seed" of one thing or another which are qualitatively different. And as these "seeds" come to gather together, they become a manifestation of the actual thing in question—a bone, or flesh, or hair. Thus bone is composed only of bone "seeds," gold only of gold "seeds." But bone seeds and gold seeds are in fact different quantitative arrangements of the "portions" of everything. Is there any analogue to this in contemporary thinking about the makeup and intelligibility of the world of our experience? There is, of course, and perhaps the first and most obvious is the relationship between atoms and the protons and neutrons that make them up. Protons *qua* protons are qualitatively homogeneous. Electrons are similarly homogeneous. But according to their quantitative arrangement or structure they become now a hydrogen atom, now an oxygen atom, etc. There are, of course, important differences from Anaxagoras' view, and in any case so little survives of Anaxagoras' account of the nature of the "portions" and "seeds" that one is forced to speculate. But it is reasonable to suppose that Anaxagoras was applying the same *principle* as does modern science, that of accounting for qualitative difference in essentially quantitative terms, and that he was doing so in such a way as to respond to the accepted demands of his predecessors, to explain the heterogeneity of the world in terms which did not involve an unacceptable creation *ex nihilo*. We have discussed in earlier chapters the historical and philosophic significance of this mode of explanation. What we see in Anaxagoras is a development of this mode in a way which moves increasingly toward the version of that explanation offered by modern science.

But if what we have discussed so far were all that Anaxagoras offered, we would also seem to have a falling off from the genuine achievement of Parmenides and Heraclitus, and even, if these interpretations are correct, from the majority of Anaxagoras' predecessors. For according to the interpretations, these men were not concerned simply or even most significantly with the actual structure of the physical world; always at issue in their reflections was the question of intelligibility itself, the question of the possibility, the manner, and the significance of the *intelligibility* of the world to finite man. Anaxagoras, too, would seem to pay heed to this issue in his teaching concerning *Nous*, mind or thought, although if we are persuaded by Plato's Socrates, his efforts in this direction were rather meager.[3] Let us turn to a consideration of this important aspect of Anaxagoras' philosophy.

Anaxagoras' materialist metaphysics so far lacks an account both of intelligibility and of how the "combinations" of portions into seeds ever come about, a problem the parallel of which we saw Empedocles explain by the agency of Love and Strife. Both these lacunae Anaxagoras attempts to fill by the power of *Nous,* mind or thought. *Nous* is both the original agent which sets in motion the process which gives rise to our present world, and it is also the principle of intelligibility by which the world becomes accessible to us. But mind would seem to have two manifestations here. Mind insofar as it functions as what Aristotle was later to call the "first mover" or "first cause" we could perhaps call "universal mind";[4] it is not personal or individual. On the other hand, mind as the principle of motion and life occasionally enters into or participates in individual entities, namely those which have life, and it is by and through *Nous* that those creatures think and thus that the world becomes to some extent intelligible. It is not entirely clear whether the institution of the motion which formulates seeds and things was performed only once, originally, by *Nous,* or whether *Nous*, as it were, acts in the world again and again; but the second function of *Nous,* to make possible life, thought, and intelligibility, certainly suggests its continued presence. Whatever the case, it is clear that *Nous* is meant to function both as first cause of the world, that is, as *arche* in the modern causal sense, and as what Aristotle called final cause, or teleological cause, the *arche* in the sense of that in terms of which and by which a thing can be understood. It is especially the latter function which Plato's Socrates expected to find fulfilled in Anaxagoras, and in which he was so disappointed. What Socrates saw in *Nous* was the possibility of a genuine teleology, an account, that is, of why it is *best* that the world be as it is.[5] Instead, as he relates, although Anaxagoras begins in this direction, he soon abandons it for what Socrates considers inadequate mechanical explanations. Hegel puts this issue nicely in his commentary on the passage from the *Phaedo*:

> Plato here correctly places the two kinds of reason and cause in opposition to one another—the cause proceeding from ends, and the inferior, subject, and merely external causes of chemistry, mechanism, etc.—in order to show the discrepancy between them, as here exemplified in the case of a man with consciousness.[6]

The issue here is of decisive importance to an understanding of the very nature of understanding itself. It was Socrates' view that any genuine understanding of something, any adequate account or *logos* of it, be it the shape of the earth or the nature of piety, must include an account of the *value* of the thing, whether it is good or wicked, in what way it is *best* that it is as it is. Without inclusion of an account of value, no *logos* of anything can be complete or satisfactory. Socrates claimed to find in Anaxagoras' doctrine of *Nous* the basis of such an account, but argued that Anaxagoras unfortunately abandoned such a potential in favor of "mere" mechanical explanations. Now there seems to be general agreement both among ancient and modern commentators that Socrates is at least correct that Anaxagoras does not sustain his interest in teleological explanation. What is *not* agreed upon is whether this abandonment was a defect. For it has been the widely accepted view, ever since the seventeenth-century founders of science first made it explicit, that science if it is to attain genuinely certain knowledge must abandon any attempt to give teleological explanation.[7] "Avoid value judgments" has since been the virtual first commandment of every modern discipline that wanted to claim to be a science, from physics to political science to literary criticism. From the modern standpoint, then, what Socrates considered Anaxagoras' mistake was in fact his virtue, and it was rather the insistence of Socrates, Plato, and Aristotle that an account of anything must include a teleological explanation which set back the path of true science for centuries. Whether we agree with the Socratic view or the spokesmen for modern science depends upon the view we adopt as to what counts as making something intelligible and so, ultimately, of what counts as the genuine *arche*, or origin, of things. With the help of Plato's Socrates this very issue becomes an issue for thought in the philosophy of Anaxagoras.

In a way, it is not difficult to understand why Anaxagoras' teaching on *Nous* would not preserve the interest in teleology. For, like Empedocles, Anaxagoras makes thought material—not the blood around our heart but the "finest of all things, and the purest."[8] As such, Anaxagoras' teaching bears a rather complex relation to Parmenides. For the materiality of *Nous* offers, on the one hand, the "sameness" of thought and that which it knows, thus following the principle of "like knows like" which Parmenides so firmly established, and also continued the great emphasis on thought and the closeness of its affinity with the origin of things, indeed its sameness with the origin of things, upon which Parmenides insisted. At the same time, if we can interpolate somewhat, that same materiality would seem to put Anaxagoras with Empedocles in denying the *ideality* of Being and of thought so strongly implicit in Parmenides' poem. It remains for Socrates and Plato to reinstate that ideality while preserving the affinity between thought and Being in a new and more complex way.

Nevertheless, it remains a signal contribution of Anaxagoras that he raised this affinity of thought and Being to a higher level of explicitness than perhaps any of his predecessors. Again, Hegel puts this point nicely in his discussion of the superiority of Anaxagoras' *Nous* to such origins as earth, water, fire, and air.

> Anaxagoras now says that it is not gods, sensuous principles, elements, or thoughts—which really are determination of reflection—but that it is the Universal, Thought itself, in and for itself, without opposition, all embracing, which is the substance or the principle.[9]

Even more explicitly than Parmenides in his famous but ambiguous Fragment 5, even more explicitly than Heraclitus in his aphorisms concerning the *Logos*, Anaxagoras virtually identifies Being and intelligibility, and so insists, even if he did not in the end successfully follow his own teaching, that the origin of things is bound up most fundamentally not with their physical constitution but with their intelligibility. However critical we may want to be of modern versions of what is now called idealism, we can now see that the most fundamental insight which makes not only idealism but almost all modern metaphysics possible, the affinity of Being and intelligibility, the view that the Being of anything is what it is intelligible as, this insight is a legacy of the Pre-Socratics.

Anaxagoras

Anaxagoras was born in Clazomenae in Asia Minor, not far from Heraclitus' native city of Ephesus. He flourished around 460 B.C. He came to Athens as a man and became a teacher of several famous students, apparently including Pericles the statesman and Euripides the tragic poet. Socrates, according to Plato's *Phaedo,* read Anaxagoras' book as a young man but had serious doubts about its value. Anaxagoras was banished from Athens in old age, apparently because of the atheism implicit in his claim that the sun was not a god but hot, molten rock.

ANAXAGORAS: FRAGMENTS*

1.   (*Opening sentences from his book 'On Natural Science'*): All Things were together, infinite in number and in smallness. For the Small also was infinite. And since all were together, nothing was distinguishable because of its smallness. For Air and Aether dominated all things, both of them being infinite. For these are the most important (*Elements*) in the total mixture, both in number and in size.

2.   Air and Aether are separated off from the surrounding multiplicity, and that which surrounds is infinite in number.

3.   For in Small there is no Least, but only a Lesser: for it is impossible that Being should Not-Be; and in Great there is always a Greater. And it is equal in number to the small, but each thing is to itself both great and small.

4.   Conditions being thus, one must believe that there are many things of all sorts in all composite products, and the seeds of all Things, which contain all kinds of shapes and colours and pleasant savours. And men too were fitted together, and all other creatures which have life. And the men possessed both inhabited cities and artificial works just like ourselves, and they had sun and moon and the rest, just as we have, and the earth produced for them many and diverse things, of which they collected the most useful, and now use them for their dwellings. This I say concerning Separation, that it must have taken place not only with us, but elsewhere.

Before these things were separated off, all things were together, nor was any colour distinguishable, for the mixing of all Things prevented this, (*namely*) the mixing of moist and dry and hot and cold and bright and dark, and there was a great quantity of earth in the mixture, and seeds infinite in number, not at all like one another. For none of the other things either is like any other. And as this was so, one must believe that all Things were present in the Whole.

5.   These things being thus separated off, one must understand that all

---

* From Kathleen Freeman, *Ancilla to the Pre-Socratic Philosophers*.

things are in no wise less or more (for it is not possible for them to be more than All), but all things are forever equal (*in quantity*).

6. And since there are equal (*quantitative*) parts of Great and Small, so too similarly in everything there must be everything. It is not possible (*for them*) to exist apart, but all things contain a portion of everything. Since it is not possible for the Least to exist, it cannot be isolated, nor come into being by itself; but as it was in the beginning, so now, all things are together. In all things there are many things, and of the things separated off, there are equal numbers in (*the categories*) Great and Small.

7. So that the number of the things separated off cannot be known either in thought or in fact.

8. The things in the one Cosmos are not separated off from one another with an axe, neither the Hot from the Cold, nor the Cold from the Hot.

9. Thus these things circulate and are separated off by force and speed. The speed makes the force. Their speed is not like the speed of any of the Things now existing among mankind, but altogether many times as fast.

10. How can hair come from not-hair, and flesh from not-flesh?

11. In everything there is a portion of everything except Mind; and some things contain Mind also.

12. Other things all contain a part of everything, but Mind is infinite and self-ruling, and is mixed with no Thing, but is alone by itself. If it were not by itself, but were mixed with anything else, it would have had a share of all Things, if it were mixed with anything; for in everything there is a portion of everything, as I have said before. And the things mixed (*with Mind*) would have prevented it, so that it could not rule over any Thing in the same way as it can being alone by itself. For it is the finest of all Things, and the purest, and has complete understanding of everything, and has the greatest power. All things which have life, both the greater and the less, are ruled by Mind. Mind took command of

the universal revolution, so as to make (*things*) revolve at the outset. And at first things began to revolve from some small point, but now the revolution extends over a greater area, and will spread even further. And the things which were mixed together, and separated off, and divided, were all understood by Mind. And whatever they were going to be, and whatever things were then in existence that are not now, and all things that now exist and whatever shall exist—all were arranged by Mind, as also the revolution now followed by the stars, the sun and moon, and the Air and Aether which were separated off. It was this revolution which caused the separation off. And dense separates from rare, and hot from cold, and bright from dark, and dry from wet. There are many portions of many things. And nothing is absolutely separated off or divided the one from the other except Mind. Mind is all alike, both the greater and the less. But nothing else is like anything else, but each individual thing is and was most obviously that of which it contains the most.

13.   And when Mind began the motion, there was a separating-off from all that was being moved; and all that Mind set in motion was separated (*internally*); and as things were moving and separating off (*internally*), the revolution greatly increased this (*internal*) separation.

14.   Mind, which ever Is, certainly still exists also where all other things are, (*namely*) in the multiple surrounding (*mass*) and in the things which were separated off before, and in the things already separated off.

15.   The dense and moist and cold and dark (*Elements*) collected here, where now is Earth, and the rare and hot and dry went outwards to the furthest part of the Aether.

16.   From these, while they are separating off, Earth solidifies; for from the clouds, water is separated off, and from the water, earth, and from the earth, stones are solidified by the cold; and these rush outward rather than the water.

17.   The Greeks have an incorrect belief on Coming into Being and Passing Away. No Thing comes into being or passes away, but it is mixed together or separated from existing Things. Thus they would be cor-

rect if they called coming into being 'mixing', and passing away 'separation-off'.

18.   It is the sun that endows the moon with its brilliance.

19.   We give the name Iris to the reflection of the sun on the clouds. It is therefore the sign of a storm, for the water which flows round the cloud produces wind or forces out rain.

* * *

21.   Through the weakness of the sense-perceptions, we cannot judge truth.

21a.   Visible existences are a sight of the unseen (*i.e. the present gives a view of the future*).

TESTIMONIA ON ANAXAGORAS BY PLATO

Then I heard someone who had a book of Anaxagoras, as he said, out of which he read that mind was the disposer and cause of all, and I was quite delighted at the notion of this, which appeared admirable, and I said to myself: If mind is the disposer, mind will dispose all for the best, and put each particular in the best place; and I argued that if any one desired to find out the cause of the generation or destruction or existence of anything, he must find out what state of being or suffering or doing was best for that thing, and therefore a man had only to consider the best for himself and others, and then he would also know the worse, for that the same science comprised both. And I rejoiced to think that I had found in Anaxagoras a teacher of the causes of existence such as I desired, and I imagined that he would tell me first whether the earth is flat or round; and then he would further explain the cause and the necessity of this, and would teach me the nature of the best and show that this was best; and if he said that the earth was in the centre, he would explain that this position was the best, and I should be satisfied if this were shown to me, and not want any other sort of cause. And I thought that I would then go on and ask him about the sun and moon and stars, and that he would explain to me their comparative swiftness, and their returnings and various states, and how their several affections, active and passive, were all for the best. For I could not imagine that when he spoke of mind as the disposer of them, he would give any other account of their being as they are, except that this was best; and I thought that when he had explained to me in detail the cause of each and the cause of all, he would go on to explain to me what was best for each and what was best for all. I had hopes which I would not have sold for much, and I seized the books and read them as fast as I could in my eagerness to know the better and the worse.

What hopes I had formed, and how grievously was I disappointed! As I proceeded, I found my philosopher altogether forsaking mind or any other principle of order, but having recourse to air, and ether, and water, and other eccentricities. I might compare him to a person who began by maintaining generally that mind is the cause of the actions of Socrates, but who, when he endeavoured to explain the causes of my several actions in detail, went on to show that I sit here because my body is made up of bones and muscles; and the bones, as he would say, are hard and have ligaments which divide them, and the muscles are elastic, and they cover the bones, which have also a covering or environment of flesh and skin which contains them; and as the bones are lifted at their joints by the contraction or relaxation of the muscles, I am able to bend my limbs, and this is why I am sitting here in a curved posture;—that is what he would say, and he would have a similar explanation of my talking to you, which he would attribute to sound, and air, and hearing, and he would assign ten thousand other causes of the same sort, forgetting to mention the true cause, which is, that the Athenians have thought fit to condemn me, and accordingly I have thought it better and more right to remain here and undergo my sentence; for I am inclined to think that these muscles and bones of mine would have gone off to Megara or Boeotia—by the dog of Egypt they would, if they had been guided only by their own idea of what was best, and if I had not chosen as the better and nobler part, instead of playing truant and running away, to undergo any punishment which the state inflicts. There is surely a strange confusion of causes and conditions in all this. It may be said, indeed, that without bones and muscles and the other parts of the body I cannot execute my purposes. But to say that I do as I do because of them, and that this is the way in which mind acts, and not from the choice of the best, is a very careless and idle mode of speaking. I wonder that they cannot distinguish the cause from the condition, which the many, feeling about in the dark, are always mistaking and misnaming. And thus one man makes a vortex all round and steadies the earth by the heaven; another gives the air as a support to the earth, which is a sort of broad trough. Any power which in disposing them as they are disposes them for the best never enters into their minds, nor do they imagine that there is any superhuman strength in that; they rather expect to find another Atlas of the world who is stronger and more everlasting and more containing than the good is, and are clearly of the opinion that the obligatory and containing power of the good is as nothing; and yet this is the principle which I would fain learn if any one would teach me. . . . (*Phaedo,* 97-99)

TESTIMONIA ON ANAXAGORAS BY ARISTOTLE

. . . Now Anaxagoras opposes Empedocles' view of the elements. Empedocles says that fire and earth and the related bodies are elementary bodies of which all things are composed; but this Anaxagoras denies. His elements are the homoeomerous things, viz. flesh, bone, and the like. Earth and fire are mixtures, composed of them and all the other seeds, each consisting of a collection of all the homoeomerous bodies, separately invisible; and that explains why from these two bodies all others are generated. (To him fire and *aither* are the same thing.) (*De Caelo*, 302*a* 28)

. . . Thus Empedocles holds that the corporeal elements are four, while all the elements—including those which initiate movement—are six in number; whereas Anaxagoras agrees with Leucippus and Democritus that the elements are infinite.

(Anaxagoras posits as elements the 'homoeomeries', viz. bone, flesh, marrow, and everything else which is such that part and whole are the same in name and nature. . . .) (*De Generatione et Corruptione*, 314*a* 16)

Anaxagoras gives an absurd account of why the infinite is at rest. He says that the infinite itself is the cause of its being fixed. This because it is *in* itself, since nothing else contains it—on the assumption that wherever anything is, it is there by its own nature. But this is not true: a thing could be somewhere by compulsion, and not where it is its nature to be. (*Physica*, 205*b* 1)

As regards Anaxagoras, if one were to suppose that he said there were two elements, the supposition would accord thoroughly with an argument which Anaxagoras himself did not state articulately, but which must have accepted if any one had led him on to it. True, to say that in the beginning all things were mixed is absurd both on other grounds and because it follows that they must have existed before in an unmixed form, and because nature does not allow any chance thing to be mixed with any chance thing, and also because on this view modifications and accidents could be separated from substances (for the same things which are mixed can be separated); yet if one were to follow him up, piecing together what he means, he would perhaps be seen to be somewhat modern in his views. For when nothing was separated out, evidently nothing could be truly asserted of the substance that then existed. I mean, e.g., that it was neither white nor black, nor grey nor any other colour, but of necessity colourless; for if it had been coloured, it would have had one of these colours. And similarly, by this same argument, it was flavourless, nor had it any similar attribute; for it could not be either of any quality or of any size, nor could it be any definite kind of thing. For if it were, one of the particular forms would have belonged to it, and this is impossible, since all were mixed together; for the particular form would necessarily have been already separated out, but he says all were mixed except reason, and this alone was unmixed and pure. From this it follows, then, that he must say the principles are the One (for this is simple and unmixed) and the Other, which is of such a nature as we suppose the indefinite to be before it is defined and partakes of some form. (*Metaphysica*, 989*a* 30)

The second set assert that the contrarieties are contained in the one and emerge from it by segregation, for example Anaximander and also all those who assert that 'what is' is one and many, like Empedocles and Anaxagoras; for they too produce other things from their mixture by segregation. These differ, however, from each other in that the former imagines a cycle of such changes, the latter a single series. Anaxagoras again made both his 'homoeomerous' substances and his contraries infinite in multitude, whereas Empedocles posits only the so-called elements.

The theory of Anaxagoras that the principles are infinite in multitude was probably due to his acceptance of the common opinion of the physicists that nothing comes into being from not-being. For this is the reason why they use the phrase 'all things were together' and the coming into being of such and such a kind of thing is reduced to change of quality, while some spoke of combination and separation. Moreover, the fact that the contraries proceed from each other led them to the conclusion. The one, they reasoned, must have already existed in the other; for since everything that comes into being must arise either from what is or from what is not, and it is impossible for it to arise from what is not (on this point all the physicists agree), they thought that the truth of the alternative necessarily followed, namely that things come into being out of existent things, i.e. out of things already present, but imperceptible to our senses because of the smallness of their bulk. So they assert that everything has been mixed in everything, because they saw everything arising out of everything. But things, as they say, appear different from one another and receive different names according to the nature of the particles which are numerically predominant among the innumerable constituents of the mixture. For nothing, they say, is purely and entirely white or black or sweet, bone or flesh, but the nature of a thing is held to be that of which it contains the most. (*Physica*, 187a 20)

So, too Anaxagoras is right when he says that Mind is impassive and unmixed, since he makes it the principle of motion: for it could cause motion in this sense only by being itself unmoved, and have supreme control only by being unmixed. (*Physica*, 256b 24)

The exception is Anaxagoras; he alone says that Mind is impassible, and has nothing in common with anything else. (*De Anima*, 405b 19)

Anaxagoras, as we said above, seems to distinguish between soul and mind, but in practice he treats them as a single substance, except that it is mind that he specially posits as the principle of all things; at any rate what he says is that mind alone of all that is is simple, unmixed, and pure. He assigns both characteristics, knowing and origination of movement, to the same principle, when he says that it was mind that set the whole in movement. (*De Anima*, 405a 13)

When one man (Anaxagoras) said, then, that reason (Mind) was present—as in animals, so throughout nature—as the cause of order and of all arrangement, he seemed like a sober man in contrast with the random talk of his predecessors. (*Metaphysica,* 984b 15)

Now it is the opinion of Anaxagoras that the possession of these hands is the cause of man being of all animals the most intelligent. (*De Partibus Animalium,* 687a 7)

TESTIMONIA ON ANAXAGORAS BY DIOGENES LAERTIUS*

Anaxagoras, the son of Hegesibulus or Eubulus, was a native of Clazomenae. He was a pupil of Anaximenes, and was the first who set mind above matter, for at the beginning of his treatise, which is composed in attractive and dignified language, he says, "All things were together; then came Mind and set them in order." This earned for Anaxagoras himself the nickname of Nous or Mind, and Timon in his *Silli* says of him:

> Then, I ween, there is Anaxagoras, a doughty champion, whom they call Mind, because forsooth his was the mind which suddenly woke up and fitted closely together all that had formerly been in a medley of confusion.

He was eminent for wealth and noble birth, and furthermore for magnanimity, in that he gave up his patrimony to his relations. For, when they accused him of neglecting it, he replied, "Why then do you not look after it?" And at last he went into retirement and engaged in physical investigation without troubling himself about public affairs. When some one inquired, "Have you no concern in your native land?" "Gently," he replied, "I am greatly concerned with my fatherland," and pointed to the sky. . . .

He declared the sun to be a mass of red-hot metal and to be larger than the Peloponnesus, though others ascribe this view to Tantalus; he declared that there were dwellings on the moon, and moreover hills and

* From R. D. Hicks, *Lives of Eminent Philosophers*.

ravines. He took as his principles the homoeomeries or homogeneous molecules; for just as gold consists of fine particles which are called gold-dust, so he held the whole universe to be compounded of minute bodies having parts homogeneous to themselves. His moving principle was Mind; of bodies, he said, some, like earth, were heavy, occupying the region below, others, light like fire, held the region above, while water and air were intermediate in position. For in this way over the earth, which is flat, the sea sinks down after the moisture has been evaporated by the sun. In the beginning the stars moved in the sky as in a revolving dome, so that the celestial pole which is always visible was vertically overhead; but subsequently the pole took its inclined position. He held the Milky Way to be a reflection of the light of stars which are not shone upon by the sun; comets to be a conjunction of planets which emit flames; shooting-stars to be a sort of sparks thrown off by the air. He held that winds arise when the air is rarefied by the sun's heat; that thunder is a clashing together of the clouds, lightning their violent friction; an earthquake a subsidence of air into the earth.

Animals were produced from moisture, heat, and an earthy substance; later the species were propagated by generation from one another, males from the right side, females from the left. . . .

Of the trial of Anaxagoras different accounts are given. Sotion in his *Succession of the Philosophers* says that he was indicted by Cleon on a charge of impiety, because he declared the sun to be a mass of red-hot metal; that his pupil Pericles defended him, and he was fined five talents and banished. Satyrus in his *Lives* says that the prosecutor was Thucydides, the opponent of Pericles, and the charge one of treasonable correspondence with Persia as well as of impiety; and that sentence of death was passed on Anaxagoras by default. When news was brought him that he was condemned and his sons were dead, his comment on the sentence was, "Long ago nature condemned both my judges and myself to death"; and on his sons, "I knew that my children were born to die."

Some, however, tell this story of Solon, and others of Xenophon. That he buried his sons with his own hands is asserted by Demetrius of Phalerum in his work *On Old Age*. Hermippus in his *Lives* says that he was confined in the prison pending his execution; that Pericles came forward and asked the people whether they had any fault to find with him in his own public career; to which they replied that they had not. "Well," he continued, "I am a pupil of Anaxagoras; do not then be carried away by slanders and put him to death. Let me prevail upon you to release him." So he was released; but he could not brook the indignity he had suffered and committed suicide. Hieronymus in the second book of his *Scattered Notes* states that Pericles brought him into court so weak and wasted from illness that he owed his acquittal not so much to the merits of his case as to the sympathy of the judges. So much then on the subject of his trial.

He was supposed to have borne Democritus a grudge because he had failed to get into communication with him. At length he retired to Lampsacus and there died. And when the magistrates of the city asked if there was anything he would like done for him, he replied that he would like them to grant an annual holiday to the boys in the month in which he died; and the custom is kept up to this day. . . .

Notes: VIII

1. *Cf.* G. S. Kirk and J. E. Raven, *The Pre-Socratic Philosophers* (Cambridge, England, Cambridge University Press, 1960), p. 380.

2. Anaxagoras, Fragments 6, 11, 12.

3. Plato, *Phaedo,* 97c ff.

4. G. F. Hegel, *Lectures on the History of Philosophy,* trans. by E. S. Haldane (New York, Humanities Press, 1963), Vol. I, p. 320 ff.

5. Plato, *Phaedo,* 97c ff.

6. Hegel, *op. cit.,* p. 342.

7. *See,* for example, René Descartes, *Meditations On First Philosophy,* in *Philosophical Works of Descartes,* trans. by E. S. Haldane and G. R. T. Ross (New York, Dover Publications, 1955), Vol. 1, p. 173, Meditation IV.

8. Anaxagoras, Fragment 12.

9. Hegel, *op. cit.,* p. 320. *See also* pp. 330, 331.

The Atomists

E VEN more obviously than the philosophy of Anaxagoras, the atomist doctrines of Democritus and Leucippus[1] bear a striking similarity to the more complex and empirically documented theories of modern science. It is thus as the progenitors of modern science that the atomists are usually and justly praised and evaluated.[2] It is possible to go into considerable detail, as many have done, in the reconstruction of their account of the makeup of the physical world. There are, however, two other aspects to their view on which we will concentrate in this interpretative essay. The first is the ethical doctrine of Democritus, which, in the opinion of most commentators unfortunately, constitutes the major position of the extant fragments. Second is the curious story recounted by Diogenes Laertius that Plato was so opposed to Democritus' philosophy that he tried to buy up all of Democritus' books and burn them![3] Now we may take this as an exaggeration of the possible truth that Plato had a strong dislike of Democritus' philosophy. Although many of Plato's philosophic predecessors are mentioned and discussed in the dialogues, including many whom he criticizes, Democritus, who was a contemporary of Socrates and probably a late contemporary of Plato himself, is pointedly ignored. The question is, what is there in Democritus' philosophy which Plato might find so extraordinarily objectionable? It is generally agreed that the ethical teaching is, in fact, strongly conventional and even conservative, in many cases rather similar to ethical views articulated in the dialogues. And what, after all, is so inherently objectionable about the metaphysical doctrine of atomism which seems such a clear progenitor of modern science? The guiding interpretative problem of this essay will be the attempt to view the atomists from the standpoint of this question: "Why should Plato have found the atomists' philosophy so distasteful?"

Let us begin by discussing briefly the most philosophically significant aspects of the theory of atoms itself. This significance can best be understood from two standpoints: the aforementioned extent to which it prefigures the view of modern science and the extent to which it constitutes a response to the legacy of Heraclitus and Parmenides, to the demand, that is, both to account for the phenomenal world and to obey the demands laid down by Parmenides concerning the nature of Being. In the first regard, what is especially significant about the atoms is that they differ only in quantitatively and, at least in principle, exactly measurable ways—according to size, shape, and weight; but they are qualitatively homogeneous. This affords again, at least theoretically, the possibility of a mathematically exact account of the structure of the cosmos—the goal of science, one might say, to this day. The things of our experience, including not just entities but "qualities" such as sweet and sour, hot and cold, and color, are formed by various conglomerations of these atoms.[4] Thus, for example, what is sweet is composed of atoms which are round and quite large, what is sour of atoms which are "bulky, jagged, and many angled, without curves."[5] In general, *any* entity or quality in the world of our experience can be exactly accounted for in terms of the size and shape of its constituent atoms, and their arrangement and position in relation to one another. Further, and also in keeping with the aims of modern science, the atomists offer a thoroughgoing mechanistic account of the universe. No gods or universal Mind arrange the atoms or first set things in motion; there is no teleological claim that the atoms are or ought to be arranged according to what is "best," but conglomerations of atoms form into and dissolve from things and qualities "according to necessity,"[6] which under the circumstances seems to mean very much the same as "by chance."

At the same time, each individual atom, since it is the *arche* of things, or Being, bears many of the characteristics of Being upon which Parmenides insisted. Each is, of course, a one, an indivisible unity. Each atom, as Being, does not itself change, that is, it undergoes no internal change. It is imperishable, neither having come to be nor passing away. Things that do come to be, change, and pass away do so thanks to the coming together and dissolution of conglomerations of atoms, but the atoms themselves are changeless.

Our senses present us with things and qualities. According to Democritus these are not the true reality; the atoms invisible to the senses are the real. Thus "Sweet exists by convention, bitter by convention, colour by convention; atoms and Void alone exist in reality."[7] As a consequence, Democritus accepts another important Parmenidean tenet: the untrustworthiness of the senses as the source of an account of Being. "One must learn by this rule that man is severed from reality."[8] We thus see yet another important acceptance of that proposition which seems to have pervaded early philosophic thought and given decisive direction to later philosophic thinking: What "appears" is not necessarily most fundamental; an adequate account of appearances, an account which "saves the phenomena," must, strange as it seems, go beyond or perhaps beneath appearance to the more fundamental but less visible origin, or *arche*. The acceptance of that proposition, it is worth noting, is as strong in contemporary scientific accounts, even those with so-called empirical support, as it was for Democritus.

We have seen that Democritus accepts the Parmenidean view that the atoms, as Being, cannot undergo change. How, then, account for the motion and change of the world of experience? In order to do so, Democritus must break in a decisive way with one of the most fundamental of all Parmenidean teachings: the view that only Being can be, that "nothing" cannot be. Let us first understand the immediate occasion for the denial of this principle, and then consider its broader significance. The atoms are "what is," or Being. They do not change. In order for motion to occur, therefore, there must be a kind of "empty space" through which the atoms, internally changeless, might move in order to come together and dissolve into the changing things of our experience. Democritus called this empty space "the void." But if the atoms are Being, the void must be not-being. Hence the famous line in Fragment 156: "Nothing exists just as much as . . . atoms and Void alone exist in reality."[9] We can at very least say this much; If the atoms are Being, then in order to explain the motion and change of the world, it must be asserted that that which is *other* than Being exists. This in itself is a radical break with Parmenides. It is tempting to go further, as we have above, and see in this the assertion of the coprimordiality of Being and Nothing. The alternative is to see implicit in Democritus a distinction which is generally attributed first to Plato in the *Sophist*: the distinction between non-being, *i.e.*, that which is not the same as Being, and *nothing*, that which has no being at all. Whichever of these two alternatives we choose—and Fragment 156 strongly militates in favor of the former—Democritus' effort to account for motion raises a metaphysical or ontological issue of the first magnitude both intrinsically and in its historical significance: the question of the co-presence, relationship, and indeed the "being" of Being and Nothing. Evidently the is-sue was present with Parmenides, but that philosopher responded to it by utterly denying the intelligibility and so the being of "what is not." More specifically, he denied the "way of non-being" as a fruitful path of inquiry. Democritus reinstitutes it not only as a path of inquiry but as a necessary aspect of an adequate account of the world. Subsequently, from Plato and Aristotle, through such seventeenth-century philosophers as Descartes, Spinoza, and Leibniz, through Kant, Hegel, Nietzsche, to the twentieth-century philosophies of Heidegger and Sar-tre, this issue has been a central one in philosophy. In the more scien-tific-minded tradition of analytic philosophy, the same kind of issue manifests itself in different terminology as the logical problem of "nega-tion" and the "logic of negative facts." The problem in all its manifesta-tions might be stated broadly in a Parmenidean way. If all there is is Being, if there is nothing else but Being, do we not find ourselves in a radical monism which makes the intelligibility even of Being im-possible? On the other hand, given the plausible affinity between Being and intelligibility, is it possible to speak intelligibly about non-being at all? To be sure, Democritus did not take up the issue in such general terms. His explicit concern was rendering an adequate account of mo-tion in the physical world, and to do so he found it necessary to argue for the "being" of "the void," or non-being. But in reflecting on the broader consequences of his doing so, we can begin to see the intercon-nection between that specific issue and the immense general issue for philosophy which is in large measure the legacy of Parmenides.

So far, Democritus' atomism would seem more a matter for thought for a philosopher like Plato than a position he would find detestable. Evidently, then, we have not begun to penetrate, in this general and reasonably orthodox account of atomism, what there is about it that Plato might have found so objectionable. There are several apparently minor points, however, that have already been mentioned which might offer us our first clues. The first is the antiteleological character of the mechanistic account offered by Leucippus and Democritus. As the quote from the *Phaedo* regarding Anaxagoras' philosophy makes ini-tially clear, it is the Socratic or Platonic view that no account of the world can be adequate, no account of anything *in* the world can be ade-quate, which does not at least consider the issue of value; as Socrates puts it in a somewhat exaggerated example, if someone claims that the world is round, Socrates wants to know why it is *best* that the world is round.[10] More generally, in the "ontology," the "logos of Being" set out in the *Republic* in terms of the so-called theory of Forms, or theory of Ideas, Socrates offers an account of the Forms which arranges them in an apparent hierarchy. The Forms themselves are the principles of intelligibility by which the things of the world of appearances get their intelligibility and being. But strangely enough, there is one Form which occupies an analogous status towards the *other* Forms: It is the Form which gives the *other* Forms their being and makes them intelligible. That Form is the famous "Idea of the Good."[11] Whatever the detailed significance of this difficult teaching, it certainly suggests at least this much: that for Socrates and Plato, the question of value is at the absolute fundament of an account of the world. There is no issue more fundamental than the issue of value; no aspect of the world, no matter for thought, can be discussed adequately if one has decided in advance that it is "beyond good and evil." Why should this insistence be so important? As suggested in the chapter on Heraclitus, if there are *issues* that are considered "beyond good and evil," then it is at least likely that there will be *actions* given the same status, either the action of the investigator investigating the issue or some action closely related to, or possibly a consequence of, the issue itself. Two brief recent examples should suffice. Modern science, as indicated, has argued implicitly or explicitly since the seventeenth century that "scientific knowledge" of the world involves "no value judgments." Few would argue seriously, for instance, that when accounting for the difference between a hydrogen and an oxygen atom one ought to include a discussion of which is "better" or which "more beautiful." However, the inference has often been drawn from this value-neutral status of a scientific account of a phenomenon that the act of scientific investigation *itself* was value-neutral, that is, to use recent examples, that the investigation into the development of destructive weapons or germ warfare should proceed with the same freedom from ethical questioning as does the search for a cure for cancer. A second example might be the existentialist conception of "authentic action" as action in which one is truly "one's own self" (*Eigentlichkeit*—the German word for authenticity). With the insistence by Heidegger and other philosophers that the "ontological" issue of authenticity is prior to or more fundamental than the "ontic" question of good and evil, we are forced to allow for at least the theoretical possibility that Hitlerlike actions can be as authentic—and who knows? perhaps even more so—than Christlike actions. It is the unacceptability of situations such as these two examples as an account of human experience that has led philosophers such as Plato to insist on the absolute fundamentality of the issue of value in ontology.

The mechanistic atomism of Leucippus and Democritus offers a metaphysical basis for the kind of view opposed by Plato in at least two obvious ways. First, it is "value-free"—the shape, size, and arrangement of atoms is the fundamental *logos* of the world, not the question of value. The question of value, it would seem, is "ontic," or conventional, although the way in which Democritus works this out is complex, as we shall see. Second, the *thoroughgoing* character of the mechanism means that the birth, death, and activity of human beings has a status no higher in the scheme of things than that of a blade of grass. Both are ultimately to be accounted for in terms of atoms and the void. Indeed, the world itself, the conglomeration of atoms that presently exists, could fall apart at any moment for mechanical reasons, not as a "punishment of the gods" or whatever. As the Christian Bishop, Hippolytus, complained, "This man ridiculed everything—as if all human concerns were absurd!"[12]

A second source of Platonic dissatisfaction with Democritus' view might derive from the relativism of perception explicitly defended by Democritus and the relativism of value strongly implied. The general statement of the relativity of what appears is well stated in Theophrastos' account of Democritus; to quote just enough to make the point:

> An indication that the aforementioned qualities (hot, cold, bitter, sweet, etc.) do not exist in nature is that things do not appear the same to all living creatures, but what is sweet to us is bitter to others, and to still others sour or pungent or astringent; and so with the rest.
>
> Moreover, he says that men "alter in makeup" according to age and condition—from which it is clear that a man's bodily state is a cause of what appears to him.[13]

As an account of *perception,* this is an insightful account whose consequences are still with us today. One of the most basic problematics of the phenomenological movement in philosophy today is the nature and significance of what they call the constitutive power of consciousness. It is as clear and as problematic to us as it was to Democritus that what appears to us often owes as much to *our* contribution as to its own nature as a "thing in itself."[14] Plato himself discusses a similar view at considerable length and with sensitivity in his dialogue *Theaetetus*.[15]

It is when the relativity of *value* is inferred from the relativity of perception that many thinkers, including Plato, become alarmed. Democritus seems to fall prey to this inference, which does not seem to be a necessary one. Thus Fragment 4 and 188 both essentially say: "Pleasure and absence of pleasure are the criteria of what is profitable and what is not."[16] But pleasure, as we all know and as Democritus knew well, is one of the most relative of things: "For all men, good and true are the same; but pleasant differs for different men."[17] This is an interesting fragment, for on the surface it contradicts the contention that Democritus infers from the relativity of perception the relativity of value. The good and the true are the same for all men. But note how this fits with Fragments 4 and 188. Pleasure and lack of pleasure are the criteria of the profitable and the unprofitable, but pleasure and its lack differ among men. It would seem to follow therefore that what is profitable differs among men. How could what is good for men be the same, but what is profitable differ according to the criterion of pleasure? The logically consistent reply, and the reply implicit in large numbers of Democritus' fragments, is this: The good is the same for all men in the sense that it is good for them to pursue pleasure and avoid displeasure or pain. But what *is* good or profitable for individual men varies according to what pleases them. What is good for all is to follow pleasure. The relativism of value which Democritus infers from his atomism is now joined to an inferred hedonism or adherence to the principle that the good is the pleasurable. We must now consider in more detail the extremely sophisticated version of hedonism that Democritus presents.

Democritus' hedonistic ethics is not at all an "eat, drink, and be merry . . ." view. On the contrary, he recommends a rather contemplative, almost ascetic, life dominated by the virtue of *sophrosyne* ("moderation") which would probably seem dull to more free-spirited hedonists. This, however, is not a denial of hedonism but a sophistication. Democritus thinks that he knows that the long-run pleasure will be greater in a life of moderation than one of intense pursuit of intense pleasure. A few representative fragments will make this clear.

> Cheerfulness is created for men through moderation of enjoyment and harmoniousness of life.[18]

> Moderation (*sophrosyne*) multiplies pleasures, and increases pleasure.[19]

> If one oversteps the due measure, the most pleasurable things become most unpleasant. [20]

To be sure, Democritus' hedonism is respectable and conventional to the point of tediousness. But it remains the case that in his view even the virtues are praised in the light of the pleasure that adherence to them will produce. One should be moderate (*sophron*) not because it is intrinsically good to be *sophron*, but because being so is more pleasant—from which it would seem to follow that if Democritus were shown that *sophrosyne* was unpleasant, he would cease to consider it a virtue. And in any case, has not Democritus already asserted that what is pleasant for one person is not pleasant for another? Suppose moderation happens to be extremely unpleasant for someone. Is there anything in Democritus' philosophy which suggests that one should continue to be moderate? On the contrary. We can now begin to see why Plato might have objected so strenuously to Democritus' view: Notwithstanding the eminently respectable ethical consequences which Democritus draws from his hedonism—that one ought to be *sophron*, just, contemplative, etc., because they are more pleasant—there is latent in his view the justification for a very different ethic indeed.

Even and especially the role of *reason* is subordinated in Democritus' philosophy to the principle of pleasure. One ought to be wise, to lead a contemplative life, because it is most pleasurable.[21] As J. M. Robinson observes, the implications of this view can be brought out by a comparison of the role of reason in Heraclitus[22] or, I would add, Parmenides. For these men, reason was embedded in the very nature of the world, and the challenge for the thinking man was to gain access to or get in attunement with the *rational* character of the world, and so to become part of the reason of nature. Both men might agree with Hegel's view that the world is through and through rational. For Democritus, however, reason is essentially a skill possessed by man, a skill to be used most basically for the *calculation of pleasure*. Reason is funlamentally calculation, and what it can best, that is, most profitably calculate, is pleasure. There are many fragments which support this, but perhaps the most striking is Democritus' application of the principle of the rational calculation of pleasure to the problem of child rearing:

> Whoever wants to have children should, in my opinion, choose them from the family of one of his friends. He will thus obtain a child such as he wishes, for he can select the kind he wants. And the one that seems fittest will be most likely to follow on his natural endowment. The difference is that in the latter way one can take one child out of many who is according to one's liking; but if one begets a child of one's own, the risks are many, for one is bound to accept him as he is.[23] . . .

The objection that Plato might have had to Democritus' philosophy might thus be summed up as follows: Plato often and explicitly argues in the dialogues against the Sophists, who taught, in one way or another, a doctrine of ethical relativism often coupled with hedonism and a conception of reason as calculation or rhetoric. These men for the most part argued straightforwardly for the relativist view; it was not grounded in a more comprehensive philosophic conception of the structure of reality, or Being. As such, it was a simpler, or at least more clearly defined task to refute them. Democritus, on the other hand, by claiming to derive his relativism and hedonism as consequences of his atomistic mechanism, offers a metaphysical foundation for the very position which the Sophists defended and which Socrates and Plato so violently opposed.[24] At least from a philosophic standpoint, then, Democritus was all the more dangerous than the Sophists, dangerous because his defense of a potentially destructive philosophy was more thorough, and so more persuasive to young minds who might be tempted by it.[25]

And yet, as we have seen and as everyone seems to agree, atomism is very much a prototype of modern science. And it is safe to say that hedonistic relativism is by no means absent from our own cultural situation. Could these two contemporary phenomena be related? A consideration of the opposition between Democritus and Plato might well lead us to a very serious and possibly painful reflection on some of the most cherished aspects of our own contemporary culture. Perhaps the way can be prepared for such a reflection by the last two chapters of this book, the Sophists, who are the more popular spokesmen for the consequences of Democritus' view, and Plato, who so strongly opposed them.

Leucippus and Democritus

Both Leucippus and Democritus came from Abdera, although Leucippus was probably born in either Elea or Miletus. Leucippus flourished around 430 B.C., Democritus, supposedly his pupil, around 420 B.C. It is noteworthy that this date makes Democritus a contemporary of Socrates. Because only one of Leucippus' fragments survives, very little is known of him, except that he founded the philosophic school of atomism. Democritus, because so much more of his work survives, is the more famous of the two. In the opinion of many, it is only because of the dominance of Socrates and Plato, and their noteworthy silence on the atomists, that atomism did not receive the wider consideration that it deserves.

A. Leucippus

LEUCIPPUS: FRAGMENT*

Nothing happens at random; whatever comes about is by rational necessity.

TESTIMONIA ON LEUCIPPUS BY DIOGENES LAERTIUS**

Leucippus was born at Elea, but some say at Abdera and others at Miletus. He was a pupil of Zeno. His views were these. The sum of things is unlimited, and they all change into one another. The All includes the empty as well as the full. The worlds are formed when atoms fall into the void and are entangled with one another; and from

* From Philip Wheelwright, *The Pre-Socratics*.
** From R. D. Hicks, *Lives of Eminent Philosophers*.

their motion as they increase in bulk arises the substance of the stars. The sun revolves in a larger circle round the moon. The earth rides steadily, being whirled about the centre; its shape is like that of a drum. Leucippus was the first to set up atoms as first principles. Such is a general summary of his views; on particular points they are as follows.

He declares the All to be unlimited, as already stated; but of the All part is full and part empty, and these he calls elements. Out of them arise the worlds unlimited in number and into them they are dissolved. This is how the worlds are formed. In a given section many atoms of all manner of shapes are carried from the unlimited into the vast empty space. These collect together and form a single vortex, in which they jostle against each other and, circling round in every possible way, separate off, by like atoms joining like. And, the atoms being so numerous that they can no longer revolve in equilibrium, the light ones pass into the empty space outside, as if they were being winnowed; the remainder keep together and, becoming entangled, go on their circuit together, and form a primary spherical system. This parts off like a shell, enclosing within it atoms of all kinds; and, as these are whirled round by virtue of the resistence of the centre, the enclosing shell becomes thinner, the adjacent atoms continually combining when they touch the vortex. In this way the earth is formed by portions brought to the centre coalescing. And again, even the outer shell grows larger by the influx of atoms from outside, and, as it is carried round in the vortex, adds to itself whatever atoms it touches. And of these some portions are locked together and form a mass, at first damp and miry, but, when they have dried and revolve with the universal vortex, they afterwards take fire and form the substance of the stars.

The orbit of the sun is the outermost, that of the moon nearest to the earth; the orbits of the other heavenly bodies lie between these two. All the stars are set on fire by the speed of their motion; the burning of the sun is also helped by the stars; the moon is only slightly kindled. The sun and the moon are eclipsed <when . . . , but the obliquity of the zodiacal circle is due> to the inclination of the earth to the south; the regions of the north are always shrouded in mist, and are extremely cold and frozen. Eclipses of the sun are rare; eclipses of the moon constantly occur, and this because their orbits are unequal. As the world is born, so, too, it grows, decays and perishes, in virtue of some necessity, the nature of which he does <not> specify.

TESTIMONIA ON LEUCIPPUS BY ARISTOTLE

Leucippus, however, thought he had a theory which harmonized with sense-perception and would not abolish either coming-to-be and passing-away or motion and the multiplicity of things. He made these concessions to the facts of perception: on the other hand, he conceded to the Monists that there could be no motion without a void. The result is a theory which he states as follows: 'The void is a "not-being", and no part of "what is" is a "not-being"; for what "is" in the strict sense of the term is an absolute *plenum*. This *plenum*, however, is not "one": on the contrary, it is a "many" infinite in number and invisible owing to the minuteness of their bulk. The "many" move in the void (for there is a void): and by coming together they produce "coming-to-be", while by separating they produce "passing-away". Moreover, they act and suffer action wherever they chance to be in contact (for *there* they are not "one"), and they generate by being put together and becoming intertwined. (*De Generatione et Corruptione*, 325a 24)

. . . Leucippus and his associate Democritus say that the full and the empty are the elements, calling the one being and the other non-being—the full and solid being being, the empty non-being (whence they say being no more is than non-being, because the solid no more is than the empty); and they make these the material causes of things. And as those who make the underlying substance one generate all other things by its modifications, supposing the rare and the dense to be the sources of the modifications, in the same way these philosophers say the differences in the elements are the causes of all other qualities. These differences, they say, are three—shape and order and position. For they say the real is differentiated only by 'rhythm' and 'inter-contact' and 'turning'; and of these rhythm is shape, inter-contact is order, and turning is position; for A differs from N in shape, AN from NA in order, I from H in position. The question of movement—whence or how it is to belong to things—these thinkers, like the others, lazily neglected. (*Metaphysica*, 985b 4)

. . . Thus Empedocles holds that the corporeal elements are four, while all the elements—including those which initiate movement—are six in number; whereas Anaxagoras agrees with Leucippus and Democritus that the elements are infinite.

(Anaxagoras posits as elements the 'homoeomeries', viz. bone, flesh, marrow, and everything else which is such that part and whole are the same in name and nature; while Democritus and Leucippus say that there are indivisible bodies, infinite both in number and in the varieties of their shapes, of which everything else is composed—the compounds differing one from another according to the shapes, 'positions', and 'groupings' of their constituents.) (*De Generatione et Corruptione*, 314*a* 16)

B. Democritus

DEMOCRITUS: FRAGMENT*

3.   The man who wishes to have serenity of spirit should not engage in many activities, either private or public, nor choose activities beyond his power and natural capacity. He must guard against this, so that when good fortune strikes him and leads him on to excess by means of (*false*) seeming, he must rate it low, and not attempt things beyond his powers. A reasonable fullness is better than overfullness.

4.   Pleasure and absence of pleasure are the criteria of what is profitable and what is not.

* * *

6.   One must learn by this rule that Man is severed from reality. (*From 'On the Forms'*.)

7.   We know nothing about anything really, but Opinion is for all individuals an inflowing (*? of the Atoms*). (*From 'On the Forms'*.)

8.   It will be obvious that it is impossible to understand how in reality each thing is. (*From 'On the Forms'*.)

* * *

*   From Kathleen Freeman, *Ancilla to the Pre-Socratic Philosophers*.

9.   Sweet exists by convention, bitter by convention, colour by convention; atoms and Void (*alone*) exist in reality . . . We know nothing accurately in reality, but (*only*) as it changes according to the bodily condition, and the constitution of those things that flow upon (*the body*) and impinge upon it.

10.   It has often been demonstrated that we do not grasp how each thing is or is not.

*   *   *

11.   There are two sorts of knowledge, one genuine, one bastard (*or 'obscure'*). To the latter belong all the following: sight, hearing, smell, taste, touch. The real is separated from this. When the bastard can do no more—neither see more minutely, nor hear, nor smell, nor taste, nor perceive by touch—and a finer investigation is needed, then the genuine comes in as having a tool for distinguishing more finely. (*From 'The Canon'*).

*   *   *

31.   Medicine heals diseases of the body, wisdom frees the soul from passions.

32.   Coition is a slight attack of apoplexy. For man gushes forth from man, and is separated by being torn apart with a kind of blow.

33.   Nature and instruction are similar; for instruction transforms the man, and in transforming, creates his nature.

34.   Man is a universe in little (*Microcosm*).

GNOMAE

35.   If any man listens to my opinions, here recorded, with intelligence, he will achieve many things worthy of a good man, and avoid doing many unworthy things.

*   *   *

37.   He who chooses the advantages of the soul chooses things more divine, but he who chooses those of the body, chooses things human.

38.   It is noble to prevent the criminal; but if one cannot, one should not join him in crime.

39.   One must either be good, or imitate a good man.

40.   Men find happiness neither by means of the body nor through possessions, but through uprightness and wisdom.

41.   Refrain from crimes not through fear but through duty.

* * *

45.   The wrongdoer is more unfortunate than the man wronged.

46.   Magnanimity consists in enduring tactlessness with mildness.

47.   Well-ordered behaviour consists in obedience to the law, the ruler, and the man wiser (*than oneself*).

48.   When inferior men censure, the good man pays no heed.

49.   It is hard to be governed by one's inferior.

50.   The man completely enslaved to wealth can never be honest.

51.   In power of persuasion, reasoning is far stronger than gold.

* * *

53.   Many who have not learnt Reason, nevertheless live according to reason.

* * *

55.   One should emulate the deeds and actions of virtue, not the words.

* * *

57.   Good breeding in cattle depends on physical health, but in men on a well-formed character.

* * *

59.   Neither skill nor wisdom is attainable unless one learns.

60.   It is better to examine one's own faults than those of others.

* * *

62.   Virtue consists, not in avoiding wrong-doing, but in having no wish thereto.

* * *

64.   Many much-learned men have no intelligence.*

65.   One should practise much-sense, not much-learning.*

* * *

69.   For all men, good and true are the same; but pleasant differs for different men.

70.   Immoderate desire is the mark of a child, not a man.

71.   Untimely pleasures produce unpleasantnesses.

72.   Violent desire for one thing blinds the soul to all others.

* * *

* Cf. Heraclitus, Frg. 40.

74.   Accept no pleasure unless it is beneficial.

75.   It is better for fools to be ruled than to rule.

*   *   *

80.   It is shameful to be so busy over the affairs of others that one knows nothing of one's own.

*   *   *

83.   The cause of error is ignorance of the better.

*   *   *

86.   It is greed to do all the talking and not be willing to listen.

*   *   *

92.   Accept favours in the foreknowledge that you will have to give a greater return for them.

93.   When you do a favour, study the recipient first, lest he prove a scoundrel and repay evil for good.

94.   Small favours at the right time are greatest to the recipients.

*   *   *

96.   The generous man is he who does not look for a return, but who does good from choice.

*   *   *

98.   The friendship of one intelligent man is better than that of all the unintelligent.*

* Cf. Heraclitus, Frg. 49.

99.   Life is not worth living for the man who has not even one good friend.

*   *   *

102.   In all things, equality is fair, excess and deficiency not so, in my opinion.

*   *   *

105.   Physical beauty is (*merely*) animal unless intelligence be present.

*   *   *

107.   Not all one's relatives are friends, but only those who agree with us about what is advantageous.

*   *   *

108.   Good things are obtained with difficulty if one seeks; but bad things come without our even seeking.

*   *   *

110.   A woman must not practise argument: this is dreadful.

111.   To be ruled by a woman is the ultimate outrage for a man.

112.   It is the mark of the divine intellect to be always calculating something noble.

*   *   *

(End of the Gnômae)

116.   I came to Athens and no one knew me.

117.   We know nothing in reality; for truth lies in an abyss.

118.   (*I would*) rather discover one cause than gain the kingdom of Persia.

119.   Men have fashioned an image of Chance as an excuse for their own stupidity. For Chance rarely conflicts with Intelligence, and most things in life can be set in order by an intelligent sharpsightedness.

* * *

125.   Colour exists by convention (*usage*), sweet by convention, bitter by convention.
    (*Reply of the senses to Intellect*): 'Miserable Mind, you get your evidence from us, and do you try to overthrow us? The overthrow will be your downfall'.

* * *

127.   Men get pleasure from scratching themselves: they feel an enjoyment like that of lovemaking.

* * *

145.   Speech is the shadow of action.

146.   The Reason within the soul, accustoming itself to derive its pleasures from itself.

* * *

148.   The navel forms first in the womb, as an anchorage against tossing and wandering, a cable and a rope for the fruit, engendered and future.

* * *

154.   We are pupils of the animals in the most important things: the spider for spinning and mending, the swallow for building, and the songsters, swan and nightingale, for singing, by way of imitation.

155.   If a cone were cut by a plane parallel to the base,* what ought one to think of the surfaces resulting from the section: are they equal or unequal? If they are unequal, they will make the cone have many steplike indentations and unevennesses; but if they are equal, the sections will be equal, and the cone will appear to have the same property as a cylinder, being made up of equal, not unequal, circles, which is most absurd.

*   *   *

156.   Naught exists just as much as Aught.

*   *   *

159.   (*Democritus said*): If the body brought a suit against the soul, for all the pains it had endured throughout life, and the illtreatment, and I were to be the judge of the suit, I would gladly condemn the soul, in that it had partly ruined the body by its neglect and dissolved it with bouts of drunkenness, and partly destroyed it and torn it in pieces with its passion for pleasure—as if, when a tool or a vessel were in a bad condition, I blamed the man who was using it carelessly.

*   *   *

164.   Living creatures consort with their kind, as doves with doves, and cranes with cranes, and similarly with the rest of the animal world. So it is with inanimate things, as one can see with the sieving of seeds and with the pebbles on beaches. In the former, through the circulation of the sieve, beans are separated and ranged with beans, barley-grains with barley, and wheat with wheat; in the latter, with the motion of the wave, oval pebbles are driven to the same place as oval, and round to round, as if the similarity in these things had a sort of power over them which had brought them together.

165.   I say the following about the Whole . . . Man is that which we all know.

* 'By which is clearly meant a plane indefinitely near to the base.' Heath, *Greek Mathematics*, 1, pp. 179-80.

* * *

169.   Do not try to understand everything, lest you become ignorant of everything.

170.   Happiness, like unhappiness, is a property of the soul.

171.   Happiness does not dwell in flocks of cattle or in gold. The soul is the dwelling-place of the (*good and evil*) genius.

172.   Those same things from which we get good can also be for us a source of hurt, or else we can avoid the hurt. For instance, deep water is useful for many purposes, and yet again harmful; for there is danger of being drowned. A technique has therefore been invented: instruction in swimming.

173.   For mankind, evil comes out of what is good, if one does not know how to guide and drive correctly. It is not right to place such things in the category of evil, but in that of good. It is possible also to use what is good for an evil end* if one wishes.

* * *

175.   But the gods are the givers of all good things, both in the past and now. They are not, however, the givers of things which are bad, harmful or non-beneficial, either in the past or now, but men themselves fall into these through blindness of mind and lack of sense.

176.   Chance is generous but unreliable. Nature, however, is self-sufficient. Therefore it is victorious, by means of its smaller but reliable (*power*) over the greater promise of hope.

* * *

---

* The MS. reading ἀλκήν is emended by Diels-Kranz ἀλκῇ and translated: 'It is possible to use what is good as a help against what is evil.'

179. If children are allowed not to work,* they cannot learn letters or music or gymnastic, nor that which above all things embraces virtue, (namely) reverence. For it is precisely from these studies that reverence usually grows.

180. Education is an ornament for the prosperous, a refuge for the unfortunate.

* * *

187. It is right that men should value the soul rather than the body; for perfection of soul corrects the inferiority of the body, but physical strength without intelligence does nothing to improve the mind.

188. The criterion of the advantageous and disadvantageous is enjoyment and lack of enjoyment.

189. The best way for a man to lead his life is to have been as cheerful as possible and to have suffered as little as possible. This could happen if one did not seek one's pleasure in mortal things.

* * *

191. Cheerfulness is created for men through moderation of enjoyment and harmoniousness of life. Things that are in excess or lacking are apt to change and cause great disturbance in the soul. Souls which are stirred by great divergences are neither stable nor cheerful. Therefore one must keep one's mind on what is attainable, and be content with what one has, paying little heed to things envied and admired, and not dwelling on them in one's mind. Rather must you consider the lives of those in distress, reflecting on their intense sufferings, in order that your own possessions and condition may seem great and enviable, and you may, by ceasing to desire more, cease to suffer in your soul.

---

* It seems best to take ἀπιόντας after the intrans. ἀνιέντες, as a consecutive infinitive: 'If children are left free so as not to work.' Kranz translates: 'If we do not leave children free to work.'

For he who admires those who have, and who are called happy by other mortals, and who dwells on them in his mind every hour, is constantly compelled to undertake something new and to run the risk, through his desire, of doing something irretrievable among those things which the laws prohibit. Hence one must not seek the latter, but must be content with the former, comparing one's own life with that of those in worse cases, and must consider oneself fortunate, reflecting on their sufferings, in being so much better off than they. If you keep to this way of thinking, you will live more serenely, and will expel those not-negligible curses in life, envy, jealousy and spite.

* * *

193.   It is the business of intelligence to guard against a threatened injustice, but it is the mark of insensibility not to avenge it when it has happened.

194.   The great pleasures come from the contemplation of noble works.

* * *

199.   People are fools who hate life and yet wish to live through fear of Hades.

200.   People are fools who live without enjoyment of life.

201.   People are fools who yearn for long life without pleasure in long life.

* * *

207.   One should choose not every pleasure, but only that concerned with the beautiful.

208.   The self-control of the father is the greatest example for the children.

* * *

211.   Moderation multiplies pleasures, and increases pleasure.

*   *   *

214.   The brave man is not only he who overcomes the enemy, but he who is stronger than pleasures. Some men are masters of cities, but are enslaved to women.

*   *   *

226.   Freedom of speech is the sign of freedom; but the danger lies in discerning the right occasion.

*   *   *

232.   Of pleasures, those that come most rarely give the greatest enjoyment.

233.   If one oversteps the due measure, the most pleasurable things become most unpleasant.

*   *   *

235.   All who derive their pleasures from the stomach, overstepping due season in eating or drinking or sexual pleasure, have pleasures that are but brief and short-lived, (*that is*), only while they are eating and drinking, but pains that are many. For this desire is always present for the same things, and when people get what they desire, the pleasure passes quickly, and they have nothing good for themselves except a brief enjoyment; and then again the need for the same things returns.

236.   It is hard to fight desire; but to control it is the sign of a reasonable man.

*   *   *

242.   More men become good through practice than by nature.

* * *

245.   The laws would not prevent each man from living according to his inclination, unless individuals harmed each other; for envy creates the beginning of strife.

* * *

267.   Rule belongs by nature to the stronger.

* * *

273.   A woman is far sharper than a man in malign thoughts.

* * *

275.   The rearing of children is full of pitfalls. Success is attended by strife and care, failure means grief beyond all others.

276.   I do not think that one should have children. I observe in the acquisition of children many great risks and many griefs, whereas a harvest is rare, and even when it exists, it is thin and poor.

277.   Whoever wants to have children should, in my opinion, choose them from the family of one of his friends. He will thus obtain a child such as he wishes, for he can select the kind he wants. And the one that seems fittest will be most likely to follow on his natural endowment. The difference is that in the latter way one can take one child out of many who is according to one's liking; but if one begets a child of one's own, the risks are many, for one is bound to accept him as he is.

278.   For human beings it is one of the necessities of life to have children, arising from nature and primeval law. It is obvious in the other animals too: they all have offspring by nature, and not for the sake of any profit. And when they are born, the parents work and rear each as best they can and are anxious for them while they are small, and if anything happens to them, the parents are grieved. But for man it has now become an established belief that there should be also some advantage from the offspring. . . .

TESTIMONIA ON DEMOCRITUS BY ARISTOTLE

He [Democritus] says one thing cannot be made out of two nor two out of one; for he identifies substances with his indivisible magnitudes. (*Metaphysica*, 1039a 9)

. . . . Democritus seems to think there are three kinds of difference between things; the underlying body, the matter, is one and the same, but they differ either in rhythm, i.e. shape, or in turning, i.e. position, or in inter contact, i.e. order. (*Metaphysica*, 1042b 12)

Democritus, for his part, asserts the contrary, namely that no element arises from another element. Nevertheless for him the common body is a source of all things, differing from part to part in size and in shape. (*Physica*, 203a 33)

'Democritus thinks the nature of the eternal entities consists of small substances infinite in number; as a place for them he supposes something else infinite in size, and to this he applies the names "void", nothing", and "the infinite", while to each of the substances he applies the names "thing", "solid", and "real". He thinks the substances are so small as to escape our senses, but have all sorts of shapes and figures, and differences of size. From these substances, as from elements, are generated and compounded visible and sensible masses. The substances are at variance and move in the void because of their dissimilarity and the other aforesaid differences, and as they move they impinge on each other and are so completely interlocked that they touch one another or get near one another; but a single substance is never in reality produced from them by this interlocking; for it would be very naïf to suppose that two or more things could ever become one. The fact that substances stay with one another for some time the Atomists ascribe to the bodies fitting into one another and catching hold of one another; for some of them are scalene, others hook-shaped, others concave, others convex, and others have numberless other differences. He thinks they cling to one another and remain together until some stronger force arriving from the environment shakes them asunder and separates them.'

He ascribes the genesis and the separation opposed to it not only to animals but also to plants and to worlds, and comprehensively to all sensible bodies. If, then, genesis is combination of atoms, and destruction separation of them, then even according to Democritus 'genesis' must be change of quality. (From Aristotle's lost work *On Democritus*)

All thinkers then agree in making the contraries principles, both those who describe the All as one and unmoved (for even Parmenides treats hot and cold as principles under the names of fire and earth) and those too who use the rare and the dense. The same is true of Democritus also, with his plenum and void, both of which exist, he says, the one as being, the other as not-being. Again he speaks of differences in position, shape, and order, and these are genera of which the species are contraries, namely, of position, above and below, before and behind; of shape, angular and angle-less, straight and round. (*Physica*, 188b 18)

It is just this that enables Democritus to show that all things cannot have had a becoming: for time, he says, is uncreated. (*Physica*, 251b 15)

And again, they say that many of the other animals receive impressions contrary to ours; and that even to the senses of each individual, things do not always seem the same. Which, then, of these impressions are true and which are false is not obvious; for the one set is no more true than the other, but both are alike. And this is why Democritus, at any rate, says that either there is no truth or to us at least it is not evident.

And in general it is because these thinkers suppose knowledge to be sensation, and this to be a physical alteration, that they say that what appears to our senses must be true; for it is for these reasons that both Empedocles and Democritus and, one may almost say, all the others have fallen victims to opinions of this sort. (*Metaphysica*, 1009b 7)

. . . This is what led Democritus to say that soul is a sort of fire or hot substance; his 'forms' or atoms are infinite in number; those which are spherical he calls fire and soul, and compares them to the motes in the air which we see in shafts of light coming through windows; the mixture of seeds of all sorts he calls the elements of the whole of Nature (Leucippus gives a similar account); the spherical atoms are identified with soul because atoms of that shape are most adapted to permeate everywhere, and to set all the others moving by being themselves in movement. This implies the view that soul is identical with what produces movement in animals. That is why, further, they regard respiration as the characteristic mark of life; as the environment compresses the bodies of animals, and tends to extrude those atoms which impart movement to them, because they themselves are never at rest, there must be a reinforcement of these by similar atoms coming in from without in the act of respiration; for they prevent the extrusion of those which are already within by counteracting the compressing and consolidating force of the environment; and animals continue to live only as long as they are able to maintain this resistance. (*De Anima*, 404*a* 1)

. . . Democritus roundly identifies soul and mind, for he identifies what appears with what is true—that is why he commends Homer for the phrase 'Hector lay with thought distraught'; he does not employ mind as a special faculty dealing with truth, but identifies soul and mind. (*De Anima*, 404*a* 28)

. . . There is a consequent diversity in their several accounts of soul; they assume, naturally enough, that what is in its own nature originative of movement must be among what is primordial. That has led some to regard it as fire, for fire is the subtlest of the elements and nearest to incorporeality; further, in the most primary sense, fire both is moved and originates movement in all the others.

Democritus has expressed himself more ingeniously than the rest on the grounds for ascribing each of these two characters to soul; soul and mind are, he says, one and the same thing, and this thing must be one of the primary and indivisible bodies, and its power of originating movement must be due to its fineness of grain and the shape of its atoms; he says that of all the shapes the spherical is the most mobile, and that this is the shape of the particles of both fire and mind. (*De Anima*, 405*a* 2)

TESTIMONIA ON DEMOCRITUS BY DIOGENES LAERTIUS*

. . . Afterwards he [Democritus] met Leucippus and, according to some, Anaxagoras, being forty years younger than the latter. But Favorinus in his *Miscellaneous History* tells us that Democritus, speaking of Anaxagoras, declared that his views on the sun and the moon were not original but of great antiquity, and that he had simply stolen them. Democritus also pulled to pieces the views of Anaxagoras on cosmogony and on mind, having a spite against him, because Anaxagoras did not take to him. If this be so, how could he have been his pupil, as some suggest?

According to Demetrius in his book on *Men of the Same Name* and Antisthenes in his *Successions of Philosophers,* he travelled into Egypt to learn geometry from the priests, and he also went into Persia to visit the Chaldaeans as well as to the Red Sea. Some say that he associated with the Gymnosophists in India and went to Aethiopia. . . .

. . . Demetrius goes on: "It would seem that he also went to Athens and was not anxious to be recognized, because he despised fame, and that while he knew of Socrates, he was not known to Socrates, his words being, 'I came to Athens and no one knew me.' "

"If the *Rivals* be the work of Plato," says Thrasylus, "Democritus will be the unnamed character, different from Oenopides and Anaxagoras, who makes his appearance when conversation is going on with Socrates about philosophy, and to whom Socrates says that the philosopher is like the all-round athlete. And truly Democritus was versed in every department of philosophy, for he had trained himself both in physics and in ethics, nay more, in mathematics and the routine subjects of education, and he was quite an expert in the arts." From him we have the saying, "Speech is the shadow of action." . . .

His character can also be seen from his writings. "He would seem," says Thrasylus, "to have been an admirer of the Pythagoreans. Moreover, he mentions Pythagoras himself, praising him in a work of his own entitled *Pythagoras*. He seems to have taken all his ideas from him and, if chronology did not stand in the way, he might have been thought his pupil." . . .

---

* From R. D. Hicks, *Lives of Eminent Philosophers.*

He would train himself, says Antisthenes, by a variety of means to test his sense-impressions by going at times into solitude and frequenting tombs. The same authority states that, when he returned from his travels, he was reduced to a humble mode of life because he had exhausted his means; and, because of his poverty, he was supported by his brother Damasus. But his reputation rose owing to his having foretold certain future events; and after that the public deemed him worthy of the honour paid to a god. There was a law, says Anthisthenes, that no one who had squandered his patrimony should be buried in his native city. Democritus, understanding this, and fearing lest he should be at the mercy of any envious or unscrupulous prosecutors, read aloud to the people his treatise, the *Great Diacosmos*, the best of all his works; and then he was rewarded with 500 talents; and, more than that, with bronze statues as well; and when he died, he received a public funeral after a lifetime of more than a century. . . .

Aristoxenus in his *Historical Notes* affirms that Plato wished to burn all the writings of Democritus that he could collect, but that Amyclas and Clinias the Pythagoreans prevented him, saying that there was no advantage in doing so, for already the books were widely circulated. And there is clear evidence for this in the fact that Plato, who mentions almost all the early philosophers, never once alludes to Democritus, not even where it would be necessary to controvert him, obviously because he knew that he would have to match himself against the prince of philosophers, for whom, to be sure, Timon has this meed of praise:

> Such is the wise Democritus, the guardian of discourse, keen-witted disputant, among the best I ever read. . . .

. . . Moreover, Hippocrates being accompanied by a maidservant, on the first day Democritus greeted her with "Good morning, maiden," but the next day with "Good morning, woman." As a matter of fact the girl had been seduced in the night.

Of the death of Democritus the account given by Hermippus is as follows. When he was now very old and near his end, his sister was vexed that he seemed likely to die during the festival of Thesmophoria and she would be prevented from paying the fitting worship to the goddess. He bade her be of good cheer and ordered hot loaves to be brought to him every day. By applying these to his nostrils he contrived to outlive the festival; and as soon as the three festival days were passed he let his life go from him without pain, having then, according to Hipparchus, attained his one hundred and ninth year. . . .

His opinions are these. The first principles of the universe are atoms and empty space; everything else is merely thought to exist. The worlds are unlimited; they come into being and perish. Nothing can come into being from that which is not nor pass away into that which is not. Further, the atoms are unlimited in size and number, and they are borne along in the whole universe in a vortex, and thereby generate all composite things—fire, water, air, earth; for even these are conglomerations of given atoms. And it is because of their solidity that these atoms are impassive and unalterable. The sun and the moon have been composed of such smooth and spherical masses [*i.e.* atoms], and so also the soul, which is identical with reason. We see by virtue of the impact of images upon our eyes.

All things happen by virtue of necessity, the vortex being the cause of the creation of all things, and this he calls necessity. The end of action is tranquillity, which is not identical with pleasure, as some by a false interpretation have understood, but a state in which the soul continues calm and strong, undisturbed by any fear or superstition or any other emotion. This he calls well-being and many other names. The qualities of things exist merely by convention; in nature there is nothing but atoms and void space. These, then, are his opinions. . . .

Notes: IX

1. There is only one extant fragment of Leucippus. I am following convention by interpreting the two philosophers as sharing essentially the same view.

2. *See,* especially, J. M. Robinson's excellent account in *An Introduction to Early Greek Philosophy* (Boston, Houghton Mifflin Co., 1968), pp. 195-238.

3. Diogenes Laertius, *Lives of Eminent Philosophers,* trans. by R. D. Hicks (Harvard University Press and The Loeb Classical Library, 1935), Vol. II, Chap. IX, 40.

4. *E.g.*, Theophrastos, *De Caus. Plant.* VI 1 6 (D-K 68A29).

5. *Ibid.*

6. Leucippus, Fragment 2 (D-K).

7. Democritus, Fragment 9 (D-K).

8. *Ibid.*, Fragments 6, 11, 125.

9. *Ibid.*, Fragment 9.

10. Plato, *Phaedo,* 97e.

11. Plato, *Republic,* 505 ff., 509 ff.

12. Hippolytus, *Refutation of All Heresies,* i 13. 4 (D-K 68A40), cited in Robinson, *op. cit.,* p. 214.

13. Theophrastos, *De Sensu,* 60-64 (D-K 68A135).

14. The modern formulation of this problem owes much, of course, to Kant's *Critique of Pure Reason.*

15. Plato, *Theaetetus,* 151e ff.

16. The word translated as "profitable" is *symphoros,* which can also mean "useful" or "suitable."

17. Democritus, Fragment 69.

18. *Ibid.*, Fragment 191.

19. *Ibid.*, Fragment 211.

20. *Ibid.*, Fragment 233.

21. *Ibid.*, Fragments 126, 37, 146, 118.

22. Robinson, *op. cit.,* p. 228.

23. Democritus, Fragment 277. *Cf.* Fragments 275, 276, 278, 112, 119, 146, 191, 233, 236.

24. This, to repeat, in spite of the fact that Democritus' own specific ethical maxims were quite respectable.

25. It is, of course, possible to understand Plato's dialogues as refuting this position without mentioning Democritus by name.

Philosophy as Rhetoric—The Sophists

D EMOCRITUS' atomism included, as we saw, a rather sophisticated and plausible doctrine of the relativism of sense perception; but Democritus drew from this the inference of a more problematic relativism of all value. He thought to avoid falling into a radical relativism, the view that all value is relative and that there is *no* objective standard of value, by appealing to the principle of advantage or profit (*sympheron*): *All* men do in fact seek their own advantage; the objective standard of what is "good" is "what is to my advantage." Further, what is to the advantage of someone is reflected in, indeed determined by, the arrangement of the atoms which constitute his soul.

The difficulty even with this sophisticated version of relativism is that its proposed standard, the principle of advantage, is itself problematic, all too liable to degenerate into relativism or conventionalism itself. It is notoriously difficult to say what one's "advantage" really is, and even more difficult to argue convincingly that what is to one's "advantage" is objectively determined for all. The problematic character of Democritus' position was amply illustrated by the fact that the ethical or moral standpoint that he proposed as "advantageous" and therefore "most pleasant," namely, a rather conventional call to moderation and contemplation, was by no means the only ethic that could plausibly be derived from his fundamental position.

Nevertheless, this position was first developed into a fully stated ethic and pragmatic philosophy by a group of men who came to be called Sophists, practitioners or professors of wisdom. It is instructive that Protagoras, who is generally considered the first of the Sophists, was from Democritus' city of Abdera, and was reported by some to have actually studied with Democritus.[1] Whether or not this is true, it is clear that Protagoras' thought bears a close resemblance to Democritus' in many ways. His account of matter and the senses, although not the dominant issue that it was for Democritus, attests to this similarity:

All matter is in a state of flux. A fluctuating thing may attain its shape, however, because the changes may be such that the additions compensate for the losses. It is our sense impressions of the thing that get modified, because affected by age and other bodily conditions.[2]

There are intelligible principles inherent in the matter of every phenomenon; because matter is essentially the sum of all the seemings that it has for any and all persons.[3]

But the most striking way in which Protagoras developed the standpoint of Democritus was in his account of human experience and man's relationship to and comportment toward his world. His position is expressed in his most famous fragment, which is often considered the cornerstone of all sophistry:

Man is the measure of all things: of things that are, that they are, of things that are not, that they are not.[4]

This statement is often considered to be the classic statement of the principle of relativism, and the Sophists are praised or blamed as the real founders of this famous and, today, dominant position. But it is by no means clear what kind of relativism this is, and whether in particular it degenerates into the kind of nihilism alluded to in the previous chapter. To take up this issue, let us consider first one of the most famous interpretations of this principle, that of Socrates and Plato, who were both vehemently opposed to sophistry.

In broad outline, the Socratic-Platonic objection to sophistry is threefold. First, the Sophists claimed, implicitly in their title and explicitly in their speeches, to be wise. For a variety of complex reasons, which we shall presently take up, Socrates thought this claim suspicious. Second, the Sophists claimed to be able to *teach* this wisdom. The objection that Socrates had against this claim was that it implied that wisdom was a *techne,* an art or skill such as carpentry or shoe-making or medicine, which could indeed be taught. Finally, as a consequence of the latter, the Sophists considered themselves justified in charging fees for the dispensing of this wisdom. Perhaps the clearest statement of these objections to sophistry is in Plato's dialogue *Protagoras.*[5]

Now, why should Socrates object so strenuously to the Sophists' claim to be wise? For Socrates, wisdom means in some sense "knowledge of the structure of the whole," or just simply "knowledge of the whole." As he elaborates this conception of wisdom in the dialogues, at least two things become clear. First, the implication for the question of value is that there are somehow objective standards of value which Socrates called Ideas, or Forms, which give individual instances of these values their intelligibility and their being. This is an extremely complex issue which we certainly cannot adequately touch upon here. But we can surely say this much. If the standard for "what justice is" is "the Form Justice" or "justice itself," if the standard for what equality is is "the Form Equality" or "equality itself," if the standard of "what goodness is" is "the Idea of the Good," then it cannot be the case that "man is the measure of all things." Man is not the measure; Being is. A second consequence of Socrates' conception of wisdom, at least as he interpreted it, was that knowledge of the structure of the whole would only be possible if one were in every way complete. But man is in his very nature incomplete or, as this point is expressed in the *Symposium,* erotic; as existentialist philosophers emphasize today, man is finite. As such, wisdom, at least *this* kind of wisdom, is impossible for man. Only the gods can be wise.[6] There is, as Socrates argues in the *Apology,* a *kind* of wisdom possible for man, namely, self-knowledge interpreted as knowledge of one's limits, of one's incompleteness, or *aporia*. This "Socratic wisdom" becomes in the *Apology* the foundation of his conception of the philosophic life. But Socrates detected in the Sophists' claims to wisdom a claim to wisdom in the divine sense, and this act of *hybris* seemed to him unjustified and dangerous. But it was not simply an unjustified claim to knowledge to which Socrates objected. Given Protagoras' famous dictum, given the conception of wisdom that it embodied, Protagoras' claim to wisdom would have been justified, and it was to this implication that Socrates objected. For if man is the measure of all things, that meant that there were no standards—Forms, or Ideas—by which actions could be evaluated. If there is no objective standard of justice, of equality, of goodness, then there could be no question of "knowing" those standards, as Socrates held. But if there are no standards to know, what knowledge would constitute wisdom? As Protagoras himself suggests in Plato's *Protagoras,* "man is the measure of all things" implies that what any man *thinks* is just, equal, or good *is* just, equal, or good *for him*. If there are no standards but everything is relative in this sense, then the important thing to know evidently would not be "what justice is." What *would* be worthwhile, what would indeed be the highest knowledge in a world where people's *opinion* is the standard of what a thing is, is knowledge of how to *persuade* people to believe what one believes about justice, equality, goodness, or whatever. Since there are no objective standards, it is not even an issue whether what one believes, say, justice, to be is "really true." What counts in such a situation is that one knows how to persuade others to his opinion. "Wisdom," from this standpoint, is not "knowledge of the structure of the whole" but "knowledge of how to persuade," or rhetoric. And rhetoric *is* a *techne*, an art or skill; and as such, it obviously can be taught, and one who could teach it would seem to be justified both in charging a fee and in claiming to be wise. Thus what Socrates really objected to was the claim that man is the measure of all things; if this were true, the other Sophist claims followed. To him it seemed to imply the view that any behavior was equally justifiable as long as one were a sufficiently crafty rhetorician to win his case. "Reason" in this view becomes not that mode of thinking which leads to insight into truth; "reason" becomes indistinguishable from rhetorical skill, and this seemed to Socrates to be an utterly unacceptable account of human experience.

The condemnation of sophistry presented throughout the Platonic dialogues has certainly been the main factor in giving the term "sophistry" the pejorative connotation that it has had since Plato's time. This is strange when we consider that the main thesis of sophistry as so understood, the principle of relativism, is probably the dominant world view of our own culture. Appeals to the claim "it's all relative" are regularly offered as the height of sophistication, whether we are talking about the comparative ethical systems of different cultures or differences in musical taste. It is therefore not surprising that there have been significant voices raised against this extremely negative interpretation of the Sophists popularized in the Platonic dialogues. We must therefore turn to a consideration of what some have thought the more positive aspects of the Sophists' position.

Although these interpretations have argued against this view, it is easy to see the Pre-Socratic philosophers as being primarily if not exclusively concerned with knowledge of the physical world. Even if this is not entirely true, it remains the case that the Sophists did raise the issue of man's *relation* to the world, and in particular his relation to his fellowman, to paramount philosophic importance. For Democritus, the doctrine of relativism was an aspect of, an inference from, his more fundamental doctrine of atomism. For Protagoras, it was the basis of his entire philosophic position. At least one positive implication of Protagoras' doctrine is this: The most fundamental concern for man is not the physical world as it is in itself, or even justice and goodness as they are "in themselves," but the physical world, justice, and goodness *for man*. Most generally, it is not "the world" but human experience of the world that is the real matter for human thought. Lazlo Versenyi puts this important and extremely influential point succinctly:

> Protagoras announces a practical program: the things we are concerned with are *chremata*, i.e. things we are related to. There is no point in speaking grandly about what things may or may not be in themselves. What we have to take into account and concentrate on is what they are for us, in the world we live in, in a world in which our relationship to things, our living in the world, is decisive. . . . Pointing to the world in which our relationships, attitudes, and opinions are decisive, our concerns of utmost concern, he recalled man to himself.[7]

Versenyi's very language serves to remind the reader familiar with contemporary philosophy of the debt that one of the most important existentialist thinkers owes to this Sophist insight: This refers to Martin Heidegger's now classic analysis of human being as Being-in-the-world, and even of his technical distinctions between presence-at-hand and readiness-to-hand, Care, Concern, and Solicitude, whose power is built so heavily on this insight.[8] In fact, with the massive exception of modern science up until the development of considerations such as Heisenberg's uncertainty principle, it is possible to say that the concern not with the world as it is in-itself but as it is for human experience has been, in its many guises, the fundamental concern of Western man's pursuit of knowledge. With the investigations of Heisenberg and others in our own century, even the claim of science to yield utterly unbiased knowledge in which the nature of the observer (the scientist) is irrelevant has been called into serious question. We can easily see how this reaction might develop. We have seen through the course of these studies how again and again in a variety of ways the Pre-Socratic philosophers found it necessary to draw some kind of distinction between phenomena, things as they appear to us, and an *arche*, or origin, which lies beneath appearance. If my interpretations were correct, this step was taken not in order to abandon appearance, not because it was decided that human experience was not important or not what needed to be explained. Rather, the step was taken out of a claimed necessity of thought, out of the decision that the world as it appears to humans could not be adequately accounted for in its own terms, that the world of our experience is grounded in an *arche*, or origin, to which we must gain access if "this world" is to be rendered intelligible. Nevertheless, it can easily enough appear that such a distinction between "appearance" and "reality" is drawn out of the sentiment that "our world" is really not important or even ultimately "real," out of a desire, that is, to take some sort of leap to "another world." From this standpoint, Protagoras' dictum "man is the measure of all things" can be interpreted, as Versenyi interprets it, as a healthy recall to this world from the abstruseness of other-worldly philosophy. Whether or not the interpretation of previous philosophy implicit in this view is correct, it is certainly the case that the Sophists made philosophic concerns more anthropomorphic, not only for themselves but even for their staunch opponents such as Socrates and Plato.

But Protagoras did more than affirm with renewed vigor that human experience should be man's fundamental concern. Expanding Democritus' view that the way we perceive the world has at least something to do with the arrangement of our own atoms, Protagoras developed the groundwork for the issue that has come to be known as subjectivity or subjectivism, the view that, in some sense or other, the experienced world is "constituted" by the being who experiences it. To explain: One possible and initially plausible view of man's experience of the world makes him essentially a passive recipient. The world which we perceive is the world "in itself," the very same world as would be there if no being were observing it. In short, the observer merely receives external impressions; he does not act on those impressions. Such a view is evidently the view upon which the possibility of "impartial" and so "objective" scientific investigation is based. But it is not long before it occurs to us that at very least in the realm of sense perception, our senses seem to contribute something. To use favorite Democritean examples, the same wine that tastes sweet to us when we are healthy tastes bitter when we are fevered. Considerations such as these can get generalized to the view that in fact the world as it is "in itself" is not the world as viewed by man, that human consciousness *acts* on what its sensory organs take in, or even that the way we perceive things *is* the way they are. And this is at least one possible interpretation of "man is the measure of all things, of things that are, that they are, of things that are not, that they are not." No less important a philosopher than Hegel interprets this to be the genuine significance of Protagoras' position.

> Since man, as subject, is the measure of everything, the existent is not alone, but is for my knowledge. Consciousness is really the producer of the content in what is objective, and subjective thinking is thus really active. And this view extends even to the most modern philosophy, as when, for instance, Kant says that we only know phenomena, i.e., that what seems to us to be objective reality, is only to be considered in its relation to consciousness, and does not exist without this relation.[9]

In our own century it can almost be said that the philosophic movement of phenomenology is founded on this issue, which they refer to as intentionality or the "constitution of objects" on the part of consciousness.

If this view or anything like it was the actual intention of Protagoras, then his view does not obviously fall into the kind of destructive relativism of which he is accused by Socrates in the dialogues. On such a view, what is "true" might well be "relative" to man, but nevertheless true for all men. Or on a more particular level, the goodness or wickedness of a certain act may be relative to a given set of circumstances, but true for any man who finds himself in those circumstances. There are thus many ways of construing Protagoras' dictum, and its precise meaning surely cannot be gleaned from the fragment itself. However, Socrates' "radicalization" of the dictum, even if in the end unfair to Protagoras, succeeds in raising a problem which must be faced by any modified version of the dictum, including the most contemporary: It is one thing to demand that philosophy concern itself with human experience; but can it be inferred from this that an account of man can be given without "going beyond man," without, that is, referring to origins, *archai*, or standards of intelligibility, of reason and of conduct of which man is *not* the measure? As a contemporary existentialist might formulate the question, Is Being in the end indistinguishable from *human* being? Protagoras would seem to offer a view which answers this in the affirmative. And Plato, to whom we shall turn in the next chapter, offers perhaps *the* classic statement of its denial.

Again we see that the terms of a decisively influential philosophic theme are set in the very beginnings, chronologically and ontologically, of philosophy.

The other philosopher often considered one of the founders of sophistry is Gorgias. Perhaps even more than Protagoras, Gorgias emphasized the importance of the *techne* of argument, or rhetoric. In particular, he made significant developments in the technique of antilogical argument, or arguing validly for both sides of a disputed question. It was this sort of ability which Aristophanes criticized so bitterly in his satire of sophistry, the *Clouds,* as "making the weaker argument appear the stronger." Nevertheless, there are several issues raised by Gorgias' use of antilogy which must be considered.

The most significant of his works in this regard is entitled, rather startlingly, *On Non-Being or On Nature.* Gorgias is reported to have received early training in Eleatic thought. But his arguments in this work take a basic Eleatic form of argument and prove three theses utterly unacceptable to Eleatic philosophy itself, namely (1) Nothing exists; (2) If anything exists, it could not be thought or known; (3) If anything existed and could be thought or known, it could not be communicated. Now as Versenyi and others observe, it is highly dubious that Gorgias really believed these theses.[10] It is much more likely that the work is a parody on the Eleatic position designed to show that the same kind of argument employed to prove the Eleatic theses that only Being is, that thought and Being are the same, etc., could be employed to prove precisely the opposite.

Now if we suppose that this was Gorgias' explicit intention in the work, he makes a point worth considering, for it forces us to rethink Parmenides' poem to see to what extent the truth of his position really depends on the validity of the argument he presents. The previous interpretation of Parmenides tended to minimize this dependence, but in the work of Parmenides' student and successor, Zeno, the problem becomes even more acute; it is safe to say that Gorgias places Zeno in an even more serious predicament than Parmenides.

But like all important contributions to thought, Gorgias' argument contains nuances that go far beyond its primary intention. On the one hand, as Versenyi points out,[11] Gorgias' argument stands to the Eleatic ones very much as the opposed positions in the Antinomies of Kant,[12] and serve the same formal purpose: They show that the truth of a certain position—say the Eleatic one—cannot depend on the validity of the argument by which it is presented, since the same form of argument can be used to prove its opposite. And this conclusion can it-self be extended to the inference which Hegel derives:

> With such reasoning men can easily get so far as to know (where they do not, it is owing to the want of education—but the Sophists were very well educated) that if arguments are relied upon, every-thing can be proved by argument, and arguments for and against can be found for everything; . . .[13]

Now what is the significance of this inference? If men had not realized this before, Parmenides and Zeno demonstrated once and for all the power of the *form of arguments* in convincing oneself of the truth of one's position. Ever since Parmenides, most philosophers have agreed upon at least this much: that if one's position is true, one should be able to strongly support, if not conclusively prove, one's position by an argument (in Greek a *logos*, the evident root of our word "logic"). Rarely since Parmenides has there been a philosopher who thought it sufficient simply to utter his position, without argumentative support. But reflection on Gorgias' contribution warns us that no amount of valid argument can ever establish the *truth* of our position, and that if we allow ourselves to get too intoxicated with the validity of arguments and their persuasive power, we may forget the supposedly origin-al motivation of our enterprise—the quest for truth. A brief perusal of a few contemporary philosophical journals will be ample testimony that such a warning is to this day needful of occasional repetition.

Gorgias, strangely enough for one who claimed to teach rhetoric, in fact points to the limitations of argument, and so, more narrowly, of what we call logic. As long as this does not lead to the opposite extreme, a disdain for argument, there is no reason to believe that such a lesson is not healthy. Unfortunately, an awareness of the limitations of argument can and has led men, even of our own time, to a much more serious predicament: a crisis of reason, or a failure of confidence in the justification for being rational. Today this loss of faith in rationality, whose manifestations, sophisticated and vulgar, are everywhere, is often called nihilism.[14] How could such a crisis come about? Without con-sidering in detail the question of the nature of reason, a topic which would demand volumes to consider adequately, we might at least sug-gest this much in the light of the present studies: For Parmenides and Heraclitus, reason—*logos* or *nous*—whatever its precise nature, was embedded in the *arche*, or origin of things, indeed in a fundamental way identical with it. To be reasonable—to get in attunement with the *Logos* or to "follow the course" of Parmenides' poem—*was* to gain access to Being. We saw that Democritus reduced reason—perhaps some would want to say refined it—to a calculative technique (*techne*) for the calculation of pleasures. The Sophists, who were Democritus' philosophic descendants, reformulated his view in the more concrete terms of rhetoric. Being reasonable is arguing validly or, what in the end is more important, arguing persuasively. If *this* is what reason is, then when the limitations of argument are pointed out, this becomes tantamount to a statement of the limitations of reason. If we view this situation in a certain rather negative mood, it is easy to see how from it the crisis of reason in our own time could occur.

Such is at least one way that a loss of confidence in reason *could* arise, although there are certainly other ways and more complicated versions of this one. But it is at least possible that Socrates and Plato recognized some such danger in the Sophist position, for, as we shall see, their own positive response to their criticism of sophistry certainly included an attempted return to the Heraclitean-Parmenidean insistence that reason is embedded in the origin of things.

Evidently enough, a recurring theme in the reflection on the Sophists here offered has been the extent to which the position articulated by them—whether we consider it from the standpoint of relativism or of the nature of reason, or of the crisis of confidence in reason—is remarkably similar to the dominant attitudes on these themes in our own time. This is all the more ironic in view of the pejorative connotation which the term sophistry has even in our own time.[15] We will conclude this chapter by noting yet another affinity to our own time, yet another challenge to our own fond prejudices, cited by Hegel. The view of the Sophists, especially the emphasis on rhetorical skill rather than actual knowledge of the subjects in question, seems peculiarly and deplorably appropriate in a democracy, where not just knowledgeable experts but all citizens have equal voice in the affairs of the city. In a situation where the participants were all knowledgeable—say in a conference of surgeons on the problems of a certain operation—the role of rhetoric (as opposed to actual knowledge of the issues) would be minimized. But as the number of participants in a discussion increases, and especially as the demands for demonstration of knowledge—expertise—about the subject diminish or become blurred—as is the case in a democratic form of government—the ability to persuade regardless of the truth of one's position becomes increasingly important. Surely no more disturbing testimony to this could be offered than the fact that in recent years our own Presidential campaigns have been virtually turned over to specialists in advertising.

It is a common opinion among us that our cultural beliefs and values were significantly established by the great Greek philosophers, Plato and Aristotle. Alfred North Whitehead articulated this view in his famous statement that the history of philosophy is "a series of footnotes to Plato." We turn next to Plato's dialogue *Charmides*. But as we do so, it is perhaps worthwhile to ponder the thought-provoking and ironic extent to which we today in myriad ways are the spiritual descendants not of Plato and Aristotle whom we praise, but of the Sophists whom we damn.

Protagoras and Gorgias

Protagoras of Abdera (about 480-411 B.C.) and Gorgias of Leontini (about 483-375 B.C.) were the acknowledged founders of the Sophist movement. The Sophists, a group of men who arose in the late fifth century B.C., were really the first professional teachers. The word *sophistes* means, in Greek, something like "professional wise man" or "wisdom expert." The Sophists thus claimed to be wise, to be able to teach their wisdom, and therefore to be justified in charging money for their services. As we shall see, they were strongly opposed by Socrates and Plato, who contributed significantly to the pejorative connotation that the term "sophist" still has.

A. Protagoras

PROTAGORAS: FRAGMENT*

1. (*From 'Truth' or 'Refutatory Arguments'*). Of all things the measure is Man, of the things that are, that they are, and of the things that are not, that they are not.

* * *

* From Kathleen Freeman, *Ancilla to the Pre-Socratic Philosophers*.

3. (*From a treatise entitled 'Great Logos'*). Teaching needs endowment and practice. Learning must begin in youth.

4. (*From 'On the Gods'*). About the gods, I am not able to know whether they exist or do not exist, nor what they are like in form; for the factors preventing knowledge are many: the obscurity of the subject, and the shortness of human life.

* * *

6b.   To make the weaker cause the stronger.

TESTIMONIA ON PROTAGORAS BY DIOGENES LAERTIUS*

Protagoras, son of Artemon or, according to Apollodorus and Dinon in the fifth book of his *History of Persia,* of Maeandrius, was born at Abdera (so says Heraclides of Pontus in his treatise *On Laws,* and also that he made laws for Thurii) or, according to Eupolis in his *Flatterers,* at Teos; for the latter says:

Inside we've got Protagoras of Teos.

He and Prodicus of Ceos gave public readings for which fees were charged, and Plato in the *Protagoras* calls Prodicus deep-voiced. Protagoras studied under Democritus. The latter was nicknamed "Wisdom," according to Favorinus in his *Miscellaneous History.*

Protagoras was the first to maintain that there are two sides to every question, opposed to each other, and he even argued in this fashion, being the first to do so. Furthermore he began a work thus: "Man is the measure of all things, of things that are that they are, and of things that are not that they are not." He used to say that soul was nothing apart from the senses, as we learn from Plato in the *Theaetetus,* and that everything is true. In another work he began thus: "As to the gods, I have no means of knowing either that they exist or that they do not exist. For many are the obstacles that impede knowledge, both the obscurity of the question and the shortness of human life." For this introduction to his book the Athenians expelled him; and they burnt his

---

* From R. D. Hicks, *Lives of Eminent Philosophers.*

works in the market-place, after sending round a herald to collect them from all who had copies in their possession.

He was the first to exact a fee of a hundred minae and the first to distinguish the tenses of verbs, to emphasize the importance of seizing the right moment, to institute contests in debating, and to teach rival pleaders the tricks of their trade. Furthermore, in his dialectic he neglected the meaning in favour of verbal quibbling, and he was the father of the whole tribe of eristical disputants now so much in evidence; insomuch that Timon too speaks of him as

> Protagoras, all mankind's epitome,
> Cunning, I trow, to war with words.

He too first introduced the method of discussion which is called Socratic. Again, as we learn from Plato in the *Euthydemus,* he was the first to use in discussion the argument of Antisthenes which strives to prove that contradiction is impossible, and the first to point out how to attack and refute any proposition laid down: so Artemidorus the dialectician in his treatise *In Reply to Chrysippus.* He too invented the shoulder-pad on which porters carry their burdens, so we are told by Aristotle in his treatise *On Education*; for he himself had been a porter, says Epicurus somewhere. This was how he was taken up by Democritus, who saw how skillfully his bundles of wood were tied. He was the first to mark off the parts of discourse into four, namely, wish, question, answer, command; . . .

TESTIMONIA ON PROTAGORAS BY PLATO

Thank you, Socrates, for your consideration of me. For certainly a stranger finding his way into great cities, and persuading the flower of the youth in them to leave the company of their other kinsmen or acquaintance, and live with him, under the idea that they will be improved by his conversation, ought to be very cautious; great jealousies are occasioned by his proceedings, and he is the subject of many enmities and conspiracies. I maintain the art of the Sophist to be of ancient date; but that in ancient times the professors of the art, fearing this odium, veiled and disguised themselves under various names, some under that of poets, as Homer, Hesiod, and Simonidès, some as hierophants and prophets, as Orpheus and Musaeus, and some, as I observe, even under the name of gymnastic-masters, like Iccus of Tarentum, or the more recently celebrated Herodicus, now of Selymbria and formerly of Megara, who is a first-rate Sophist. Your own Agathocles pretended to be a musician, but was really an eminent Sophist; also Pythocleides the Cean; and there were many others; and all of them, as I was saying, adopted these arts as veils or disguises because they were afraid of the envy of the multitude. But that is not my way, for I do not believe that they effected their purpose, which was to deceive the government, who were not blinded by them; and as to the people, they have no understanding, and only repeat what their rulers are pleased to tell them. Now to run away, and to be caught in running away, is the very height of folly, and also greatly increases the exasperation of mankind; for they regard him who runs away as a rogue, in addition to any other objections which they have to him; and therefore I take an entirely opposite course, and acknowledge myself to be a Sophist and instructor of mankind; such an open acknowledgment appears to me to be a better sort of caution than concealment. Nor do I neglect other precautions, and therefore I hope, as I may say, by the favour of heaven that no harm will come of the acknowledgment that I am a Sophist. And I have been now many years in the profession—for all my years when added up are many—and there is no one here present of whom I might not be the father. Wherefore I should much prefer conversing with you, if you do not object, in the presence of the company. . . .

Protagoras answered: Young man, if you associate with me, on the very first day you will return home a better man than you came, and better on the second day than on the first, and better every day than you were on the day before. . . .

When Protagoras heard me say this, he replied: You ask questions fairly, and I like to answer a question which is fairly put. If Hippocrates comes to me he will not experience the sort of drudgery with which other Sophists are in the habit of insulting their pupils; who, when they have just escaped from the arts, are taken and driven back into them by these teachers, and made to learn calculation, and astronomy, and geometry, and music (he gave a look at Hippias as he said this); but if he comes to me, he will learn that which he comes to learn. And this is prudence in affairs private as well as public; he will learn to order his own house in the best manner, and he will be best able to speak and act in the affairs of the state.

Do I understand you, I said; and is your meaning that you teach the art of politics, and that you promise to make men good citizens?

That, Socrates, is exactly the profession which I make.

Then, I said, you do indeed possess a noble art, if there is no mistake about this; for I will freely confess to you, Protagoras, that I have a doubt whether this art is capable of being taught, and yet I know not how to disbelieve your assertion. And I ought to tell you why I am of opinion that this art cannot be taught or communicated by man to man. . . . (*Protagoras*, 316-319)

Soc. And so you say that perception is knowledge?

Theaet. Yes.

Soc. I think that you have delivered yourself of a very important doctrine about knowledge, which is indeed that of Protagoras, who has another way of expressing the same thing when he says that man is the measure of all things, of the existence of things that are, and of the non-existence of things that are not: You have read that?

Theaet. Yes, I have read that, again and again.

Soc. Does he not mean to say that things are to you such as they appear to you, and are to me such as they appear to me, for you and I are men?

Theaet. Yes, that is what he says.

Soc. Such a wise man has doubtless a meaning: let us try to understand him; the same wind is blowing, and yet one of us may be cold and the other not, or one may be slightly and the other very cold?

Theaet. Very true.

Soc. Now is the wind, regarded not in relation to us but absolutely, cold or not; or are we to say, with Protagoras, that the wind is cold to him who is cold, and not to him who is not?

Theaet. I suppose the last.

Soc. This is what appears to each of them?

Theaet. Yes.

Soc. And "appears to him" means the same as "he perceives"?

Theaet. True.

Soc. Then appearance and perception coincide in this instance of hot and cold, and in similar instances; for things appear, or may be supposed to be, to each one such as he perceives them?

Theaet. Yes.

Soc. Then perception is always of existence, and being the same as knowledge is unerring?

Theaet. That is clear.

Soc. Now, I verily and indeed suspect that Protagoras, who was an almighty wise man, spoke these things in a parable to the common herd, like you and me, but he told the truth, "his truth," in secret to his own disciples.

Theaet. What do you mean, Socrates?

Soc. I am about to speak of an illustrious philosophy, in which all things are said to be relative; you cannot rightly call anything by any name, such as great or small, or heavy or light, for the great will be small and the heavy light,—there is no one or some or any sort of nature, but out of motion and change and admixture all things are becoming, which "becoming" is by us incorrectly called being, but is really becoming, for nothing really is, but all things are becoming. Summon all philosophers,—Protagoras, Heraclitus, Empedocles, and the rest of them, one after another, with the exception of Parmenides, and they will agree with you in this. Summon the great masters of either kind of poetry,—Epicharmus, the prince of Comedy, and Homer of Tragedy; when the latter sings of—

"Ocean the birth of gods, and mother Tethys,"—

does he not mean that all things are the offspring of flux and motion?

Theaet. Yes, that is his meaning. . . .

Soc. Shall I tell, Theodorus, what amazes me in your acquaintance Protagoras?

Theod. What is that?

Soc. I say nothing against his doctrine, that what appears is to each one, but I wonder that he did not begin his great work on Truth with a declaration that a pig or a dog-faced baboon, or some other stranger monster which has sensation, is the measure of all things; then, when we were reverencing him as a god, he might have condescended to inform us that he was no wiser than a tadpole and did not even aspire to be a man—would not this have produced an overpowering effect? For if truth is only sensation, and one man's discernment is as good as another's, and no man has any superior right to determine whether the opinion of any other is true or false, but each man, as we have several times repeated, is to himself the sole judge, and everything that he judges is true and right, why should Protagoras be preferred to the place of wisdom and instruction, and deserve to be well paid, and we poor ignoramuses have to go to him, if each one is the measure of his own wisdom? Must he not be talking "ad captandum" in all this? I say nothing of the ridiculous predicament in which my own midwifery and the whole art of dialectic is placed; for the attempt to supervise or refute the notions or opinions of others would be a tedious and enormous piece of folly, if to each man they are equally right; and this must be the case if Protagoras' Truth is the real truth, and the philosopher is not merely amusing himself by giving oracles out of the shrine of his book. . . .

. . . But O, my good sir, he will say, come to the point in a more generous spirit; and either show, if you can, that our sensations are not relative and individual, or, if you admit that they are individual, prove that this does not involve the consequence that the appearance becomes, or, if you like to say, is, to the individual only. As to your talk about pigs and baboons, you are yourself a pig, and you make my writings the sport of other swine, which is not right. For I declare that the truth is as I have written, and that each of us is a measure of existence and of non-existence. Yet one man may be a thousand times better than another in proportion as things are and appear different to him. And I am far from saying that wisdom and the wise man have no existence; but I say that the wise man is he who makes the evils which appear and are to a man, into goods which are and appear to him. And I would beg you not to press my words in the letter, but to take the meaning of them as I will explain them. Remember how I said before, that to the sick man his food appears to be and is bitter, and to the man in health the opposite of bitter. Now I cannot conceive that one of these men can be or ought to be made wiser than the other; nor can you assert that the sick man because he has one impression is foolish, and the healthy man because he has another is wise; but the one state requires to be changed into the other, the worse into the better. As in education, a change of state has to be effected, and the sophist accomplishes by words the change which the physician works by the aid of drugs. Not that any one ever made another think truly, who previously thought falsely. For no one can think what is not, or think anything different from that which he feels, and which is always true. But as the inferior habit of mind has thoughts of a kindred nature, so I conceive that a good mind causes men to have good thoughts; and these which the inexperienced call true, I maintain to be only better, and not truer than others. And, O my dear Socrates, I do not call wise men tadpoles; far otherwise; I say that they are the physicians of the human body, and the husbandmen of plants—for the husbandmen also take away the evil and disordered sensations of plants, and infuse into them good and healthy sensations as well as true ones; and the wise and good rhetoricians make the good intead of the evil to seem just to states; for whatever appears to be just and fair to a state, while sanctioned by a state, is just and fair to it; but the teacher of wisdom causes the good to take the place of the evil, both in appearance and in reality. And the sophist who is able to train his pupils in this spirit is a wise man, and deserves to be well paid by them. And in this way one man is wiser than another; and yet no one thinks falsely, and you, whether you will or not, must endure to be a measure. . . . (Theaetetus, 152, 161, 166-167)

TESTIMONIA ON PROTAGORAS BY ARISTOTLE

The saying of Protagoras is like the views we have mentioned; he said that man is the measure of all things, meaning simply that that which seems to each man also assuredly is. If this is so, it follows that the same thing both is and is not, and is bad and good, and that the contents of all other opposite statements are true, because often a particular thing appears beautiful to some and the contrary of beautiful to others, and that which appears to each man is the measure. (Metaphysica, 1062b 12)

. . . Again, if all contradictory statements are true of the same subject at the same time, evidently all things will be one. For the same thing will be a trireme, a wall, and a man, if of everything it is possible either to affirm or to deny anything (and this premiss must be accepted by those who share the views of Protagoras). For if any one thinks that the man is not a trireme, evidently he is not a trireme; so that he also is a trireme, if, as they say, contradictory statements are both true. And we thus get the doctrine of Anaxagoras, that all things are mixed together; so that nothing really exists. (Metaphysica, 1007b 18)

. . . This sort of argument illustrates what is meant by making the worse argument seem the better. Hence people were right in objecting to the training Protagoras undertook to give them. It was a fraud; the probability it handled was not genuine but spurious, and has a place in no art except Rhetoric and Eristic. (Rhetoric, 1402a 23)

B. Gorgias

GORGIAS: FRAGMENT*

IIa.   *(The 'Defence of Palamêdês': summary).***

(1)   This trial is concerned not with death, which comes to all, but with honour: whether I am to die justly or unjustly, under a load of disgrace.

(2)   You have the power to decide the issue; you can kill me easily if you wish, whereas I am powerless.

(3)   If the accuser Odysseus were bringing the charge because he knew or believed me to be betraying Greece to the barbarians, he would be the best of men, as ensuring the safety of his country, his parents and all Greece, as well as the punishment of the traitor; but if he has concocted this charge through malice, he is equally the worst of men.

(4)   Where shall I begin my defence? A cause unsupported by proof engenders fear, and fear makes speech difficult, unless truth and necessity instruct me—teachers more productive of risk than of the means of help.

(5)   The accuser cannot know for certain that I committed the crime, because I know for certain that I did not. But if he is acting on conjecture, I can prove in two ways that he is wrong.

(6)   First, I cannot have committed the crime. Treasonable action must begin with discussion; but discussion implies a meeting, which was impossible since no one could come to me and I could not go to anyone, nor could a written message be sent.

(7)   Nor was direct communication possible between myself, a Greek, and the enemy, a barbarian, since we did not understand each other's language, and an interpreter would have meant having an accomplice.

(8)   But even supposing communication could have been arranged, it would have been necessary to exchange pledges, such as hostages (which was impossible),

(9)   or perhaps money. A small sum would not have sufficed in such

* From Kathleen Freeman, *Achilla to the Pre-Socratic Philosophers*.
** This speech has at first sight little philosophical interest; but its influence on forensic oratory, and therefore doubtless on education, cannot be over-estimated.

a great undertaking; a large sum could not have been transported without the help of many confederates.

(10)   Conveyance of money would have been impossible at night because of the guards, and by daylight because all could see. Nor could I have gone out, or the enemy have come into the camp. Nor could I have concealed any money received.

(11)   But suppose all this achieved—communication established and pledges exchanged—action had then to follow. This had to be done with or without confederates. If with confederates, were they free or slaves? If any free man has information, let him speak. Slaves are always untrustworthy: they accuse voluntarily to win freedom, and also under compulsion when tortured.

(12)   Nor could the enemy have entered by my help, either by the gates or over the walls, because of the guards; nor could I have breached the walls, as in camp everybody sees everything. Therefore all such action was completely impossible for me.

(13)   What motive could I have had? Absolute power over yourselves or the barbarians? The former is impossible in view of your courage, wealth, prowess of body and mind, control of cities.

(14)   Rulership over the barbarian is equally impossible. I could not have seized it or won it by persuasion, nor would they have handed it to me voluntarily: no one would choose slavery instead of kingship, the worst instead of the best.

(15)   Nor was wealth my motive. I have moderate means, and do not need more. Wealth is needed by those who spend much; not by those who are masters of their natural pleasures, but by those who are enslaved by pleasures, or wish to buy honour with riches. I call you to witness that my past life proves me not to be one of these.

(16)   My motive cannot have been ambition: honour accrues to virtue, not to a betrayer of Greece. Besides, I had honour already, from you for my wisdom.

(17)   Safety cannot have been the motive. The traitor is the enemy of all: law, justice, the gods, his fellow-men.

(18)   Another motive could be the desire to help friends and injure enemies; but I would have been doing the reverse.

(19)   The remaining possibility would be a wish to avoid trouble or danger. But if I betrayed Greece, I should have betrayed myself and all that I had.

(20)   My life would have been unbearable in Greece; and if I stayed

among the barbarians, I would have thrown away all the rewards of my past labours, through my own action, which is worst.

(21)   The barbarians too would have distrusted me; and if one loses credit, life is intolerable. The loss of money or throne or country can be retrieved; but the loss of credit is irretrievable. It is thus proved that I neither could nor would have betrayed Greece.

(22)   I now address my accuser: do you base your accusation on knowledge or conjecture? If on knowledge, either this is your own or hearsay. If it is your own, give exact details of time, place, method; if hearsay, produce your witness.

(23)   It is your place to produce witnesses, not mine: no witness can be produced for what did not happen; but for what did happen, it is easy and essential to produce witnesses. But you cannot produce even false witnesses.

(24)   That you have no knowledge of your accusations is clear. Hence they must be conjectural, and you are the most villainous of men, to bring a capital charge relying on opinion—which is a most unreliable thing—and not knowing the truth. Conjecture is open to all in everything, and you are no wiser than anyone else in this. One must believe, not conjecture, but truth.

(25)   You are accusing me of two opposites, wisdom and madness: wisdom in that I am crafty, clever, resourceful; madness in that I wished to betray Greece. It is madness to attempt what is impossible, disadvantageous, disgraceful, injurious to friends and helpful to enemies, and likely to make one's life intolerable. But how can one believe a man who in the same speech, to the same audience, says the exact opposite about the same things?

(26)   Do you consider the wise to be foolish or sensible? If you say 'foolish', this is original but untrue. If 'sensible', then sensible men do not commit the greatest crimes, or prefer evil to the good they have. If I am wise, I did not err. If I erred, I am not wise. Therefore you are proved a liar on both counts.

(27)   I could bring counter-accusations, but I will not. I would rather seek acquittal through my virtues than your vices.

(28)   (*To the jury*): I must now speak of myself, in a way that would not be suitable except to one accused. I submit my past life to your scrutiny. If I mention my good deeds, I pray that no one will resent this: it is necessary in order that I may refute serious charges with a true statement of merits known to you.

(29)   Above all, my past life has been blameless. My accuser can bring no proof of this charge, so that his speech is unsubstantiated obloquy.

(30)   I claim also to be a benefactor of Greece, present and future, by reason of my inventions, in tactics, law, letters (the tool of memory), measures (arbiters of business dealings), number (the guardian of property), beacon-fires (the best and swiftest messengers), and the game of draughts as a pastime.

(31)   I mention these things to show that in devoting my thoughts to them I am bound to abstain from wicked deeds.

(32)   I deserve no punishment from young or old. I have been considerate to the old, helpful to the young, without envy of the prosperous, merciful to the distressed; not despising poverty, nor preferring wealth to virtue; useful in counsel, active in war, fulfilling commands, obeying the rulers. But it is not for me to praise myself; I do so under the compulsion of self-defence.

(33)   Lastly I shall speak of you to you. Lamentations, prayers, and the petitions of friends are useful when judgement depends on the mob; but before you, the foremost of the Greeks, I need not use these devices, but only justice and truth.

(34)   You must not heed words rather than facts, nor prefer accusations to proof, nor regard a brief period as more instructive than a long one, nor consider calumny more trustworthy than experience. Good men avoid all wrong-doing, but above all what cannot be mended; things can be righted by forethought, but are irrevocable by afterthought. This happens when men are trying a fellow-man on a capital charge, as you now are.

(35)   If words could bring the truth of deeds clearly and certainly before their hearers, judgement would be easy; since this is not so, I ask you to preserve my life, await the passage of time, and pass your judgement with truth. You run the great risk of a reputation for injustice; to good men, death is preferable to a bad reputation: one is the end of life, the other is a disease in life.

(36)   If you put me to death unjustly, you will bear the blame in the eyes of all Greece, as I am not unknown and you are famous. The blame will be yours, not my accuser's, because the issue is in your hands. There could be no greater crime than if you as Greeks put to death a Greek, an ally, a benefactor of yours and of Greece, when you can show no cause.

(37)   Here I stop. A summary of a long speech is worth while when

one is speaking to a jury of inferiors; but before the leaders of Greece it is uncalled-for, as is the exhortation to pay attention or to remember what has been said.

*   *   *

12.   One must destroy one's adversaries' seriousness with laughter, and their laughter with seriousness. . . .

*   *   *

26.   Being is unrecognisable unless it succeeds in seeming, and seeming is weak unless it succeeds in being. . . .

TESTIMONIA ON GORGIAS BY PLATO

Soc. Come, then, and let us see what we really mean about rhetoric; for I do not know what my own meaning is as yet. When the assembly meets to elect a physician or a shipwright or any other craftsman, will the rhetorician be taken into counsel? Surely not. For at every election he ought to be chosen who has the greatest skill; and, again, when walls have to be built or harbors or docks to be constructed, not the rhetorician but the master workman will advise; or when generals have to be chosen and an order of battle arranged, or a position taken, then the military will advise and not the rhetoricians: would you admit that, Gorgias? As you profess to be a rhetorician and a maker of rhetoricians, I shall do well to learn the nature of your art from you. And here let me assure you that I have your interest in view as well as my own. For I dare say that some one or other of the young men present might like to become your pupil, and in fact I see some, and a good many too, who have this wish, but they would be too modest to question you. And therefore when you are interrogated by me, I would have you imagine that you are interrogated by them. "What is the use of coming to you, Gorgias?" they will say, "about what will you teach us to advise the State? about the just and unjust only, or about those other things also which Socrates has just mentioned?" How will you answer them?

Gor. I like your way of leading us on, Socrates, and I will endeavor to reveal to you the whole nature of rhetoric. You must have heard, I think, that the docks and the walls of the Athenians and the plan of the harbor were devised in accordance with the counsels, partly of Themistocles, and partly of Pericles, and not at the suggestion of the builders.

Soc. Certainly, Gorgias, that is what is told of Themistocles, and I myself heard the speech of Pericles when he advised us about the middle wall.

Gor. And you will observe, Socrates, that when a decision has to be given in such matters the rhetoricians are the advisers; they are the men who win their point.

Soc. I had that in my admiring mind, Gorgias, when I asked what is the nature of rhetoric, which always appears to me, when I look at the matter in this way, to be a marvel of greatness.

Gor. A marvel indeed, Socrates, if you only knew how rhetoric comprehends and holds under her sway all the inferior arts. And I will give you a striking example of this. On several occasions I have been with my brother Herodicus or some other physician to see one of his patients, who would not allow the physician to give him medicine, or apply the knife or hot iron to him; and I have persuaded him to do for me what he would not do for the physician just by the use of rhetoric. And I say that if a rhetorician and a physician were to go to any city, and there had to argue in the Ecclesia or any other assembly as to which should be elected, the physician would have no chance; but he who could speak would be chosen if he wished, and in a contest with a man of any other profession the rhetorician more than any one would have the power of getting himself chosen, for he can speak more persuasively to the multitude than any of them, and on any subject. Such is the power and quality of rhetoric, Socrates. And yet rhetoric ought to be used like any other competitive art, not against everybody,—the rhetorician ought not to abuse his strength any more than a pugilist or pancratiast or other master of fence; because he has powers which are more than a match either for enemy or friend, he ought not therefore to strike, stab, or slay his friends. And suppose a man who has been the pupil of a palaestra and is a skillful boxer, and in the fullness of his strength he goes and strikes his father or mother or one of his familiars or friends, that is no reason why the trainer or master of fence should be held in detestation or banished,—surely not. For they taught this art for a good purpose, as an art to be used against enemies and evil-doers, in self-defense, not in aggression, and others have perverted their instructions, making a bad use of their strength and their skill. But not on this account are the teachers bad, neither is the art in fault or bad in itself; I should rather say that those who make a bad use of the art are to blame.

And the same holds good of rhetoric; for the rhetorician can speak against all men and on any subject, and in general he can persuade the multitude of anything better than any other man, but he ought not on that account to defraud the physician or any other artist of his reputation merely because he has the power: he ought to use rhetoric fairly, as he would also use his combative powers. And if after having become a rhetorician he makes a bad use of his strength and skill, his instructor surely ought not on that account to be held in detestation or banished. For he was intended by his teacher to make a good use of his instructions, and he abuses them. And therefore he is the person who ought to be held in detestation, banished, and put to death, and not his instructor. . . . (*Gorgias,* 455-457)

Notes: X

1. Diogenes Laertius, *Lives of Eminent Philosophers,* trans. by R. D. Hicks (New York, Harvard University Press and The Loeb Classical Library, 1935), Vol. II, Chap. IX, p. 50.

2. Sextus Empiricus, quoted in *The Pre-Socratics,* Philip Wheelwright, ed. (New York, Odyssey Press, 1966), p. 239.

3. *Ibid.*

4. Protagoras, Fragment 1 (D-K).

5. *See also* Plato, *Apology, Gorgias, Sophist, Euthydemus, Theaetetus, Hippias Major, Hippias Minor.*

6. Plato, *Symposium,* 204a.

7. Lazlo Versenyi, *Socratic Humanism,* (New Haven, Conn., Yale University Press, 1963), pp. 12, 13. Versenyi's defense of the Sophists, pp. 1-72, is well-stated and challenging.

8. Martin Heidegger, *Being and Time,* trans. by John Macquarrie and Edward Robinson (New York, Harper and Row, 1962).

9. G. F. Hegel, *Lectures on the History of Philosophy,* trans. by E. S. Haldane (New York, Humanities Press, 1963), IV p. 374.

10. Versenyi, *op. cit.,* p. 40. *See* especially footnote 31 for others who hold this view.

11. *Ibid.,* p. 40.

12. Immanuel Kant, *Critique of Pure Reason,* trans. by N. K. Smith (New York, Macmillan and Co., 1961), pp. 384 ff.

13. Hegel, *op. cit.,* p. 368.

14. The best book in my opinion on this issue is Stanley Rosen, *Nihilism: A Philosophical Essay* (New Haven, Conn., Yale University Press, 1969).

15. *Cf*. Hegel, *op. cit*., p. 367.

The New Beginning

THE Pre-Socratic works are fragmentary; at times, such as in the cases of Thales, Anaximander, and Anaximenes, we are limited to one or two lines on which to base our reflections. But when we turn to Plato we have whole works to consider, and immensely complex ones at that. Even the so-called early Platonic dialogues, of which the *Charmides* is an example, supposedly written before Plato's philosophical maturity, emerge, upon serious reflection, as immensely complex and sophisticated works. For this reason, one cannot even approach a thorough interpretation of a dialogue in a few pages. Instead, we shall consider the *Charmides* only from the standpoint which has been the dominant theme of this book, the question of the origins of philosophy. In what sense does the *Charmides* respond to, or perhaps exhibit, the theme of the origins of philosophy? This question turns us first and most strikingly to the problem of the dialogue form itself.

Why did Plato choose to present his philosophical writing in the form of dialogues? Neither before nor since Plato has this been a common form of philosophic writing. Because most philosophers are concerned in their writing to present their own philosophic views clearly and persuasively, the treatise form, written in the first person, has been the dominant and indeed most "natural" choice of format for philosophic writing. To be sure, Parmenides had written his philosophic poem, Heraclitus had written for the most part in cryptic dictums; nevertheless, the dominant form of philosophic writing employed by the Pre-Socratics had been the well-known "Concerning Nature" treatises.

Plato's choice of the dialogue should therefore be no less thought-provoking from the standpoint of his own predecessors than it is today. The standard explanation, in my opinion, does not so much resolve as beg the question. Plato was both a great artist and a great philosopher, we are told, and it is therefore not surprising—perhaps even psychologically inevitable—that he should have presented his philosophy in such a poetic style. In short, the dialogue form and the elements which it introduces—personalities, locations, interaction between participants—can safely be ignored when considering Plato's philosophy. Plato's philosophy is, on this view, confined to the arguments presented by men in the dialogues, and a philosophic consideration of the dialogue is thus tantamount to an analysis of the meaning, validity, and soundness of those arguments. But Plato is hardly the only gifted writer in the history of philosophy, and others have been able to subjugate this artistic flair to the demands of philosophic rigor when they deemed it necessary. Are we justified in attributing such a lack of *sophrosyne* to the author of the *Charmides?* Many have thought not, and there are a considerable number of philosophers who have attempted to show how the dialogue form functions *philosophically* in Plato's works; they argue that the choice of the dialogue is a *philosophic,* and not primarily artistic, decision on Plato's part.[1] A reflection on the dialogue form and its relation to the origins of philosophy supports the latter claim, but, more importantly, it helps us to think more fruitfully about the philosophic significance of any dialogue we consider, and in particular the *Charmides.*

The dialogue form itself is origin-al in at least three ways. The first and perhaps least important is that Plato first used it significantly—it was his genius which saw its possibilities for philosophic presentation. Second, the dialogue by its very form refers to the origins of philosophy in that it reveals the occasion, the concrete experience, out of which the specific philosophic speech of any dialogue arises, and thereby suggests that a reflection upon the origin of philosophic speech in this sense, a reflection, that is, on the existential situation which occasions that speech, is important to an understanding of the speech itself. Third, the dialogue form, especially as Plato employs it, serves to origin-ate philosophy by forcing—or enticing—the reader to philosophize on his own. The dialogues are invitations to philosophy.

Let us begin with a reflection on the second point, that the dialogue form refers to the origins of philosophy. Consider, by contrast, a typical example of a philosophic treatise, say, Kant's *Critique of Pure Reason.* The opening line of the introduction reads simply, "There can be no doubt that all our knowledge begins with experience."[2] Kant, interestingly enough, begins by referring to origins, not specifically of philosophy but of all knowledge. Yet there is nothing in the introduction or in the rest of the work to suggest the relevance of the experience out of which the *First Critique* arose. If anything, the implication of a treatise is that the situations which occasioned the philosophic thought are ir-relevant to an understanding of the thought itself. Philosophic writing, in this sense at least, is "abstract." It could have been written, ideally, by a "pure mind." Strangely enough, this ideal is stated best not in a treatise but in Descartes' *Meditations on First Philosophy*, which, ironically enough, begins by presenting the dramatic situation—undramatic though it is—out of which they arise. In the first para-graph of *Meditation I*, Descartes characterizes his situation:

> Today, then, since very opportunely for the plan I have in view I have delivered my mind from every care [and am happily agitated by no passions] and since I have procured for myself an assured leisure in a peaceable retirement, I shall at last seriously and freely address myself to the general upheaval of all my former opin-ions.[3]

Descartes' intention, which in a way is the intention of much of sub-sequent modern philosophy, is to strip away not only the relevance of the particular situation but even of all of his former opinions as well. In accord with the distinction between the mind and the body which Descartes apparently draws, he conceives philosophic writing as the en-terprise of a mind without the influence of a body.

It is here that the contrast with the dialogue form becomes especially visible. By placing every dialogue in a specific situation, at a specific time, with specific individuals involved, Plato suggests that to "deliver my mind from every care" or be "agitated by no passions" in order to "overthrow all my former opinions" would be not only impossible but undesirable. Philosophic thought, like all human thought, *does* originate in specific situations, and those situations, as the dialogues themselves amply demonstrate, shed considerable light on the philosophic thought itself. Let us consider in this light the relevance of the dramatic situation of the *Charmides*, turning first to the cast of characters. Because a thorough statement of our interpretation of the setting would require a lengthy exposition, let us confine ourselves for the most part to raising the most interesting questions.

There are four main participants in the *Charmides*: Chaerephon, Critias, Charmides, and Socrates. Chaerephon, who plays an apparently insignificant introductory role, is known primarily for two traits. He is a fanatical devotée of Socrates, and he is a staunch defender of the democracy which was overthrown by the Thirty Tyrants in 404 B.C.

Critias and his nephew Charmides, in fact, become two of the leaders of the Thirty Tyrants. Charmides is the head of the ten who rule the Peireias, and Critias was known as the most vicious of the Thirty. Critias himself is also a Sophist and a special follower of the more well-known Sophist, Prodicus. Over the course of time he develops a very tense relationship with Socrates, based primarily, according to Xenophon, on the fact that Socrates once publicly reprimanded Critias for his vulgar behavior toward his beloved Euthydemus.[4] Critias and Charmides are also, strangely enough, related to Plato, who is Charmides' nephew. So Socrates conducts this dialogue in strange company. His fanatic devotée, Chaerephon, staunch defender of democracy, is present along with Critias and Charmides who, however friendly and promising they may appear now, are both made of the stuff of tyranny. We can then ask, what is the political significance of this dialogue? More specifically, is *sophrosyne* a political virtue, peculiar to one regime or the other? What are we to make of Charmides' apparent promise and exemplary behavior in the light of his subsequent development? Are there traces of this future in his present behavior? If so, does it shed any light on the inadequacy of his responses to the question "what is *sophrosyne*?"[5] What of Critias' apparently praiseworthy concern with his nephew's welfare and virtue, as well as that the argument be kept on a high plane, seeking truth rather than victory? Are there indications in the dialogue of *his* subsequent development? And what of Socrates himself? Is his interest in Charmides genuine or ironic? Why does he use such patently invalid arguments to refute Charmides' definitions? Why, for that matter, does he conduct himself in such a way as to almost deserve the reprimand from Critias implying that he is guilty of sophistry?

Turning to the situation which gives rise to the discussion of *sophrosyne*, the following issues seem especially noteworthy. Socrates has returned the very evening of the dialogue from a battle in the war between Athens and Sparta in which the Athenians apparently suffered a serious defeat;[6] it is also, possibly, the very battle in which Socrates distinguished himself for his courage, according to Alcebiades in the *Symposium*.[7] What are we to make of Socrates' extraordinary calm and even nonchalance in such a situation? Is it an exhibition of *sophrosyne*, and, if so, is such a manifestation discussed explicitly?

When Socrates finally meets Charmides, his behavior, especially in the light of his behavior under the stress of battle, is strange indeed. He claims to become "inflamed with passion,"[8] and to have difficulty controlling himself, but responds to this passion with a speech not of seduction but of *sophrosyne*. The question is immediately raised as to the connection between eros and *sophrosyne,* and by extension, since eros is closely connected in other dialogues with philosophy,[9] between *sophrosyne* and philosophy. This connection becomes most important when *sophrosyne* is characterized later in the dialogue[10] as the very kind of self-knowledge which Socrates, in the *Apology*, describes as his own philosophic enterprise.

But surely the most important and problematic aspect of the dramatic background of this dialogue concerns Charmides' recurring morning headaches, Socrates' participation in Critias' lie that he is a physician with a cure for headache, and the very strange nature of the cure itself. What, if anything, does this episode have to do with *sophrosyne,* either with the explicit definitions offered or with *sophrosyne* as it or its lack is exhibited by the participants? If this episode has nothing to do with *sophrosyne*, then surely those interpreters are correct who say that such artistic accouterments can be ignored. But it is at least possible—and elsewhere we will exhibit this in detail[11]—that Plato wants to show us that the situation has very much to do with the thought that emerges, and so more generally that philosophy does and *ought* to arise out of—that is, originate in—specific human experience. Perhaps most especially, philosophy originates—contrary to Descartes' opinion—in human opinion, and although it certainly attempts to go beyond opinion, it always recognizes its origin there. Perhaps for this reason, Socrates begins his questioning of Charmides by asking, "What, in your opinion, is *sophrosyne*?"[12]

All of this is to say that at least one locus of the origin of philosophy is in human experience itself, and Plato considers this origin so important as to refer to it nor merely in speech but "existentially" in every one of his written works. Plato is at least in partial accord therefore with the interpretation of the origin of philosophy offered in the Introduction and based on Aristotle's view that "philosophy begins in wonder." But this should hardly be surprising. Not only was Aristotle a student of Plato's; it was Socrates who first gave voice to the origin of philosophy in wonder in Plato's dialogue, *Theaetetus*.[13]

The dialogue also refers to the origins of philosophy, as earlier suggested, by itself originating philosophy in the reader. It does so much more obviously and effectively than does the typical philosophic treatise. On the one hand, this suggests a genuine concern on Plato's part to function as an originator of philosophy. But not surprisingly, this tendency of the dialogue to lead the reader to philosophize is not simply a noble pedagogic concern divorced from Plato's philosophic interests; it is embedded in the very conception of philosophy which Socrates defends and exhibits, and in the following way.

Consider for a moment the implied stance taken by Parmenides when he reports the revelation of the goddess, or by Kant or Hegel when they set out their conceptions of the nature of man and the world. Such thinkers always exhibit at least an implied claim to wisdom, to knowing and articulating the structure of the whole. Even if they modestly allow that they may be mistaken, it remains the case that philosophic speech of this sort exhibits at least the tentative claim to wisdom in the aforementioned sense. Socrates, on the other hand, regularly denies such wisdom. The stance that he regularly takes is not claimed wisdom but *aporia*. In perhaps its most famous formulation in the *Apology*, Socrates explains this stance of *aporia* in terms of the "riddle" of the Delphic oracle that "no man is wiser than Socrates."[14] Socrates discovers through discussion with other men who claim to be wise that he is wiser than them by virtue of the fact that he knows he is not wise. When asked about piety, or *sophrosyne*, Socrates does not give a speech saying what it is but begins with the admission that he is in *aporia*, "at a loss" as to what the issue is, and from there Socrates begins not to pontificate but to question, as exemplified in the *Charmides*. We shall want to say more presently about the aporetic stance as a characterization of philosophy, but we can now note this consequence for the dialogue form itself. Because Socrates does not claim wisdom about what *sophrosyne* is—to use the present issue—but questions about it, and because such questioning reveals that Socrates' correspondents do not know either, even though, like Critias, they may think that they know, the dialogue itself does not end typically with a "conclusion." The final definition of *sophrosyne* is not accepted; at the end of the dialogue, we are still in *aporia*, although hopefully of a more profound sort than when we started. It is thus not available to the reader simply to accept the doctrine of the *Charmides* without thinking about it. The most natural and intended response to the *Charmides* is for the reader to continue wondering and reflecting about *sophrosyne* himself. But this is to say that the dialogue leads the reader to philosophize himself; the very conception of philosophy as embodying *aporia* means that the dialogue originates philosophy in the reader: "Form" and "content," philosophy and pedagogy, are united and even indistinguishable.

It is easy to fail to appreciate the genuine significance of Socrates' philosophic stance of *aporia*. To state simply that "I know that I am not wise," "I know that I do not know," does not seem especially impressive. But as Socrates interprets and exhibits it, it is a most difficult and worthwhile achievement, tantamount to the achievement of philosophy. For *aporia is* a mode of knowledge; it is in fact knowledge of what one knows and what one does not know, that is, knowledge of one's limits or, as the existentialists might put it more expansively, knowledge of the horizon within which human being occurs. But this is to say that Socratic *aporia* is self-knowledge, which Socrates regularly insists is the goal of his philosophic enterprise. Socrates is wise not in the "divine" sense of knowledge of the structure of the whole, but wise in the sense that he has self-knowledge, knowledge of human being as in *aporia*, that is, as incomplete, striving for completeness, or, as this is expressed in the *Symposium*, as erotic.[15] This means, in fact, that as a consequence, the philosophic stance of *aporia* has its origins in human nature itself. The recognition of one's lack of wisdom and the questioning movement toward wisdom exhibited by Socrates is itself a manifestation of man's primordial incompleteness, or partiality, and the erotic striving to attain completeness, a conception of human nature hilariously presented by Aristophanes' speech in the *Symposium* and preserved by Socrates in his speech. And so the thesis which was defended earlier, that philosophy has its origins in human nature itself, is supported in the Platonic dialogues both explicitly and implicitly by the Socratic questioning stance. It is not difficult to see, either, how closely related this stance of *aporia* is to the wonder which Socrates and Aristotle agree is the origin of philosophy. When one wonders that things are as they are, one recognizes the incompleteness of his knowledge, and it is literally the most *natural* thing to do to question; the preservation of this questioning stance is Socratic philosophy. Philosophy thus both originates in human nature and, as the quest for self-knowledge, questions after those origins. In this light, the status of *sophrosyne* as it is discussed in the *Charmides* becomes especially interesting. For one of the most important characterizations of *sophrosyne* there offered is precisely self-knowledge, and Socrates' elaboration of the meaning of *sophrosyne* as self-knowledge reads exactly like his conception of philosophy. He says:

> Then the *sophron* man, and only he, will know himself, and be able to examine what he knows or does not know, and to see what others know and think that they know and do really know, and what they do not know and fancy that they know when they do

not. No other person will be able to do this. And this is to be *sophron* and *sophrosyne* and self-knowledge—for a man to know what he knows and what he does not know. That is your meaning?[16]

Could it be that when thought through, *sophrosyne* is identical with philosophy, interpreted as the questioning after that origin which originates philosophy itself—human being? Such is a central matter for thought in reflecting on the *Charmides*.

But Socrates exhibits in this dialogue a concern with origins of a very different sort which demands consideration. He several times expresses great concern for Charmides' lineage, and even suggests that the nobility of his lineage should imply that Charmides himself will be noble.[17] Socrates regularly exhibits this interest in lineage in other dialogues.[18] Now there is of course immense irony, at least on Plato's part, in Socrates' praise of Charmides' noble lineage. Charmides and Critias in fact become tyrants. The same family that gave us the great law-giver, Solon, and the great philosopher, Plato, also gives us the tyrants Charmides and Critias. Lineage, the episode implies, is *not* a trustworthy or even relevant sense of origins, especially when one is talking about the origin of nobility or philosophy. If we remember that it is Plato who is writing these words, we can perhaps see in them the implication on his part that his *own* philosophic originator was not his relatives or lineage but his teacher, Socrates.

This essay has hardly touched upon the actual arguments put forward in the *Charmides* in support of various "definitions" of *sophrosyne*. Rather, it has concentrated on certain aspects of the dialogue form itself, both as preparation for a study of the arguments themselves, and especially as those aspects refer to origins. The dialogue exhibits philosophy as both having its *arche*, or origin, in human nature, and at the same time as questing toward an understanding of those origins, or self-knowledge. This might be expressed by saying that in a way, the *arche* and the *telos* of philosophy are the same. According to a fragment of Alcmaeon, a relatively unknown Pre-Socratic philosopher, "Men die for this reason, that they cannot join together the beginning and the end."[19] Whatever Alcmaeon may have meant by this, it is true to say that men are philosophical because they desire to do so. The Platonic dialogues are perhaps the most successful philosophic works ever written because they again and again succeed in both referring to the origins of philosophy and originating that movement toward those origins which is philosophy itself. They thus show that philosophy is literally the natural consequence, perhaps the culmination, of what it means to be a human being. Man, and perhaps man alone, is original in the manifold sense that has been set out in this book; and perhaps that is why man and man alone is philosophical.

Socrates and Plato

The pervasive influence of Socrates and his student Plato on the whole of Western culture is acknowledged everywhere, although the judgment as to the final value of that influence is considerably more controversial. Socrates was born around 471-472 B.C. and died in Athens in 399 B.C., condemned to death by the Athenians on charges of impiety and corruption of the youth. He made a point of never writing anything, and the reasons indicated in Plato's *Phaedrus* for this decision may be genuine. Plato, on the other hand, did write some thirty-five dialogues, and his writings, along with those of Xenophon and the comic poet Aristophanes, are the main source of our knowledge of Socrates. The *Charmides,* here presented in the standard translation by Benjamin Jowett, is supposedly one of Plato's "early" dialogues, written when he was quite young. But as is obvious, it is no less a great dialogue for having been written by a young genius.

The dialogue is presented in its entirety. But with regard to the reading of this standard translation, two notes of considerable importance must be made.

First, a reader without a Greek text would get the impression that the dialogue begins with a discussion of "temperance," gradually develops into a discussion of "temperance and wisdom," and moves finally into an almost exclusive concern with "wisdom." This is entirely wrong and is the most serious fault of the translation. The dialogue, from first to last, from "a kind of quietness" to "the science of itself and of other sciences" is about the Greek virtue of *sophrosyne*, which is sometimes translated as "temperance," "self-control," "moderation," or even "integrity." But this very dialogue is an attempt to work out the meaning of *sophrosyne*; the best translation, therefore, might leave the word untranslated, and let its meaning, or meanings, emerge in the dialogue. In any case, the reader without Greek should remember that whether the translation reads "temperance," "temperance or wisdom" (or, adverbially, "temperately or wisely"), or "wisdom," the discussion is about *sophrosyne.*

Second, there is, especially in the latter half of the dialogue, much use and discussion of the word "science," which is an oft-used translation of the Greek word *episteme.* To be sure, most translators finally decide upon "science" as the best translation of *episteme,* but with justifiable qualms. The chief difficulty is that the twentieth-century reader will almost certainly understand by "science" something closely akin to modern natural or experimental science; this is misleading. What *episteme* does seem to share with the word "science" are the notions of rigor and completeness. *Episteme* is knowledge that can be demonstrated, of which a *logos,* or account, can be given, and it carries with it the ideal of completeness. If the reader will think of these notions, and not so much of experimentation and methodology, he will be less misled by the discussion of "science."

PLATO'S CHARMIDES

Yesterday evening I returned from the army at Potidaea, and having been a good while away, I thought that I should like to go and look at my old haunts. So I went into the palaestra of Taureas, which is over against the temple adjoining the porch of the King Archon, and there I found a number of persons, most of whom I knew, but not all. My visit was unexpected, and no sooner did they see me entering than they saluted me from afar on all sides; and Chaerephon, who is a kind of madman, started up and ran to me, seizing my hand, and saying, How did you escape, Socrates?—(I should explain that an engagement had taken place at Potidaea not long before we came away, of which the news had only just reached Athens.)

You see, I replied, that here I am.

There was a report, he said, that the engagement was very severe, and that many of our acquaintance had fallen.

That, I replied, was not far from the truth.

I suppose, he said, that you were present.

I was.

Then sit down, and tell us the whole story, which as yet we have only heard imperfectly.

I took the place which he assigned to me, by the side of Critias the son of Callaeschrus, and when I had saluted him and the rest of the company, I told them the news from the army, and answered their several enquiries.

Then, when there had been enough of this, I, in my turn, began to make enquiries about matters at home—about the present state of philosophy, and about the youth. I asked whether any of them were remarkable for wisdom or beauty, or both. Critias, glancing at the door, invited my attention to some youths who were coming in, and talking noisily to one another, followed by a crowd. Of the beauties, Socrates, he said, I fancy that you will soon be able to form a judgment. For those who are just entering are the advanced guard of the great beauty, as he is thought to be, of the day, and he is likely to be not far off himself.

Who is he, I said; and who is his father?

Charmides, he replied, is his name; he is my cousin, and the son of my uncle Glaucon: I rather think that you know him too, although he was not grown up at the time of your departure.

Certainly, I know him, I said, for he was remarkable even then when he was still a child, and I should imagine that by this time he must be almost a young man.

You will see, he said, in a moment what progress he has made and what he is like. He had scarcely said the word, when Charmides entered.

Now you know, my friend, that I cannot measure anything, and of the beautiful, I am simply such a measure as a white line is of chalk; for almost all young persons appear to be beautiful in my eyes. But at that moment, when I saw him coming in, I confess that I was quite astonished at his beauty and stature; all the world seemed to be enamoured of him; amazement and confusion reigned when he entered; and a troop of lovers followed him. That grown-up men like ourselves should have been affected in this way was not surprising, but I observed that there was the same feeling among the boys; all of them, down to the very least child, turned and looked at him, as if he had been a statue.

Chaerephon called me and said: What do you think of him, Socrates? Has he not a beautiful face?

Most beautiful, I said.

But you would think nothing of his face, he replied, if you could see his naked form: he is absolutely perfect.

And to this they all agreed.

By Heracles, I said, there never was such a paragon, if he has only one other slight addition.

What is that? said Critias.

If he has a noble soul; and being of your house, Critias, he may be expected to have this.

He is as fair and good within, as he is without, replied Critias.

Then, before we see his body, should we not ask him to show us his soul, naked and undisguised? he is just of an age at which he will like to talk.

That he will, said Critias, and I can tell you that he is a philosopher already, an also a considerable poet, not in his own opinion only, but in that of others.

That, my dear Critias, I replied, is a distinction which has long been in your family, and is inherited by you from Solon. But why do you not call him, and show him to us? for even if he were younger than he is, there could be no impropriety in his talking to us in the presence of you, who are his guardian and cousin.

Very well, he said; then I will call him; and turning to the attendant, he said, Call Charmides, and tell him that I want him to come and see a physician about the illness of which he spoke to me the day before yesterday. Then again addressing me, he added: He has been complaining lately of having a headache when he rises in the morning: now why should you not make him believe that you know a cure for the headache?

Why not, I said; but will he come?

He will be sure to come, he replied.

He came as he was bidden, and sat down between Critias and me. Great amusement was occasioned by every one pushing with might and main at his neighbour in order to make a place for him next to themselves, until at the two ends of the row one had to get up and the other was rolled over sideways. Now I, my friend, was beginning to feel awkward; my former bold belief in my powers of conversing with him had vanished. And when Critias told him that I was the person who had the cure, he looked at me in such an indescribable manner, and was just going to ask a question. And at that moment all the people in the palaestra crowded about us, and, O rare! I caught a sight of the inwards of his garment, and took the flame. Then I could no longer contain myself. I thought how well Cydias understood the nature of love, when, in speaking of a fair youth, he warns some one 'not to bring the fawn in the sight of the lion to be devoured by him,' for I felt that I had been overcome by a sort of wild-beast appetite. But I controlled myself, and when he asked me if I knew the cure of the headache, I answered, but with an effort, that I did know.

And what is it? he said.

I replied that it was a kind of leaf, which required to be accompanied by a charm, and if a person would repeat the charm at the same time that he used the cure, he would be made whole; but that without the charm the leaf would be of no avail.

Then I will write out the charm from your dictation, he said.

With my consent? I said, or without my consent?

With your consent, Socrates, he said, laughing.

Very good, I said; and are you quite sure that you know my name?

I ought to know you, he replied, for there is a great deal said about you among my companions; and I remember when I was a child seeing you in company with my cousin Critias.

I am glad to find that you remember me, I said, for I shall now be more at home with you and shall be better able to explain the nature of the charm, about which I felt a difficulty before. For the charm will do more, Charmides, than only cure the headache. I dare say that you have heard eminent physicians say to a patient who comes to them with bad eyes, that they cannot cure his eyes by themselves, but that if his eyes are to be cured, his head must be treated; and then again they say that to think of curing the head alone, and not the rest of the body also, is the height of folly. And arguing in this way they apply their methods to the whole body, and try to treat and heal the whole and the part together. Did you ever observe that this is what they say?

Yes, he said.

And they are right, and you would agree with them?

Yes, he said, certainly I should.

His approving answers reassured me, and I began by degrees to regain confidence, and the vital heat returned. Such, Charmides, I said, is the nature of the charm, which I learned when serving with the army from one of the physicians of the Thracian king Zamolxis, who are said to be so skilful that they can even give immortality. This Thracian told me that in these notions of theirs, which I was just now mentioning, the Greek physicians are quite right as far as they go; but Zamolxis, he added, our king, who is also a god, says further, 'that as you ought not to attempt to cure the eyes without the head, or the head without the body, so neither ought you to attempt to cure the body without the soul; and this,' he said, 'is the reason why the cure of many diseases is unknown to the physicians of Hellas, because they are ignorant of the whole, which ought to be studied also; for the part can never be well unless the whole is well.' For all good and evil, whether in the body or in human nature, originates, as he declared, in the soul, and overflows from thence, as if from the head into the eyes. And therefore if the head and body are to be well, you must begin by curing the soul; that is the first thing. And the cure, my dear youth, has to be effected by the use of certain charms, and these charms are fair words; and by them temperance is implanted in the soul, and where temperance is, there health is speedily imparted, not only to the head, but to the whole body. And he who taught me the cure and the charm at the same time added a special direction: 'Let no one,' he said, 'persuade you to cure the head, until he has first given you his soul to be cured by the charm. For this,' he said, 'is the great error of our day in the treatment of the human body, that physicians separate the soul from the body.' And he added with emphasis, at the same time making me swear to his words, 'Let no one, however rich, or noble, or fair, persuade you to give him the cure, without the charm.' Now I have sworn, and I must keep my oath, and therefore if you will allow me to apply the Thracian charm first to your soul, as the stranger directed, I will afterwards proceed to apply the cure to your head. But if not, I do not know what I am to do with you, my dear Charmides.

Critias, when he heard this, said: The headache will be an unexpected gain to my young relation, if the pain in his head compels him to improve his mind: and I can tell you, Socrates, that Charmides is not only pre-eminent in beauty among his equals, but also in that quality which is given by the charm; and this, as you say, is temperance?

Yes, I said.

Then let me tell you that he is the most temperate of human beings, and for his age inferior to none in any quality.

Yes, I said, Charmides; and indeed I think that you ought to excel others in all good qualities; for if I am not mistaken there is no one present who could easily point out two Athenian houses, whose union would be likely to produce a better or nobler scion than the two from which you are sprung. There is your father's house, which is descended from Critias the son of Dropidas, whose family has been commemorated in the panegyrical verses of Anacreon, Solon, and many other poets, as famous for beauty and virtue and all other high fortune: and your mother's house is equally distinguished; for your maternal uncle, Pyrilampes, is reputed never to have found his equal, in Persia at the court of the great king, or on the continent of Asia, in all the places to which he went as ambassador, for stature and beauty; that whole family is not a whit inferior to the other. Having such ancestors you ought to be first in all things, and, sweet son of Glaucon, your outward form is no dishonour to any of them. If to beauty you add temperance, and if in other respects you are what Critias declares you to be, then, dear Charmides, blessed art thou, in being the son of thy mother. And here lies the point; for if, as he declares, you have this gift of temperance already, and are temperate enough, in that case you have no need of any charms, whether of Zamolxis or of Abaris the Hyperborean, and I may as well let you have the cure of the head at once; but if you have not yet acquired this quality, I must use the charm before I give you the medicine. Please, therefore, to inform me whether you admit the truth of what Critias has been saying;—have you or have you not this quality of temperance?

Charmides blushed, and the blush heightened his beauty, for modesty is becoming in youth; he then said very ingenuously, that he really could not at once answer, either yes, or no, to the question which I had asked: For, said he, if I affirm that I am not temperate, that would be a strange thing for me to say of myself, and also I should give the lie to Critias, and many others who think as he tells you, that I am temperate: but, on the other hand, if I say that I am, I shall have to praise myself, which would be ill manners; and therefore I do not know how to answer you.

I said to him: That is a natural reply, Charmides, and I think that you and I ought together to enquire whether you have this quality about which I am asking or not; and then you will not be compelled to say what you do not like; neither shall I be a rash practitioner of medicine: therefore, if you please, I will share the enquiry with you, but I will not press you if you would rather not.

There is nothing which I should like better, he said; and as far as I am concerned you may proceed in the way which you think best.

I think, I said, that I had better begin by asking you a question; for if temperance abides in you, you must have an opinion about her; she must give some intimation of her nature and qualities, which may enable you to form a notion of her. Is not that true?

Yes, he said, that I think is true.

You know your native language, I said, and therefore you must be able to tell what you feel about this.

Certainly, he said.

In order, then, that I may form a conjecture whether you have temperance abiding in you or not, tell me, I said, what, in your opinion, is Temperance?

At first he hesitated, and was very unwilling to answer: then he said that he thought temperance was doing things orderly and quietly, such things for example as walking in the streets, and talking, or anything else of that nature. In a word, he said, I should answer that, in my opinion, temperance is quietness.

Are you right, Charmides? I said. No doubt some would affirm that the quiet are the temperate; but let us see whether these words have any meaning; and first tell me whether you would not acknowledge temperance to be of the class of the noble and good?

Yes.

But which is best when you are at the writing-master's, to write the same letters quickly or quietly?

Quickly.

And to read quickly or slowly?

Quickly again.

And in playing the lyre, or wrestling, quickness or sharpness are far better than quietness and slowness?

Yes.

And the same holds in boxing and in the pancratium?

Certainly.

And in leaping and running and in bodily exercises generally, quickness and agility are good; slowness, and inactivity, and quietness, are bad?

That is evident.

Then, I said, in all bodily actions, not quietness, but the greatest agility and quickness, is noblest and best?

Yes, certainly.

And is temperance a good?

Yes.

Then, in reference to the body, not quietness, but quickness will be the higher degree of temperance, if temperance is a good?

True, he said.

And which, I said, is better—facility in learning, or difficulty in learning?

Facility.

Yes, I said; and facility in learning is learning quickly, and difficulty in learning is learning quietly and slowly?

True.

And is it not better to teach another quickly and energetically, rather than quietly and slowly?

Yes.

And which is better, to call to mind, and to remember, quickly and readily, or quietly and slowly?

The former.

And is not shrewdness a quickness or cleverness of the soul, and not a quietness?

True.

And is it not best to understand what is said, whether at the writing-master's or the music-master's, or anywhere else, not as quietly as possible, but as quickly as possible?

Yes.

And in the searchings or deliberations of the soul, not the quietest, as I imagine, and he who with difficulty deliberates and discovers, is thought worthy of praise, but he who does so most easily and quickly?

Quite true, he said.

And in all that concerns either body or soul, swiftness and activity are clearly better than slowness and quietness?

Clearly they are.

Then temperance is not quietness, nor is the temperate life quiet,—certainly not upon this view; for the life which is temperate is supposed to be the good. And of two things, one is true,—either never, or very seldom, do the quiet actions in life appear to be better than the quick and energetic ones; or supposing that of the nobler actions, there are as many quiet, as quick and vehement: still, even if we grant this, temperance will not be acting quietly any more than acting quickly and energetically, either in walking or talking or in anything else; nor will the quiet life be more temperate than the unquiet, seeing that temperance is admitted by us to be a good and noble thing, and the quick have been shown to be as good as the quiet.

I think, he said, Socrates, that you are right.

Then once more, Charmides, I said, fix your attention, and look within; consider the effect which temperance has upon yourself, and the nature of that which has the effect. Think over all this, and, like a brave youth, tell me—What is temperance?

After a moment's pausè, in which he made a real manly effort to think, he said: My opinion is, Socrates, that temperance makes a man ashamed or modest, and that temperance is the same as modesty.

Very good, I said; and did you not admit, just now, that temperance is noble?

Yes, certainly, he said.

And the temperate are also good?

Yes.

And can that be good which does not make men good?

Certainly not.

And you would infer that temperance is not only noble, but also good?

That is my opinion.

Well, I said; but surely you would agree with Homer when he says,

"Modesty is not good for a needy man"?

Yes, he said; I agree.

Then I suppose that modesty is and is not good?

Clearly.

But temperance, whose presence makes men only good, and not bad, is always good?

That appears to me to be as you say.

And the inference is that temperance cannot be modesty—if temperance is a good, and if modesty is as much an evil as a good?

All that, Socrates, appears to me to be true; but I should like to know what you think about another definition of temperance, which I just now remember to have heard from some one, who said, 'That temperance is doing our own business.' Was he right who affirmed that?

You monster! I said; this is what Critias, or some philosopher has told you.

Some one else, then, said Critias; for certainly I have not.

But what matter, said Charmides, from whom I heard this?

No matter at all, I replied; for the point is not who said the words, but whether they are true or not.

There you are in the right, Socrates, he replied.

To be sure, I said; yet I doubt whether we shall ever be able to discover their truth or falsehood; for they are a kind of riddle.

What makes you think so? he said.

Because, I said, he who uttered them seems to me to have meant one thing, and said another. Is the scribe, for example, to be regarded as doing nothing when he reads or writes?

I should rather think that he was doing something.

And does the scribe write or read, or teach you boys to write or read, your own names only, or did you write your enemies' names as well as your own and your friends'?

As much one as the other.

And was there anything meddling or intemperate in this?

Certainly not.

And yet if reading and writing are the same as doing, you were doing what was not your own business?

But they are the same as doing.

And the healing art, my friend, and building, and weaving, and doing anything whatever which is done by art,—these all clearly come under the head of doing?

Certainly.

And do you think that a state would be well ordered by a law which compelled every man to weave and wash his own coat, and make his own shoes, and his own flask and strigil, and other implements, on this principle of every one doing and performing his own, and abstaining from what is not his own?

I think not, he said.

But, I said, a temperate state will be a well-ordered state.

Of course, he replied.

Then temperance, I said, will not be doing one's own business; not at least in this way, or doing things of this sort?

Clearly not.

Then, as I was just now saying, he who declared that temperance is a man doing his own business had another and a hidden meaning; for I do not think that he could have been such a fool as to mean this. Was he a fool who told you, Charmides?

Nay, he replied, I certainly thought him a very wise man.

Then I am quite certain that he put forth his definition as a riddle, thinking that no one would know the meaning of the words 'doing his own business.'

I dare say, he replied.

And what is the meaning of a man doing his own business? Can you tell me?

Indeed, I cannot; and I should not wonder if the man himself who used this phrase did not understand what he was saying. Whereupon he laughed slyly, and looked at Critias.

Critias had long been showing uneasiness, for he felt that he had a reputation to maintain with Charmides and the rest of the company. He had, however, hitherto managed to restrain himself; but now he could no longer forbear, and I am convinced of the truth of the suspicion which I entertained at the time, that Charmides had heard this answer about temperance from Critias. And Charmides, who did not want to answer himself, but to make Critias answer, tried to stir him up. He went on pointing out that he had been refuted, at which Critias grew angry, and appeared, as I thought, inclined to quarrel with him; just as a poet might quarrel with an actor who spoiled his poems in repeating them; so he looked hard at him and said—

Do you imagine, Charmides, that the author of this definition of temperance did not understand the meaning of his own words, because you do not understand them?

Why, at his age, I said, most excellent Critias, he can hardly be expected to understand; but you, who are older, and have studied, may well be assumed to know the meaning of them; and therefore, if you agree with him, and accept his definition of temperance, I would much rather argue with you than with him about the truth or falsehood of the definition.

I entirely agree, said Critias, and accept the definition.

Very good, I said; and now let me repeat my question—Do you admit, as I was just now saying, that all craftsmen make or do something?

I do.

And do they make or do their own business only, or that of others also?

They make or do that of others also.

And are they temperate, seeing that they make not for themselves or their own business only?

Why not? he said.

No objection on my part, I said, but there may be a difficulty on his who proposes as a definition of temperance, 'doing one's own business,' and then says that there is no reason why those who do the business of others should not be temperate.

Nay, said he; did I ever acknowledge that those who do the business of others are temperate? I said, those who make, not those who do.

What! I asked; do you mean to say that doing and making are not the same?

No more, he replied, than making or working are the same; thus much I have learned from Hesiod, who says that 'work is no disgrace.' Now do you imagine that if he had meant by working and doing such things as you were describing, he would have said that there was no disgrace in them—for example, in the manufacture of shoes, or in selling pickles, or sitting for hire in a house of ill-fame? That, Socrates, is not to be supposed: but I conceive him to have distinguished making from doing and work; and, while admitting that the making anything might sometimes become a disgrace, when the employment was not honourable, to have thought that work was never any disgrace at all. For things nobly and usefully made he called works; and such makings he called workings, and doings; and he must be supposed to have called such things only man's proper business, and what is hurtful, not his business: and in that sense Hesiod, and any other wise man, may be reasonably supposed to call him wise who does his own work.

O Critias, I said, no sooner had you opened your mouth, than I pretty well knew that you would call that which is proper to a man and that which is his own, good; and that the makings (ποίησεις) of the good you would call doings (πράξεις) for I am no stranger to the endless distinctions which Prodicus draws about names. Now I have no objection to your giving names any signification which you please, if you will only tell me what you mean by them. Please then to begin again, and be a little plainer. Do you mean that this doing or making, or whatever is the word which you would use, of good actions, is temperance?

I do, he said.

Then not he who does evil, but he who does good, is temperate?

Yes, he said; and you, friend, would agree.

No matter whether I should or not; just now, not what I think, but what you are saying, is the point at issue.

Well, he answered; I mean to say, that he who does evil, and not good, is not temperate; and that he is temperate who does good, and not evil: for temperance I define in plain words to be the doing of good actions.

And you may be very likely right in what you are saying; but I am curious to know whether you imagine that temperate men are ignorant of their own temperance?

I do not think so, he said.

And yet were you not saying, just now, that craftsmen might be temperate in doing another's work, as well as in doing their own?

I was, he replied; but what is your drift?

I have no particular drift, but I wish that you would tell me whether a physician who cures a patient may do good to himself and good to another also?

I think that he may.

And he who does so does his duty?

Yes.

And does not he who does his duty act temperately or wisely?

Yes, he acts wisely.

But must the physician necessarily know when his treatment is likely to prove beneficial, and when not? or must the craftsman necessarily know when he is likely to be benefited, and when not to be benefited, by the work which he is doing?

I suppose not.

Then, I said, he may sometimes do good or harm, and not know what he is himself doing, and yet, in doing good, as you say, he has done temperately or wisely. Was not that your statement?

Yes.

Then, as would seem, in doing good, he may act wisely or temperately, and be wise or temperate, but not know his own wisdom or temperance?

But that, Socrates, he said, is impossible; and therefore if this is, as you imply, the necessary consequence of any of my previous admissions, I will withdraw them, rather than admit that a man can be temperate or wise who does not know himself; and I am not ashamed to confess that I was in error. For self-knowledge would certainly be maintained by me to be the very essence of knowledge, and in this I agree with him who dedicated the inscription, 'Know thyself!' at Delphi. That word, if I am not mistaken, is put there as a sort of salutation which the god addresses to those who enter the temple; as much as to say that the ordinary salutation of 'Hail!' is not right, and that the exhortation 'Be temperate!' would be a far better way of saluting one another. The notion of him who dedicated the inscription was, as I believe, that the god speaks to those who enter his temple, not as men speak; but, when a worshipper enters, the first word which he hears is 'Be temperate!' This, however, like a prophet he expresses in a sort of riddle, for 'Know thyself!' and 'Be temperate!' are the same, as I maintain, and as the letters imply [σωφρόνει, γνῶθι σαυτόν], and yet they may be easily misunderstood; and succeeding sages who added 'Never too much,' or, 'Give a pledge, and evil is nigh at hand,' would appear to have so misunderstood them; for they imagined that 'Know thyself!' was a piece of advice which the god gave, and not his salutation of the worshippers at their first coming in; and they dedicated their own inscription under the idea that they too would give equally useful pieces of advice. Shall I tell you, Socrates, why I say all this? My object is to leave the previous discussion (in which I know not whether you or I are more right, but, at any rate, no clear result was attained), and to raise a new one in which I will attempt to prove, if you deny, that temperance is self-knowledge.

Yes, I said, Critias; but you come to me as though I professed to know about the questions which I ask, and as though I could, if I only would, agree with you. Whereas the fact is that I enquire with you into the truth of that which is advanced from time to time, just because I do not know; and when I have enquired, I will say whether I agree with you or not. Please then to allow me time to reflect.

Reflect, he said.

I am reflecting, I replied, and discover that temperance, or wisdom, if implying a knowledge of anything, must be a science, and a science of something.

Yes, he said; the science of itself.

Is not medicine, I said, the science of health?

True.

And suppose, I said, that I were asked by you what is the use or effect of medicine, which is this science of health, I should answer that medicine is of very great use in producing health, which, as you will admit, is an excellent effect.

Granted.

And if you were to ask me, what is the result or effect of architecture, which is the science of building, I should say houses, and so of other arts, which all have their different results. Now I want you, Critias, to answer a similar question about temperance, or wisdom, which, according to you, is the science of itself. Admitting this view, I ask of you, what good work, worthy of the name wise, does temperance or wisdom, which is the science of itself, effect? Answer me.

That is not the true way of pursuing the enquiry, Socrates, he said; for wisdom is not like the other sciences, any more than they are like one another: but you proceed as if they were alike. For tell me, he said, what result is there of computation or geometry, in the same sense as a house is the result of building, or a garment of weaving, or any other work of any other art? Can you show me any such result of them? You cannot.

That is true, I said; but still each of these sciences has a subject which is different from the science. I can show you that the art of computation has to do with odd and even numbers in their numerical relations to themselves and to each other. Is not that true?

Yes, he said.

And the odd and even numbers are not the same with the art of computation?

They are not.

The art of weighing, again, has to do with lighter and heavier; but the art of weighing is one thing, and the heavy and the light another. Do you admit that?

Yes.

Now, I want to know, what is that which is not wisdom, and of which wisdom is the science?

You are just falling into the old error, Socrates, he said. You come asking in what wisdom or temperance differs from the other sciences, and then you try to discover some respect in which they are alike; but they are not, for all the other sciences are of something else, and not of themselves; wisdom alone is a science of other sciences, and of itself. And of this, as I believe, you are very well aware: and that you are only doing what you denied that you were doing just now, trying to refute me, instead of pursuing the argument.

And what if I am? How can you think that I have any other motive in refuting you but what I should have in examining into myself? which motive would be just a fear of my unconsciously fancying that I knew something of which I was ignorant. And at this moment I pursue the argument chiefly for my own sake, and perhaps in some degree also for the sake of my other friends. For is not the discovery of things as they truly are, a good common to all mankind?

Yes, certainly, Socrates, he said.

Then, I said, be cheerful, sweet sir, and give your opinion in answer to the question which I asked, never minding whether Critias or Socrates is the person refuted; attend only to the argument, and see what will come of the refutation.

I think that you are right, he replied; and I will do as you say.

Tell me, then, I said, what you mean to affirm about wisdom.

I mean to say that wisdom is the only science which is the science of itself as well as of the other sciences.

But the science of science, I said, will also be the science of the absence of science.

Very true, he said.

Then the wise or temperate man, and he only, will know himself, and be able to examine what he knows or does not know, and to see what others know and think that they know and do really know; and what they do not know, and fancy that they know, when they do not. No other person will be able to do this. And this is wisdom and temperance and self-knowledge—for a man to know what he knows, and what he does not know. That is your meaning?

Yes, he said.

Now then, I said, making an offering of the third or last argument to Zeus the Saviour, let us begin again, and ask, in the first place, whether it is or is not possible for a person to know that he knows and does not know what he knows and does not know; and in the second place, whether, if perfectly possible, such knowledge is of any use.

That is what we have to consider, he said.

And here, Critias, I said, I hope that you will find a way out of a difficulty into which I have got myself. Shall I tell you the nature of the difficulty?

By all means, he replied.

Does not what you have been saying, if true, amount to this: that there must be a single science which is wholly a science of itself and of other sciences, and that the same is also the science of the absence of science?

Yes.

But consider how monstrous this proposition is, my friend: in any parallel case, the impossibility will be transparent to you.

How is that? and in what cases to you mean?

In such cases as this: Suppose that there is a kind of vision which is not like ordinary vision, but a vision of itself and of other sorts of vision, and of the defect of them, which in seeing sees no colour, but only itself and other sorts of vision: Do you think that there is such a kind of vision?

Certainly not.

Or is there a kind of hearing which hears no sound at all, but only itself and other sorts of hearing, or the defects of them?

There is not.

Or take all the senses: can you imagine that there is any sense of itself and of other senses, but which is incapable of perceiving the objects of the senses?

I think not.

Could there be any desire which is not the desire of any pleasure, but of itself, and of all other desires?

Certainly not.

Or can you imagine a wish which wishes for no good, but only for itself and all other wishes?

I should answer, No.

Or would you say that there is a love which is not the love of beauty, but of itself and of other loves?

I should not.

Or did you ever know of a fear which fears itself or other fears, but has no object of fear?

I never did, he said.

Or of an opinion which is an opinion of itself and of other opinions, and which has no opinion on the subjects of opinion in general?

Certainly not.

But surely we are assuming a science of this kind, which, having no subject-matter, is a science of itself and of the other sciences?

Yes, that is what is affirmed.

But how strange is this, if it be indeed true; we must not however as yet absolutely deny the possibility of such a science; let us rather consider the matter.

You are quite right.

Well then, this science of which we are speaking is a science of something, and is of a nature to be a science of something?

Yes.

Just as that which is greater is of a nature to be greater than something else?

Yes.

Which is less, if the other is conceived to be greater?

To be sure.

And if we could find something which is at once greater than itself, and greater than other great things, but not greater than those things in comparison of which the others are greater, then that thing would have the property of being greater and also less than itself?

That, Socrates, he said, is the inevitable inference.

Or if there be a double which is double of itself and of other doubles, these will be halves; for the double is relative to the half?

That is true.

And that which is greater than itself will also be less, and that which is heavier will also be lighter, and that which is older will also be younger: and the same of other things; that which has a nature relative to self will retain also the nature of its object: I mean to say, for example, that hearing is, as we say, of sound or voice. Is that true?

Yes.

Then if hearing hears itself, it must hear a voice; for there is no other way of hearing.

Certainly.

And sight also, my excellent friend, if it sees itself must see a colour, for sight cannot see that which has no colour.

No.

Do you remark, Critias, that in several of the examples which have been recited the notion of a relation to self is altogether inadmissible, and in other cases hardly credible—inadmissible, for example, in the case of magnitudes, numbers, and the like?

Very true.

But in the case of hearing and sight, or in the power of self-motion, and the power of heat to burn, this relation to self will be regarded as incredible by some, but perhaps not by others. And some great man, my friend, is wanted who will satisfactorily determine for us, whether there is nothing which has an inherent property of relation to self, or some things only and not others; and whether in this class of self-related things, if there be such a class, that science which is called wisdom or temperance is included. I altogether distrust my own power of determining these matters: I am not certain whether there is such a science of science at all; and even if there be, I should not acknowledge this to be wisdom or temperance, until I can also see whether such a science would or would not do us any good; for I have an impression that temperance is a benefit and a good. And therefore, O son of Callaeschrus, as you maintain that temperance or wisdom is a science of science, and also of the absence of science, I will request you to show in the first place, as I was saying before, the possibility, and in the second place, the advantage, of such a science; and then perhaps you may satisfy me that you are right in your view of temperance.

Critias heard me say this, and saw that I was in a difficulty; and as one person when another yawns in his presence catches the infection of yawning from him, so did he seem to be driven into a difficulty by my difficulty. But as he had a reputation to maintain, he was ashamed to admit before the company that he could not answer my challenge or determine the question at issue; and he made an unintelligible attempt to hide his perplexity. In order that the argument might proceed, I said to him, Well then, Critias, if you like, let us assume that there is this science of science; whether the assumption is right or wrong may hereafter be investigated. Admitting the existence of it, will you tell me how such a science enables us to distinguish what we know or do not know, which, as we were saying, is self-knowledge or wisdom: so we were saying?

Yes, Socrates, he said; and that I think is certainly true: for he who has this science or knowledge which knows itself will become like the knowledge which he has, in the same way that he who has swiftness will be swift, and he who has beauty will be beautiful, and he who has knowledge will know. In the same way he who has that knowledge which is self-knowing, will know himself.

I do not doubt, I said, that a man will know himself, when he possesses that which has self-knowledge: but what necessity is there that, having this, he should know what he knows and what he does not know?

Because, Socrates, they are the same.

Very likely, I said; but I remain as stupid as ever, for still I fail to comprehend how this knowing what you know and do not know is the same as the knowledge of self.

What do you mean? he said.

This is what I mean, I replied: I will admit that there is a science of science;—can this do more than determine that of two things one is and the other is not science or knowledge?

No, just that.

But is knowledge or want of knowledge of health the same as knowledge or want of knowledge of justice?

Certainly not.

The one is medicine, and the other is politics; whereas that of which we are speaking is knowledge pure and simple.

Very true.

And if a man knows only, and has only knowledge of knowledge, and has no further knowledge of health and justice, the probability is that he will only know that he knows something, and has a certain knowledge, whether concerning himself or other men.

True.

Then how will this knowledge or science teach him to know what he knows? Say that he knows health;—not wisdom or temperance, but the art of medicine has taught it to him;—and he has learned harmony from the art of music, and building from the art of building,—neither, from wisdom or temperance: and the same of other things.

That is evident.

How will wisdom, regarded only as a knowledge of knowledge or science of science, ever teach him that he knows health, or that he knows building?

It is impossible.

Then he who is ignorant of these things will only know that he knows, but not what he knows?

True.

Then wisdom or being wise appears to be not the knowledge of the things which we do or do not know, but only the knowledge that we know or do not know?

That is the inference.

Then he who has this knowledge will not be able to examine whether a pretender knows or does not know that which he says that he knows: he will only know that he has a knowledge of some kind; but wisdom will not show him of what the knowledge is?

Plainly not.

Neither will he be able to distinguish the pretender in medicine from the true physician, nor between any other true and false professor of knowledge. Let us consider the matter in this way: If the wise man or any other man wants to distinguish the true physician from the false, how will he proceed? He will not talk to him about medicine; and that, as we were saying, is the only thing which the physician understands.

True.

And, on the other hand, the physician knows nothing of science, for this has been assumed to be the province of wisdom.

True.

And further, since medicine is science, we must infer that he does not know anything of medicine.

Exactly.

Then the wise man may indeed know that the physician has some kind of science or knowledge; but when he wants to discover the nature of this he will ask, What is the subject-matter? For the several sciences are distinguished not by the mere fact that they are sciences, but by the nature of their subjects. Is not that true?

Quite true.

And medicine is distinguished from other sciences as having the subject-matter of health and disease?

Yes.

And he who would enquire into the nature of medicine must pursue the enquiry into health and disease, and not into what is extraneous?

True.

And he who judges rightly will judge of the physician as a physician in what relates to these?

He will.

He will consider whether what he says is true, and whether what he does is right, in relation to health and disease?

He will.

But can any one attain the knowledge of either unless he have a knowledge of medicine?

He cannot.

No one at all, it would seem, except the physician can have this knowledge; and therefore not the wise man; he would have to be a physician as well as a wise man.

Very true.

Then, assuredly, wisdom or temperance, if only a science of science, and of the absence of science or knowledge, will not be able to distinguish the physician who knows from one who does not know but pretends or thinks that he knows; or any other professor of anything at all; like any other artist, he will only know his fellow in art or wisdom, and no one else.

That is evident, he said.

But then what profit, Critias, I said, is there any longer in wisdom or temperance which yet remains, if this is wisdom? If, indeed, as we were supposing at first, the wise man had been able to distinguish what he knew and did not know, and that he knew the one and did not know the other, and to recognize a similar faculty of discernment in others, there would certainly have been a great advantage in being wise; for then we should never have made a mistake, but have passed through life the unerring guides of ourselves and of those who are under us; and we should not have attempted to do what we did not know, but we should have found out those who knew, and have handed the business over to them and trusted in them; nor should we have allowed those who were under us to do anything which they were not likely to do well, and they would be likely to do well just that of which they had knowledge; and the house or state which was ordered or administered under the guidance of wisdom, and everything else of which wisdom was the lord, would have been well ordered; for truth guiding, and error having been eliminated, in all their doings, men would have done well, and would have been happy. Was not this, Critias, what we spoke of as the great advantage of wisdom—to know what is known and what is unknown to us?

Very true, he said.

And now you perceive, I said, that no such science is to be found anywhere.

I perceive, he said.

May we assume then, I said, that wisdom, viewed in this new light merely as a knowledge of knowledge and ignorance, has this advantage:—that he who possesses such knowledge will more easily learn anything which he learns; and that everything will be clearer to him, because, in addition to the knowledge of individuals, he sees the science, and this also will better enable him to test the knowledge which others have of what he knows himself; whereas the enquirer who is without this knowledge may be supposed to have a feebler and weaker insight? Are not these, my friend, the real advantages which are to be gained from wisdom? And are not we looking and seeking after something more than is to be found in her?

That is very likely, he said.

That is very likely, I said; and very likely, too, we have been enquiring to no purpose; as I am led to infer, because I observe that if this is wisdom, some strange consequences would follow. Let us, if you please, assume the possibility of this science of sciences, and further admit and allow, as was originally suggested, that wisdom is the knowledge of what we know and do not know. Assuming all this, still, upon further consideration, I am doubtful, Critias, whether wisdom, such as this, would do us much good. For we were wrong, I think, in supposing, as we were saying just now, that such wisdom ordering the government of house or state would be a great benefit.

How so? he said.

Why, I said, we were far too ready to admit the great benefits which mankind would obtain from their severally doing the things which they knew, and committing the things of which they are ignorant to those who were better acquainted with them.

Were we not right in making that admission?

I think not.

How very strange, Socrates!

By the dog of Egypt, I said, there I agree with you; and I was thinking as much just now when I said that strange consequences would follow, and that I was afraid we were on the wrong track; for however ready we may be to admit that this is wisdom, I certainly cannot make out what good this sort of thing does to us.

What do you mean? he said; I wish that you could make me understand what you mean.

I dare say that what I am saying is nonsense, I replied; and yet if a man has any feeling of what is due to himself, he cannot let the thought which comes into his mind pass away unheeded and unexamined.

I like that, he said.

Hear, then, I said, my own dream; whether coming through the horn or the ivory gate, I cannot tell. The dream is this: Let us suppose that wisdom is such as we are now defining, and that she has absolute sway over us; then each action will be done according to the arts or sciences, and no one professing to be a pilot when he is not, or any physician or general, or any one else pretending to know matters of which he is ignorant, will deceive or elude us; our health will be improved; our safety at sea, and also in battle, will be assured; our coats and shoes, and all other instruments and implements will be skilfully made, because the workmen will be good and true. Aye, and if you please, you may suppose that prophecy, which is the knowledge of the future, will be under the control of wisdom, and that she will deter deceivers and set up the true prophets in their place as the revealers of the future. Now I quite agree that mankind, thus provided, would live and act according to knowledge, for wisdom would watch and prevent ignorance from intruding on us. But whether by acting according to knowledge we shall act well and be happy, my dear Critias,—this is a point which we have not yet been able to determine.

Yet I think, he replied, that if you discard knowledge, you will hardly find the crown of happiness in anything else.

But of what is this knowledge? I said. Just answer me that small question. Do you mean a knowledge of shoemaking?

God forbid.

Or of working in brass?

Certainly not.

Or in wool, or wood, or anything of that sort?

No, I do not.

Then, I said, we are giving up the doctrine that he who lives according to knowledge is happy, for these live according to knowledge, and yet they are not allowed by you to be happy; but I think that you mean to confine happiness to particular individuals who live according to knowledge, such for example as the prophet, who, as I was saying, knows the future. Is it of him you are speaking or of some one else?

Yes, I mean him, but there are others as well.

Yes, I said, some one who knows the past and present as well as the future, and is ignorant of nothing. Let us suppose that there is such a person, and if there is, you will allow that he is the most knowing of all living men.

Certainly he is.

Yet I should like to know one thing more: which of the different kinds of knowledge makes him happy? Or do all equally make him happy?

Not all equally, he replied.

But which most tends to make him happy? The knowledge of what past, present, or future thing? May I infer this to be the knowledge of the game of draughts?

Nonsense about the game of draughts.

Or of computation?

No.

Or of health?

That is nearer the truth, he said.

And that knowledge which is nearest of all, I said, is the knowledge of what?

The knowledge with which he discerns good and evil.

Monster! I said; you have been carrying me round in a circle, and all this time hiding from me the fact that the life according to knowledge is not that which makes men act rightly and be happy, not even if knowledge include all the sciences, but one science only, that of good and evil. For, let me ask you, Critias, whether, if you take away this, medicine will not equally give health, and shoemaking equally produce shoes, and the art of the weaver clothes?—whether the art of the pilot will not equally save our lives at sea, and the art of the general in war?

Quite so.

And yet, my dear Critias, none of these things will be well or beneficially done, if the science of the good be wanting.

True.

But that science is not wisdom or temperance, but a science of human advantage; not a science of other sciences, or of ignorance, but of good and evil: and if this be of use, then wisdom or temperance will not be of use.

And why, he replied, will not wisdom be of use? For, however much we assume that wisdom is a science of sciences, and has a sway over other sciences, surely she will have this particular science of the good under her control, and in this way will benefit us.

And will wisdom give health? I said; is not this rather the effect of medicine? Or does wisdom do the work of any of the other arts,—do they not each of them do their own work? Have we not long ago asseverated that wisdom is only the knowledge of knowledge and of ignorance, and of nothing else?

That is obvious.

Then wisdom will not be the producer of health.

Certainly not.

The art of health is different.

Yes, different.

Nor does wisdom give advantage, my good friend; for that again we have just now been attributing to another art.

Very true.

How then can wisdom be advantageous, when giving no advantage?

That, Socrates, is certainly inconceivable.

You see then, Critias, that I was not far wrong in fearing that I could have no sound notion about wisdom; I was quite right in depreciating myself; for that which is admitted to be the best of all things would never have seemed to us useless, if I had been good for anything at an enquiry. But now I have been utterly defeated, and have failed to discover what that is to which the imposer of names gave this name of temperance or wisdom. And yet many more admissions were made by us than could be fairly granted; for we admitted that there was a science of science, although the argument said No, and protested against us; and we admitted further, that this science knew the works of the other sciences (although this too was denied by the argument), because we wanted to show that the wise man had knowledge of what he knew and did not know; also we nobly disregarded, and never even considered, the impossibility of a man knowing in a sort of way that which he does not know at all; for our assumption was, that he knows that which he does not know; than which nothing, as I think, can be more irrational. And yet, after finding us so easy and good-natured, the enquiry is still unable to discover the truth; but mocks us to a degree, and has gone out of its way to prove the inutility of that which we admitted only by a sort of supposition and fiction to be the true definition of temperance or wisdom: which result, as far as I am concerned, is not so much to be lamented, I said. But for your sake, Charmides, I am very sorry—that you, having such beauty and such wisdom and temperance of soul, should have no profit or good in life from your wisdom and temperance. And still more am I grieved about the charm which I learned with so much pain, and to so little profit, from the Thracian, for the sake of a thing which is nothing worth. I think indeed that there is a mistake, and that I must be a bad enquirer, for wisdom or temperance I believe to be really a great good; and happy are you, Charmides, if you certainly possess it. Wherefore examine yourself, and see whether you have this gift and can do without the charm; for if you can, I would rather advise you to regard me simply as a fool who is never able to reason out anything; and to rest assured that the more wise and temperate you are, the happier you will be.

Charmides said: I am sure that I do not know, Socrates, whether I have or have not this gift of wisdom and temperance; for how can I know whether I have a thing, of which even you and Critias are, as you say, unable to discover the nature?—(not that I believe you.) And further, I am sure, Socrates, that I do need the charm, and as far as I am concerned, I shall be willing to be charmed by you daily, until you say that I have had enough.

Very good, Charmides, said Critias; if you do this I shall have a proof of your temperance, that is, if you allow yourself to be charmed by Socrates and never desert him at all.

You may depend on my following and not deserting him, said Charmides: if you who are my guardian command me, I should be very wrong not to obey you.

And I do command you, he said.

Then I will do as you say, and begin this very day.

You sirs, I said, what are you conspiring about?

We are not conspiring, said Charmides, we have conspired already.

And are you about to use violence, without even going through the forms of justice?

Yes, I shall use violence, he replied, since he orders me; and therefore you had better consider well.

But the time for consideration has passed, I said, when violence is employed; and you, when you are determined on anything, and in the mood of violence, are irresistible.

Do not you resist me then, he said.

I will not resist you, I replied. (*Charmides,* 153-176)

Notes: XI

1. E.g., Gerhard Krüger, *Einsicht und Leidenschaft* (Frankfurt am Main, Vittorio Klostermann, 1948); Leo Straus, *The City and Man* (Chicago, Rand McNally, 1964); Jacob Klein, *A Commentary on Plato's Meno,* (Chapel Hill, University of North Carolina Press, 1965); Stanley Rosen, *Plato's Symposium* (New Haven, Conn., Yale University Press, 1968); Paul Friedlander, *Plato,* (Princeton University Press,

1958), Vols. 2 and 3; Drew Hyland, "Why Plato Wrote Dialogues," in *Philosophy and Rhetoric*, I (1968), p. 38-50; Kenneth Dorter, "The Dramatic Aspect of Plato's *Phaedo*," *Dialogue*, VIII (1970), p. 4.

2. Immanuel Kant, *Critique of Pure Reason*, trans. by N. K. Smith (New York, Macmillan and Co., 1961), p. 4.

3. René Descartes, *Meditations on First Philosophy*, in *The Philosophical Works of Descartes*, trans. by E. S. Haldane and G. R. T. Ross (New York, Dover Publications, 1931), Vol. I, p. 144.

4. Xenophon, *Memorabilia*, I, 2, 28-32.

5. Plato, *Charmides*, 166c.

6. K. W. Luckhurst, "Note on Plato, *Charmides*, 153B" in *Classical Review* (1934), pp. 207-208. The date of the battle is 429 B.C.

7. Plato, *Symposium*, 220 ff.

8. Plato, *Charmides*, 155d.

9. *See*, for example, Plato, *Symposium* and *Phaedrus*.

10. Plato, *Charmides*, 167a.

11. In my forthcoming book on Plato's *Charmides*.

12. Plato, *Charmides*, 159a.

13. Plato, *Theaetetus*, 155d.

14. Plato, *Apology*, 21 ff.

15. *See* especially the speeches of Aristophanes and Socrates in the *Symposium*.

16. Plato, *Charmides*, 167a.

17. *Ibid.*, 155a, 157e ff.

18. Plato, *Theaetetus*, 144b, *Lysis*, 204e. In the *Symposium*, 203a, Socrates even asks Diotima who Eros' parents were.

19. Alcmaeon, Fragment 2 (D-K).

Glossary of Greek Terms

adikia: injustice, an offense
aleitheia: truth, literally "un-hiddenness"
apeiron: indefinite, undefined
aporia: state of being at a loss, hence difficulty, predicament
arche: origin, beginning, principle
daimon: a spiritual being, usually understood as in the middle between the mortal and the divine
Dike: justice, right
doxa: opinion, seeming
eidos: a form, that which is seen
episteme: knowledge for which an account (*logos*) can be given, hence, demonstrable knowledge, science
eros: love
ethos: custom, habit, character, manner
Gaia: earth, one of the earliest dieties
genesthai: to come to be, become
gigantomachia: battle of the giants, sometimes applied to the supposed opposition between Parmenides and Heraclitus
hybris: arrogance, pride
idea: form, the look or appearance of a thing
Kronos: early god in Hesiod, later interpreted as Chronos, time
logos: word, account, reason; in Heraclitus something like "law"
moira: fate, destiny
neikos: strife
nous: mind, thought, intellect
orthodoxa: right or true opinion
Ouranos: ancient diety, heaven or sky
Peitho: persuasion
phenomenon: that which appears
philotes: love

physis: nature, as in "the nature of a thing," related to growth

psyche: soul

saphes: clear

sophistes: Sophist

sophron: adjectival form of *sophrosyne*

sophrosyne: self-control, moderation, temperance, in the *Charmides*, self-knowledge

stoicheion; element

sympheron: advantage, profit

techne: skill, art, hence "technical knowledge"

telos: end, purpose, what a thing is at its best

theogony: genesis of the gods

theology: logos (account) of the gods

Xáos: chaos

Suggestions for Further Reading

Burnet, J., *Early Greek Philosophy*. New York, Meridian Books, 1957. This book is one of the earlier but still highly respected discussions from the English tradition of Pre-Socratic philosophy. Burnet emphasizes the scientific character of early Greek philosophy.

Cornford, F. M., *From Religion to Philosophy*. New York, Harper Torchbooks, 1957. This is a well-written and extremely influential statement of the view that Pre-Socratic philosophy arises out of religious myth.

Diogenes Laertius, *Lives of Eminent Philosophers*, trans. by R. D. Hicks, 2 volumes. New York, Loeb Classical Library, G. P. Putnam's Sons, 1935. This study by the third-century A.D. historian contains copious information about the Pre-Socratics, some of it interpreting their philosophy, some containing biographical data. It is not always utterly trustworthy, especially with regard to biographical information.

Hegel, G. F., *Lectures on the History of Philosophy*, trans. by E. S. Haldane, 3 volumes. New York, Humanities Press, 1963. This book, though difficult, contains extremely thought-provoking interpretations of the historical development of thought in Pre-Socratic philosophy. Hegel's own standpoint is often presupposed.

Heidegger, Martin, *Introduction to Metaphysics*, trans. by Ralph Manheim. New Haven, Conn., Yale University Press, 1959. This book, though difficult, contains imaginative and provocative interpretations of Heraclitus and Parmenides.

Heidegger, Martin, *What Is Called Thinking?*, trans. by F. D. Wieck and J. Glenn Gray. New York, Harper and Row, 1968. The second part of this book contains a detailed examination and interpretation, in Heidegger's own imaginative way, of Parmenides.

Kirk, C. S., and Raven, J. E., *The Presocratic Philosophers*. Cambridge, England, Cambridge University Press, 1960. This compendious volume contains generous discussion of the scholarly problems surrounding each of the Pre-Socratic philosophers. It also contains most of the original texts in Greek and is, therefore, a valuable book for the serious student of Pre-Socratic philosophy.

Lee, H. D. P., *Zeno of Elea*. Cambridge, England, Cambridge University Press, 1936. This is the standard scholarly edition of Zeno, giving Greek texts, English translations, and an extensive commentary.

Mourelatos, A., *The Route of Parmenides*. New Haven, Conn., Yale University Press, 1970. This thorough interpretation of Parmenides' poem offers extensive historical background and careful grammatical analysis. Some parts require knowledge of Greek for thorough understanding. This is one of the best studies of any single Pre-Socratic philosopher.

Nietzsche, Friedrich, *Philosophy in the Tragic Age of the Greeks*, trans. by Marianne Cowan. Chicago, Gateway Paperbacks, Henry Regnery Co., 1962. Nietzsche here offers one of the most imaginative, thoughtful, yet accessible interpretations of Pre-Socratic philosophy we know of. This is an immensely valuable book.

Seidel, George, O.S.B., *Martin Heidegger and the Presocratics*. Lincoln, Nebr., University of Nebraska Press, 1964. This book is a careful and well-documented interpretation of Heidegger's valuable studies in Pre-Socratic philosophy.

The Epic of Gilgamesh, trans. by N. K. Sandars. Baltimore, Penguin Books, 1960. This very readable translation also has an extremely valuable introduction which not only interprets the epic but offers extensive historical background as well.

Versenyi, Lazlo, *Socratic Humanism*. New Haven, Conn., Yale University Press, 1963. The first part of this book offers a thoughtful and provocative defense of the Sophists, the second part an interesting discussion of the extent to which Socrates can be interpreted as a humanist.

Vlastos, Gregory, "Zeno of Elea," in Paul Edwards, ed., *The Encyclopedia of Philosophy*, 8 volumes. New York, Macmillan, 1967. A good short introduction which has an interpretation of Zeno substantially different from the one in this volume.

Zeno's Paradoxes, Salmon, Wesley C., ed. Indianapolis, Ind., The Bobbs-Merrill Co., 1970. This excellent volume should be the student's first stop in a further exploration of Zeno's thought —especially because it contains an extensive (143 items) bibliography of works on Zeno.